City of Big Shoulders

City of
Big Shoulders

A HISTORY OF CHICAGO

ROBERT G. SPINNEY

NORTHERN

ILLINOIS

UNIVERSITY

PRESS

DeKalb

2000

© 2000 by Northern Illinois University Press

Published by the Northern Illinois University Press, DeKalb, Illinois 60115

Manufactured in the United States using acid-free paper

All Rights Reserved

Design by Julia Fauci

Library of Congress Cataloging-in-Publication Data

Spinney, Robert G. (Robert Guy)

City of big shoulders : a history of Chicago / Robert G. Spinney.

    p.   cm.

Includes bibliographical references and index.

ISBN-13: 978–0-87580-583-2 (pbk. : alk. paper)

ISBN-10: 0-87580-583-3 (pbk. : alk. paper)

1. Chicago (Ill.)—History. I. Title.

F548.3.S75 2000

977.3'11—dc21   99-28067

                CIP

Cover photograph courtesy of Jane Addams Memorial Collection (JAMC neg. 1394),

Wallace Kirkland Photographer, Special Collections, University Library,

University of Illinois at Chicago.

To **Myron Magnuson,**

Angelo Rentas, and

Jim Ritchhart,

good friends who made my years in Chicago gratifying.

CONTENTS

List of Illustrations   ix

List of Tables   xi

Preface   xiii

1. The Early World of Chigagou, 1600–1750   *5*

2. Chigagou Becomes Chicago, 1750–1835   *13*

3. Boom, Bust, and Recovery in Early Chicago, 1835–1850   *31*

4. Chicago Conquers the Midwest, 1850–1890   *46*

5. Life in a City on the Make, 1850–1900   *70*

6. The Fire, the Bomb, and the Fair, 1871–1893   *99*

7. The New Immigration, 1880–1920   *123*

8. Progressivism and Urban Reform, 1890–1915   *146*

9. World War I and the Roaring Twenties, 1915–1929   *165*

10. The Great Depression, World War II, and Suburban Growth, 1929–1955   *188*

11. Richard J. Daley and The City That Works, 1955–1976   *213*

12. The Transitions of the Post-Daley Years, 1976–1997   *241*

Notes   *269*

Bibliography   *285*

Index   *295*

LIST OF ILLUSTRATIONS

1. The Chicago stockyards   *58*

2. Downtown Chicago following the fire   *102*

3. The Columbian Exposition   *116*

4. Maxwell Street, c. 1910   *134*

5. Downtown Chicago, c. 1910   *154*

6. Hull-House   *159*

7. St. Valentine's Day Massacre   *178*

8. Mayor Richard J. Daley   *218*

9. Riot control jeeps for the Democratic Convention   *234*

10. Mayor Harold Washington   *250*

LIST OF TABLES

•

1. Immigration to Chicago, 1830–1980   *125*

2. European-Born Immigrants in Chicago, 1890 and 1920   *126*

3. The Changing Nature of Immigration: Old and
   New Immigration in Chicago, 1860–1920   *127*

4. Immigration to the Ten Largest U.S. Cities   *128*

5. Top Ten U.S. Cities in Value of War Supply Contracts,
   June 1940 to September 1945   *200*

6. Top Ten U.S. Cities in Value of Publicly Financed Industrial
   and Manufacturing Facilities, June 1940 to June 1945   *201*

7. Population of Chicago and Its Suburbs, 1920–1970   *211*

8. Population of the Six-County Chicago Metropolitan Area,
   1970–1990   *259*

9. Hispanic Population of Metropolitan Chicago, 1980 and 1990   *263*

10. Hispanic Communities in Chicago, 1990   *264*

PREFACE

• This book was born in my teaching on the history of Chicago at Trinity International University in Deerfield, Illinois. Chicago is a fascinating city that has attracted the attention of many capable historians. These scholars have produced an impressive array of excellent books about the Windy City, many of which deserve careful reading by any serious student of the city. However, no book currently in print filled the bill for my college course. Many of these recently published studies are outstanding treatments of specific subjects (such as Roger Biles's first-rate biography of Richard J. Daley) or lengthy and richly textured examinations of whole chunks of the city's history (such as Donald L. Miller's history of pre-1900 Chicago). For my course on the history of Chicago, however, I needed something like a textbook: a book of moderate length that told the city's story from the 1500s up to the post-machine era of the 1990s, hitting most of the main facts and introducing most of the main personages along the way. Moreover, I wanted a book aimed at my college undergraduates and other interested readers who were not professional historians—a book that indulged my preferences for narrative and amusing stories while it analyzed the formative events and trends in the city's history. History should be both entertaining and informative; this book is my attempt at that.

Readers will discover that this book is not a Chicago encyclopedia. It is by necessity a selective history that illuminates those events, personalities, developments, and institutions that are most important for understanding Chicago's history. I have felt no obligation to identify every mayor, to describe every labor strike, or to explain in detail why the Cubs have not won a World Series since before World War I. Nor is this book brimming with new conclusions and interpretations. It is a synthesis of the vast existing literature on Chicago's history, here brought together into a manageable length and a readable format. Also included in this book are extended quotations from contemporary observers and eyewitnesses, which will give the reader a sense of how Chicagoans themselves understood and experienced their history. It seems desirable that a survey of Chicago's history (like this one) should introduce the reader to Carl Sandburg's poetry, Upton Sinclair's classic novel about the meatpacking industry, and Richard J. Daley's malapropisms. I have refrained from engaging historians' debates because, although historiographical discussions are important, the burden of this book is to tell Chicago's story as briskly as possible.

This is the kind of book that my students, my wife, or my brother Karl, who is not a historian, can read with profit and hopefully with pleasure. It covers the city's entire history, places Chicago's history within the broader national context, pays attention to enduring themes like ethnicity, and embraces a more or less chronological approach for ease of reading. Meaty issues like economic development, the sociology of the political machine, and class conflict after the Great Chicago Fire are covered. Also covered are issues like the city's pursuit of clean drinking water, the butchering process in the meatpacking plants, and how Bulls basketball player Dennis Rodman helped eighty-year-old Margaret Glenn renovate her Near West Side home. It is difficult to navigate between the Scylla of dry academic tome and the Charybdis of anecdotal nostalgia, but the course is charted for this history of Chicago.

Many have contributed to this book, and they deserve recognition. Foremost are the legions of Chicago historians who have waded through newspapers, documents, personal correspondence, court papers, and interviews to write many well-researched monographs and journal articles on virtually every facet of Chicago's history. These scholars bequeathed to me a veritable arsenal of published scholarship with which to work; this synthesis relies upon and is indebted to these scholars. Much of my work was made possible by a Summer Research Grant that was graciously extended to me by Trinity International University. My colleagues there—especially Steve Pointer, Steve Fratt, Harold Baxter, Cliff Williams, Bill Graddy, Angelo Rentas, and Tom Hunt—were most supportive. I am also indebted to my Trinity students who endured early versions of this manuscript in my teaching. I promised to include their names in the preface if they provided me with editorial help on my book-in-progress. They upheld their end of the bargain splendidly, so I shall uphold mine: many thanks to Dan, Brenda, Maribeth, Ian, Andrew, Billie Jo, Jamie, Cheri, Andy, Tiffany, Amelia, Jessica, Kevin, Matt, and Tim.

City of Big Shoulders

CHICAGO

Carl Sandburg

Hog Butcher for the World,
Tool Maker, Stacker of Wheat,
Player with Railroads and the Nation's Freight Handler,
Stormy, husky, brawling,
City of the Big Shoulders:

They tell me you are wicked and I believe them, for I have seen your
painted women under the gas lamps luring the farm boys.
And they tell me you are crooked and I answer: Yes, it is true I have seen
the gunman kill and go free to kill again.
And they tell me you are brutal and my reply is: On the faces of women
and children I have seen the marks of wanton hunger.
And having answered so I turn once more to those who sneer at this my
city, and I give them back the sneer and say to them:
Come and show me another city with lifted head singing so proud to be
alive and coarse and strong and cunning.
Flinging magnetic curses amid the toil of piling job on job, here is a tall
bold slugger set vivid against the little soft cities;

Fierce as a dog with tongue lapping for action, cunning as a savage
pitted against the wilderness,
Bareheaded,
Shoveling,
Wrecking,
Planning,
Building, breaking, rebuilding,
Under the smoke, dust all over his mouth, laughing with white teeth,
Under the terrible burden of destiny laughing as a young man laughs,
Laughing even as an ignorant fighter laughs who has never lost a battle,
Bragging and laughing that under his wrist is the pulse, and under his
ribs the heart of the people,
Laughing!
Laughing the stormy, husky, brawling laughter of Youth, half-naked,
sweating, proud to be Hog Butcher, Tool Maker, Stacker of
Wheat, Player with Railroads and Freight Handler to the Nation.

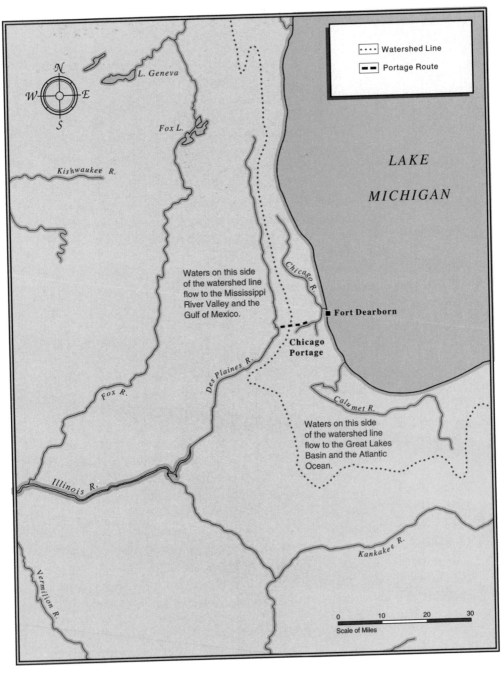

LAKE

MICHIGAN

L. Geneva

Fox L.

Kishwaukee R.

Chicago R.

■ Fort Dearborn

Waters on this side of the watershed line flow to the Mississippi River Valley and the Gulf of Mexico.

Chicago Portage

Des Plaines R.

Fox R.

Calumet R.

Waters on this side of the watershed line flow to the Great Lakes Basin and the Atlantic Ocean.

Illinois R.

Kankakee R.

Vermilion R.

········ Watershed Line
▬ ▬ Portage Route

0   10   20   30
Scale of Miles

Rivers and portage of early Chicago

CHAPTER ONE

THE EARLY

WORLD OF

CHIGAGOU,

1600-1750

•   Before there was a city of Chicago, Native Americans knew about a marshy area they called *Chigagou,* meaning "the wild-garlic place."[1] To these American Indians, Chigagou was an inhospitable place, and few wanted to live on the area's marshy land. About four miles from the Lake of the Illinois (Lake Michigan), the mud and bogs gave way to a vast, twelve-mile-wide prairie swamp. Within this swamp was a five-mile-long depression so inglorious that later settlers could think of no better name for it than Mud Lake. The soil was not especially fertile, and the long, bitterly cold winters made for short growing seasons. The flat prairie offered no hills and few trees to shield inhabitants from the howling wind; winter wind chill factors of twenty degrees below zero were as common in 1390 as they were in 1990. The combination of soggy swampland, flat prairie, and routine flooding meant that the area would suffer from drainage problems for centuries to come.[2]

The ancestors of the Native Americans who settled in this region came from Siberia. Crossing the Bering Strait, they sojourned in the territory that would be known as Alaska and western Canada before moving south. Archaeologists tell us they were originally native Siberians, Mongols, or Asians. Perhaps, then, we could call these early explorers, conquerors, and settlers Siberian Americans, the first of many immigrants to a swampy area that would someday stand as one of the largest cities in the world.

Because of the inclement environment, it is little surprise that, although many Native Americans traveled to and from the region of Chigagou, few chose to settle there. For good reason, the American Indians preferred living on dry land, especially land near trees. The few Illiniwek, or Illinois, Indians who lived in the area subsisted on both agriculture and hunting. They spent their winters huddled in log cabins covered with sewn reed mats that repelled both rain and snow. Chigagou was simply one of many small gathering places. Its geographic location suggests it was a place that American Indians passed through while traveling. Most of the Illinois lived farther south and closer to the great river that would later be known as the Mississippi River. It was here—near present-day St. Louis—that Illinois settlements dotted the land, not in the dismal swamps of Chigagou. At least for the American Indians, what distinguished the swamplands near the Lake of the Illinois from other locales was the abundance of wild garlic that thrived there.

The Illinois Indians claimed most of the surrounding area, but they established no large settlement at Chigagou. Sometime around 1650, Iroquois tribes from the territories that would become Indiana and Ohio attacked and decimated the Illinois. Only a few Illinois Indians remained, and so the neighboring Miami moved to occupy the Chigagou area. Such intertribal warfare was common among North American Indian tribes. Even in the late 1700s and early 1800s, when Native Americans in the Indiana-Illinois area found themselves warring with increasing frequency with settlers, the pace of intertribal warfare continued unabated. American Indians routinely fought among themselves even while they fought the settlers.[3]

The Miami were only the latest victors in a long process of war, defeat, and relocation. When the first French missionaries and settlers came to Chigagou in the late 1600s, it was the Miami that they encountered. According to the French, the Miami men were friendly, dark, strong, wearing little clothing, and often covered with tattoos.[4] The Miami abandoned the area around 1800, moving to warmer lands formerly held by the Iroquois. They were replaced in the Chigagou area by the Potawatomi, who had begun moving southward from the area of present-day Green Bay, Wisconsin, in the late 1600s. The Potawatomi would be the last tribe to make its home in the Chigagou area, remaining there until evicted by settlers in 1833. A multicultural people, the Potawatomi were closely related to the Chippewa and Ottawa and had also assimilated aspects of Sac (or Sauk), Fox, and Kickapoo cultures.

Because Native Americans could find plenty of other lands that were warmer, drier, less windy, and closer to major rivers, Chigagou was never the site of a major settlement. European settlers saw the area differently, however. For Europeans, the cold swamp would become one of the most important geographical spots in all of North America.

White traders quickly realized that the Chigagou swamp straddled what amounted to a mini-continental divide. East of Chigagou, rivers flowed eastward toward the Atlantic Ocean, and, west of the swamp, rivers flowed westward toward the Mississippi River. Because no river flowed from North America's Atlantic coast to the Mississippi River, Europeans could only reach the Mississippi River, and thereby access the heart of the North American continent, by an arduous overland route. But a marsh located about six miles southwest of present-day downtown Chicago, near today's Midway Airport, was a place where westward- and eastward-flowing rivers met. Flowing eastward from this marsh, which was known as the portage, was a small, lazy river that merged with several other streams and eventually emptied into Lake Michigan. On the west side of the marsh, the Des Plaines River flowed westward into the Illinois River, and the Illinois continued westward into the Mississippi River. This natural intersection of river systems created a convenient, all-water connection between the Great Lakes and the Mississippi River that would make lengthy overland journeys unnecessary. During the dry season, travelers could simply carry canoes across the short span of dried swamp, and, during the wet season, they could paddle across the flooded swamp.

Until the advent of the railroad in the mid-1800s, water travel was by far the most efficient mode of travel for settlers and traders. Overland travel was extraordinarily slow and difficult, as few roads existed, and most of these were little more than beaten trails. Mud, rivers, and forests hindered overland travel, permitting caravans of goods to travel perhaps ten or fifteen miles per day. This is why the discovery of the Chigagou portage was tantamount to discovering a gateway or an entrepôt into the vast North American interior. Europeans could now enter the North American continent at the mouth of the St. Lawrence River, travel down the St. Lawrence to the Great Lakes, cross the lakes to Chigagou, negotiate the Chigagou area's small local rivers and portage, and then link up with the Mississippi River. Once Europeans realized they could access the heart of North America via this all-water route, Chigagou took on a new importance.

Europeans first saw Chigagou in 1673. By this time, European colonists had been living in Virginia for more than sixty years and in Massachusetts for more than fifty. Although about 120,000 white immigrants called North America home by this time, most were British and therefore occupied the British-controlled lands along the Atlantic coast. By contrast, France possessed much more expansive lands in what is now Canada and the Great Lakes region.

The French had not sent families to the Americas to establish permanent colonies. Aided by the extensive lake and river system of the Great Lakes area, the French missionaries and fur trappers, seeking converts and beaver but not homesteads, reached deep into North America, while few British colonists strayed more than eighty miles from the Atlantic Ocean. In the long run, Britain's strategy of planting a self-reproducing population in the Americas would prove more effective in conquering a continent than France's strategy of sending out trappers and missionaries. Taking the exploitive (or extractive) approach was common to European conquering powers; Spain had become Europe's preeminent power in the 1500s by laying claim to the new lands its agents explored. Looking to claim the heart of the continent for France, two Frenchmen passed through Chigagou in 1673. They immediately realized the area's value.

Jacques Marquette, a Jesuit missionary for the Roman Catholic Church in his mid-thirties, and Louis Joliet, a French explorer not yet thirty years of age, had different reasons for wanting to visit the native people of the region. Marquette hoped to convert the natives to Christianity, while Joliet sought to map the vast unknown heartland of North America and to claim new territory for France. Both men were seasoned explorers, and Marquette spoke six American Indian languages. The Frenchmen were also skilled cartographers: using only a compass and an astrolabe, they would draw the first trustworthy map of this corner of the globe. After a chance meeting with several Illinois Indians on the shore of what is now Lake Superior, the two men set out to travel to the Illinois Indians' home. Joliet carried with him orders from France: find "the great river" that flowed somewhere in the west. If he found it, he could claim it and its extensive basin for his country.

During 1673, the priest-and-explorer pair, assisted by five additional travelers, traversed northern Wisconsin for a month before coming upon the Mississippi River. Traveling south by canoe on the river, they journeyed for another month and explored as far as the Arkansas River before turning back. By that time, they had concluded that the great river emptied into the Gulf of Mexico and not the Pacific Ocean, as some had conjectured. The prospect of paddling their canoes upstream for several hundred miles against the flow of the mighty Mississippi was unappealing, however, especially as the summer sun beat upon them and Marquette suffered from dysentery. Upon reaching the Illinois River, a Native American boy who was traveling with the Frenchmen suggested that the party travel up the tributary. The Illinois River would speed their return to Lake Michigan, the boy told them. Unbeknownst to the French explorers, the Illinois River proved to be a tributary of the Mississippi that cut across present-day Illinois in an east-to-west direction. The Frenchmen paddled up the Illinois River, and a party of American Indians escorted them to the Des Plaines River, another westward-flowing river that originated in a swampy pond. On the opposite side of the swamp, Native Americans directed the men to an eastward-flowing river that drained into Lake Michigan. At last they had reached their destination, and their four-month-long journey over 2,500 miles was a success.

Marquette and Joliet had been the first white men to see Chigagou and the critical portage area, and they owed their "discovery" to the Illinois Indians. Marquette described his contact with the native people: "They received us very well, and obliged me to promise that I would return to instruct them."[5] Accordingly, the French priest returned in the fall of 1674 only to become snowbound in Chigagou in the winter of 1674–1675. He spent the winter there, becoming the first European to reside in the area. He was also the first European to die there. At the age of thirty-seven, the "black robe," as the Jesuit missionaries were called, took ill and died in 1675. The Native Americans to whom he had preached buried him along Lake Michigan.

Although they were the first to map the territory, Marquette and Joliet did not "discover" Chigagou. Not only had the Native American Indians known about "the wild-garlic place" for some time, but other Europeans were in the area as well. When Marquette wintered in Chigagou in 1674–1675, for example, he met two French traders. One of these traders, Pierre Moreau, called the Mole, was a fur trader who specialized in selling liquor to the Native Americans—an illegal but financially rewarding activity. Moreau's partner is known to us only by his nickname: the Surgeon. Marquette's diaries tell us that the Mole and the Surgeon befriended the Jesuit missionary, built a cabin for him on the bank of the Chicago River, near the Damen Avenue Bridge today, so he could survive the winter, and provided food when his health failed.[6] There may have been earlier French fur trappers who had passed through Chigagou long before these Frenchmen saw the swampy land. It was Marquette and Joliet, however, who first recorded their journey in diaries, drew maps of their travels, and realized that they had passed through previously unmapped land.

Marquette was concerned about his Christian mission to the Indians, and he seemed not to realize the strategic and commercial possibilities of the Chigagou area. This was not so for Joliet, who wrote to his superiors to suggest that a canal be built through the portage and that colonies be established in the area. He explained that New France now possessed "a very great and important advantage, which perhaps will hardly be believed. It is that we could go with facility to Florida in a bark, and by very easy navigation. It would only be necessary to make a canal by cutting through half a league of prairie, to pass from the foot of the Lake of the Illinois [Lake Michigan] to the river Saint Louis [the Illinois River]."[7] French officials scoffed at Joliet's plans, however, probably finding it difficult to imagine a canal set in the barren wilderness of Chigagou. Only 6,700 Frenchmen sojourned in all of North America at the time, and France could spare none of them for highly speculative dreams like Joliet's. It would be almost a century and a half before other men would bring to fruition Joliet's proposal for a portage canal.

Despite Marquette's death and Joliet's rebuff by his superiors, Chigagou was on the map. More importantly, the rivers that linked Lake Michigan with the Mississippi River were on the map. The French realized that Chigagou and its portage gave them a strategic advantage over their bitter rivals, the British. The British had planted thriving colonies on the Atlantic coast, and those colonists now threatened to move westward and to claim more of North America. British dominance of the Atlantic seaboard prevented competing French colonies there. Chigagou and its portage allowed the French to do an "end run" around the British-controlled colonies. Chigagou could become a base of operations from which the French could access the heart of North America, travel down the Mississippi, and claim all the Mississippi basin, gaining vast new lands for the French crown and restricting Britain's westward advance across America. French control of the Mississippi River basin, therefore, was part of a seventeenth-century French containment policy aimed at limiting British expansion in North America.

France authorized two men, Robert Cavelier Sieur de La Salle and Henri de Tonty, to build a chain of forts throughout the middle of North America that would secure those lands for France. La Salle and Tonty passed through Chigagou in 1681–1682, built a stockade and cabin there, constructed several forts nearby, and explored the Mississippi River all the way to the Gulf of Mexico. They audaciously claimed the entire Mississippi River basin for France and named it Louisiana after the French king, Louis XIV. Like Joliet, La Salle grasped the strategic importance of the Chigagou portage. Holed up in a cold log hut on the portage during the winter of 1682–1683, La Salle nonetheless prophesied that the area would someday become "the gate of empire" and "the seat of commerce."[8] La Salle never lived to bask in his newfound glory as the king's agent or even to see Chigagou become anything other than a swampy frontier outpost. He was killed in 1684 by a group of frightened French colonists when he misread his maps and they became lost in the wilderness. Tonty was more fortunate: he faithfully built French forts in the Mississippi River valley until his death in 1704.

French trappers continued to work the Chigagou area while French missionaries labored among local Native Americans. As late as 1766, a British captain surveyed the area and reported that France had been busy carrying on trade "all round . . . by Land and by Water; 1st up the Mississippi and to the Lakes by the Ouisconsing, Foxes, Chigagou, and Illinois Rivers."[9] The French proved more adept at sending out pioneering fur trappers, however, than at building a permanent community. Perhaps three hundred small cabins dotted the Chigagou area in 1700. A number of French fur trappers lived there with American Indian wives and reared children. Pierre Pinet, a Jesuit missionary, opened the Mission of the Guardian Angel in Chigagou in 1696, which ministered to the small settlement. Pinet, who uncharitably described his neighbors as "hardened in profligacy," took special pride in the children he was able to baptize there. Within five years, however, Father Pinet's mission had closed—perhaps because Pinet criticized the French practice of trafficking alcohol among the Native Americans. The French settlement at Chigagou stagnated, and France's western empire never materialized. Indeed, we know little about Chigagou between 1700 and 1750, largely because Chigagou never grew into the bustling entrepôt that the French had envisioned. For almost seventy years, the area remained little more than a crossroads where a handful of trappers, explorers, missionaries, and Native Americans wintered.

Chigagou's future had looked bright in the 1680s, when France had intended to make the area the jewel of its North American possessions, the French version of New York City or Boston. But local Indians began to resent what was beginning to look like a European invasion of the area. Perhaps this is why Native Americans murdered twelve Frenchmen in 1714 in Chigagou. By 1720, Fox Indians had cut off the Europeans' access to the southern end of the portage, where the Des Plaines River leaves the swamp and begins it westward journey to the Illinois River. Local Native Americans knew that severing the Lake Michigan-to-Mississippi River waterway robbed the area of its significance.

Establishing a series of French forts in the wilderness was an extremely difficult task under the best of conditions. Such forts needed to be self-sufficient, as they had little contact with the outside world and were surrounded by sometimes hostile Native Americans. France's ability to project power abroad was waning at this time. Protracted European wars had depleted France's financial resources by 1720, and heavy taxation of the peasantry was beginning to produce social tensions. Creating an extended series of forts in North America required money, soldiers, administrative expertise, and political commitment. The French were short on all four.

Another hindrance to the development of Chigagou was that France claimed an enormous area of North America and had no need to exploit the Mississippi River valley. The vast expanses of Canada and the Great Lakes region produced fur-bearing animals in abundance and was inhabited by plenty of Native Americans in need of salvation—the two chief concerns of French adventurers. When difficulties were encountered, short-term interests such as the profitable fur trade took precedence over the long-term goal of containing Britain's westward expansion. Thus when Native Americans blocked France's access to the Des Plaines River, trappers and priests simply looked for business in the more hospitable wilderness of Canada. Other Frenchmen planted a small settlement at New Orleans.

If the French plans for a North American empire had come to fruition, hundreds of thousands of French trappers, missionaries, and settlers might have peopled the vast Mississippi River basin. Chigagou might have indeed become the hub of a vast overseas French colony, a Paris-on-Lake Michigan through which France would manage her New World domain. By imagining what might have been—what America might have looked like with Chigagou as the nerve center of a thriving mid-American French empire—we are better able to appreciate what actually did happen. As it was, the French empire never materialized, and France's grandiose plans for Chigagou fizzled. Chigagou remained a small, unimportant settlement until the 1750s. The area remained a swamp, not the linchpin of a French empire in the Mississippi River valley. Great Britain continued to focus on its colonies on the Atlantic seaboard. Nobody would have called Chigagou a city or even a town. Few could have thought that, in the next century and a half, this would be one of the largest cities in the world.

CHAPTER TWO

CHIGAGOU

BECOMES

CHICAGO,

1750 - 1835

• In the late 1700s and early 1800s, daring Americans seeking the excitement and potential wealth of the frontier headed for the remote settlement of Chigagou. Upon arriving there, they found a typical North American frontier settlement: wealthy speculators, dirty fur trappers, and fugitives from justice all sought shelter in run-down flophouses. Animals wandered about on dirt roads that sometimes choked man and beast with dust and sometimes swallowed both in mud. American Indians, French outdoorsmen, and British colonists rubbed shoulders without too many incidents. Land was cheap. Alcohol was cheaper. Philadelphia, London, and Paris were a long way away, and these restless entrepreneurs and adventurers were free to remake their lives apart from traditional mores and protocol.

The period between 1750 and 1835 was an exciting, contentious, topsy-turvy time in North America as the French, British, Anglo-American settlers, and Native Americans jockeyed for control of the continent.[1] European conflicts between the French and British were played out in America, where both the European colonists and the American Indians became (in some sense) pawns in an extended battle between two superpowers. The little settlement of Chigagou was emblematic of these power struggles, as it passed from French control to British authority and finally to American control, all within a thirty-year period. Not only did settlers face sporadic conflict with local native peoples, but their method of dealing with them would change markedly during the period. Moreover, Chigagou first began to look like an Anglo-American town in the early 1800s—a town more appropriately referred to by its Europeanized name of Chicago than its Native American name of Chigagou.

FROM FRENCH TO BRITISH TO AMERICAN CONTROL, 1754–1784

In 1750, when Chigagou was still a small, struggling frontier outpost controlled by France, Britain engaged France in a bold move calculated to gain a world empire—in India, Europe, North America, the Philippines, Cuba, and Martinique—in a series of battles that are now called the Great War for Empire. Britain's object was to strip France of her colonial possessions, to add those lands to the growing British Empire, and to supplant France as the dominant nation in the world. One aspect of this world war was the struggle over new colonies in North America, where, over the course of the eighteenth century, the British had grown stronger as French power waned. Britain called on her colonists in North America for support, and as loyal British subjects such men as Benjamin Franklin and George Washington waged war with France and her Native American allies in Pennsylvania, New York, Quebec, and Nova Scotia. American colonists hoped this conflict, which they called the French and Indian War, would weaken the Native Americans, who had been harassing settlers along the frontier and preventing them from acquiring land farther west. By 1763, Britain and her colonists were victorious. They forced France to surrender almost all her colonial possessions in North America, which more than doubled the British territory on the continent. All this was cause for rejoicing for the British and the residents of the thirteen British colonies. The French menace was gone, and the British now controlled vast new lands that could be opened to new colonists. Without their French allies, the Native Americans would presumably be weaker as well.

Britain's victory in the Great War for Empire also meant that frontier settlements like Chigagou changed hands. With the French ousted from the continent, Chigagou and its environs passed from French to British jurisdiction. Everyday life, however, did not change much for the handful of frontiersmen and Native Americans who called Chigagou home. The British were too busy consolidating control of their new worldwide empire. Tiny frontier outposts located in the middle of swamps were a low priority.

Chigagou remained a part of His Majesty's Empire for less than twenty years. During the early years of the American War for Independence, the rebellious colonists seized present-day Ohio, Indiana, Illinois, Michigan, Wisconsin, parts of Minnesota, and the Great Lakes area. It was George Rogers Clark, a twenty-six-year-old Kentuckian, who almost singlehandedly captured the vast Old Northwest for the United States.[2] He and his 175-man Kentucky militia were commissioned by the Virginia House of Burgesses, and they promptly marched westward in search of Redcoats. They captured British forts at Vincennes (on the present-day border between Illinois and Indiana, about 200 miles south of Chicago), Kaskaskia (on the present-day border between Illinois and Missouri, about 50 miles south of St. Louis), and Cahokia (adjacent to St. Louis).[3] With these conquests in hand, Clark audaciously claimed all the land from the Ohio River to the Great Lakes for the Americans. Included in this region was Chigagou.

State loyalties were stronger than national allegiances in 1778. This is why Clark claimed the southern shores of Lake Michigan for the state of Virginia, not for the infant United States of America. The Virginia House of Burgesses created the County of Illinois to govern the newly acquired lands, and thus Chigagou belonged to Virginia for several years. The British recognized Clark's victories in the 1783 Treaty of Paris that ended the War for Independence, formalizing transfer of the Old Northwest (and Chigagou) to the new United States of America. In 1784, Virginia yielded control of Illinois to the new national government. There were few residents of Illinois either to celebrate or to bemoan their second change of masters in twenty years. Virginia boasted a population of 540,000 and Pennsylvania claimed 330,000 residents in the 1780s, but only about 1,000 white settlers lived inside the borders of present-day Illinois at this time.

A PERMANENT SETTLER AND A PERMANENT FORT

It was during the War for Independence that Chigagou became home to the man who may well qualify as the settlement's first permanent resident: Jean Baptiste Pointe Du Sable. Either mulatto or black, Du Sable was born in the present-day Dominican Republic or in Haiti. Little is known of Du Sable, but a British military report refers to him as "a handsome negro" and "well-educated."[4] In 1779 he settled in Chigagou and promptly built a sumptuous house, which was twenty-two feet by forty feet long, that became the talk of the settlement. Du Sable shared his frontier palace with his wife, who was the daughter of a Potawatomi chief, and their two children for nearly twenty years.[5] This multiethnic family thrived in the multiethnic world of frontier Chigagou. One British observer referred to Du Sable as "a Black Chief" who enjoyed good relationships with the local Miami. Another traveler described Du Sable as being "a trader, pretty wealthy, . . . [who] drank freely."[6]

Du Sable's estate, located where the *Chicago Sun-Times* building stands today, was a combination of farm, trading post, and store. Du Sable owned a mill, a smokehouse, a dairy, a workshop, two barns, and herds of livestock. He probably hired workers to tend his farm, stable, and bakery. His house included such luxuries as a French walnut cabinet with four glass doors, several paintings, and a feather bed. The presence of such items on the frontier is astounding; one can only imagine the bewildered looks on the faces of fur trappers or Native Americans as they transported fine French furniture in canoes to Du Sable's home. In addition to suggesting that Du Sable was a man of both means and culture, such luxury items indicate that Chigagou was a growing settlement. Trading posts and stores like Du Sable's only thrive where there are traders and customers.

Although the Northwest Ordinance of 1787 organized the Illinois area as a U.S. possession, thereby formally placing Chigagou under U.S. control, Du Sable would have considered himself a resident of the small French–Native American frontier settlement of Chigagou, not the American town of Chicago. The settlement remained a remote frontier outpost, populated more by Native Americans and French fur trappers than by white Anglo-Americans. The United States did nothing to assert its authority in the area until 1795, when Revolutionary War veteran "Mad Anthony" Wayne defeated the Shawnee, Potawatomi, Wyandot, and Miami at the Battle of Fallen Timbers near present-day Toledo, Ohio. In the resulting Treaty of Greenville, the vanquished tribes surrendered several tracts of land. Among them was the six-square-mile tract of Chigagou, an area that comprises the heart of downtown Chicago today.[7]

In 1803, the construction of Fort Dearborn (named for Henry Dearborn, President Thomas Jefferson's Secretary of War) at Chigagou seemed to confirm the transformation of the settlement from a Native American gathering place into an American town. U.S. Army Captain John Whistler arrived in Chigagou to construct and to garrison the new fort.[8] His contingent was small: one captain, one second lieutenant, one ensign, four sergeants, three corporals, fifty-four privates, one surgeon's mate, and four musicians. Within a year, they built Fort Dearborn, a log fort sporting twelve-foot-high palisades and located near the intersection of Michigan Avenue and Wacker Drive today.

Although a U.S. soldier, Whistler himself exemplifies how the term "American" was ethnically ambiguous in the early years of the Republic.

Whistler was born in Ireland and served as a British soldier during the War for Independence. Captured by the American rebels during the fighting, he languished as a prisoner of war in American prisons. He returned to Great Britain when the war ended but realized that he missed the wide-open spaces of America. He returned to the United States with his family, settled in Maryland, and enlisted in the same U.S. Army that he had fought against only a few years earlier. Within twenty years, he was building a fort in the remote Old Northwest—an area populated largely by American Indians and French Canadians, in a frontier community where Anglo-Americans were the clear minority. His story reminds us that simply referring to someone as an American in 1800 often tells us little about that person. Whistler was indeed an American, but he was also an Irishman and a former British citizen.

The cosmopolitan Whistler must have blanched when he first saw the dreary desolateness of Chigagou. Others did. One visitor to the settlement, who stopped by to greet Whistler upon his arrival at the frontier settlement, noted, "At this time there were no buildings there [in Chigagou], except a few dilapidated log huts, covered with bark. Captain Whistler had selected one of these as a temporary, though miserable, residence for his family, his officers and men being under canvas."9 Nor were Whistler's soldiers impressed with their new home. They saw only four rude cabins at the point where the Chicago River lazily emptied into Lake Michigan. Indeed, the soldiers refused to glorify the waterway they saw by calling it a river. It was, they claimed, a muddy stream "about 30 yards wide . . . 18 feet and upwards deep, dead water, owing to its being stopped by the washing of sand from the lakes," and they pronounced the water "not fit for use."10 The soldiers were virtual prisoners in their raw, isolated outpost. It was a one-week trip to equally remote Fort Wayne, Indiana, a two-week journey to Detroit, and a two-to-three-week passage to St. Louis.

The presence of Whistler, his men, and Fort Dearborn was important to the United States for symbolic reasons. They signified the U.S. commitment to maintain control over the most remote reaches of its frontier. Although the American colonies had won their independence in the Revolutionary War, the Americans remained economically dependent on their former mother country. The British were therefore able to exact painful economic concessions from the colonists between 1783 and 1812. In addition to squeezing the Americans economically, Britain refused to vacate its western frontier posts. Throughout the period between 1783 and 1812, a handful of British agents remained in the Old

Northwest. They befriended the Native Americans and supplied them with weapons, money, and alcohol. The British surely did not want to see a virile, confident America expand its possessions across the continent, so they motivated the Indians to harass the Americans on their newly acquired frontier. Like the French before them, the British implemented a policy in North America that could be characterized as a crude sort of containment. The French hoped to control the American interior so as to contain Britain's westward expansion; now the British hoped to control the Old Northwest to restrict the westward expansion of the United States. In essence, the British fought the Americans by proxy through the American Indians.

Though the British were able to involve some tribes in their fight, many Native American Indians remained on friendly terms with the Anglo-American settlers and resisted British overtures to be paid thorns in the white settlers' sides. Two such pro-American peoples were the Potawatomi and the Miami—tribes indigenous to the Chigagou area. The Potawatomi and the Miami went so far as to side with the Americans against other local Native American peoples, most notably the Winnebago, who became de facto British mercenaries in the Old Northwest. In this context of mounting frontier insecurity, Fort Dearborn was a statement of U.S. resolve. It declared that the United States, not the British or the American Indians, controlled the area. With the arrival of U.S. troops and the establishment of Fort Dearborn, Chigagou began to be rapidly transformed into the American settlement of Chicago.[11]

Tensions between the Americans and the British-backed American Indians were minimal at first. There simply were not enough Americans in the Illinois area to alarm most Indians. At least until 1811, the soldiers at Fort Dearborn fought boredom more than they fought Indians or Redcoats. The local Potawatomi were friendly and did much business with the Anglo-Americans, so much so that the years between 1803 and 1811 might well have been the zenith of Chicago's Native American trade. Many local settlers, such as Antoine Ouilmette (for whom the settlement of Wilmette was named), were European men with American Indian wives. In this frontier settlement, lives meshed and there was virtually no segregation. Native Americans posed little threat to settlers and soldiers; whites were more likely to die from disease, childbirth, or the white-on-white violence that was common on the lawless frontier. In one prominent example of this violence, John Kinzie, a leading citizen of Chicago, stabbed a resident, Jean La Lime, to death. Kinzie fled the area for the safety of Native American lands, remained in self-imposed exile for a short time until tempers cooled, and then returned to town to resume his position as a town leader.

INDIAN WARS IN THE CHICAGO AREA

The frontier exploded in 1811 with the Battle of Tippecanoe. Under the direction of the Native American leader Tecumseh, a confederation of tribes engaged U.S. soldiers who were commanded by future president William Henry Harrison. The battle—which took place near present-day Lafayette, Indiana, only one hundred miles southeast of Chicago—ended in a decisive U.S. victory. More important, it sent shock waves across the frontier. American Indians in many places concluded that war with the American settlers was inevitable, and they therefore chose to go on the offensive. The explosive situation worsened for Americans when the young nation declared war on Great Britain in 1812. Now the United States was openly at war with both the British and many British-supplied American Indians. The British redoubled their support of their American Indian allies.

Repercussions were felt in Chicago almost immediately. In 1812, a band of British-aided Winnebago Indians raided Charles Lee's farm, which was four miles south of Fort Dearborn. Two farm laborers were shot and scalped. The entire white community, which numbered fewer than one hundred, fled to Fort Dearborn and huddled behind its wooden palisades for protection. For the next few months, the handful of non–Native American settlers in the area lived in fear. Bands of Winnebago as well as young, rebellious Potawatomi (who did not share their parents' willingness to accommodate the Anglo-Americans) roamed the frontier, stealing livestock and burning buildings. Frightened settlers knew a major attack was imminent and sought protection at the fort, but it was little more than an outpost. It never housed more than one hundred soldiers, and reinforcements were one week's march away. Such a skimpy contingent stood little chance against a concerted attack.

An American Indian war in Chicago seemed certain. Hundreds of Native Americans had flooded into Chicago from surrounding areas; most were not the friendly Potawatomi and Miami. Facing sure defeat if war were to break out, the U.S. Army made a fateful decision. It conceded that Fort Dearborn could never protect itself and the area's white settlers from an attack by the Native Americans. The army ordered Captain Nathan Heald, who had replaced Whistler one year earlier in 1811, to evacuate the fort. Heald decided to destroy all the supplies within the fort, particularly munitions and liquor, and to travel by foot and wagon to the nearest U.S. fort, which was one week away. The Army hired a rescue party of pro-American Miami, who arrived to escort the Fort Dearborn occupants safely out of the area.

Heald assembled his exit parade. Between fifteen and thirty Miami traveled at the front and tail of the procession. Heald's fifty healthy soldiers and twelve civilian males traveled in the middle. All prepared to protect the numerous women and children who joined the parade. As they departed, Native Americans swarmed into the fort and looted it. Hundreds of American Indians, vastly outnumbering the frightened Americans and Miami, watched the somber procession as it slowly moved away from Chicago. Tense moments followed, no one sure whether the party would be allowed to leave. The whites and their Miami escort were at the mercy of the angry, surrounding Indians.

The procession was only about a mile and a half from Fort Dearborn when the ambush began. About six hundred Native Americans swooped down upon the travelers. It was, in the truest sense of the word, a massacre. Of the ninety-four white Americans and Miami Indians who had attempted to flee Chicago, about sixty were killed.[12] Friendly Potawatomi broke into the killing frenzy, grabbed several white people, and whisked them away to safety. The hostile warriors then burned the wood-sided Fort Dearborn to the ground. The massacre effectively ended the settlement at Chicago. Virtually no one except Native Americans remained in the area, and Chicago reverted to Chigagou. Settlers did not return to the area for four years, in 1816.

The War of 1812 went equally badly for the United States in other theaters. The District of Columbia was invaded by the British and burned. The U.S. attempt to invade Canada, to conquer the vast British possessions there, and to hold those lands hostage failed miserably. The only significant U.S. victory in the war was at the Battle of New Orleans, but that triumph came several days after the peace treaty had been signed. Yet Great Britain agreed to a peace treaty with the United States in 1814, primarily because the British were weary from twenty years of continual war in Europe. The treaty gave nothing to either the United States or the British. Neither side made concessions, and the agreement simply restored the status quo antebellum.[13]

The true losers in the War of 1812 were the Native Americans. The British pledged in their 1814 treaty to cease inciting the American Indians to fight, which meant that British weapons, supplies, and money would no longer find a way into Native American hands. This left the Native Americans with no ally; they would now face alone the rapidly growing number of American settlers who were moving westward. Moreover, the conflicts between 1812 and 1814 marked a change in how Anglo-American settlers would deal with the Native Americans. Before 1812, many frontier settlers had freely lived in diverse, multiethnic communities that consisted of Anglo-Americans, American Indians, French settlers, and African Americans. Intermarriage and Anglo-Indian commerce were common. Whites in the region rarely attempted to evict Native Americans from parcels of land. All things changed after 1814. With conflicts such as the Fort Dearborn massacre fresh in American minds, many whites began to assume that Native Americans were bellicose and untrustworthy. Settlers hastened their efforts to push Native Americans westward. The older settlers had distinguished between the friendlier native peoples, such as the Potawatomi and the Miami, and the more hostile tribes, such as the Winnebago. The newer settlers saw no such distinction; they feared all Indians.

In 1816, the United States forced the American Indians to sign the first of several treaties that would effectively move them west of the Mississippi. In the Treaty of St. Louis, American Indians surrendered the area bounded by the southern end of Lake Michigan on the north and Kankakee and the Fox Rivers on the south. Fort Dearborn was rebuilt in 1816–1817; this time, however, it was not designed to deter Britain. The new Fort Dearborn was to be a defense against the Native Americans. An 1821 conference between Governor Lewis Cass of Michigan and local Native Americans drew 3,500 American Indians to Chicago. The conference ended with the Native Americans ceding five million acres of southwestern Michigan. In return, the American Indians received $5,000 annually for twenty years and the services of a blacksmith and a school teacher in Chicago. The agreement forced many Native Americans in Michigan to flee westward to the Chicago area.

The War of 1812 signaled another change in the relationship between Native Americans and settlers. Heretofore, American Indians had been clinging to self-sufficiency and had acted on a more equal footing with whites on the frontier. With a diminishing supply of game and the fur trade dominated by large monopolies such as John Jacob Astor's American Fur Company, however, the Native Americans were becoming increasingly dependent on the settlers. Thousands of American Indians returned to Chicago every fall to collect their government annuities. Soon this yearly ritual began to take on a carnival atmosphere. Merchants and traders flocked to Chicago so they could fleece the temporarily wealthy Native Americans. Alcohol flowed freely. The plethora of refugee American Indians in Chicago prompted one 1826 visitor to observe: "At that time, Chicago was merely an Indian agency. It contained about fourteen houses, and not more than seventy-five or one hundred inhabitants at the most. . . . The staple business seemed to be carried on by the Indians and runaway soldiers, who hunted ducks and muskrats in the marshes."[14]

A more subtle change was taking place as well. Before 1812, few Americans (and even fewer Frenchmen) viewed the American Indians as inherently inferior to Europeans. Educated Americans who had read the Enlightenment philosophers in Europe saw the Native Americans as "noble savages."[15] American Indians were regarded as uneducated, uncultured, and naive but no less human than Europeans. Accordingly, many Americans assumed that the American Indian would one day be assimilated fully into white culture. Absorption, not segregation or annihilation, would ultimately solve what Anglo-Americans called "the Indian problem." This attitude was similar to the one held by most Frenchmen, who freely intermarried with Native Americans and treated them as equals. This treatment characterized the relationship between Native Americans and non–Native Americans in Chigagou prior to 1812. When the U.S. government built Fort Dearborn in 1803, for example, it did not try to displace or to intimidate local native people. It instead created an Indian Agency at the fort with the task of securing good relations with local tribes.

By 1812, however, a new generation of Americans was beginning to regard the Native Americans as distinctly inferior. American Indians were increasingly seen as primitive and belligerent. Many people thought they could never be assimilated into "civilized society." More and more Americans talked about either killing off the American Indians or removing them to land west of the Mississippi. Andrew Jackson would emerge as the leading spokesman for this "removalist" approach to solving "the Indian problem." As president, he would oversee the first deportation of Native Americans to lands west of the Mississippi.

The change in policy from assimilation to removal was slow in coming. At least until the early 1830s, Native Americans and white settlers coexisted peacefully in Chicago. One scholar conjectures that Native Americans outnumbered Anglo-Americans by twenty to one.[16] The settlement was still a frontier outpost, so it attracted many veteran settlers who could live peaceably with American Indians such as the

Potawatomi and Miami; indeed, European-Indian marriages were quite common. It remained, in the words of one historian, "a polyglot world of Indian, French, British, and American cultures tied to a vast trading network that was no less Indian than European."[17] Adventurers in Chicago were still earning a living from the fur trade, much as French trappers had done more than one hundred years earlier.

Illinois could boast of only 40,000 white residents when it qualified for statehood in 1818, and most of these lived in the southern part of the state. At a time when New York City boasted a population of 125,000 and Philadelphia claimed 100,000 residents, John Tipton reported that Chicago in 1821 consisted of Fort Dearborn and "about 9 or 10 houses & families mostly French Trader[s] without any kind of civil government."[18] As late as 1825, when Philadelphia's population exceeded 130,000, Chicago was home to only fourteen taxpayers and thirty-five eligible voters. Several taverns and boardinghouses were located one-half mile west of the fort at Wolf Point, but the mud was so deep between these two spots that the only convenient means of traveling from one to the other was canoe or rowboat. "I passed over the ground from the fort to the Point on horseback," complained one visitor to the settlement in the 1820s. "I was up to my stirrups in water the whole distance. I would not have given sixpence an acre for the whole of it."[19] Not surprisingly, visitors to Chicago thought the settlement had little promise. When Professor William H. Keating, a mineralogist from the University of Pennsylvania, visited Chicago in 1823 and compiled a report for the Army Corps of Engineers, he had few kind words. He began by noting that the climate was wretched, the swampy soil sterile, and the surrounding scenery "monotonous and uninviting." He continued: "The village presents no cheering prospect, as . . . it consists of but few huts, inhabited by a miserable race of men, scarcely equal to the Indians from whom they are descended. Their log or bark houses are low, filthy and disgusting, displaying not the least trace of comfort. . . . As a place of business, it offers no inducement to the settler; for the whole annual shipment of the trade on the lake did not exceed the cargo of five or six schooners. . . . The dangers attending the navigation of the lake, and the scarcity of harbors along the shore, must ever prove a serious obstacle to the increase of the commercial importance of Chicago."[20] Mark Beaubien, a businessman who came to Chicago in 1826, put it more succinctly. When asked about the town he first encountered upon arriving in the area, Beaubien said, "There was no town; didn't expect no town."[21] As late as 1830, Chicago's population still had not reached one hundred. That was not Beaubien's fault, however. He fathered twenty-three children by two successive wives.

Between 1815 and 1830, it was the fur trade—and, more specifically, the American Fur Company—that invigorated Chicago. John Jacob Astor had formed his fur company in 1811, headquartered in the northern Great Lakes area, and he sent permanent fur traders to Chicago in 1817. For a few years, the American Fur Company was often the frontier settlement's sole link to the outside world. Company boats brought two kinds of items: supplies such as food and clothing for Chicago-based traders and trading goods like British playing cards and tomahawks that were exchanged with local Indians for furs. Especially valuable commodities like wine and whiskey qualified as both necessity and barter material. Fur remained a booming business until the late 1820s, when the increasing number of settlers drove both game and Native Americans out of the region. The changing character of the area made fur a dying business, and the American Fur Company presence in the Chicago-area ended in 1835.

The fur business had brought a sixteen-year-old from Vermont, Gurdon Saltonstall Hubbard, to Chicago in 1818. Hubbard was an apprentice fur trader for the American Fur Company. He was most famous, however, for two other things. Native Americans nicknamed Hubbard "The Swift Walker" because of his ability to walk fifty miles in a single day. In a frontier world devoid of roads, such a skill made the young Hubbard invaluable. Hubbard, who remained a Chicago resident until his death in 1886, moved out of the dying fur business and later became Chicago's first insurance underwriter and the owner of several local insurance companies, making him one of the most influential men in Chicago by the mid-nineteenth century.

It was during the 1830s that Chicago passed from settlement to town. With settlers pouring into Illinois, the state's population grew from 55,000 in 1820 to 157,000 in 1830, and even Chicago began to see new faces. To reach the Illinois River more easily, locals proposed building a canal through the portage. As valuable as the portage was, it remained virtually as it had been when Marquette and Joliet passed through it. It consisted of more mud than swamp, and the mud had the consistency of wet cement. Crossing the portage required several men to unload a boat's heaviest items, lash them to their backs, and carry them by foot across the portage. Several others would stay inside the boat, pushing themselves along with long poles that descended into the muck. Still other men climbed out of the boat, sunk waist deep into the mud, and struggled to drag the boat forward. Except when heavy rains had flooded the area, it often took three days to get boats and cargo through the ten-mile-long portage, after which, according to Hubbard, the travelers cursed "this miserable lake."[22]

The new canal would provide efficient transportation between the westward-flowing Des Plaines River and Lake Michigan. State officials, anticipating the growth that would accompany a canal, authorized the first formal survey of Chicago. Today's famous downtown Chicago streets—Washington, Adams, Jefferson, Madison, Jackson, Dearborn, Clark, and La Salle Streets—were plotted at this time. The ensuing auction sold 126 lots at an average price of $35 each. Most purchasers were squatters who had been living for some time on the lots they purchased, and they now enjoyed legal title to their land. In 1832, the first bridges were built over the Chicago River, and the town's first jail was constructed. Chicago's first public building was constructed as well—a pen that held the errant livestock found wandering through the town's muddy streets. The town's first newspaper, the *Chicago Democrat,* went to press in 1833.

This growth was the result of new settlers. Between 1832 and 1833, the town's population doubled to about 350. Most of these settlers were forced into makeshift, hastily constructed housing. Colbee C. Benton, a visitor from New Hampshire, noted: "The lots, many of them, are improved with temporary buildings, some not more than ten feet square, and they are scattered about like cattle on the prairie. . . . I believe there has been one hundred built this year, all without any regard to beauty, and they are set on blocks so that they can move them at the shortest notice."[23]

The shanties offered scant protection from Chicago's brutal winters. "Fortunately we had warm clothing," wrote one Chicago resident. "I actually had my cup freeze to the saucer while sitting at the table at breakfast. Stoves were not to be had."[24] One 1834 visitor wrote: "It has been so cold as almost to render writing impracticable in a place so comfortless. The houses were built with such rapidity, during the summer, as to be mere shells; and the thermometer having ranged as low as 28 below zero during several days, it has been almost impossible, notwithstanding the large fires kept up by an attentive landlord, to prevent the ink from freezing while using it."[25] The town offered few diversions for residents tired of their cramped, cold quarters. The town boasted no theaters, no concert halls, and no reading rooms. Newspapers from New York City were at least three weeks old by the time they reached Chicago. One visitor remarked that Chicagoans could only pass time by playing checkers or listening to Mark Beaubien, owner of one of the settlement's few tavern-and-hotel enterprises, play his fiddle.

Most of these new residents were Easterners looking for a fresh start and cheap land in the west. For the first time, the Americans outnumbered the French and Potawatomi in Chicago. (As late as 1826, twenty-one of thirty-five Chicago voters possessed French names.) This shift in the character of Chicago's population—a shift mirrored throughout Illinois at this time—did not bode well for local American Indians. The newer settlers had no experience dealing with the native population, and, unlike the older settlers, these eager frontiersmen seized their land aggressively, nursed a paranoia about massacres, and accepted the new thinking that Native Americans should be killed or removed, not absorbed.

The influx of new settlers led to the so-called Black Hawk War of 1832, the last significant Indian war in Illinois. White settlers in northwestern Illinois thought they had purchased land from local Sac, Fox, and Kickapoo. When Sac chief Black Hawk returned to his tribal lands, however, he informed the settlers that his people had made no such agreement. Black Hawk attempted to explain to the bewildered settlers that one cannot sell land any more than one can sell the air or rain. You can buy only what you can carry away, argued Black Hawk. Such reasoning baffled the Anglo-American settlers, whose European culture had taught them to treat land as simply another commodity to be bought and sold. Neither side had deliberately misled the other. This was a classic example of two peoples who, possessing vastly different worldviews and presuppositions, found it impossible to communicate with one another.

In Black Hawk we see all the dilemmas encountered by American Indians who hoped to deal with white settlers. An honest man, Black Hawk did not deliberately violate his treaties. Nor was he a primitive warrior who killed simply for the sake of killing, as many whites portrayed him. Black Hawk was a warrior, however, and his people—the Sac—were accustomed to war. For generations, they had made war on the neighboring Osage tribe. The Sac and the Osage did not fight over land or possessions; instead, they fought almost as a way of defining themselves. In Sac culture, war was neither bad nor something to be avoided. It was simply part of living honorably. Black Hawk and his people could not accede the white ethos that made compromise and negotiation better than war. When Black Hawk and whites negotiated, they were more likely to misunderstand one another than they were to disagree openly on substantive matters.

An aging Black Hawk and his people returned to their lands in western Illinois, despite the agreements that white settlers thought had been made. Black Hawk's intentions were, at least at this time, wholly peaceful. The Native Americans had returned to plant crops and to hunt game, which is what they had always done on their land. Black Hawk gambled that the settlers would leave his people alone if they peacefully cultivated their crops. He was wrong. The sight of bands of Native Americans heading toward their unprotected homesteads horrified many settlers. They assumed that the Native Americans were looking for war. Illinois Governor John Reynolds worsened matters when he proclaimed that his state had been invaded by Indians on the warpath. Settlers fled their farms and sought shelter in Fort Dearborn. Militias were formed, and the U.S. government sent General Winfield Scott and his soldiers from New York; Abraham Lincoln and Jefferson Davis were among the armed men sent to northern Illinois.

Assuming that war was inevitable, white settlers planned preemptive attacks. Emblematic of the entire "war" was one of Black Hawk's attempts to explain his position to local whites. He sent representatives to the whites' camp under a white truce flag, but none of the men spoke English. Black Hawk apparently did not consider that an interpreter would be needed. Frightened Illinois militiamen surrounded the three envoys. When the whites saw other Sac watching the proceedings from a nearby ridge, the militiamen suspected deceit and treachery and fired on the Native Americans. The death of the envoys understandably enraged Black Hawk and his people. A brief and lopsided war broke out between the Sac, Kickapoo, and Fox, led by Black Hawk, and the settlers aided by U.S. soldiers.

The Native Americans, who were pursued through northwestern Illinois and southern Wisconsin, were defeated in fifteen weeks. They never came closer to Chicago than Rockford, eighty miles northwest of the city. The coup de grâce came in Vernon County, Wisconsin, at the Bad Axe River, where U.S. soldiers ignored a truce flag, massacred numerous American Indian men, women, and children, and captured Black Hawk. In the subsequent 1833 Treaty of Chicago, the defeated Native Americans surrendered the last great tract of Indian land north of the Ohio River and east of the Mississippi River. U.S. Secretary of War Lewis Cass, who oversaw the treaty, judged that wholesale removal of Native Americans was "an event equally desirable for us as for them; as it is not possible that they can retain their present position much longer, pressed as they will be by our settlements, and exposed to all the evils which these produce."[26] By 1835, Native Americans were forced to move west of the Mississippi; in return, the United States agreed to make twenty annual payments of $14,000 and allocated about $230,000 for various improvements to the Native Americans' new home in Missouri.

The people most victimized by the Black Hawk War were the Potawatomi. Most had not participated in the war; indeed, the Potawatomi had for the previous fifty years sided with Chicago's Anglo-Americans against other Native American peoples. Twenty Potawatomi warriors had even fought alongside the Americans in the Black Hawk War, and the tribe was awarded cash compensation for losses suffered in battle. To most new settlers, however, all American Indians were dangerous. Treaties in 1833 forced the Potawatomi to surrender almost 800,000 acres of land and to leave Illinois along with the other Native American tribes. One local resident, who observed the treaty negotiations, bemoaned the shabby treatment of the Native Americans: "You or hardly any other man, can imagine what was done, or how ridiculously the whole thing was carried on or closed up. It should have been conducted upon the principles of truth and justice; but the whole thing was a farce, acted by those in office in our government."[27] A British traveler, Charles J. Latrobe, witnessed the proceedings as well. Noting in particular the whites' habit of supplying the American Indians with alcohol, Latrobe concluded, "The whites seemed to me more pagan than the red men."[28] The Black Hawk War effectively ended the American Indian presence in both Chicago and Illinois. Chicagoans saw their last large contingent of American Indians in 1835 when the Potawatomi came to the city for their final annual payment.

The Black Hawk War also affected the town's sizeable and influential multiethnic population, consisting primarily of people with both Native American and white ancestry. Before 1830, a settler who took a Native American wife or who was born of a Native American mother found few doors closed to him. This was not so after 1835. Many Chicagoans of mixed ancestry—such as college-educated Madore Beaubien, whose second wife was a Potawatomi woman—could not stomach the mounting disdain for Native Americans. He joined the Potawatomi in their westward trek and grew old on a reservation in Kansas. Many other

Chicagoans with Native American ancestry fled west. In fact, half of the settlers registered to vote between 1828 and 1830 were, or were thought to be, residing in western Native American territory during the 1850s.[29]

The Black Hawk War had another impact on the area: the influx of many U.S. soldiers to Illinois to fight the American Indians was followed by a deluge of settlers. Many soldiers who passed through Chicago returned home with stories about cheap land and the excitement of frontier life. The trickle of new settlers turned into a torrent. In 1833, the town's population stood at 350; by 1834, it had grown to 1,800; by 1835, more than 3,200 residents called Chicago home. "The cloud of emigrants which we then saw rising," wrote one Chicago newspaper editor, "now darkens the eastern sky, and seems still to be thickening upon us."[30] Grain and consumer goods were scarce. Local merchants thrived.

Also, attempts to land ships full of federal soldiers at Chicago during the Black Hawk War had demonstrated the city's need for a useable harbor. Sand clogged the mouth of the Chicago River, effectively prohibiting large ships from entering the river. Such ships instead anchored as far as one mile offshore; smaller vessels ferried passengers and goods into the city. With the assistance of government engineers and federal funding, the mouth of the Chicago River was dredged, a channel was cut through the sand bar, and a 1,260-foot-long pier was built. In July 1834, the schooner *Illinois* navigated the short channel and entered the river, a portent of more ships (and more commerce) to come. By 1835, the city had a harbor that could receive large ships, and 255 major vessels arrived at the city in that year alone.

Although Native Americans were for the most part removed from the Chicago area after the Black Hawk War, they have not been forgotten. Most Chicagoans cheer lustily when their professional hockey team, the Chicago Blackhawks, takes the ice. Thousands of Chicago youths proudly wear jerseys that bear the likeness of a Native American that their ancestors feared and hated. And the Potawatomi remain in the Chicago area and operate a bingo casino in nearby Milwaukee, Wisconsin. Although Native Americans no longer play the preeminent role that they had in the early days of the settlement, their influence in Chicago remains.

* * * *

By 1835, Chicago was no longer a frontier outpost composed primarily of backwoodsmen, fur trappers, and Native Americans. The American

Fur Company closed and sold its properties, as pioneers became far more plenteous than beaver and fox. When John Wentworth, a Dartmouth College graduate, came to town in the early 1830s, he was struck by the cosmopolitan atmosphere. He observed "people from almost every clime, and almost every opinion. . . . Jews, Christians, Protestants, Catholics and infidels . . . Calvinists and Arminians." He continued, "Nearly every language was represented. . . . Some were quite learned and some were ignorant."[31] Chicago was now a town. It was a small town, to be sure, but a town with bright prospects.

CHAPTER THREE

BOOM, BUST,

AND RECOVERY IN

EARLY CHICAGO,

1835 - 1850

• Judge Theophilus Smith of the Illinois Supreme Court used a barrel as his platform when he spoke to the public in 1836. The occasion was the start of construction on the long-anticipated portage canal that would link Chicago with the westward-flowing Des Plaines River. Judge Smith accepted the applause of the numerous Chicagoans who had traveled a few miles south of the town to Canalport (now the Chicago neighborhood of Bridgeport). He read the Declaration of Independence and then waxed eloquent on Chicago's possibilities. He predicted the city would boast 20,000 inhabitants in twenty years and 50,000 in fifty years. Even to Chicagoans who dreamed big dreams, Smith seemed unrealistically optimistic. After all, the current population was only 3,820. One skeptical listener teased Judge Smith by asking how big Chicago would be in one hundred years. "Yes, fellow citizens," Smith assured the doubtful listeners, "In a hundred years from this time you will have a city of 100,000!" A Chicagoan who was present that day, Fernando Jones, continues the story: "This was too much for the boys. They took him off the barrel and threw water in his face. 'Arrah,' said Jones's comrade, 'if we hadn't stopped you, you'd have made it a million.'"[1]

Many local residents were wildly optimistic about the town's prospects. They fully expected the town to grow quickly into a frontier metropolis, a city that would dominate the Old Northwest. Such booster enthusiasm was not uncommon: similar predictions accompanied nearly every new town born in the Old Northwest in the 1820s and 1830s. But level-headed observers had every reason to reject such prognostications as silly. In 1836, Chicago was small, dirty, and unattractive. Winters were bitter and long, and ice closed Lake Michigan to shipping for at least one-third of every year. The Chicago River, upon the banks of which the city was built, was little more than a lazy, dirty stream. A more likely candidate for a frontier metropolis was St. Louis. Unlike

Chicago, St. Louis was already established. Located on the Mississippi River, it was linked to New Orleans (one of the largest ports in the United States) and connected to the hinterland by countless rivers and tributaries. In a warmer clime than Chicago, St. Louis was on a waterway that remained ice-free and therefore open to shipping throughout the year. As late as 1833, both Milwaukee and Michigan City, Indiana, were larger than Chicago and seemingly faced more promising futures.

THE LAND BOOM OF THE 1830S

The removal of American Indians to the west of the Mississippi, the desire of Easterners to resettle in the Old Northwest, and President Andrew Jackson's financial policies in the 1830s combined to create the largest land speculation bonanza in U.S. history. Frontier land was in great demand, and Chicago was at the eye of the storm. Land speculators had good reason to believe that the small town of Chicago might develop quickly.

The big news was the proposed Illinois and Michigan Canal. Instead of the unpredictable portage and the small Des Plaines River, a new ninety-six-mile-long canal would link the Illinois River with the South Branch of the Chicago River. Such a canal would enable large ships to sail directly from Lake Michigan to the Mississippi, solving the portage dilemma.[2] The canal would reach ambitiously from Chicago to the north central Illinois town of La Salle, and it promised to make Chicago a commercial center overnight.

"Canal fever" in Chicago was inspired by the Erie Canal's smashing success. In 1825, New York's newly completed Erie Canal—the first major inland waterway built in the United States—linked the Hudson River and Lake Erie. The canal revolutionized the economy of the Atlantic seaboard, as New York City now enjoyed continuous water passage to the Great Lakes. The canal's chief benefit was that it lowered transportation costs dramatically. Manufactured eastern goods now moved throughout the Great Lakes region, and western agricultural produce and raw materials poured into the East. Land speculators noticed something else about the canal: it transformed the small New York hamlet of Buffalo, the western terminus of the canal, into one of the leading commercial cities in the United States.

Construction of the Illinois and Michigan Canal did not begin until 1836, and the first ship did not pass through the waterway until 1848. Locals knew the canal was coming, however. The 1830 survey of the town had been part of the Illinois Canal Commission's initial steps toward making the canal a reality. Town residents secured a $25,000 federal grant to improve Chicago's Lake Michigan harbor that year, a project that was pointless unless a canal was planned for the near future. The victory in the Black Hawk War and the subsequent Potawatomi treaty meant that one barrier had been overcome. Certain that they saw a boom town in the making, land speculators descended upon Chicago. They bought up every piece of available land at ridiculously inflated prices. By 1835, local land speculator Buckner S. Morris proclaimed that a man did poor business if he failed to make a one hundred percent profit on his land investments. Harriet Martineau visited the city in 1836 at the peak of the buying frenzy. "I never saw a busier place than Chicago was at the time of our arrival," reported Martineau. She continued: "The streets were crowded with land speculators, hurrying from one sale to another. A negro, dressed up in scarlet, bearing a scarlet flag, and riding a white horse with housings of scarlet, announced the times of sale. At every street-corner where he stopped, the crowd flocked around him; and it seemed as if some prevalent mania infected the whole people. The rage for speculation might fairly so be regarded. As the gentlemen of our party walked the streets, storekeepers hailed them from their doors, with offers of farms, and all manner of land-lots, advising them to speculate before the price of land rose higher."[3] Gurdon S. Hubbard, the young fur trader whom Indians had dubbed "The Swift Walker," became an equally swift buyer. He had purchased two town lots in 1831 for less than $80; now he sold them for $80,000. He and two partners also bought fifty acres of North Chicago land for $5,000 in 1836. A few months later, he sold half of it to New York City investors for $80,000. One Lake Street lot cost $300 in 1834 and sold for $60,000 in 1836. Another lot brought $62 in 1830 and sold for $96,700 in 1836. All told, land sales in Chicago jumped from $2.4 million in 1832 to $24.9 million in 1836. Many purchasers bought land they had never seen, and prices bore no relationship to the real economic value of the land. They instead represented investors' inflated dreams of what the land might be worth in the future.

This frenzy of land speculation was encouraged by President Andrew Jackson's war on the Bank of the United States. Jackson harbored a deep suspicion of eastern bankers, whom he believed were dominating the American economy. He broke the power of the national bank in 1832, and his actions had an enormous effect on banks nationwide. No longer reined in by the national bank, western banks extended more credit to investors while making risky investments of their own. Easy credit made "land gambling" possible, and it encouraged land speculators to pay exorbitant prices for what had been worthless land only one decade earlier. Western banks were requiring little or no collateral before making big loans, gambling on the future value of land.

In 1836, Jackson realized that western banks were engaging in unsound practices. His specie circular of that year sharply curtailed further speculation. It required public lands to be purchased with gold or silver (not with loans) and ordered western banks to redeem its paper money in gold or silver. The policy pulled the rug out from under thousands of frontier investors. Investors could no longer invest, buyers stopped buying, and property values plummeted. A sharp economic downturn ensued—the panic of 1837—followed by an economic depression in 1839–1842.

Towns such as Chicago that had seen excessive land speculation were especially hard hit. Land valued at $1,000 in 1833 was suddenly worth $50, but the investor who signed the $1,000 note still owed $1,000. Most investors defaulted on their loans. John Stephen Wright, a newcomer to Chicago who made and lost a fortune while in his twenties, assessed his brief career as a real estate tycoon this way: "I came to Chicago with nothing, failed for $100,000, and could have failed for a million if he [Jackson] had let the bubble burst in the natural way."[4] Most of the leading businessmen of 1836 were bankrupt or penniless by 1842. Chicagoan William B. Ogden wrote a friend in 1841, "Those who were richest when you left are of the poorest now. . . . Very few of the old stock of '36 are otherwise than deeply embarrassed."[5]

Ogden did his part to sustain the town during the lean years between 1836 and 1850. Reared in a well-to-do New York family, Ogden had sold real estate while still a teenager. He became a die-hard booster for the state of New York, urging the construction of new railroads lest Philadelphia bypass New York. When his brother-in-law invested in Chicago land and asked thirty-year-old Ogden to move to Chicago to oversee it, Ogden agreed. Ogden arrived in Chicago (population 3,200) in 1835 and was elected the town's first mayor in 1837. Ogden had speculated with some land purchases of his own, and, like others, lost money when the land speculation bubble burst.

As mayor, Ogden presided over Chicago's grim years, a time characterized by some as a time of hibernation. Ogden's contagious optimism helped to prevent the hibernation from becoming a suicide. In the midst of the land boom collapse, some investors counseled that the city should simply default on its obligations. Confident that better times were coming, Ogden knew that such financial irresponsibility would cripple the city for years to come. He reminded Chicagoans that "many a fortress has saved itself by the courage of its inmates and their determination to conceal their weakened condition."[6] The metaphorical use of images such as "fortress" and "inmate" suggests both the bleakness of the post-1836 years and Ogden's determination.

Times did get better, and Ogden's perseverance paid off. He became Chicago's most indefatigable booster. "Perhaps, the most striking trait of his character, was his absolute faith in Chicago," remembered one contemporary. "He saw in 1836, not only the Chicago of today, but in the future the great City of the continent. From that early day, his faith never wavered. Come good times—come bad times—come prosperity or adversity—Chicago booming, or Chicago in ashes, its great future was to him a fixed fact."[7] Theologians maintain that faith without works is dead faith, and, in that sense, Ogden possessed a living faith in Chicago. And Ogden's activities contributed heavily to Chicago's eventual prosperity. His hand was to be found in almost every early innovation, undertaking, and improvement in the town. He built the first swing bridge that spanned the Chicago River, helped plan and build parks, laid out hundreds of miles of city streets, and assisted in the acquisition of clean drinking water and a sewage system. Ogden became president of the Chicago and Michigan Steam Boat Company, a firm that provided transportation between Chicago and other lake ports. He was one of the chief promoters of the Illinois and Michigan Canal and later the first promoter of area railroads. He singlehandedly purchased one of the city's most notorious red light districts, the Sands (immediately north of the river on Michigan Avenue), allowing the mayor at the time, John Wentworth, to level the brothels and shanties. He was a silent partner in the city's Lill and Diversey Brewery, which was founded in 1838. Ogden served as the first president of the city's Rush Medical College; in 1860, he was elected to the Illinois Senate. In 1875, at age seventy, the tireless Ogden finally found time to get married. French historian Francois Guizot exaggerated only a little when, while gazing upon a portrait of Ogden, he quipped, "He built and owns Chicago."[8]

LIFE IN A SMALL FRONTIER TOWN

The land bust meant that Chicago failed to become a wilderness metropolis overnight. The town nonetheless grew modestly. Most important, Chicago still had the canal project. Indeed, the bursting of the land speculation bubble, the panic of 1837, and the depression that followed might have crippled the fledgling town of Chicago. The canal, however, proved the savior. By 1834, 150 houses and stores had been constructed along the site of the proposed canal. Construction of the canal began in 1836 with a monthly payroll of $75,000. Total sales in the town reached $1 million that same year—a modest figure, but one that distinguished the town of Chicago from the old outpost of Chigagou.

The small frontier town was home in the 1830s not only to Catholic, Presbyterian, Baptist, Methodist, and Episcopal churches but also to trendy Universalist and Swedenborgian congregations. Mark Beaubien, the tavern owner who amused patrons by playing his fiddle, still provided one of Chicago's most popular entertainments by welcoming a lively competition among performers, such as Mr. Bowers, self-proclaimed *Profeseur de Tours Amusant,* who brought his ventriloquism/fire-eating/magic show to the town. Perhaps somewhat more professional was the town's first theater, which in 1837 performed live dramas for six-week stands. A city hospital opened in 1837, and Rush Medical College opened in 1839. Two necessities for town living—a Board of Health and a volunteer fire department—were organized in 1835. All able-bodied male citizens were required to join in fighting fires; violators paid a two-dollar fine. Fire fighting in the 1830s, however, was neither an art nor a science. It was more like a comedy of errors as amateurs fought ferocious infernos in dense all-wood towns. Few were surprised when the first of many devastating fires raced through the town of Chicago in 1839.

Chicago was passing from frontier outpost to small town, yet no Chicago residents could have doubted that they still lived on the edge of the frontier. Stray dogs, cattle, and hogs roamed the busiest city streets. Those same streets were littered with the carcasses of dead animals, "putrid meat," "green putrid water and decaying vegetable matter," and livestock manure.[9] So nauseating was the smell that one 1845 visitor quipped, "Chicago should be called *the City of pestiferous odour.*"[10] At least it was fairly easy to escape the "pestiferous odour." A several-minute walk put residents on the vast prairie to the west. Once there, residents could hunt wolves within earshot of town residents. To the north, only a trail marked by blazed trees showed the way to Milwaukee.

Then there was the mud. Chicago was every bit as swampy in 1840 as it had been in 1640. If anything, the problem had grown worse. Gustav Unonius, a Swedish immigrant, called the city a "vast mud puddle" in

1845.[11] Wagons traveled daily through the deeply rutted, grassless trails that served as city streets. In 1836, Charles Cleaver saw a stagecoach buried in the mud on Clark Street, "where it remained several days, with a board driven in the mud at the side of it bearing this inscription: 'No bottom here.'"[12] Farmers drove their livestock through those same streets on their way to market. There was no asphalt or concrete in the 1840s; instead, residents tried to escape the mud by building wooden plank sidewalks. When the water and mud rose, they simply built their sidewalks higher. "In the prairie, it rains, & thaws incessantly," warned Ralph Waldo Emerson in 1853 upon a visit to Chicago, "&, if we step off the short street, we go up to the shoulders, perhaps, in mud."[13] By the 1850s, the muddy streets were so impassable that Chicagoans put wooden planks over them. This worked well enough during dry seasons. When the streets became too wet, however, the planks simply floated on top of the mud. When heavy wagons passed over the roads, the planks were forced down into the mire, and muddy water squirted upward, spraying travelers and pedestrians.

At least initially, clean drinking water was not a problem. Lake Michigan was large, close, and still relatively unpolluted. Large carts carrying wooden barrels ran back and forth from the lake throughout the day. Each barrel was outfitted with a faucet; customers brought their buckets out to the wagons, filled them, and paid the wagon driver. By the 1840s, the Chicago Hydraulic Company was providing lake water to some parts of the city through log pipes. Sewage disposal posed a more difficult problem. Rural homesteads might not need carefully planned sewage systems, but town living required a high standard of public sanitation. Drains and sewers, however, could not be dug in Chicago's swampy ground, where the water table was high. Because Chicagoans could not dig down into the swamp, they did the next best thing: they raised the city. Beginning in 1849, city residents used large mechanical jacks to raise their homes, stores, and warehouses from four to fourteen feet above ground level. New foundations were then constructed under the elevated buildings, so the buildings appeared to stand upon stilts, which created space under them for drains. Buildings were not always raised to a uniform grade. For example, one store might have its front entrance at six feet above street level, while the bakery next door had a front entrance ten feet above street level. The result was a zigzag array of sidewalks, stairs, and buildings above the perpetual and ever-deepening muck.

The town's drainage system gave Chicagoans only a Pyrrhic victory. When it worked, it simply dumped sewage into the Chicago River, and the lazy river, meandering through the city, became a putrid cesspool. It is no surprise that one European visitor observed in 1850, "Chicago is one of the shabbiest and ugliest cities I have yet seen in America."[14]

EARLY EUROPEAN IMMIGRATION TO CHICAGO

Chicago was not prohibitively ugly to everyone. By 1840, it was an attractive destination for many European immigrants. The canal company beginning work in Chicago needed the cheap labor that immigrants could provide. Work on the Illinois and Michigan Canal was backbreaking, and most of it was done manually with picks and shovels. Laborers routinely toiled for twelve hours each day and usually for six days every week. Anglo-American settlers from the East Coast disdained the low wages and hard work of canal-digging, preferring to push westward in search of farmland. Canal work was ideal, however, for unskilled and penniless immigrants who were desperate for any kind of job. And growing frontier towns such as Chicago needed trained craftsmen, artisans, and professionals. Anglo-Americans who possessed these skills tended to prefer living in the more refined eastern cities, but skilled immigrants found immediate work in frontier towns.

Irish immigrants responded to the need for laborers. Fleeing first political persecution and then famine in Ireland, thousands of Irish flocked to America before the American Civil War. Most Irish immigrants were unskilled, illiterate, and impoverished. That meant that they took the lowest paying and least desirable jobs, such as canal-digging. By 1850, 6,000 Irish had moved to Chicago to work on the canal. Most settled near Canalport, the eastern terminus of the canal. The community would later call itself Bridgeport, and it remained the heart of Chicago's Irish community for more than a century.

German immigrants were also drawn to Chicago. Unlike the Irish, many of the several thousand German immigrants who had come to the city by 1850 were skilled laborers or professionals. They established thriving businesses, succeeded financially, and became the vanguard of cultural life in late-nineteenth-century Chicago. About 7 percent of these German immigrants were Jewish; they became the city's first Jewish residents. The first synagogue in Illinois was organized in Chicago in 1851, and a local newspaper commented that year, "The Jews in our city are not numerous, but are wealthy, very respectable and public spirited."[15] Early Jewish immigrants apparently faced little anti-Semitism, and several were elected to local political offices.

Small numbers of Swedes and Norwegians also came to the city during the 1840s. As early as 1843, Chicago was a town marked by a large immigrant population: 30 percent of all Chicagoans had been born overseas. The pace of immigration quickened in the 1850s. By 1860, half of Chicago's 110,000 citizens were foreign-born, including 21,000 Germans, 20,000 Irish, and 2,200 Scandinavians.

The immigrants brought several things to Chicago. One was their purchasing power. As day laborers who had no time to grow their own food, they were the ideal consumers for Chicago merchants. Another was their demand for beer, a staple in Irish and German diets. Some Anglo-Americans regarded beer consumption as immoral, however, so Chicago's first immigrants could not purchase beer in local stores. Two immigrants opened the town's first brewery in 1839 on the corner of Pine Street (now Michigan Avenue) and Chicago Avenue; by 1857, it was the largest brewery west of Cincinnati. The Irish and German immigrants also swelled the numbers of Roman Catholics in Chicago. The preponderance of French settlers in the area gave the Catholic Church an early foothold; in 1836, a German-speaking priest joined the local French American priest in Chicago.

Immigrants also elicited anti-immigrant sentiments. One 1850 visitor to Chicago reported that her local hosts "complain about the chaotic and nasty condition in political matters brought about especially because of the strong migration of Europe's rawest populations, and the ease with which this population can obtain full rights of citizenship."[16] New immigrants to the city gained the right to vote after living in Illinois for only one year. They soon became a decisive factor in municipal elections. An 1840 edition of the *Chicago Daily American* contained an advertisement paid for by 250 area residents. The advertisement called on Congress to disfranchise all foreign-born residents of the United States who had not yet gained the right to vote. Such activities were aimed primarily at Catholics, most of whom were recent immigrants from Ireland or Germany. Many Americans, fearing that Roman Catholics would be loyal to their pope and not to the United States, merged anti-Catholic sentiment with patriotism and concerns for national security. Such sentiments were not unusual in the United States. They mounted during the 1840s and culminated in the American, or Know-Nothing, Party in the 1850s.

REFORM IN CHICAGO

In the midst of a languishing economy, Chicagoans found some comfort participating in the various reform movements that swept the nation in the 1830s and 1840s. Most were fueled by the Second Great Awakening, an enormous religious revival that swept the nation (and especially the frontier) between 1800 and 1830. The experience of Chicago's Henry Whitehead illustrates the connection between Christian revivalism and social reform. A Methodist circuit rider, Whitehead came to the city in 1833 and faithfully preached the gospel in surrounding communities. Poor health forced him to retire in the 1840s. Still a relatively young man, Whitehead sought other ways to express his Christian commitment. He stayed in Chicago and turned his attention to local temperance, antislavery, and antivice crusades in the city.

Most popular of all the reform efforts was the temperance movement. The Second Great Awakening had been spearheaded by the frontier evangelism of many Methodists and Baptists, most of whom urged teetotaling, or total abstention from alcohol, as normative Christian behavior. Beer-drinking Irish and German immigrants, most of whom were Catholic, further heightened American sensitivity to the demon rum. The temperance crusade swept America, including Chicago. A local branch of the American Temperance Society was organized in 1833, and within a decade nearly 2,000 of the city's 7,600 residents belonged to one of Chicago's four temperance societies. According to the *Chicago Daily American*, the prohibitionists were wildly successful. The newspaper reported that the societies had succeeded in "rendering not only habitual intoxication but even a single instance utterly disgraceful and without the shadow of excuse."[17] By 1845, the movement seemed to have become a victim of its own success. Temperance ceased to inspire Chicagoans, perhaps because so many residents had joined the ever-increasing number of temperance societies. There was a certain irony in the popularity of the temperance movements in Chicago, for the city owed its birth in part to the liquor. Free-flowing alcohol is what cemented the original relationships between fur trappers, settlers, soldiers, and local Indians in the 1600s and 1700s.

Perhaps the most significant reform movement, however, was abolitionism. The antislavery movement burst upon the American conscience in 1831. Before that year, slavery had been a tolerated fact of life in the United States. Slavery had not yet become a moral issue that could not be compromised. Three events in 1831 changed that: the highly publicized Nat Turner slave revolt, the beginning of David Walker's public antislavery activity, and the publication of William Lloyd Garrison's abolitionist newspaper, the *Liberator*. Slavery became a moral issue that increasingly polarized the nation. At least until 1837, however, slavery was not a pressing issue for most Chicagoans. Although statewide "Black Codes" consigned African Americans to second class status, few state residents protested their existence.[18]

True abolitionism came to Chicago in 1837, when prominent abolitionist Elijah Lovejoy was murdered in Alton, Illinois. With the issue brought so close to home, secret abolitionist meetings evolved into the Chicago Anti-Slavery Society in 1840. Three white Chicagoans led the society: Dr. Charles Volney Dyer, one of the earliest medical doctors in the city; Philo Carpenter, one of the city's first druggists; and the First Presbyterian Church's Reverend Flavel Bascome. The *Western Citizen*, the official newspaper of the Illinois Liberty Party and the voice of local abolitionist sentiment, began publishing in Chicago in 1842. Local reformers who seemed to be losing enthusiasm for the temperance issue shifted their zeal to abolitionism. Most city churches embraced the cause as one indispensable to the Christian faith, but not all Chicagoans agreed. At least two local churches—the Presbyterian and the Baptist congregations—split over the slavery issue, the minority faction in each church leaving to form independent churches that did not champion abolitionism.[19]

By the 1840s, Chicago had become a key stop on the Underground Railroad. Numerous runaway slaves passed through the city on their way to Canada and freedom. They were aided by Dyer, the "station master" of the city's Underground Railroad, and the city's growing free black population. Between 1833 and 1845, the city's African American population grew from 33 to 145; by 1850, the city's total population of 30,000 included about 400 blacks. Prominent black abolitionists in Chicago included John Jones, Abram T. Hall, Henry O. Wagoner, and William Johnson.

Antislavery men routinely helped runaways escape and thwarted slave catchers who patrolled the city. Local mobs sometimes pressured local judges to protect runaways. One such case occurred in 1846. A slave catcher from Missouri apprehended two runaway slaves in the city. As the law required, the man appeared before a local judge to present evidence that his prisoners were indeed fugitives. While the case was in progress, an armed mob released the former slaves. The mob then defied the legal authorities and sent the slaves on to safety.

If anyone doubted that Chicago was an antislavery city, that doubt was entirely eliminated in 1850. Before then, southerners had always been free to search for fugitive slaves in northern states. Northerners, however, had never been required by federal law to aid in apprehending runaways. As part of the Compromise of 1850, Congress enacted the Fugitive Slave Law. The law required northern law enforcement agencies to assist in the apprehension and return of runaway slaves. Like many Northerners, Chicagoans were outraged by the Fugitive Slave Law. Assisting slave owners to recapture their slaves would implicate Chicagoans in the sinful business of slavery. The Chicago City Council responded to the act by resolving that city police need not comply with the federal law. The local black community went further. It created a "black police force" of seven divisions; each division consisted of six persons who patrolled the city each night looking for slave catchers.

Thus, while Chicagoans attended Know-Nothing meetings that nurtured anti-Irish sentiments, they also crusaded against slavery. These two campaigns are not as incongruous as they might appear. White abolitionists in antebellum America rarely advocated social equality or what we now call civil rights for slaves in the South. They merely detested slavery. Most white Chicagoans probably would have desired to confer upon freed slaves only second-class status as citizens. That is why, for example, Chicago's free blacks (even wealthy, influential African Americans such as Jones, Hall, Wagoner, and Johnson) could not vote until after the Civil War. Few local whites embraced the cause of full social and political equality.

THE TRANSPORTATION PROBLEM

In the years following the land speculation disaster, Chicago's economy continued to grow. The city's population stabilized at around 4,000 between 1836 and 1840 but then began to grow steadily: 6,200 in 1842, 8,000 in 1844, 14,000 in 1846, 20,000 in 1848, and 30,000 in 1850. The states that provided the most settlers for Chicago were (in order) New York, Pennsylvania, Connecticut, Massachusetts, and Vermont; less than 2 percent of the city's 1850 residents hailed from southern states. When construction on the Illinois and Michigan Canal was halted in 1842 for a year, the city immediately fell into a depression. The District Court of Illinois was forced to hold a special three-month session in 1843 so it could dispose of all the local bankruptcy cases the economic crisis had created. Business soon recovered. By 1847, Chicago was a thriving frontier city. It was home to ten drug stores, seventeen hardware stores, twenty-five cobblers, sixty-five grocery stores, fifty-six attorneys, four public schools with ten teachers and 1,500 pupils, and fifteen private schools with twenty teachers and 1,000 pupils. "It is a remarkable thing," wrote Harriet Martineau of Chicago in 1840, "to meet such an assemblage of educated, refined, and wealthy persons as may be found there, living in small, inconvenient houses on the edge of the wind prairie."[20] Founded as the city's third newspaper, the *Chicago Daily Tribune* (later the *Chicago Tribune*) competed with the *Chicago Democrat* and the *Chicago Journal* for readers. Although not a metropolis or a major city, Chicago was no longer a frontier village.

The buoyant Chicago economy was fueled by two factors. First, the number of city residents was continually growing. Second, farmers from northern Illinois and northwestern Indiana did business in Chicago. Because Chicago was linked to New York City via an all-water route that made New York-to-Chicago travel possible in six days by 1840, it offered unbeatably low prices for goods and top dollar for farmers' produce. Area farmers preferred doing business in Chicago. The lack of good roads, however, meant that only a relatively small number of outlying farmers could sell their produce and livestock in Chicago. The same geographical phenomena that made Illinois and Indiana prime farm land—abundant rainfall and the absence of hills—also made the dirt roads in these areas virtually unusable during much of the year. One farmer explained in 1848, "On the outskirts of town . . . the highways were impassable, except in winter when frozen, or in summer when dry and pulverized into the finest and most penetrating of dust. At all other seasons they were little less than quagmires."[21] Another visitor described the situation more bluntly: the roads leading to the city were "about as bad as could be imagined"—a strong statement to make in the 1830s when roads everywhere were notoriously primitive.[22] This is why one Chicago merchant routinely closed his shop on rainy spring afternoons. "People from the country," he observed, "never thought of coming to Chicago during the reign of mud, except for very urgent reasons."[23]

When farmers did brave the mud to come to Chicago, they came in horse-drawn wagons. That meant they could never bring with them (or return with) more than one wagonload of goods. Farmers with especially big crops or in need of many supplies would make several trips to Chicago. Consider the case of Lester Harding, a farmer who lived seventy miles west of Chicago in Paw Paw, Illinois. Grain dealers in Chicago would buy his wheat for seventy to eighty-five cents per bushel, whereas he could only sell it for fifty cents per bushel in Paw Paw. Transporting his entire 1847 harvest to Chicago, however, required at least four separate trips. Each trip took a minimum of five days. Farmer Harding spent almost one month of each year driving his wagon back and forth across terrible roads, often in inclement autumn weather.

The twin realities of poor roads and limited wagon capacities restricted the business between Chicago and its hinterlands. Farmers were reluctant to devote all their efforts to a single cash crop such as wheat. Doing so would mean dependence upon Chicago for nonfarm goods as well as many long trips to Chicago to sell their harvest. Most Illinois and Indiana farmers in the 1840s, therefore, remained subsistence farmers who were close to self-supporting. They were not dependent on Chicago; the city merely provided conveniences or supplementary income. As long as Chicago did not develop complementary economic relationships with area farmers (that is, farmers growing cash crops for sale in Chicago and Chicago merchants selling manufactured goods to rural customers), the city remained much like other frontier towns. It was not a city that maximized the possibilities inherent in urban-rural economic relationships. Before 1848, no American city had taken advantage of such opportunities.

Chicagoans knew that better transportation would improve their lives. That is why they eagerly awaited the completion of the Illinois and Michigan Canal. Water transportation was infinitely preferable to land transportation. Besides being easier, cheaper, and quicker, the barges carried much larger cargoes than did horse-drawn wagons. With a completed canal, area farmers would need only to transport their goods to the nearest canal site. Farmers could likewise purchase goods and have them delivered via the canal. The canal would not only make existing economic relationships more efficient and profitable but, perhaps more important, it would also bring more of the hinterland into the city's economic web.

Thus Chicago was a logical host for the national River and Harbor Convention in 1847. Ten thousand national leaders packed into the city to proclaim the virtues of better transportation—which, in 1847, meant water transportation. The national Whig Party had long advocated government-supported internal improvement projects (for example, canals, river dredging, and turnpikes).[24] But President James K. Polk, a Democrat, rejected such projects as wasteful and unimportant. For Chicagoans, the Whigs' internal improvements meant the difference between a mediocre economy and a thriving one. Judge Jesse B. Thomas explained in his report to the convention that the current transportation problem limited the city's commerce. The city, he complained, was still "merely the centre of a local retail trade of a few hundred miles of extent."[25]

Chicagoans, like Judge Thomas, complained about their transportation problems, primarily because they sought still more economic growth. By any measure, Chicago's growth between 1830 and 1850 was spectacular. The city went from little more than a fur trading outpost to a respectable, if modest, town in twenty years. It even surpassed Judge Theophilus Smith's seemingly insane predictions from atop a barrel in 1836. He had foreseen 20,000 inhabitants by 1856, but by 1850 30,000 Americans called the city home. But no one could have foreseen the growth that the city would experience in the second half of the nineteenth century. Largely as a result of creating one of the most efficient transportation networks in the world and placing itself at the hub of that network, Chicago went from being a frontier town to a world-class metropolis in fifty years.

CHAPTER FOUR

CHICAGO

CONQUERS

THE MIDWEST,

1850-1890

• German chancellor Otto von Bismarck, a European statesman accustomed to the cultural glories of Paris and Rome, the Byzantine heritage of Moscow and Kiev, and the industrial and technological wonders of London and his own Berlin, commented in 1870, "I wish I could go to America, if only to see that Chicago."[1] In 1850, Chicago had been a thriving but unspectacular frontier town, the unglamorous home of thirty thousand residents and miles of mud. "Chicago is one of the most miserable and ugly cities which I have yet seen in America," observed Fredrika Bremer, a Swedish novelist upon her 1853 visit to the city.[2] Why, therefore, did the cosmopolitan Bismarck desire to visit Chicago? Because, by 1870, Chicago was being transformed into an extraordinary city.

The transformation of Chicago—by 1900, Chicago's population would grow to 1.7 million, making it the second largest city in the United States—was centered in the nineteenth-century American attitude toward business and profits. French political scientist Emile Boutmy made this observation in the late 1800s regarding Americans' relationship with their land: "Their one primary and predominant object is to cultivate and settle these prairies, forests, and vast waste lands. The striking and peculiar characteristic of American society is, that it is not so much a democracy as a huge commercial company for the discovery, cultivation, and capitalization of its enormous territory. . . . The United States are primarily a commercial society . . . and only secondarily a nation."[3]

Perhaps Americans bristled at Boutmy's charge that they were first and foremost acquisitive capitalists. With regard to Chicago between 1850 and 1900, however, Boutmy was certainly right. During those years, Chicago emerged as perhaps the preeminent "commercial company" in the world. Several visitors to the city during this time commented on this phenomenon. A Swedish visitor in 1850 observed, "The city seems to consist mainly of stores. One sees almost no pretty country houses with gardens inside or outside of the city which otherwise is so common in American towns. . . . And it seems from everything that people come here to trade, to make money, but not to live."[4] Another European visitor in 1855 said, "Of Chicago itself, what can I say? It seems mad after money. It is an extraordinary fact. It is the entrepôt of the west, and must continue to increase."[5] In 1864, a visiting journalist concluded, "It would seem that materialism was the leading characteristic of Chicago, and that she had learned to be forever content with the greatest warehouse, the tallest grain elevators, the biggest pork trade, the largest and handsomest stores and fancy dwellings, the most overgrown of hotels, the most railroads, and most street bridges of any city in the Union."[6] The London Times stated bluntly in 1887 that "a paramount devotion to the Almighty Dollar" is one of "the prominent characteristics of Chicago." All these observers agreed on one thing: Chicago was a town where people could and did make money.

CANALS, RAILROADS, AND CHICAGO'S ECONOMIC BREAKTHROUGH

In 1848, Chicago was poised for a season of economic expansion unparalleled in American history. The foundation upon which Chicago's economy was built was the lucrative New York City trade. Merchants there controlled a significant portion of all commerce in both the northeast (from Maryland to Maine) and the Great Lakes region, due to the Erie Canal. The canal had revolutionized not merely New York City's trade but virtually the entire U.S. economy as well. The vast agricultural areas of the Old Northwest could now provide food for Easterners. Eastern farmers, who could not compete with the larger farms and the economies of scale of Minnesota, Indiana, and Iowa, abandoned farming for manufacturing. The result was a reciprocal trading relationship between the Old Northwest and the East. Farmers in the Old Northwest produced food for eastern markets; manufacturers in the East produced consumer goods for western farmers, who were now devoting their time to cash crops. Quirks of geography—the Mohawk Pass in upstate New York, a lack of any mountain barrier, and the Great Lakes—cemented this relationship between the Northeast and the Old Northwest.

Between 1830 and 1848, Chicago's port on the Great Lakes allowed the city to participate in this profitable east-west trade. A host of other cities in the Old Northwest also profited from this trade—among them Cleveland, Toledo, Detroit, Port Huron, Green Bay, Sheboygan, Milwaukee, Muskegon, and Grand Haven. None of those cities possessed any decisive economic advantages over the others. All enjoyed low shipping rates to and from New York City. All controlled a fairly limited regional market, extending perhaps one hundred miles inland from the Great Lakes. It is fair to say that all of these cities were poised for a season of economic expansion unparalleled in American history. If any one of these cities developed an extensive and efficient transportation system that reached deep into its hinterland, and thereby enticed more farmers to do business there, that city would tap an enormously profitable market.

It was Chicago that enjoyed the economic breakthrough. The ninety-six-mile Illinois and Michigan Canal, begun in 1836, was finally completed in 1848. It immediately improved business in Chicago. Corn shipments to the city increased eightfold in the canal's first year of operation, because many farmers chose to market in Chicago rather than in St. Louis. Chicago's lumber business doubled in 1848 as Michigan and Wisconsin lumbermen anticipated more Chicago customers. The waterway did boost business markedly, but what made the canal valuable was not how it created a speedy, all-water route linking Lake Michigan and the Mississippi River but how it replaced the slow, muddy roads that linked Chicago to its hinterlands. Now Illinois farmers needed only to take their harvest to ports along the canal. Likewise, they could purchase cheap Chicago products that had been shipped down the canal.

The new canal probably tripled the geographical area controlled by Chicago merchants. This gave Chicago's businessmen a decided advantage over merchants in other Great Lakes port cities. Chicago's merchants now enjoyed both a greater volume of sales to the hinterlands and the economies of scale that resulted from more farm goods passing through the city. Farmers in the Chicago environs also benefited from the canal. Lower transportation costs meant they enjoyed greater profit margins on their produce and lower prices on their purchased goods.

Chicagoans barely had time to enjoy their new canal, however, for it became obsolete almost as soon as it was completed. A new invention—the railroad—proved better suited to solve the transportation dilemma faced by Chicago-area farmers. Chicago's first mayor, William B. Ogden, had originally suggested building a regional railroad line in 1836. Ogden's plan was to link Chicago to northern Illinois and especially the mining town of Galena (located in extreme northwestern Illinois, less than five miles from the Mississippi River). Like the canal, however, the railroad project suffered following the panic of 1837. The first ten-mile section of the Galena and Chicago Union Railroad began operating in 1848. By 1850, track had reached Elgin, which was 40 miles west of Chicago. Rockford—80 miles northwest of the city—enjoyed rail service by 1852. By 1853 trains ran regularly to Freeport, the western terminus of the railroad and nearly 110 miles northwest of Chicago.[8] Because railroad construction was a business venture, some distrustful rural people became alarmed. One tavernkeeper who lived sixty miles northwest of Chicago assailed the railroads as "undemocratic aristocratic institutions that would ride roughshod over the people and grind them to powder."[9] Many rural farmers, however, welcomed an alternative to slow, muddy roads; Ogden sold 1,200 shares in his railroad company, many of them to farmers who bought only one or two shares. By 1857, an incredible three thousand miles of railroad track were connected to Chicago and nearly one hundred trains entered and left the city daily.

Railroads revolutionized commerce in Chicago in several ways. By greatly expanding the geographical area that city merchants controlled, they stimulated economic development. One government economist in 1881 identified the city's geographical market as nearly unlimited: "In the sense of being a primary market for the purchase and sale of agricultural products of the western and Northwestern States and Territories, and for supplying general merchandise throughout this region, the range of the trade of Chicago embraces Illinois, Wisconsin, Northern Michigan, Iowa, Northern Missouri, Kansas, Nebraska, Colorado, the Territory of Dakota, the Indian Territory [Oklahoma], New Mexico, and the other Territories as far west as the eastern borders of the States of California and Oregon, an area constituting more than one-half of the territorial limits of the United States exclusive of Canada."[10] The Chicago market had reached maybe one hundred miles inland as late as 1840, but by 1880 it reached all the way to Oregon. With such a large market, the city was able to maximize its peculiar commercial relationship with New York City and the East.

The railroads routed most of the east-west rail travel through the city. Virtually no railroad company operated lines both east and west of Chicago, at least until well after the Civil War. This meant that nearly all railroad lines east and west of Chicago terminated in the city. The railroads effectively channeled commerce into Chicago. Even passengers on long journeys would disembark in Chicago and spend some time (and money) in the city before transferring to another train. Chicago's status as terminus for both eastern and western railroad lines had enormous economic ramifications: because the terminus always garnered the lowest railroad freight rates, farmers had a strong economic incentive to ship their produce there.

Railroads were also far more efficient than canals. Canals needed water and usually linked rivers; railroads were liberated from such constraints. Railroads were therefore able to do a thorough job of connecting rural farms with Chicago. Unlike canals, railroads did not freeze in the winter or become so muddy as to be impassable in the spring, which effectively lengthened the business year in Chicago. Moreover, rail transportation was infinitely faster than both canal and horse-and-wagon transportation, which minimized produce spoilage en route to market.

Less than ten years after the Illinois and Michigan Canal opened, locals already knew that the future belonged to the railroad. A local newspaper predicted in 1852 that Chicago would become "the commercial metropolis of the Mississippi Valley," basing its claim on the convergence of myriad railroad lines on the city.[11] *Chicago Magazine* in 1857 went so far as to refer to the once coveted Illinois and Michigan Canal as "an old fogy institution—one of the things that were, to be superseded by new inventions."[12] It was the railroad, not the canal, that made Chicago a frontier metropolis.

The railroad allowed Chicago to supplant its rival, St. Louis, as the greatest city in mid-America. Founded in 1764 three hundred miles southwest of Chicago, St. Louis had quickly established itself as the premier Midwest city in the United States. St. Louis was located at the confluence of the Mississippi and Missouri Rivers, which gave the city unparalleled advantages in an age when river travel reigned supreme. Indeed, St. Louis was a thriving commercial center for more than half a century before Chicago elected its first mayor. When the steamboat reached its zenith in the 1840s, St. Louis's ascendancy seemed assured. Nearly all river trade in mid-America passed through the city, and any American in 1840 would have said that the Gateway to the West was St. Louis (except, of course, for the relentless boosters in Chicago). Like Chicago's businessmen, St. Louis's commercial leaders realized that the new railroad could easily revolutionize transportation and sought to build railroads. But the businessmen were hamstrung by a Missouri legislature that was reluctant to spend state money on internal improvements such as railroads. Missouri legislators delayed endorsing railroad construction for several critical years; when they finally allocated funds for railroad construction in 1851, their Jacksonian Democrat leanings led them to attach such strings to the grants (for example, mandating eventual state ownership of the railroads) that railroad investors were reluctant to build. Chicago also enjoyed geographical advantages, as it was much closer than St. Louis to the established New York City-Erie Canal-Great Lakes transportation system. Moreover, the St. Louis commercial-civic elite was no match for the combined economic resources of Chicago and New York businessmen. Before the railroads were built, Chicago already enjoyed a close relationship with New York's business community, in part because New Yorkers stood to profit from trade that passed through the Erie Canal (and hence through Chicago) and in part because many prominent Chicagoans were transplanted New Yorkers.

These dynamics combined to give Chicago a critical head start on St. Louis when it came to railroad construction. Railroad track quickly radiated out of Chicago, crossed the Mississippi River, and captured what had been exclusive St. Louis markets. St. Louis businessmen took their fight against the railroads into the courtroom, alleging that railroad bridges spanning the Mississippi River (and their supports anchored in the river bottom) created dangerous river eddies that jeopardized water traffic. Sharp railroad lawyers such as Abraham Lincoln defeated these challenges, and Chicago conquered St. Louis in the battle for hinterland markets.

The railroad's effect on the city was immediate and significant. Business boomed almost overnight. People flocked to the city, causing the population to skyrocket from 30,000 in 1850 to 110,000 in 1860. A British visitor to the city in 1856 exclaimed: "Ever since I came into the States, I have been hearing of Chicago, as the great feature of the new Western World, and was therefore prepared for a wonderful city. But the reality exceeded my expectations. It is a city, not in growth, but in revolution; growth is much too slow a word for the transformation of a hamlet of log-huts into a western New York, in the space of a few years."13 Historian William Cronon offers this judgment: "Chicago became the link that bound the different worlds of east and west into a single system. In the most literal sense, from 1848 to the end of the nineteenth century, it was where the West began."14 No other city in the Old Northwest controlled the commerce of such a large geographical area. No other city enjoyed Chicago's unique position as the breaking point between the eastern and western railroad systems. These factors would allow Chicago to dominate four businesses in particular: the grain (and especially wheat) trade, the lumber industry, the meatpacking business, and the mail-order catalog business.

THE GRAIN TRADE

Before the railroads, Old Northwest and western farmers commonly had grown corn and wheat. Corn was more popular, for, unlike other crops, corn was filling enough to constitute a meal in itself if necessary. No further processing was needed: corn could be picked and immediately roasted or boiled. A corn crop's yield by weight far surpassed the yields of other crops, and it stored well. Corn surpluses were never wasted, as they could be fed to livestock. The drawback to corn was that it brought a low price on the market.

Wheat was a more lucrative cash crop. Wheat was in constant demand in both America and Europe and therefore brought high prices. Wheat was difficult to harvest, however, and wheat in the field was easily damaged. If too top-heavy, it could fall to the ground and spoil. If overripe, its quality would be diminished. Wheat farmers normally faced a two- or three-day window for harvesting their wheat crop at precisely the right moment. A delay of several days—perhaps due to poor weather, sickness, or a shortage of labor—might make the difference between a good wheat crop and a failed one. Moreover, wheat, unlike corn, did not store well, and surplus wheat was often useless. If the trip to market took too long, it might spoil en route. Not surprisingly, the self-sufficient Old Northwest farmer of 1840 grew much corn and little wheat. Wheat was too risky, while corn was a safe bet. Of course, there was a great deal of money to be made if the farmer grew nothing but wheat, harvested it promptly, and transported it to market quickly. The Chicago market paid top dollar for the golden grain.

The dilemmas of both harvesting and transporting wheat were solved in the 1850s. First came Cyrus McCormick's mechanical reaper. McCormick had moved from Virginia to Chicago in 1847, opened his factory, and produced 450 reapers that year. They were an instant success. McCormick's reapers worked well on the large, flat wheat farms of the Old Northwest. They harvested wheat much more quickly than men could harvest by hand, and McCormick guaranteed that they would cut at least one-and-a-half acres of wheat per hour. Rapid harvesting minimized crop spoilage. Farmers were no longer dependent on large labor crews; one man could harvest vast fields.

But McCormick had to develop a way to convince farmers to spend their money on his new invention. After all, farmers had never seen a mechanical reaper, did not think they needed one, and did not know how to operate one. A McCormick reaper in 1860 cost $120, which made it one of the largest of all farm investments. Moreover, farmers only had cash after selling their harvest at market, not during the harvest, precisely the time when they could use the reaper most. McCormick solved those problems by pioneering two staples of American business: advertising and credit. He sent commission salesmen into the hinterlands armed with advertisement flyers, testimonials from pleased customers, and sample reapers. Farmers were required to make a $30 down payment to purchase their reaper; the balance came due after the harvest, when cash was available. McCormick even offered a money-back guarantee on his reaper, promising to refund the full purchase price if the machine broke down or failed to cut wheat as rapidly as advertised. McCormick might still have had a difficult time selling his reaper, given the machine's weight and bulk. Farmers could never transport one in their wagons for any great distance. That problem, like many others, was solved by the railroad. Sales reached 2,000 in 1855 and 4,000 in 1856. The McCormick reaper rapidly became an indispensable tool for Old Northwest farmers; in 1890 alone, 150,000 reapers were sent out to farmers worldwide.

Once harvested, the railroad brought wheat to market quickly, limiting spoilage. With the uncertainties of wheat farming solved, wheat production skyrocketed. Many Old Northwest and western farmers forsook corn to grow wheat, and the volume of wheat marketed in Chicago soared. As late as 1850, St. Louis had handled twice as much wheat and flour as Chicago; by 1856, Chicago's wheat sales far outstripped those of St. Louis. Chicago even bypassed the Russian cities of Odessa and Arkhangelsk as the largest wheat market in the world.

Other factors contributed to Chicago's burgeoning wheat trade. City merchants perfected the steam-powered grain elevator in the 1850s, a machine that mechanically removed grain from railroad cars, stored it in warehouses, and transferred it to ships and railroad cars bound for New York. Before 1850, a crew of Irish dock workers might work all day to load a ship with 7,000 bushels of wheat; in the 1850s, that same amount of grain could be loaded in one hour by one man working a mechanized grain elevator. These mammoth grain houses—some 120 feet high—made the movement of grain quick and inexpensive. In 1857, it cost half a penny to move a bushel of grain through Chicago but seven cents in St. Louis. During the Crimean War in Europe (1853–1854), U.S. wheat exports to Europe doubled in volume and tripled in value, and heightened European demand for wheat caused domestic U.S. wheat prices to climb by 50 percent. Overall, the amount of grain marketed in Chicago increased from 2 million bushels in 1856 to 50 million bushels in 1861. With the already profitable wheat even more valuable, few farmers could resist growing the cash crop.

Between 1848 and 1856, a group of grain traders known as the Chicago Board of Trade also standardized the buying and selling of grain in the city. Before 1850, the relatively low volume of grain sales made face-to-face transactions manageable: farmers brought grain to the city in bags, found a potential buyer, displayed the grain to the buyer, and exchanged grain for cash. These personal transactions became impractical, however, as the volume of grain and the number of sellers and buyers increased after 1850. The Board of Trade rationalized this process by having farmers deliver their grain to a central receiving depot. The grain was then examined, graded by quality and type (for example, red winter wheat, spring wheat, inferior spring wheat), and sorted by the Board of Trade. The farmer was given a receipt for his grain that indicated quantity and grade. The grain of various farmers was then mixed together, the only distinction being the grain's grade. Purchasers bought grain by grade—without ever actually seeing the individual farmer's wheat or corn—and were given receipts that were redeemable in grain. This process enabled the Board of Trade to streamline the grain buying and selling process, as farmers need never haggle over prices with purchasers. It also created a new form of currency, the grain receipt, that soon gave rise to the grain futures market, where shrewd grain brokers bought grain and brought it to market weeks or months later. It was in this manner that the Board of Trade brought order to what had become a potentially chaotic situation, as millions of bushels of grain passed through the city. By 1865, Chicago dominated the nation's wheat market.

THE LUMBER BUSINESS

The need for lumber in the Midwest was great. The prairies were ideal for large wheat crops in part because they were treeless, but prairie farmers desperately needed lumber for homes, barns, fences, and heating fuel. Lumber was so scarce prior to 1850 that farmers returning home from Chicago would tear up pieces of the wood plank toll roads they traveled and throw them into the backs of their wagons. The railroads themselves also created a demand for lumber. Railroad track construction required wooden railroad ties—more than 1,000 ties (each measuring about eight inches by six inches by eight feet) for each mile of track. Too, the growing city of Chicago needed its own lumber. Before 1870, nearly all city structures, such as homes, wharves, warehouses, stores, and sidewalks, were made of wood.

Chicago soon came to dominate the region's lumber market, for several reasons. Chicago merchants could exploit an abundant supply of high-quality lumber. Much of upstate Wisconsin, Michigan, and Minnesota boasted virgin forests. The most attractive lumber for building was the plentiful white pine, and, unlike hardwoods such as oak, maple, and elm, white pine floated. Lumberjacks could float trees to Lake Michigan via the area's numerous rivers, mill the lumber in lakeside sawmills, and cheaply transport the lumber to Chicago on barges. Moreover, the white pines eyed by mid-nineteenth-century lumbermen were breathtaking in size, averaging fifty feet in height and sometimes reaching two hundred feet.

Also, there was never a shortage of men to harvest the trees. Most logging work needed to be done in the winter when the soggy northlands of Wisconsin, Michigan, and Minnesota were frozen. Only on hard, frozen soil could lumbermen transport felled trees to rivers, and it was during the winter months that the Old Northwest had the greatest supply of available labor. Many farmers who might otherwise remain idle from November through April traveled north to work in lumbering camps.

Further, the extensive railroad network that fanned out from Chicago might have been built with shipping grain in mind, but it proved invaluable in transporting lumber into the hinterlands. Lumber from a variety of locations around the Great Lakes headed to market in Chicago. City merchants bought the lumber, sold it to customers, and shipped it via westbound trains throughout the Old Northwest and Great Plains states.

As with the city generally, transportation was the key to the rapid development of Chicago's lumber industry. The birth of Chicago's lumber business can be dated to the 1848 completion of the Michigan and Illinois Canal. Within a year, the canal doubled the amount of lumber that passed through the city. By the late 1850s, the railroads made the city the largest lumber market in the world. By 1867, more than two hundred lumber-bearing vessels unloaded in the city on a typical day in the seven-month-long "lumber season." Indeed, the bulk of Lake Michigan ships docking in Chicago carried, not grain, but wood. In 1872, for example, nine thousand of the thirteen thousand ships that entered the Chicago River carried lumber.

The city's lumber business grew even larger after the Civil War. By 1870, Chicago's lumber business enjoyed a near monopoly on lumber sales as far away as Nebraska and Kansas, and it even penetrated markets as far west as Colorado and Wyoming. The city shipped 220 million board feet of lumber in 1860, doubled that amount to 580 million board feet in 1870, and then doubled that amount again to 1 billion board feet in 1880.

Such a vast lumber business created what amounted to a minitown within Chicago. Chicago-bound ships laden with lumber sailed into the city and down the Chicago River's South Branch. There the ships encountered a mile-long stretch of riverfront owned by the city's lumber merchants. Hundreds of small unloading canals and wharves awaited incoming ships, which backed up to railroad tracks. Gangs of lumberyard workers unloaded the ships' cargoes, adding to what was probably the world's largest inventory of milled lumber. (The lumberyard stretched south of Twenty-second Street and west of Halsted Street.) By one estimate, five hundred million board feet of lumber (the equivalent of 250,000 trees) were stacked in Chicago in 1884. By day, workers frantically unloaded ships and loaded railroad cars; by night, security guards protected the treasure from thieves and arsonists.

Lumber remained an important business in Chicago into the 1900s. The trade, however, peaked and began to taper off in the mid-1880s. By then, railroads were running directly to the Great Lakes sawmills and lumber camps. Lumbermen no longer needed to ship lumber through Chicago; they could sell retail from their sawmills. At the same time, the diminishing stock of white pine in the Great Lakes area created competition from two directions. Frederick Weyerhauser established a rival lumber distribution center in southwestern Wisconsin and eastern Iowa. He accessed untapped forests and began harvesting Douglas firs from the Pacific Northwest. Southern logging companies began felling and marketing yellow pine, a wood both stronger and more attractive than white pine. The market for lumber in Chicago itself, however, remained healthy well into the 1900s as the city's teeming population built inexpensive wood bungalows.

THE MEATPACKING INDUSTRY

Other cities had grain elevators and lumberyards, but no city had anything like Chicago's Union Stock Yards. All visitors to the city—even princes, writers, and intellectuals—examined the world famous stockyard, making it the city's leading tourist attraction. As many as 10,000 visitors per day came to gawk at the stockyard. In 1887, one British observer said about Chicago, "Great as this wonderful city is in everything, it seems that the first place among its strong points must be given to the celerity and comprehensiveness of the Chicago style of killing hogs."[15] What made the Chicago meatpacking industry unique was the way that it surrealistically converted killing animals into a highly rational business. Butchering became a science, so much so that Chicago meatpackers were said to make use of every part of the hog except the squeal.

Before the Civil War, Chicago possessed no "meat industry." Like most cities, its local meat needs were met by numerous competing stockyards. The lack of a centralized stockyard proved inconvenient to both livestock sellers and buyers. Nor did many Chicagoans engage in meat processing, which in the 1850s was limited almost entirely to the preserving of pork. Chicago's many stockyards sold live pigs, cattle, and sheep to city butchers; butchers took them back to their shops, killed them, prepared the meat, and sold it fresh.

The Civil War changed that. With more than one million men in uniform, the Union army demanded an unprecedented amount of processed meat. Chicago, with a railroad network that reached far into the hinterlands, answered the call. Pigs poured into the city by rail; pickled, smoked, and salted ham left by rail. Between 1859 and 1863, Chicago's output of processed pork grew sixfold. By 1862, the city was the largest meatpacking city in the world and had earned the title of Porkopolis.

The Chicago Pork Packers' Association and the nine largest area railroads convened a historic conference in 1864. They lamented the decentralized, inefficient character of the city's multiple stockyards. Even with a chaotic hodgepodge of stockyards scattered throughout the city, Chicago had assumed control of the nation's meatpacking market. What could the city do if it rationalized and consolidated its meat processing industry?

The conferees made those dreams a reality. They purchased a one-half-square-mile tract of land four miles south of downtown, west of Halsted Street and between Thirty-ninth and Forty-seventh Streets. The Union Stock Yards opened in late 1865. The yard contained three miles of water troughs and ten miles of feed troughs for its inmates. Nearly thirty miles of drainage pipes carried the stockyard's offal into the Chicago River's South Branch (which soon became so polluted that it was referred to as Bubbly Creek). By 1868, the stockyard consisted of 2,300 pens on one hundred acres of land, and it was able to hold 21,000

The immense Chicago stockyards, here seen in a panoramic 1901 photograph. Over 25,000 workers labored at the stockyards by this time, butchering 13,000 hogs daily

cattle, 75,000 hogs, 22,000 sheep, and 200 horses simultaneously. Animals at the stockyard occasionally consumed one hundred tons of hay daily. Railroads enjoyed easy access to the pens, and the stockyard even included a posh 260-room hotel for buyers and sellers. Meatpacking houses, such as those operated by Swift and Armour, were conveniently located adjacent to the stockyard.

Once they arrived at the Union Stock Yards, cattle, pigs, and sheep were soon slaughtered. Chicago meatpackers mastered the art of butchering livestock efficiently and quickly using assembly line techniques long before they were used to build automobiles. Live animals were snatched up and secured by their hind feet to overhead conveyors. Arthur Holitischer, a German visitor to the city in 1912, described what happened next: "There is the big wooden wheel. Hogs hang from it and struggle. A short, thickset fellow stands beside it with a sharp steel lance. When the wheel swings the underbelly of a hog into place, he makes the first cut, slicing down from above. The writhing victim only now realizes

and processing cattle at a rate of more than one per minute. Chicago Historical Society, IChi-04081

its fate, screams in anguish like a burned child, squirts a thin hot red stream into the butcher's face, over his body, and onto his murderous hands, and is moved by a chain to the next butcher."[16] The animals proceeded down the so-called disassembly line, where they were bled, skinned or scraped, and butchered.

In 1892, Chicago meatpackers butchered about 13,000 hogs daily. Hundreds of men—an army of 25,000 was employed in the meatpacking business by 1893—hacked away at the suspended carcasses, each with his own job. Blood was drained off, fat went into lard vats, and small parts went to fertilizer tanks. Cattle were the most difficult to work with, because of their size. They hung stationary over the butchering floor while teams of men ran from one suspended bovine to the next, and in this manner eighty cattle per hour were killed, gutted, skinned, and butchered. Butchered animals were plunged immediately into vast chilling rooms, some of which, such as those of the Armour meatpacking plant, covered thirty to forty acres.

This cold efficiency and rationality delighted some and horrified others. Chicagoans tended to look at the matter pragmatically: animals had to be butchered, and the task should be done in such a way as to maximize profit. Some observers, however, were appalled at what they regarded as Chicagoans' callousness. British author Rudyard Kipling, for example, saw in Chicago and especially in the city's meatpacking business all that he despised most about America. During an 1889 stay in the city, he toured the Union Stock Yards, as did all other dignitaries. He afterward likened the city to the Bible's scarlet whore of Babylon, an inhuman figure found in the Book of Revelation who is unmoved by death:

> And then the same merciful Providence . . . sent me an embodiment of the city of Chicago, so that I might remember it forever. . . . And there entered that vermillion hall a young woman of large mould, with brilliantly scarlet lips, and heavy eyebrows, and dark hair that came in a "widow's peak" on the forehead . . . she was dressed in flaming red and black, and her feet . . . were cased in red leather shoes. She stood in a patch of sunlight, the red blood under her shoes, the vivid carcasses tacked around her, a bullock bleeding its life away not six feet away from her, and the death factory roaring all around her. She looked curiously, with hard, bold eyes, and was not ashamed. Then said I: "This is a special Sending. I have seen the City of Chicago!" And I went away to get peace and rest.[17]

Kipling's melodrama notwithstanding, he highlights the fact that late-nineteenth-century Victorian sensibilities were out of place in this grasping frontier metropolis.

Building the Union Stock Yards and organizing the butchering process was the first step Chicago took in conquering the American meat market. The second step was adapting meat preservation techniques to beef. Though pigs were butchered and processed (usually by pickling in salt or vinegar) in the Union Stock Yards, Chicagoans still sent live cattle by rail to butchers in eastern cities. As more and more cattle were shipped into Chicago, however, meatpackers sought a way to butcher cattle in Chicago and to ship prepared meat to the East. Consumers' preferences posed a problem: Americans preferred their beef fresh, not salted. The refrigerated railroad car, perfected by Gustavus F. Swift in the 1870s, solved the problem. Capable of carrying butchered beef to eastern markets without spoiling, Swift's refrigerated car used ice and brine packed into the roof of a specially designed car to cool its contents; vents pushed incoming air around the ice, and the chilled air (being heavier than warmer air in the car) dropped to the car's floor. The train stopped several times on its eastward journey to replenish the supply of ice. By 1880, Swift's chief rival, meatpacker Philip Armour, was using his design. The volume of eastbound processed beef exceeded the volume of live cattle for the first time in the 1880s.

Refrigerated cars were not the end of the battle, however. Easterners were reluctant to purchase beef that had been butchered a thousand miles away. Eastern butchers, their livelihood in jeopardy because Chicago beef was 5 to 10 percent cheaper than their own, fanned consumer fears. They denounced Chicago's processed beef as unsafe for human consumption. Shunned from eastern butcher shops, Chicago's meatpackers muscled into the market. "If you're going to lose money, lose it," Swift told his eastern marketers. "But don't let 'em nose you out."[18] Agents therefore sold Chicago beef straight out of the railroad car or directly from Swift's and Armour's refrigerated warehouses for ridiculously low prices. The Chicago packers lost money on these initial sales, but eastern consumers bought the promotional-priced beef, realized it was comparable to butcher shop beef, and demanded the inexpensive Chicago beef in the future.

By the late 1880s, Chicago dominated the nation's meat industry. Amazingly, the Chicago meatpackers' profit did not come from consumable meat. Philip Armour claimed that he lost $10.21 on every head of cattle sold in the East if he counted only his meat sales. Only 55 percent of every steer was consumable beef, however. The hide, skull, hooves, internal organs, cartilage, and bones—which made up the remaining 45 percent—were nonconsumable. Independent butchers discarded this waste because their volume of butchering did not make salvaging such products worthwhile. In Chicago, however, so many cattle were butchered that these unwanted products could be accumulated and used to make margarine, brushes, combs, bouillon, musical instrument strings, fertilizer, glue, buttons, chess pieces, and neat's-foot oil. Armour even created a laboratory at his plant where the linings from hogs' stomachs were used to make pepsin, a digestive aid. Armour estimated that on the same steer on which he lost $10.21 on the beef he sold, he also earned a profit of $10.80 on the by-products that had heretofore been discarded. This gave him a net profit of 59 cents per steer. In other words, the Chicago meatpackers made their profit on what the local butcher had always thrown away.

A net profit of 59 cents per steer is a slim profit margin. That meant that meatpacking workers were usually paid low wages. At least initially—from 1865 until about 1880—the packing companies hired many skilled German and Irish butchers. Although the meatpacking industry was the first to use the modern moving production line, butchering proved a process that was difficult to mechanize. Instead of mechanization, the packers after 1880 resorted to a minute division of labor that allowed them to use unskilled immigrant laborers. This pushed wages down to extremely low levels, so much so that the wives of meatpacking workers were forced to take in boarders to make ends meet. (When World War I cut off the supply of single male workers, many of these women reluctantly joined their husbands in the meatpacking plants.) By all estimates, workers living in the meatpacking company neighborhoods—notably Back of the Yards and Canaryville—lived difficult lives on the brink of poverty. Worker health was poor: in the Armour canning plant's paint room, for example, immigrant girls inhaled so much paint that their sputum was blue. Housing was also deplorable: when local reformers documented the tenement problem among poor Chicagoans, the stockyard neighborhoods were omitted from the study because housing conditions there were so horrendous that investigators judged them to be unrepresentative. The meatpacking business was seasonal (work was especially slow during the summer), so many workers were laid off during slow times. Perhaps one-third of the meatpacking industry's workers were "casual workers" in 1900, which meant that they did not work a steady five or six days per week but instead worked only when they were needed. When some workers went on strike in 1886 to gain an eight-hour workday, they were blacklisted by the packers and denied employment. To a large extent, the triumph of the city's meatpacking business came on the backs of poor immigrant workers.

By 1893, one-fifth of the city's population was somehow connected to the meatpacking industry. After 1900, other locales began to cut into Chicago's control of the nation's meat supply. As late as World War I, however, Chicago was still processing fifteen million animals per year and nine million pounds of beef per day during the war's peak. From 1860 until 1920, Chicago was indisputably America's Porkopolis and Beefopolis.

THE MAIL-ORDER CATALOG BUSINESS

The grain, lumber, and meatpacking businesses had several things in common. All capitalized on the unique economic relationship between

Chicago and its rural hinterlands. All depended on the railroad, linking the countryside and the city in unprecedented ways. A fourth "industry" that shared these characteristics was the Chicago mail-order catalog businesses. This distinctly American invention married urban and rural America as had never been done before. The catalog allowed rural farmers in Iowa to be almost as much a part of the Chicago economy as residents on downtown State Street.

In 1872, Chicagoan Aaron Montgomery Ward opened the first mail-order retail company in America. Ward arrived in Chicago in 1865 at the age of thirty-three and worked for two years as a clerk at the early Marshall Field and Palmer Potter retail store. Later, work as a traveling salesman throughout the Midwest's farm country for a St. Louis merchant inspired him to go into the retail sales business for himself. Montgomery Ward and Company was founded upon a shrewd marketing strategy. In the 1870s, a growing number of midwestern farmers believed they were being exploited by predatory middlemen. These middlemen bought farm products cheap, transported them to the city, and resold them to urban merchants at high prices. They also bought consumer goods in the cities, marked them up, and sold them to farmers, again taking a hefty profit. Disgruntled farmers organized protests to express their disdain for the rapacious middlemen, whom they regarded as parasites. Sometimes called the Grange or Alliance Movement, this farmer solidarity movement reached its crescendo in the 1890s with the rise of the Populist Party.

Ward and his mail-order company targeted these farmers. He was prepared to open business in late 1871, but the Great Chicago Fire destroyed his entire stock of merchandise. Ward was unfazed. He regrouped, reinvested another $2,400, and began business six months later in 1872. Ward bought consumer goods in mass quantities, which enabled him to buy at the lowest possible prices. By buying directly from Ward, farmers could bypass the greedy middleman and pay low wholesale prices. Ward presented himself as a friend of the farmer, obtained official endorsements from farmer organizations, and even advertised his mail-order business as "The Original Wholesale Grange Supply House." He mailed his first "catalog," an eight-by-twelve-inch sheet of paper with 163 items, to forty farmers. The response was overwhelmingly positive. Ward's prices were far below those of rural merchants, country stores, or traveling salesmen. Indeed, they were so low that the *Chicago Tribune* suspected the company of fraud. No legitimate merchant could offer prices as low as Ward's, the newspaper warned. Ward's unconditional money-back guarantee, however, allayed farmers' fears. Any rural customer could examine his purchase at the post office; if he was not satisfied, he could return it for a full refund.

Montgomery Ward and Company was an overnight success. Ward expanded his catalog to eight pages in 1874 and to seventy-two pages in 1875. By the end of the 1880s, Ward's catalog (now 540 pages long) was earning him a gold mine. It advertised 24,000 items and kept three hundred Chicago-based clerks busy with more than one million dollars in annual business. To rural Americans who lived miles from even a small, poorly stocked country store, the Montgomery Ward catalog offered an amazing assortment of consumer goods. In the 1882 catalog, for example, pages 230 and 231 offered Scandinavian padlocks, a carpet sweeper, a "White Mountain Potato Parer," a combination apple parer-slicer-corer, a cherry stoner, pot cleaners, an assortment of copper rivets with burrs, an ice cutter, a lemon squeezer, and a can opener. By 1900, the Montgomery Ward catalog was 1,200 pages long and contained 70,000 items. That year, two thousand clerks in Ward's Chicago headquarters did business with two million rural customers.

Richard Sears and Alvah Roebuck took the mail-order enterprise even further. Legend has it that Sears thumbed through Ward's catalog, slammed it down, and exclaimed, "That's the game I want to get into—the biggest game in the United States today!" Sears and Roebuck (both of whom were still in their twenties) founded Sears, Roebuck and Company in Chicago in 1893. Like Ward, Sears and Roebuck targeted rural Americans, selling them anything and everything. Like Ward, Sears and Roebuck bought in huge quantities and therefore offered rural Americans unbeatable prices. The new mail-order company, however, had a significant advantage over the older Montgomery Ward Company. Sears had, in the words of one historian, "a natural instinct for advertising—a seemingly innate gift for exciting in the minds of prospective customers a desire to purchase merchandise they had never before thought they either needed or wanted."[19]

The Sears and Roebuck catalog, for which Sears himself wrote all the text, combined hucksterism and hyperbole. The catalogs did not simply present goods for sale; they convinced customers to buy goods. Sears knew that rural Americans suffered from a sense of inferiority, the result of urban Americans dismissing them as hicks and hayseeds. Sears would offer farmers all the stylish items that city dwellers enjoyed. Sears also knew that he had to earn the confidence of his rural customers if his mail-order business was to succeed, and he spared no lengths to build that trust. Sears once saw a trolley conductor drop and break his Sears watch. He took the astonished conductor to his store, offered him a free watch, and proclaimed that Sears and Roebuck guaranteed their watches not to fall out of peoples' pockets. Before long, rural Americans were writing intimate letters to Sears, treating him as though he were a trusted family friend. Some letters asked Sears for advice regarding child rearing; others asked Sears for spouses.

Like Ward's, Sears's catalog was enormous. The initial 1893 catalog was 196 pages long and contained everything from clothing to saddles to pianos. The 1897 catalog mushroomed to 786 pages and contained food, drugs, refrigerators, farm implements, books, and the famous Heidelberg Belt, an electric men's corset guaranteed to cure impotency. Roebuck grew alarmed at the dizzying pace of business growth; lacking Sears's verve, he sold out in 1897. Sears pressed on. The 1900 catalog exceeded 1,100 pages and contained virtually every consumer good imaginable. The catalog eventually included a line drawing that allowed readers to test themselves for astigmatism; next to the figure, various corrective eyeglasses were sold.

Sears's salesmanship and farmers' confidence in the Chicago merchant resulted in enormous profits. To be sure, Sears offered unbeatable prices. For example, a sewing machine in the 1890s often cost about $50; Sears and Roebuck's sewing machines sold for as little as $10.45 (Sears was selling 100,000 sewing machines annually by 1902). The company registered greater gross sales than Montgomery Ward for the first time in 1900. Sales reached $16 million in 1902 and a staggering $50 million in 1907. When Sears and his 9,000 employees moved into a new forty-acre building on Chicago's West Side in 1906, Sears, Roebuck and Company was the largest retail business in the world.

Beyond selling goods and turning profits, however, the mail-order catalog business revolutionized life in rural America. Farmers no longer had to shop at small, one-room general stores that boasted minimal inventories. Did a farmer need a new hat? One page in the 1886 Montgomery Ward catalog offered him regulation Patrons of Husbandry hats, basic men's hats, three grades of men's wool hats, two grades of men's fur hats, and two grades of men's cloth caps. Isolated farmers throughout the Midwest could enjoy at least some of the comforts of city dwellers. As one Nebraska farm woman put it, "The Montgomery Ward catalog . . . was a real link between us and civilization."[20] Perhaps most important, the catalogs also cemented the economic relationship between Chicago and its rural hinterlands. With Ward's and Sears's catalogs on their parlor table, the Nebraska farm family that lived five hundred miles away was a fully integrated participant in the Chicago economy.

A NEW CONCEPT OF TIME

Shipping grain, stacking lumber, slaughtering hogs, and selling through mail-order catalogs at a breakneck pace could only occur in a culture where—to use that quintessential American cliché—time was money. Chicagoans talked incessantly of business. They hurried back and forth in order to make quick deals. They subordinated beauty and leisure to the greater values of profit and efficiency. They worked long shifts and infrequently took days off. Chicago's culture of work may well have driven other late-nineteenth-century American cities, but European visitors were nonetheless astounded at the frantic pace of life they witnessed in Chicago.[21]

One example of this frantic pace was the typical downtown Chicago lunch. Europeans were accustomed to lengthy and leisurely noon meals, and the most accomplished European businessman found time to relax over a multicourse luncheon. This was not so in Chicago. Downtown businessmen regarded lunch as a hindrance, not an oasis. They hung signs on their office doors that read "Closed for Lunch—Back in Ten Minutes" and raced through their meals. They sat on stools, bellied up to barlike counters, gulped down Spartan lunches, and charged back to work. Europeans regarded this as barbarism.

Continental observers were also stunned at the behavior of pedestrians in Chicago. Ernst von Hesse-Wartegg, a visitor from Germany, describes one instance. As he was walking along a sidewalk near the Chicago River, the people around him began to run. Afraid that he would be trampled, von Hesse-Wartegg ran along with the throng. When he heard a ship's whistle approaching, he realized why he was part of a stampede. Ships regularly plied the Chicago River during business hours, forcing the city's many swing bridges to open, cutting off street and pedestrian traffic for several minutes. The German visitor was now part of a mad dash to reach the bridge ahead of the ship. Just as he raced onto the swing bridge, the pavement separated under his feet. An iron gate popped up behind him, dooming those left behind to waste precious minutes. People beside him jumped for the bridge; most made it, but one fell into the murky Chicago River below. Von Hesse-Wartegg held on as the bridge swung him out into the center of the river. Such a fast-paced and hectic life was unheard of Europe, but it was so common as to go unnoticed in a commercial dynamo like Chicago.

To Europeans, fast lunches and sidewalk stampedes were only the most obvious examples of Chicagoans' different work culture. They also noted how Chicagoans reached business agreements. In Europe, the business deal was only culminated after several days of talking, dining, conversing, and confidence-building, a ritual that ended with the signing of a formal document. In Chicago, the business deal took three minutes and a quick handshake. Europeans also marveled at the balloon-frame construction techniques used in the city. In Europe, skilled craftsmen took months to construct homes with painstakingly cut wood and precisely mortised joints. In Chicago, construction crews erected houses in days with hastily sawn lumber and nails. Europeans pointed out that European homes had a much better chance of lasting several hundred years than did their American counterparts, but Americans craved the quickly built and relatively inexpensive balloon-frame house. In similar fashion, Europeans looked on incredulously as downtown sky-scrapers were built in months instead of in years. Chicago builders worked around the clock, using artificial light and heat to expedite construction. So amazing were these rapid construction techniques that J. Hayes Sadler, the British consul in Chicago, began including downtown building reports in his consular dispatches to London.

What Europeans such as Sadler were witnessing in Chicago was a different concept of time and a different work culture. Chicago was a commercial center first and foremost. It was not unusual to take a quick lunch, to jump for the moving swing bridge, or to build a house in ten days. It was not unusual for employers to demand a twelve-hour work-day and a six-day workweek. It was not unusual for workers to sacrifice time with the family for extra work and extra pay. This was the norm, which meant it became expected and routine. Chicago civic leaders made sure that new immigrants to the city understood this. When Frances K. Wetmore, a member of the city's board of education, collected lessons for her book *A First Book in English for Non-English Speaking Adults,* she included this pointed lesson on time:

> I look at my watch.
> It is half past four.
> I am sure my watch is right.

> Last week I took my watch to the jeweler.
> It ran too slow.
> It lost five minutes every day.
> It made me late to work.
> The time-keeper docked me for lost time.
> I had less pay, because I lost time.[22]

To European observers accustomed to the much slower work rhythms of the Old Country, such a dizzying fast pace—indeed, even the concept of "losing time," as expressed in Wetmore's lesson—seemed uncivilized. But to Chicagoans who for the first time enjoyed the creature comforts offered by a modern industrial society, such a pace seemed the very essence of civilization.

* * * *

Chicago's grain, lumber, meat, and mail-order businesses help explain how Chicago grew from a frontier town in 1850 to the nation's second largest city in 1900, but they were by no means the only factors in Chicago's growth. For example, by 1890 Chicago boasted the third-highest number of manufacturing workers in the nation (behind New York City and Philadelphia) and was second only to New York City in the value of products manufactured. Chicago was home to thriving businesses in printing and publishing, foundry and machine shop products, clothing, lumber, and furniture. Between 1880 and 1915, the South Chicago-Calumet area became one of the steel capitals of the world, and the steel industry ultimately spawned the northwestern Indiana city of Gary (so named for U.S. Steel chairman and Chicago lawyer Elbert H. Gary). As early as 1871, more ships were arriving in Chicago than were docking in New York City, Philadelphia, Baltimore, Charleston, San Francisco, and Mobile combined. Of particular importance were the grain, lumber, and meat industries, because these were the juggernaut businesses that drove Chicago's spectacular economic growth. Without them—and without the railroads that made these industries thrive—Chicago might well have been a modest Midwest city. With them, Chicago became a prairie metropolis and the Gateway to the West.

The ultimate irony is that nothing about this economic growth was "natural." What originally brought Europeans to Chicago were its natural endowments, namely, the eastward-flowing Chicago River, the portage, and the westward-flowing Des Plaines and Illinois Rivers. Nature had ordained that the all-water route from the Great Lakes to the

Mississippi River pass through the locale that became Chicago. What made Chicago America's second largest city and an economic dynamo, however, were the railroad, the mechanical reaper, the Union Stock Yards, and the mail-order house. These things owed little to Nature. As Garry Wills has written, "The city was an act of will, a *défi*, an imposition, a triumph over circumstance. There was nothing 'natural' about it."[23]

CHAPTER FIVE

LIFE IN A CITY

ON THE MAKE,

1850-1900

• Chicago's remarkable economic growth was accompanied by a meteoric increase in population. In 1850, the city was home to 30,000 residents. That number rose to 110,000 in 1860, 309,000 in 1870, 500,000 in 1880, 1,100,000 in 1890 (a total that made Chicago the second largest city in the United States), and 1,700,000 in 1900. As critical as economic growth was in the city, however, Chicagoans' lives consisted of more than marketing grain, selling lumber, processing meat, and filling catalog orders. They threw themselves into political battles as they shaped their rapidly growing city. They also created institutions ranging from water pumping stations to Young Men's Christian Association (Y.M.C.A.) buildings to meet their needs. Like most Americans, they worshiped, amused themselves in their free time, and continually struggled with ethnic relationships.

THE POLITICS OF REFORM AND ETHNICITY

During the latter half of the 1800s, American politics were driven by ethnocultural issues. These were social issues rooted in Americans' differing cultural mores. For example, some Americans sought laws that protected the Christian Sabbath by prohibiting alcohol consumption on Sundays, while others claimed a right to drink beer on their one nonworking day. One's ethnicity was often a good indicator of one's position in these debates. Protestant Anglo-Americans tended to favor more moralistic positions, while immigrants and Catholics tended to favor more nonrestrictive or permissive policies.

These ethnic, cultural, and religious concerns were intertwined in post–Civil War America, so that political debates over how much a saloon license would cost (expensive licenses drove saloon keepers out of business) often mirrored deeper debates about the relationship between

Anglo-Americans and immigrants. Not surprisingly, these ethnocultural issues mobilized voters, led to passionate disagreements, and created an urban political environment that was highly volatile.[1] Brief mayoral terms further encouraged that volatility. Mayors originally served one-year terms before the term was lengthened to two years. Political power changed hands often as mayors fell out of favor quickly.

Ethnocultural issues were most important in ethnically diverse locales like Chicago. In 1850, 54 percent of all Chicagoans had been born outside of North America, and, on one day in 1857, 3,400 new immigrants arrived in the city by train. By 1890, 80 percent of all Chicagoans either had been born overseas or were children of foreign-born parents. Germans (many of whom lived on the North Side in what became known as Old Town) were the largest ethnic group in pre-1890 Chicago, followed by the Irish (who congregated in Bridgeport on the Southwest Side), Bohemians (who lived on the Near West Side in what was later called Pilsen), and Scandinavians (who lived on the Near North Side by the Chicago River). Ethnic allegiances proved enduring. Nearly all of Chicago's ethnic groups published their own native-language newspapers. Germans maintained four newspapers, Swedes three, Norwegians one, Danes two, Czechs/Bohemians three, Italians two, Poles three, and Jews four. These ethnic newspapers suggest that Chicago was actually a collection of distinct communities and not one "melting pot" city.

Ethnocultural issues were also class issues. Few doubted then or now that a wide gulf separated the wealthiest Chicagoans (almost all of whom were Anglo-Americans) and the poorest (who were usually foreign-born immigrants). In 1848 and 1849, the wealthiest 1 percent of the city's population possessed a staggering 52 percent of the city's wealth, and the richest 10 percent controlled 94 percent of the wealth. Seventy-four percent of the city's heads of families—most of whom were immigrants or sons of immigrants—owned no land or commercial wealth and few personal belongings. Ethnic and class issues were thus inextricably connected.

By the 1850s, ethnocultural issues were at the center of the local political arena. The *Chicago Tribune*—an unashamedly Anglo-American and Protestant newspaper that frequently criticized immigrants—blamed mounting city tensions on the drinking habits of the Irish Catholics, most of whom saw nothing wrong with drinking whiskey and beer. The *Literary Budget*, a small city magazine, agreed with the *Tribune* and routinely told its readers about an alleged Roman Catholic plot to subvert individual liberty worldwide. It pointed out that 625 of the city's 675 liquor establishments were owned by immigrants. When a prominent Catholic planned a visit to the city in 1854, the *Tribune* warned of an impending Catholic conquest. According to the newspaper, "Inquisitions, with all the concomitants, of prisons, racks, thumb screws, and all the instruments of torture . . . applied to poor heretics in Spain by order of the holy Apostolic Catholic Church" could one day "include the land of Washington."[2]

The local Know-Nothing, or American, Party capitalized on this blending of prohibition and anti-Catholic sentiment. Named for their evasive response to inquiries regarding their quasi-secretive organization, the Know-Nothings were a nativistic political party that despised Irish Catholics. Members pledged never to vote for foreign-born or Catholic candidates. Chicago Know-Nothings (who were not committed in principle to prohibition) made common cause with the city's many temperance societies and in 1855 swept the city elections. Know-Nothings were elected to the mayor's office, several administrative positions, and seven of ten Common Council seats.[3] New mayor Levi D. Boone declared war on beer—which was another way of declaring war on the city's immigrants. Boone immediately raised the annual liquor license fee by 600 percent, from $50 to $300, and banned alcohol sales on Sunday. Eighty new Anglo-American police officers were hired to enforce the laws.

The Sunday-closing law was an inconvenience to the city's many Irish saloon keepers, many of whom installed heavy curtains over their windows and admitted customers secretly, creating a forerunner of the speakeasies that would become famous in the 1920s. The increased license fee, however, could drive them out of business. Also threatened were the city's numerous German tavern keepers. Germans—most of whom were not Catholic—thirsted for what they called the German national beverage, or lager beer. On Sundays they enjoyed taking their families to outdoor beer gardens, where they listened to bands and visited with friends. Rowdy drunkenness was rare, but a beer or two helped achieve the states of *Gemütlichkeit* (a German word meaning "being socially and emotionally expansive") and *Geselligkeit* ("voluntary sociability") that, at least for the German immigrants, were indispensable to good living. The new Sunday-closing laws and higher license fees endangered this mainstay of German life. City saloon keepers defied Boone's new law, and Chicago police arrested two hundred of them.

What ensued was a full-scale ethnic riot in the city, known as the Lager Beer Riot of 1855. A group of Germans and Irish marched to the city courthouse, demanding release of their saloon keepers. Police lost control of the mob, scuffling began, and gunshots rang out. One man was killed, and several were injured. Armed soldiers were called in, and quasi-martial law was imposed. By the next morning, more than fifty rioters had been arrested. After some Germans who reappeared at the courthouse with weapons were persuaded to return home, the Lager Beer Riot was over.

The riot marked the demise of the Know-Nothing Party. Always more concerned with Irish Catholics than with the wealthier and more respected Protestant Germans, the Know-Nothings' alliance with temperance advocates had alienated the city's German population. The mayor's clumsy handling of the Lager Beer Riot also alienated many Anglo-American prohibitionists in the city. As much as they disliked alcohol, they had not anticipated riots and bloodshed. Boone was ousted from office in 1856 with few remaining allies. What followed was a seesaw battle for political power. Voters alternately elected reform and antireform mayors, and mayors took turns foundering on the shoals of highly charged social issues.

Boone was replaced by Thomas Dyer. Dyer's 1856 inaugural parade—which included the city's prostitutes riding in open carriages—announced that he would end the moralizing days of the Know-Nothings. The permissive Dyer lasted one year in office; he was replaced by "Long John" Wentworth, a reform mayor. Wentworth hired a spy to scout out the city's red light district, which was located near the present-day Tribune Tower. He then attacked the flophouses in an 1857 raid, destroyed nine buildings, and burned six others. However, Wentworth brought no lasting change to the city that some Americans called "the wickedest city in the country." By 1860, the vice district had reestablished itself along Randolph Street between State and Dearborn Streets. Francis C. Sherman, who was elected mayor in 1862 during the Civil War, was flexible and tolerant. Unlike Wentworth, he did not impose his prohibitionist convictions upon others. No wartime crackdowns on beer or Sunday drinking occurred.

Perhaps the war-related economic boom distracted both Sherman and the city's reformers. Untouched by the war's carnage, Chicago, the hub of the nation's expanding railroad grid, played a key role in providing clothing and food for the Union's enormous army. Before the war, St. Louis and Cincinnati, Chicago's two chief competitors, had economies dependent upon extensive trade with southern states. The long Civil War deprived these two cities of their valuable southern markets. This was a loss Chicago did not face. The war added 80,000 new residents to the city (raising the population from 110,000 to 190,000) and boosted the economy with war-related work. In 1862 alone, the Union army's quartermaster in Chicago spent more than $4.7 million in the city on war supplies. The city's clothing business grew from $2.5 million at the war's outset to $12 million in 1863, and shoe and boot manufacturers saw their business swell from $2.5 million at the beginning of the war to $14 million in 1864. Grain exports grew during the war's first two years from 31 million to 65 million bushels. "Without McCormick's invention," said U.S. Secretary of War Edwin Stanton, referring to Cyrus McCormick's mechanical wheat reaper, "the North could not win and . . . the Union would be dismembered."[4]

Some Chicagoans resorted to creative means to profit from the war. Enlistees were paid cash bonuses by the federal government for volunteering for military service. Edward Jones enlisted, collected his bonus, deserted, enlisted again, collected another bonus, deserted again, and repeated the ruse until he had collected eight enlistment bonuses. Another Chicagoan, the aptly named Con Brown, claimed to have enlisted twenty times and acquired $8,000 in bonuses. Local vice boss Mike McDonald organized a gang of men who would enlist in the Union army, pocket the $500 bounty for doing so, desert the army after boot camp, and then return to Chicago to reenlist and to reclaim another bounty. McDonald split the take with the bounty jumpers.

Camp Douglas, a prison camp located just south of the downtown area, between Thirty-first Street, Thirty-third Street, Giles, and Cottage Grove Avenue, interned twelve thousand Confederate prisoners of war. City residents often traveled to the camp on Sundays, some to bring medicine, food, blankets, and clothing to the prisoners and some to climb the observation tower for a fee of ten cents to gawk at the unfortunate Rebel soldiers. In 1864, Confederate President Jefferson Davis sent some of his top spies to Chicago to organize a prison break. The plot called for cutting telegraph wires and burning railroad depots. A Union double agent foiled the plot, however, and Chicagoans were therefore never deprived of their Sunday excursions to Camp Douglas.

The Civil War provided ample opportunity for ethnic tensions to manifest themselves. The city's most powerful and visible citizens (most of whom were Anglo-Americans) tended to be Unionists, while the Irish and Germans tended to be antiwar Copperheads. Chicago's immigrants probably took a dim view of the war because, like immigrants throughout the North, they were the individuals who actually fought and died in the Union armies. Wealthy Americans nationwide fulfilled their military obligations by hiring men (usually poor immigrants) to serve in their places; in 1864, such replacements commanded fees of $1,200 ($1,000 was a comfortable annual salary for a skilled professional). About half of the 26,000 Chicago soldiers who served in the Civil War were German Americans, and one-third were Irish. The depth of Copperhead sentiment in the city became obvious when the U.S. military suspended publication of a local antiwar newspaper, the *Chicago Times*, in 1863. President Abraham Lincoln rescinded the closure and the *Times* continued to publish, but editor Wilbur F. Storey was physically assaulted several times for his Copperhead leanings.

The number of replacement soldiers and enlistees was sufficient to spare Chicago from forced conscription in 1862 and 1863. In 1864, however, the federal government began drafting soldiers from the city. Many Chicagoans resisted the draft calls and beat enrollment officers who came to locate draft-age men. The city never saw the full-scale draft riots that occurred in New York City, but on at least one occasion a mob of Chicagoans attacked military officials and forced them to release a group of captured draft evaders whom they were escorting to an induction center.

Following the Civil War, some immigrants in Chicago won praise for their devotion to the war effort. In 1865, former mayor John Wentworth applauded Chicago's German Jewish community for its patriotism. In his accolades of the community, he stated, "A few years hence, there was a cry raised that 'foreigners' could not be trusted, and an attempt was made to disenfranchise you, but when at last the time came that tried men's souls—when native-born Americans [Southerners] proved false to their allegiance to their flag, and tried their utmost to tear down and trample under foot the noble structure their fathers fought and died to rear up, then you 'foreigners' came forward and showed yourselves true men. You have done honor to your native and to your adopted countries. I say it: you have proved that this country owes its existence to foreign immigrants."[5]

German Jews emerged from the war more widely accepted among Chicago's Anglo-Americans, but the Irish did not. They also served loyally during the war but remained pariahs. In 1868 the *Chicago Evening Post* was still publishing scathing anti-Irish invectives: "The country has survived the Irish emigration—the worst with which any other country was ever afflicted. The Irish fill our prisons, our reform schools, our hospitals. . . . Scratch a convict or a pauper and the chances are that you tickle the skin of an Irish Catholic . . . made a criminal or a pauper by the priest and politician who have deceived him and kept him in ignorance, in a word, a savage, as he was born."[6] Although the war lessened ethnic tensions for some groups, for other Chicagoans it only deepened divisions between themselves and Anglo-Americans.

The cycle of political reform and antireform continued after the war. In the aftermath of the catastrophic 1871 fire, the city turned to a nonpolitician who had proved himself capable of managing a large business: *Chicago Tribune* publisher Joseph Medill. Although a committed prohibitionist, Medill had no intention of addressing such no-win issues as alcohol and vice control. As mayor, he sought only to rebuild a Chicago devastated by the fire. Early in his term, however, he reluctantly found himself embroiled in a debate over the Sunday closing of saloons and his authority to revoke saloon licenses. With his worst fears confirmed about the city's penchant for making vice the focus of all local politics, Medill abandoned his office. He suddenly announced he was ill and embarked on an extended tour of Europe. According to one historian, Medill was "sick at the thought of compromise with immigrant voters."[7] Medill only returned to Chicago after his term had expired. His opponents gloried in what they called their triumph over puritan rule; they celebrated by electing Harvey D. Colvin, a good friend of city crime boss Mike McDonald, mayor in 1874.

Medill's ouster coincided with an unprecedented event in Chicago politics: the creation of a German American and Irish American political alliance. This coalition transformed Chicago politics. After 1875, successful mayors were those who did not attack vice outright but rather managed it. Such a mayor was Carter Henry Harrison I. A Kentucky gentleman, Yale graduate, and lawyer who came to the city in 1855, Harrison served four consecutive mayoral terms between 1879 and 1887 and was reelected again in 1893 as the city prepared for the world's fair. Harrison was the archetypical late-nineteenth-century charismatic mayor: on the one hand, he was sufficiently elite to win the support of wealthy "silk stocking" businessmen; on the other, he was sufficiently earthy and affable to avoid alienating the city's growing ethnic population. In particular, he allied himself with the Irish. It was under Harrison that the Irish came to control the local Democratic Party. Though Harrison dispensed low-level patronage jobs to his Irish supporters (by 1900, for example, the Irish would claim six times as many police officers as the next largest ethnic group), he did not run a disciplined urban political machine. That would not come until the 1930s. He instead held together his coalition of wealthy businessmen and ethnic voters by dint of his magnetic personality and his personal control of 15,000 patronage jobs. The legendary Harrison charisma allowed him, for example, to support labor unions in the city (which won him praise from ethnic workers) and simultaneously to retain his support among Chicago's leading bankers, merchants, and real estate tycoons.

The passing of the mayor's office from Joseph Medill, who was a prohibitionist Republican, to Carter Harrison, a latitudinarian Democrat, several years later sheds light on the essential differences between these two major political parties in the late 1800s. The Republican Party tended to be the party of moral reform and won a wide following among native Anglo-Americans, businessmen, and Christian social activists, while the Democratic Party billed itself as the party of personal liberty and appealed to immigrants, the working class, and liberals. John Joseph "Bathhouse" Coughlin, one of Chicago's most powerful politicians in the late 1800s and early 1900s, defined the Republican and Democratic parties in a homey but perceptive manner: "A Republican is a man who wants you t' go t' church every Sunday. A Democrat says if a man wants t' have a glass of beer on Sunday, he can have it." Such party distinctions, however, often broke down at the local level. In Chicago, few candidates ran primarily as Democrats or Republicans. Most belonged to local parties or tickets such as the Citizens' Union, the People's Party, the Citizens' Association, the Municipal Reform Club, and the Anti-Machine Ticket. When Medill ran for mayor in 1871, for instance, it had been a Carter Harrison-led group of commercial-civic elite who slated the *Tribune* editor on a bipartisan ticket. Local politics centered around personality, vice, beer, and social control laws, not party affiliation.

Harrison's determination to give the common man what he wanted led to his philosophy of running a wide-open city. He allowed Chicagoans both to make money and to spend it any way they wished. Business flourished under Harrison's rule, but so did saloons, gambling joints, and brothels. Harrison regarded such vices as inevitable. Futile attempts to eradicate them only alienated people. "You can't make people moral by ordinance and it is no use trying," explained Harrison. "This is a free town."[8] Moreover, one-fourth of the city council's seats were held by saloon keepers in the 1880s and 1890s, and nearly one-half of the Democratic Party's precinct captains in 1900 were saloon keepers. Harrison needed to make them happy if he hoped to win the ethnic vote or to fashion a working coalition among the city's aldermen. Instead of closing these putative dens of iniquity, Harrison compelled the vice merchants to keep their businesses hidden. Bars were made secluded, quiet, and respectable. Prostitutes stayed off the streets or at least within designated areas. Gambling was done discreetly. Minors were kept out of the city's vice district, which was confined to the notorious First Ward (bounded by Clark, Polk, Dearborn, and Harrison Streets). Critics charged that Harrison made Chicago the Gomorrah of the West. What especially galled them was the brazenness with which Harrison tolerated gambling and alcohol. When a group of ministers asked if he knew that busy gambling houses were operating near the downtown area, Harrison responded that he had been there recently and had enjoyed himself immensely. The mayor's many supporters pointed out that Harrison was impeccably honest, kept most parties happy, lessened ethnic tensions, forced vice off the streets, and created the stability that allowed businesses to thrive.

One thing that even moralizing Republican prohibitionists did not protest in the late 1880s was the widespread use of narcotics such as morphine, cocaine, and opium. In Chicago, as elsewhere, few understood the health hazards posed by these narcotics in the late nineteenth and early twentieth centuries, and such drugs were legal not only in Chicago but nationwide. More than merely legal, they were easily obtainable from drug stores, department stores, tobacco shops, bookstores, and mail-order catalogs. They were inexpensive (half a day's wage purchased enough opium to supply an addict for several weeks) and could be found in such common items as infant's "soothing syrup" and Coca-Cola. "You have no idea what amount of morphine is consumed in this city daily," the Chicago *Daily News* stated in 1876. "Young men use opium on the tips of their cigars to flavor the tobacco. . . . Young women cannot go to a ball without taking a dose of morphine to nerve them, and make them bright and agreeable. Young men chew opium with their tobacco. Young women take morphine in their coffee and tea."[9] The Chicago *Medical Review* reported in 1880 that fifty local druggists each supplied an average of five addicts with sufficient narcotics to maintain their habit. It is one of the ironies of the late 1800s that moral reformers insisted upon the outlawing of beer but paid little attention to addictive narcotics.

Moral-reform politics in Chicago were coming to an end by the 1880s. Politicians might not have liked vice, but, like Harrison, they were learning to accept it as a fact of urban life. In the 1850s, successful politicians were reformers, such as Wentworth, who waged war on immorality and thereby won the support of the Protestant Anglo-Americans. By the

1880s, successful politicians were realists, such as Harrison, who took the polyglot city for what it was and tried to make as many people happy as possible. Victor Lawson, publisher of an anti-Harrison newspaper, explained Harrison's key to political success: "I never knew a man who possessed in such a marked degree the politician's prime quality of keeping in touch with the masses and commanding their affection. . . . Realizing fully the extent to which the population of Chicago is foreign born he devoted himself to gaining the support of men of every nationality."[10] In this era of ethnocultural politics, winning the ethnic vote required, among other things, the toleration of alcohol, gambling, and other pastimes. Most Chicago mayors after 1890 would follow Harrison's example, not Wentworth's.

PUBLIC POLICY AND URBAN SERVICES

Despite the blustery, nativistic world of Chicago's electoral politics, the city did address substantive public policy issues. Ethnocultural issues generated publicity and mobilized voters, but most municipal money went toward providing urban services. Unglamorous matters such as sewers, waste removal services, water pumping stations, and fire departments were (and still are) perhaps the most important business of municipal government in Chicago (or in any other city). Rural farmers might function fairly well without sewage systems, but not city dwellers. Such services were necessary if thousands of people were to live in close quarters.

The city did a creditable job of providing public services. Street lights appeared in 1850, although they illuminated mostly unpaved streets. As late as 1871, only 88 of the city's 530 miles of streets had been surfaced. By that year, though, the city had constructed twenty-seven bridges across the Chicago River as well as two "toll tunnels" that went under the river. A paid police department was organized in 1855, and expenditures on public health rose from $2,000 in 1851–1852 to $81,000 in 1868–1869. Some of that money went toward paying city food inspectors, who discovered in 1867 that 7 percent of all the meat sold by local butchers was unfit to eat.

As late as 1900, few Chicagoans were wealthy enough to enjoy private indoor baths. The city began providing free public baths (which were little more than primitive showers) in 1894, offering bathers free soap, a towel, and twenty minutes of bathing time. In 1903, police protected a half-finished bathhouse from angry area residents who threatened to storm the facility. They were mollified once they were assured that the presence of a bathhouse did not mean they would be forced to bathe. By 1910, fifty public bathhouses, charging a modest five-cent fee, averaged 30,000 patrons per year.

One area of perpetual concern to city politicians was fire fighting. The devastating fire of 1857—just one of many citywide fires—convinced city leaders that better fire protection was needed. Accordingly, they replaced their colorful, numerous, and inept volunteer fire companies with a full-time fire department in 1858. In addition to paying firemen, the city purchased its first steam-powered fire engine, a marvel of modern ingenuity called "Ye Great Skwirt 'Long John.'" The city also purchased something called a hydropult that promised to throw water an incredible fifty feet. Even with these devices, a squad of firemen that numbered 201 by 1871, and an annual budget of $400,000 that year, the new "professional" fire department enjoyed little more success than the old volunteer companies. Another catastrophic fire raced through the city in 1868, a precursor to the Great Chicago Fire of 1871. When yet another fire leveled much of the city in 1874, local insurance companies (who had been devastated by the 1871 fire) threatened to stop insuring Chicago businesses. Such an embargo would have crippled the city. Chicago leaders renewed their commitment to fire prevention, and by 1893 the city employed more than one thousand firemen.

Chicago's early city school system received high marks from contemporaries. Besides upholding high academic standards, by the 1860s they also included enrichment offerings such as graded courses in music. The schools also maintained strict discipline over their charges. Students were sent home if their hands were dirty or if their hair was uncombed, and the city's schools averaged twenty floggings per day in 1868. In 1864, evening classes were officially added to accommodate the city's many immigrants.

At least some school teachers worked long days. Mary Towne was employed by the city as a substitute teacher in the normal day schools and a regular instructor in the evening school. "Started this a.m. at 7 1/2 & have just returned at 5 3/4," wrote Towne to her family in 1868. "Shall just have time to eat a hearty supper of poached or fried eggs & cold ham and leave in time to reach school-house at 7. Pretty close work isn't it?, but pays well."[11] She earned $1.50 per day substituting and $2 per night for her evening school job. She was paid nothing for the monthly Saturday "teacher institutes" she was required to attend.

Fortunate scholars could matriculate into one of the city's three major colleges: Northwestern University (established in 1851), the University of Chicago (1857), and St. Ignatius College (1869), which later became Loyola University. All three were private schools. Northwestern had been founded for Methodist youth who needed what the founders called "sanctified learning." The state legislature, accommodating the desires of the schools' founders to create a wholesome environment for young men, passed restrictive laws forbidding the sale of alcohol within four miles of the school's campus in Evanston. This made Evanston a "dry" town on the outskirts of a very "wet" city, a circumstance that encouraged the Women's Christian Temperance Movement to locate its headquarters in Evanston. The University of Chicago went bankrupt in 1886, but, with the financial support of John D. Rockefeller and Marshall Field's contribution of land for a campus, the university reopened in 1892 with the goal of becoming a world-class institution. President William Rainey Harper purposed to create a Harvard in the West; to that end, he brought a stellar faculty to the school. Eight of the school's initial faculty members were former college presidents.

Few projects required more effort than the city's battle with sewerage, trash, and drinking water. Before the mid-1850s, the city (like all other North American cities) had no comprehensive sewer system. The garbage, industrial waste, and human and animal excrement created by 100,000 Chicagoans and their animals were thrown into streets, vacant lots, or the Chicago River. In addition to household waste was industrial waste. One local meatpacking house might easily have 120 wagonloads of waste to dispose of each day. It is little surprise that disease was rampant in the city. In 1854, a cholera epidemic killed 6 percent of all Chicagoans. "The death cart," wrote one Chicagoan, "was seen continually in the streets."[12] It was thought that Chicago had the highest death rate of any city in the country.

The city responded to this crisis by building the first integrated sewer system in the nation in 1856. Unfortunately, less than 15 percent of the city was connected to sewers by 1866. Moreover, the city's sewer mains simply emptied their filth into the Chicago River. The lazy Chicago River, possessing only the weakest of currents, gradually flowed eastward through the downtown area into Lake Michigan. The river became a putrid, smelly, disease-carrying garbage ditch. The editor of the *Democrat,* a Chicago newspaper, described the Chicago River in 1858: "On examining the water along the banks of the river, I found it to be a mass of blood, grease, animal entrails, etc., the color being so dark as to be almost opaque when pored into a glass vessel."[13] The filthy river posed an additional problem: where would Chicagoans find clean drinking water? By the 1860s, the city required 18 million gallons of fresh water per day. Both the river and the lake's shoreline, however, had become contaminated with sewage.

City engineers crafted two remarkable solutions to the problem of water quality. First, they did the extraordinary: in the late 1860s, city engineers built a two-mile-long tunnel that reached out under Lake Michigan. One end of the tunnel was onshore and accessible through a ninety-foot-deep vertical shaft. The brick-and-cement reinforced tunnel itself was five feet in diameter and thirty to sixty feet below the lake bottom. The other end of the tunnel turned upward and penetrated the lake bottom. Water from Lake Michigan flowed through the tunnel to the city's water company. City leaders hoped that the mouth of this water supply pipe would be sufficiently far from the city's shoreline to access clean water. City residents would be drinking water straight from Lake Michigan, but at least it would be fairly clean water.

There were problems with this solution, however, especially when it came to the engineers' attempt to put a filter over the water supply pipe's lake bottom mouth. Until the filter was perfected, Chicagoan's drank more than water from the lake. Historian Bessie Louise Pierce describes this problem nicely: "Chicago housewives sometimes found it almost impossible to keep small fish from squirming out of the hydrant into their cooking receptacles. . . . Even the temperate threatened to cook food in lager beer or ale. 'Dead fish, newts, and various specimens of watery animalculae known to the books,' were said to make bathing a fisherman's pastime, while quenching one's thirst gave one a strangely ticklish sensation as 'finny fellows' wriggled down the throat."[14] Even fishy water, however, was an improvement over what Chicagoans had been forced to drink.

City engineers then did what many had deemed impossible: they reversed the flow of the Chicago River in 1871. By dredging the river in strategic places, they were able to reverse the river's current. Before 1870, the river had meandered in an easterly direction and flowed into Lake Michigan. This dumped much of the city's garbage into the lake and frequently contaminated the city's drinking water. Now the river (and the city's garbage) flowed westward, away from Lake Michigan and away from the city, toward the town of Joliet.

Unfortunately for Chicago (but fortunately for Joliet), the river reversal project was only successful for one year. Heavy rains and land developers' drainage projects refilled the Chicago River with silt, halting the westward flow of water. In 1879, record rains so flooded the area's rivers that the Chicago River pushed its garbage out into Lake Michigan and past the city's drinking water intake crib. City residents resorted to boiling their drinking water. Heavy rains in 1885 did the same thing, this time bringing epidemics to the city that killed perhaps 10 percent of the population. The city returned to the river reversal project in earnest in 1889 with the construction of a massive canal that extended twenty-eight miles southwest of the city to Lockport (just east of Joliet). This second canal was so large and deep—160 feet wide and 30 feet deep at some points—that it inexorably drained water away from Chicago. When completed in 1900, the resulting Chicago Sanitary and Ship Canal provided a permanent solution to the city's garbage disposal and drinking water problem. The state of Missouri protested that the river reversal project subjected them to the horrors of Chicago's garbage, but Chicago maintained—and scientists of that day agreed—that rivers cleansed themselves after several miles of flow by diluting the garbage. In 1955, the American Society of Civil Engineers proclaimed the canal one of the seven wonders of American engineering.

Land developers used the city's inability to deliver pure drinking water, its less-than-ideal sewage system, and its chronic health problems to help sell new suburban developments. Perhaps most notable of these early suburbs was Riverside, a community constructed in the 1860s on sixteen hundred acres located nine miles west of downtown. Developers hired famed landscape architect Frederick Law Olmstead to help design the community and ended up building an oasis of lavishness west of the city. Chicago offered congested city blocks, dirty roads, and alleys for children to play in; Riverside boasted seven hundred acres of parks, eighty miles of paved sidewalks, and publicly maintained playgrounds. The newly constructed railroads that brought livestock into the city also transported Riverside commuters, who could reach the city within thirty-five minutes by train. Promoters highlighted Riverside's investment potential and reminded Chicagoans that suburban living had become a status symbol among the well-to-do. Developers also made a special point to emphasize Riverside's health benefits. The suburb obtained pure drinking water from its own well, disposed of waste with an underground drainage system, and even piped gas to each homesite. Promotional literature explained that Riverside was "the most pleasant, healthful, and desirable place of residence attainable anywhere" and that it offered a "soothing and recuperating influence upon business and professional men overtasked by duties in the city."[15]

AMUSEMENTS AND RECREATION

In Chicago during the second half of the nineteenth century, often one person's amusement was another's sin. In 1889 a guidebook to the city's nine hundred brothels was published that helped visitors identify "the quiet, respectable and legitimate establishments" that were "safe" and "first-class."[16] Had a pollster spoken with Chicagoans in the years between 1850 and 1900, he probably would have discovered that many Chicagoans sought recreation at saloons, beer gardens, variety shows in saloon music halls, public dance halls, and melodrama and minstrel shows. In the late 1800s, the variety show evolved into the vaudeville or burlesque show. Many regarded the new burlesque shows at the Opera House as a form of legitimate amusement. The *Chicago Times* demurred, calling the performances "immoral" and reporting that "scantily-clad" girls were "capering lasciviously and uttering gross indecencies." One of the actresses responded by ambushing the newspaper's publisher and horsewhipping him. Although the woman was arrested and fined, three thousand Chicagoans flocked to her next performance and cheered lustily.

The city offered more wholesome forms of amusement as well, such as the many traveling circuses and animal shows that passed through the city. As early as 1853, P. T. Barnum's circus gave three daily performances during its visits to Chicago. Other circuses competed with Barnum's collection of animals, midgets, jugglers, and Siamese twins. One circus claimed to give culture-starved Chicagoans a chance to see the Sacred White Elephant of Siam, although the beast required an occasional touching-up with some handy white paint. During the 1880s, the Wild West Shows also passed through the city regularly. Chicagoans saw men such as Buffalo Bill Cody rope cattle, perform trick shots with rifles and pistols, and reenact Indian battles.

In the 1870s, many Chicagoans were intrigued by a new sport called baseball. A local team, the Chicago White Stockings, was assembled in 1870. Crowds numbering in the thousands turned out to watch the White Stockings play teams such as the Brooklyn Atlantics. In order to make the White Stockings more competitive, team president William Hulbert lured New York star Albert G. Spalding to the team in 1876. The White Stockings created a sensation when they paid Spalding the outrageous sum of $2,000 annually (plus 25 percent of all gate receipts) for playing just one game. (By comparison, a female school teacher in Chicago earned about $900 per year.)

The National League of Professional Base Ball Clubs was created in 1876, and Chicago won the first championship. By the mid-1880s, the *Chicago Tribune* could talk about the city's "many baseball-maniacs." One four-game series with a New York team drew forty thousand Chicagoans. One newspaper told its readers in 1888 that professional baseball was "a tremendous source of revenue" and that the White Stockings was its "richest corporation. . . . The Chicago club is purely a money-making concern. . . . It is organized as any other corporation, by people of wealth . . . who . . . haul in such profits yearly as would . . . make even bonanza kings envious."[17]

Spalding went on to become the White Stockings' player-manager and then its president. He made the Chicago White Stockings the most successful professional baseball team in America by 1890. Among other things, Spalding oversaw construction of new baseball parks in the city for his team. These parks included such luxuries as private boxes, free scorecards, and a "neatly-furnished toilet room with a private entrance for ladies."[18] Always looking for a way to make a buck, Spalding turned his ball fields into amusement parks in the off-season. (He constructed a sixty-five-foot-high toboggan slide that provided customers with a seven-hundred-foot ride for only a quarter.) Spalding also opened a sporting goods store that bore his name in the city. Baseball was so popular that the city gained its second professional team in 1890. A revolt among professional ball players led to new teams, one of which was managed by Charles A. Comiskey. Comiskey stole many of the White Stockings' players, located his team on the city's South Side, in the heart of its Irish neighborhood, and began playing in a rival league.[19] Comiskey also stole the White Stockings' team name, as his upstart team became known as the White Stockings. Chicago's original North Side team was demoralized. It did not regroup until the late 1890s, and it was eventually renamed the Cubs.

Baseball thrived in part because it had little competition. Professional football did not appear until 1920. American teams did not join the National Hockey League until the 1920s. Basketball boasted no professional league until the 1940s. Thus in Chicago and in other large cities, baseball became the first popular professional sport. It is especially important to consider baseball's social impact on ethnically diverse cities like Chicago. The baseball park was a place (and perhaps the only place) where all Chicagoans—Anglo-Americans, Germans, the Irish, Italians, Jews, the wealthy and the poor, the educated and the illiterate—met on equal terms. Chicagoans who had little in common shared a common experience: they could root for the home team. The White Stockings and the Cubs probably eased the assimilation process for many Chicagoans.

The most popular sporting event in the city was not baseball, however. It was horse racing. Chicagoans flocked to the area's several racetracks and wagered on the races. The tracks proved so popular that by the 1880s many of the city's gambling houses switched from numbers games (similar to today's lotteries) to racetrack bookmaking. Garfield Park became such a notorious hangout for the city's gamblers that the city closed it in 1892. The track's owners defied the closing notice, continued to schedule races, and locked the police out of the park. Chicago police raided the track for several consecutive days and ultimately arrested more than fifteen hundred Chicagoans. For the most part, however, city leaders allowed horse racing (and wagering) to continue. Legalized horse racing was a way of managing the gambling problem.

By the 1890s, new forms of recreation were available to city residents. Trendy Chicagoans experimented with the bicycling craze. Many bought their bicycles for one hundred dollars at the city's Arnold, Schwinn & Company, which was founded in Chicago in 1895. By the mid-1890s there were at least five hundred cycling clubs in the city, each with its own uniforms, colors, and cycling caps. Enthusiasts pedaled from Michigan Avenue to their clubhouses on the outskirts of the city or participated in the Chicago-to-Pullman road race. Trendier Chicagoans enjoyed lawn tennis. Others watched Northwestern University and the University of Chicago square off in the city football championship. Northwestern had been playing intercollegiate football since 1882. When the University of Chicago reopened in 1892, it hired Amos Alonzo Stagg as a full-time coach and fielded a football team that first year (although the thirty-year-old Stagg was forced into service as a player-coach). A fourteen-year series between Northwestern and Chicago ensued. Ten thousand paying fans attended the 1900 game and perhaps invented the football ritual now known as tailgating. The University of Chicago's stunning 2–0 upset of the University of Michigan in 1905, which was seen by twenty-seven thousand fans in the city, capped off an undefeated season and earned the Maroons both the Big Ten championship and the unofficial national championship. Stagg continued to coach at the University of Chicago for forty-one years and during that time made the school one of the nation's pre-1935 football powerhouses. Stagg also helped make college football one of the hottest entertainment events in early-twentieth-century Chicago.

These diversions were most popular among the upper classes. Blue-collar entertainment came in the form of the first amusement park in the nation: Paul Boynton's Water Chutes, which he opened in 1894 at Sixty-first Street and Drexel Boulevard. (Boynton then opened the Coney Island amusement park in New York City in 1895.) Chicago's Riverview Park, at one time the world's largest amusement park, opened in 1904 on seventy-two acres at Belmont and Western Avenues. The immigrant, the poor Anglo-American, and the African American were all welcome at Riverview. "Everybody's equal on a roller coaster," quipped Harry G. Traver, builder of the park's famous Bobs ride. "They all shriek at the same time."[20] Riverview remained one of the most popular city attractions until it closed in 1967. Black Chicagoans frequented the Château de Plaisance on the South Side, a combination dance floor, roller-skating rink, and restaurant that was owned and operated by African Americans. Chicago's working classes frequented city movie theaters, which came to the city after 1900 and numbered 116 by 1907. At least initially, the well-to-do refused to attend the moving pictures. They thought it too dangerous to sit in a darkened room with so many people, especially so many working-class people. Theater owners attempted to allay those anxieties by building posh, ornate, lavish theaters that counteracted the popular perception that motion pictures were a primarily working-class entertainment.

RELIGION

By 1890, the impact of immigration was evident in Chicago's religious profile. The city's Roman Catholics, most of whom were immigrants or of immigrant stock, totaled 262,000. That made Chicago second only to New York City as the largest Catholic city in the United States. Chicago's 35,000 Lutherans, who made up 30 percent of the city's 117,000 Protestants, formed the largest Lutheran community in the nation. Also significant were the city's 9,200 Jews, which made Chicago home to the nation's second largest Jewish community. Thirty-five percent of the city's 1890 citizens were members of religious congregations, while another 21 percent affiliated themselves with congregations without becoming members.

Two somewhat innovative theological trends emerged in the city. One was the advent of liberal Protestantism. Two prominent Protestant ministers—David Swing (pastor of the fashionable Fourth Presbyterian

Church) and Hiram W. Thomas (pastor of Park Avenue Methodist Episcopal Church and later First Methodist Church)—led this movement. Both ministers were gifted speakers, highly educated, and extremely popular within their congregations. Both also challenged orthodox tenets of the Christian faith. Presbyterian officials charged Swing with compromising the Presbyterian Church's theologically conservative confession of faith and denying the Bible's inerrancy. The Synod of Illinois sustained the heresy charge in 1874, and Swing was ousted from the Chicago Presbytery. Thomas denied that Jesus Christ died to atone for men's sins and instead taught that Jesus's death served to persuade men that they too should die for righteous principles. Thomas also rejected the doctrine of biblical inerrancy. The local Methodist conference expelled Thomas from the denomination in 1881 after a trial.

These were scandalous teachings in 1880. Swing and Thomas had ministered in mainline denominations that, at least until 1875, had remained quite conservative. They responded to their censures by forming new Chicago churches that attracted many of their old congregants. From their pulpits, Swing and Thomas continued preaching what amounted to a new and theologically liberal message. Their influence became clear during Chicago's 1893 World Columbian Exposition. The World's Fair convened a Parliament of Religions as an international summit meeting of religious representatives. Swing was among those Chicago ministers who planned the meeting. The Reverend John Henry Barrows, minister of Chicago's First Presbyterian Church, opened the parliament with a call to put aside doctrinal differences: "We are not here as Baptists and Buddhists, Catholics and Confucians, Parsees and Presbyterian Protestants, Methodists and Moslems; we are here as members of a Parliament of Religions, over which flies no sectarian flag, which is to be stampeded by no sectarian war-cries, but where for the first time in a large council is lifted up the banner of love, fellowship, and brotherhood."[21] This was the inclusive and nondoctrinal message that Swing and Thomas had popularized in Chicago.

If Chicago became a hotbed of liberal Protestantism, it also became a quasi Holy Land for conservative, or evangelical, Protestants. Indeed, one local religious leader—more theologically orthodox than Swing and Thomas—derided the Columbian Exposition's Parliament of Religions, which called for an end to doctrinal differences, as an "ecclesiastical menagerie" that "belittled and disgraced" the Lord Jesus Christ.[22] The key figure in the city's evangelical Christian community was Dwight L. Moody, who came to Chicago in 1856 from Massachusetts. The twenty-one-year-old shoe salesman started the Illinois Street Mission as a downtown Sunday School class. Moody rounded up unchurched city children, enticed them with sweets, brought them to his mission, and preached the gospel to them. He also rewarded good attendance with gifts of new suits of clothing. Unlike Swing and Thomas, Moody preached the old gospel of sin, Hell, salvation, and Heaven.

Moody was perhaps the first evangelist to use what are today called "seeker-sensitive" strategies. Moody believed that sermons bored listeners quickly; accordingly, he kept his messages short and used many visual aids. Moody was also convinced that the right music created an atmosphere propitious for conversions. To that end, he hired a piano accompanist, Ira D. Sankey, and had Sankey write many evangelistic hymns for use in revival meetings. Unsatisfied with the drab Y.M.C.A. building in which he was meeting, Moody built one that included exercise rooms and a residence hall. One historian called Moody's building "the first fully-equipped Y.M.C.A. building in the United States."[23] Largely due to Moody's influence, the Chicago Y.M.C.A. attempted to create a "Christian clubhouse" environment that would offer city men an alternative to saloons, beer gardens, and gambling halls. By 1894, the Chicago Y.M.C.A. boasted bowling alleys, a swimming pool, lockers, steam baths, an indoor running track, a darkroom, a restaurant, woodworking shops, handball and tennis courts, and a small observatory. The building had become, in the words of one historian, a piece of evangelical equipment.[24] The 1894 Y.M.C.A. building also boasted signs forbidding vagrants and loiterers, demonstrating the Y.M.C.A.'s commitment to reaching the respectable, middle-class infidel, not the poverty-stricken and homeless city vagabond. Moody's remaking of the Y.M.C.A. worked: membership exceeded expectations by 50 percent by the mid-1890s. If sinners would not come to church, Moody would take the church to them. He outfitted horse-drawn "Gospel wagons" that prowled Chicago streets and brought his ministry to citizens' front doors.

Moody was ministering to 750 children by 1865. Adults wanted to hear Moody as well, and he soon became America's foremost Protestant evangelist. His fame as a revivalist grew, resulting in an 1876 tour of Great Britain and the United States. The internationally renowned Moody returned to Chicago and established both a church (today's Moody Church) and a Bible training school, the Moody Bible Institute. By 1886, perhaps 260,000 Chicagoans had attended the revivals of Moody and other evangelical Protestants. As his earthly life neared an end, Moody spearheaded an enormous citywide evangelistic campaign to coincide with the 1893 world's fair in Chicago. The millions of visitors to the city posed an opportunity that Moody could not pass up. The evangelists, however, fared better among the middle class than among the poor and the immigrants. In the working-class neighborhoods, Roman Catholic mission outreaches, which first opened in the 1880s, proved more successful. The Catholics matched the Protestants numbers, reaching about 250,000 blue-collar Chicagoans.

Another evangelist, Billy Sunday, made Chicago his home in the late 1800s. Sunday was a professional baseball player with the Chicago White Stockings. He claimed that his first experience with God's miraculous power came at the end of the 1886 baseball season, while he was playing center field in a tight game with the Detroit Tigers. A Tiger batter belted a long drive to deep center field. In the early days of baseball, there were no outfield fences that separated spectators from the playing field; spectators simply sat beyond the reach of what they thought would be the batters' longest hits. In this case, however, the fleet-footed Sunday burst through the startled fans and leaped over benches as he tracked down the mammoth blast. Running "as though wings were carrying [him]," Sunday caught the ball on the fly and saved the game for the White Stockings. "Though the deduction is hardly orthodox," Sunday later explained, "I am sure the Lord helped me catch that ball, and it was my first experience in prayer."[25]

Like Moody, Sunday was a conservative Protestant who preached traditional fire-and-brimstone messages. Like Moody, Sunday was determined not to bore his listeners. One of the most dramatic preachers in turn-of-the-century America, Sunday used his considerable athletic talents in the pulpit. Sunday's biographer explains: "Some of the platform activities make spectators gasp. He races to and fro on the platform. Like a jack knife, he fairly doubles up in emphasis. One hand smites the other. . . . No posture is too extreme for this restless gymnast. . . . In a dramatic description of the marathon he pictures the athlete falling prostrate at the goal and—thud!—there lies the evangelist prone on the platform. . . . It seems almost impossible for him to stand up behind the pulpit and talk only with his mouth."[26] Together, Moody's and Sunday's grassroots preaching led to converts by the thousands.

Was Chicago an unusually religious city in the latter half of the 1800s? One visitor in the 1860s noticed that business in the Anglo-American neighborhoods and the central business district ceased on Sunday in observance of the Christian Sabbath: "The Traveler who stays over a Sunday in Chicago witnesses as complete a suspension of labor as in Boston or Philadelphia. A great majority of the eager and busy population on that day resigns itself to the influence of its instructors; and the hundred and fifty churches are filled with attentive people."[27] But in the city's working-class neighborhoods, religious interest was less noticeable. A survey of one hundred families from blue-collar neighborhoods revealed ten families that attended church and only two that were church members. When English reformer William Stead spoke to a gathering of Chicago workers in 1893, he was warned not to mention religion. "Not five percent of these men ever go to a place of worship," he was told. "If you say anything about God or Christ or the churches, you will be hissed off the platform."[28] Hard-working immigrants often believed that evangelical Protestants in general and revivalists in particular were in league with the oppressive business owners against whom they struggled. For this reason, irreligion was often widespread among working-class Chicagoans.

CHICAGO PERSONALITIES

Chicago's Myra Bradwell was the first female lawyer in Illinois. Bradwell's husband was a local judge, and Myra Bradwell studied law on her own in order to assist her husband. Her years of unofficial clerking with her husband gave Bradwell a thorough legal education. Accordingly, she took the state bar exam and passed it—the first woman in the state to do so. Bradwell then founded the *Chicago Legal News*. When Bradwell applied to the state bar, however, she was denied her license to practice law in Illinois. She appealed to the Illinois State Supreme Court in 1869. The court's decision says much about attitudes toward women in the late nineteenth century. The Supreme Court upheld the bar's decision and refused to grant Bradwell a license because "of the disability imposed by . . . your married condition." The court went on to state: "Applications of the same character have occasionally been made by persons under twenty-one years of age, and have always been denied upon the same ground—that they are not bound by contracts, being under a legal disability in that regard. Until such disability shall be removed by legislation, the court regards itself powerless to grant your application."[29] The "disability" to which the court referred was a married woman's lack of legal standing in contracts. This is why the court compared women to children: neither could make contracts, own property, sue, or be sued. As long as Illinois law defined married women as residents with no legal status, the state supreme court could offer no assistance to Bradwell.

Undeterred, Bradwell appealed her case to the U.S. Supreme Court. The highest court in the United States affirmed the Illinois court's decision in 1873, maintaining that being a lawyer was not "one of the privileges of women citizens." The Supreme Court argued that barring women from the legal profession actually did them a favor: "The peculiar qualities of womanhood, its gentle graces, its tender susceptibilities, its purity, its delicacy, its emotional impulses, its subordination of hard reason to sympathetic feeling are surely not qualifications for forensic strife. Nature has tempered women as little for judicial conflicts of the courtroom as for the physical conflicts of the battlefield. Woman is moulded for gentler and better things, and it is not the saints of the world who chiefly give employment to our profession."[30] Bradwell despaired of gaining admittance to the bar. She turned to helping another Illinois woman, Alta M. Hulett, and the two women pursued a different strategy. They prepared a bill for the Illinois state legislature that made it illegal to deprive citizens of employment because of their gender. The legislature passed the bill, and Hulett was admitted to the bar in 1873. Bradwell turned her attention to the *Chicago Legal News*. On its own initiative, the Illinois State Supreme Court granted Bradwell a license in 1890.

Another well-known Chicagoan, Marshall Field, became a multimillionaire by selling atmosphere, glamor, and class as much as by selling clothing and shoes. Marshall Field's downtown retail store was only a few miles from the city's bustling rail yards, slaughterhouses, mail-order businesses, and lumber yards. Women who entered the store, however, were whisked into a different universe. Field began business by selling his dry goods in a building of mammoth proportions that reached from State Street to Wabash Avenue. Its sheer size made it the largest retail store on earth in the late 1800s. Field employed ninety thousand workers during the peak retail season, some of whom operated the store's fifty-three elevators, medical dispensary, post office, or telephone switchboard (the largest private switchboard in the world). When Field learned that women were leaving his store at noon for lunch, he added a tea room next to the women's furs. He later expanded the tea room into an entire floor of posh restaurants and eventually added a nursery, writing rooms complete with complimentary stationery and pens, a customer's parlor and library, meeting rooms for women's civic organizations, and a checkroom for coats.

Field succeeded in creating an urban refuge for middle- and upper-class Chicago women. Their husbands had downtown dinner and smoking clubs; they had Marshall Field's store. Field did not cater to the commoner and working-class women; they had Ernest J. Lehmann's department store, which sold a variety of goods at bargain prices and was located at the other end of Chicago's Ladies' Half Mile. Field, however, stocked his store with fine linen handkerchiefs, silk scarves, imported Parisian gloves, custom-made Oriental rugs, and designer evening gowns. He jealously protected his store's fashionable image, firing any worker who was caught drinking, gambling, or associating with labor union officials. Field would open a "bargain basement" in the late 1800s and a separate men's store at a different location in the early 1900s, but it was the women's store on State and Washington Streets that made Marshall Field famous. A woman strolling through Field's palatial emporium "found herself in fairyland."[31]

Field offered more than glamor. His store built upon the so-called Chicago ideas of Field's predecessor, Potter Palmer, and pampered the female customer. Field's store eliminated haggling over prices by setting one low, fixed price on goods. A liberal return policy—unusual for this time—encouraged impulse buying. Field drilled two maxims into the minds of his sales clerks: the customer is always right, and you must always give the lady what she wants. Greeters met customers by name. "Bundle boys" carried purchased goods to waiting carriages; if the lady of the house did not care to make the journey to the store, she could telephone her order and have it delivered to her home. Marshall Field found a niche in Chicago and capitalized on it, making his name a household word by the 1870s.

George Pullman also made a name for himself in Chicago. A cabinet-maker and construction contractor in his home state of New York, Pullman came to Chicago in 1855. In Chicago he found an unusual outlet for his construction experience: he mastered the art of using jacks to raise Chicago's buildings out of the mud. He had not forgotten, however, the bone-jarring railroad cars he rode in from New York to Chicago. Those uncomfortable, unheated cars consisted solely of wooden benches. Passengers slept sitting up (if they slept at all) and raced into terminals during brief stops to gulp down quick meals, since food was not served in transit. Recalling the railroad cars that made long rail travel a dreadful experience, Pullman tinkered with redesigning the cars while he raised buildings. In 1864, he finished work on an elaborate, comfortable sleeping car. Pullman justifiably called it a palace on wheels. It boasted soft cloth-covered seats, heaters, fine woodwork, carpeting, classy oil lamps, velvet curtains, potted plants, and comfortable beds that could be hidden during waking hours in hinged upper berths. It was also, however, an expensive car. Pullman's chances of marketing it on a large scale seemed remote until the assassination of President Abraham Lincoln. Pullman offered his luxury sleeper car to bring Lincoln's body home to Illinois. As the funeral train slowly passed through numerous American cities, people saw both the slain president and Pullman's impressive sleeper car.

That trip made Pullman's sleeper car a success. He formed the Pullman Palace Car Company in 1867, and his Chicago factory made a handsome profit. As railroad travel increased in the 1870s, nearly all rail companies purchased the Pullman sleeper car. Business flourished, which meant many jobs for Chicagoans and especially for black Chicagoans. Indeed, the Pullman Company was the largest private employer of African Americans nationwide in 1900. Unlike many of his contemporaries, Pullman contributed significant sums of money to the city's largely black South Side community. The interracial Provident Hospital, for example, was founded with a large gift from Florence Pullman, George Pullman's elder daughter, in 1891. Pullman was so respected in Chicago's black community that when the black-led Brotherhood of Sleeping Car Porters first came to Chicago in 1925, influential black leaders Robert Abbott (publisher and editor of the *Chicago Defender*), Jesse Binga (head of Binga State Bank), and Reverend Archibald James Carey (pastor of Quinn Chapel African Methodist Episcopal Church) sided with Pullman against the racially militant union.

Pullman's happy relationship with Chicago was sorely tested in 1877. This was the year of the Great Railroad Strike, a nationwide strike that saw more than one hundred thousand workers walk off their jobs for several days. It was the closest thing to a general strike and outright class warfare that the United States would ever see. Workers brandishing meat cleavers and clubs stalked the streets of Chicago; police beat back strikers with gunfire. Three days of street battles resulted in thirty Chicagoans dead and two hundred wounded. Industrialists such as Pullman who employed large numbers of unskilled and semiskilled laborers were terrified. They were on the defensive, vastly outnumbered by the thousands of urban workers. Employers seemed unable to control the tenor of labor relations, while left-leaning labor activists were ascendent. Pullman questioned whether he could truly control his Pullman Palace Car Company in such a hostile, unstable, and dangerous environment.

Pullman hit upon a novel idea. He would reassert and maintain control over his company and his employees by building a town especially for them. He bought 3,600 acres of deserted marshes fifteen miles south of downtown Chicago near Lake Calumet. In 1879, he began construction on what became the town of Pullman, Illinois. By the mid-1880s, his town consisted of the new Pullman Car factory and 1,800 buildings. The town boasted the Pullman church, the Pullman stables, the Pullman hotel, the Pullman library, theaters, a post office, stores, parks, a free kindergarten, good schools, athletic facilities, and homes for the five thousand families who were employed at the Pullman Company. Saloons were barred from the town. Employee homes were clean and cheery. Every home had running water, indoor toilets, and gas heat; every home fronted paved and lit streets. No cholera, typhoid, or yellow fever were reported in the town, a fact that gave Pullman what was believed to be the lowest death rate for any community of its size in the world. Workers enjoyed the convenience of living close to their factory. Here was none of the disorder, chaos, and unpredictability of Chicago. "The most perfect city in the world," exclaimed one London journalist.[32]

At least initially, the model town of Pullman seemed an extraordinary success. It even spawned copycat model towns, such as Harvey, Illinois, founded by Chicago businessman and prominent Christian leader Turlington W. Harvey, a close associate of Dwight Moody. Harvey, with Moody's enthusiastic backing, attempted to build a Christian community twenty-one miles south of downtown Chicago, about six miles south of Pullman. He purchased seven hundred acres of uninhabited land, incorporated his town in 1891, and saw five thousand people swarm to his community within two years. Harvey was above all else a temperance town; it was upon this foundation that Harvey, Moody, and others hoped that a Christian utopia would be born. Moody enthusiastically promoted the town of Harvey during his revival crusades, describing it as "an earthly paradise which had never been defiled by painted windows and the music of gurgling bottles."[33] Turlington W. Harvey himself wrote the restrictive covenants that encumbered all land purchases in his town. Forbidden were "any bone-boiling establishment or factory, or saloon of any kind, or . . . any other dangerous, vexatious or offensive . . . establishment whatsoever . . . nor any gambling to be carried on thereon, nor any house or any other place of lewd and immoral practice hereupon."[34] Though Harvey, Illinois, received its share of notoriety, the town of Pullman was larger and better established, and thus became more famous.

Pullman's paternalism and greed eventually poisoned his experiment with a company town. Worker welfare was not Pullman's primary objective. He built his town so he could exercise dictatorial control over his workers and his company. He prohibited labor organizers, socialists, and other troublemakers from entering the town. Pullman, who referred to his employees as his children, required his workers to live in the Pullman homes. He charged them rent that was 20 percent higher than comparable rents in Chicago and evicted workers who agitated for better working conditions. He even charged a steep fee to residents who wished to use the community library, and he made the church pay rent. Pullman could have afforded to be more generous; by 1890, he enjoyed a virtual monopoly on sleeper cars in America. Yet he insisted on squeezing every last cent out of his workers. The result was growing discontent on the part of his employees, a discontent rooted in Pullman's greed and oppressive control. Professor Richard T. Ely, after an 1885 visit to Pullman, described the town as a feudalistic community, with Pullman as the lord and his employees as the serfs. "Here is a population of eight thousand souls," wrote Ely, "where not one single resident dare speak his opinion about the town in which he lives. One feels that one is mingling with a dependent, servile people."[35]

The cruelest blow came in 1893. In the midst of a national depression, Pullman fired thousands of his employees, cut wages 25 percent for those he retained, and refused to reduce rents in his town. In response, Pullman's workers organized, protested, and finally went on strike in 1894. The local strike spread nationwide and involved 125,000 workers as American Railway Union members refused to handle any trains that included Pullman cars. President Grover Cleveland ordered soldiers into the city, and violence erupted. "All southern Chicago seemed afire," wrote famed journalist Ray Stannard Baker. "I saw long freight trains burning on side-tracks. I saw Pullman cars that had been gutted by fire. I saw attacks by strikers on non-union men, and fierce conflicts between strikers and the police and deputies."[36] With assistance from the federal government, Pullman crushed the strike. But labor unrest and violence had come to Pullman's allegedly perfect town. A federal government report later condemned Pullman for his refusal to negotiate with workers and for charging exorbitant rents in his town. Pullman died in 1897, more villain than hero to many Americans. Over the next ten years, courts forced the sale of Pullman, Illinois, to its residents.

Theodore Dreiser was sixteen years old when he first saw Chicago.

The Indiana native later described the city as "a spectacle of raw, necessary life."[37] Dreiser worked briefly as a Chicago newspaperman before moving to New York City and writing his first novel. Published in 1900, *Sister Carrie* was a story about an eighteen-year-old girl who came to Chicago. Carrie Meeber was not the virtuous heroine so common to late-nineteenth-century novels; instead, Dreiser cast her as a grasping, self-seeking woman determined to live the good life. She succeeded in the rough-and-tumble world of Chicago—but only by becoming the mistress of several wealthy men and flouting standards of decency and morality. Many see in *Sister Carrie* a poignant message: big cities like Chicago offer prosperity to some but crush others.

Some despised *Sister Carrie* for its amorality, harshness, pessimistic realism, and graceless prose. Others extolled the novel for the way it portrayed life as it really was in big American cities. H. L. Mencken, for example, praised the novel for capturing "the gross, glittering, excessively dynamic, infinitely grotesque, incredibly stupendous drama of American life."[38] Dreiser's book inaugurated a literary outpouring in the city that came to be known as the Chicago Renaissance or the Chicago School of literature. Writers such as Edgar Lee Masters, Floyd Dell, Vachel Lindsay, and Sherwood Anderson flourished in the city, as did literary journal publishers such as Margaret Anderson, Harriet Monroe, and Ben Hecht.

Dreiser's naturalism influenced many Chicago writers, among them Nelson Algren and Saul Bellow. It also influenced Carl Sandburg, who moved to Chicago in 1913 at age thirty-five. He had been somewhat of a drifter until then, but the bright lights of Chicago and his job as a newspaperman turned him into one of America's preeminent poets and writers. Sandburg published his first collection of poems in 1916 and never stopped writing thereafter. Sandburg offers in his early poetry a vivid and realistic portrayal of life in Chicago in the early 1900s. Some disdain Sandburg's poetry, considering it excessively vulgar and harsh. Others praise Sandburg for his candid description of Chicago's brutality, power, ugliness, and energy. One of Chicago's most oft-heard nicknames—"the City of Big Shoulders"—was born in his ode to the city, published in 1914.

> Hog Butcher for the World,
> Tool Maker, Stacker of Wheat,
> Player with Railroads and the Nation's Freight Handler;
> Stormy, husky, brawling,
> City of the Big Shoulders.

In this poem, Sandburg goes on to concede that his Chicago is wicked, crooked, and brutal. But he exults that it is also alive—alive with energy, opportunity, and accomplishments. Its earthiness and authenticity is precisely what makes the city "a tall bold slugger set vivid against the little soft cities," to use Sandburg's words. What was life like in this late-nineteenth-century city on the make? Sandburg was right in describing it as life marked by vibrancy, difficulty, grit, vice, recreation, activity, defeat, and success. It was, as the next chapter suggests, a city of catastrophes, conflicts, and triumphs.

CHAPTER SIX

THE FIRE,

THE BOMB,

AND THE FAIR,

1871 - 1893

• During the years between 1871 and 1893, three events served both to define Chicago and to reveal the city to the nation. Observers seeking the "real" Chicago might have done better to examine the city's railroads, its grain industry, its ethnocultural politics, or its acquisition of clean drinking water. These did not capture the public's imagination, however, nor did they make for good stories in the era's newspapers. The Great Chicago Fire of 1871, the Haymarket Bombing of 1886, and the World's Columbian Exposition of 1893, however, were nothing if not enthralling stories. Americans often learned about Chicago through these events. For them and for us, they provide windows through which to view late 1800s Chicago.

THE FIRE

Perhaps the most famous Chicagoan is not a person at all. Perhaps it is Mrs. O'Leary's cow, the alleged culprit behind the Great Chicago Fire of October 8–9, 1871. But the blame for the destruction of the city should not be laid on an animal. Large fires were a fact of life in nineteenth-century cities. Nearly all buildings at this time were built of wood. Few had fire-resistant walls or roofs, and most were constructed close to (if not touching) adjacent buildings. Cities used wood planks to pave their roads, which further blanketed cities with wood. (Chicago had fifty-five miles of planked streets in 1871.) Wooden bridges spanned rivers and canals, thus neutralizing the only natural "fire breaks" within cities. Roofs were made of highly flammable tar and pine chips; the chips were easily dislodged and blown about by the wind once they caught fire. Large quantities of hay and straw were kept in cities. Nearly all homes relied upon open flames (for example, coal and kerosene) for heating, cooking, and lighting.

All American cities experienced massive urban fires: New York City in 1835, Pittsburgh in 1845, and Philadelphia in 1865. Chicago itself routinely endured fires that devastated large portions of the city. Only one month before the Great Fire of 1871, the *Chicago Tribune* warned Chicagoans about their "miles of fire-traps, pleasing to the eye, looking substantial, but all sham and shingles."[1] Only demolishing existing buildings and rebuilding them with fireproof materials and fire walls would have remedied the situation, but that would have been unthinkably impractical.

The only force that stood between Chicago and a massive inferno was the 185-man fire department. Armed with steam-powered water pumpers that were only slightly better than bucket brigades, mid-nineteenth-century urban fire departments relied upon rapid response, and not high technology, to fight fires. Watchmen perched high in the courthouse's cupola kept a twenty-four-hour vigil over the city, and each firehouse had its own observation tower as well. When flames were spotted, the watchmen pinpointed the fire's location with the aid of mariner's spyglasses and notified nearby firehouses. Speed was the key: firemen could control a blaze if they responded within a few minutes.

An unusually dry summer and fall in 1871 made Chicago especially ripe for a major fire. On October 7—the day before the Great Chicago Fire began—a fire destroyed twenty acres west of the city's downtown area. Half of the city's fire department worked on the blaze and extinguished it only after fifteen hours of effort. This latest of innumerable city fires was the worst ever recorded in city history, but the October 7 fire held that distinction for just one day.

On the night of October 8—a Sunday night—Chicago residents' worst fears were realized. The Great Chicago Fire began in the O'Leary's barn at about 9:00 P.M. that evening. The barn was located near the intersections of Jefferson and Taylor Streets, less than one mile southwest of downtown. Perhaps a cow really did start the blaze by kicking over a lantern, but no one knows with certainty. Regardless of how the fire began, it quickly spread. A twenty-mile-per-hour wind drove the fire straight toward the city. Exhausted firemen, still recovering from fighting the previous day's blaze, were slow to respond to this fire. Also preventing a rapid response to the fire was a watchman's misjudgment of its precise location; he incorrectly sent the initial alarm to the wrong firehouse. Most Chicagoans were unconcerned. One city resident did not even bother to go out and look at the blaze at first: "Why should I care as long as our house is not on fire? There is a fire every Monday and Thursday in Chicago!"[2] Although seven fire companies arrived at the O'Leary barn within forty-five minutes, they arrived too late. They encountered a fire of mammoth proportions. By 11:00 P.M., the fire department declared the blaze out of control.

Terror-stricken Chicagoans fled down crowded streets before the advancing flames. At times, the flames marched through the city as fast as a man could run. "You couldn't see anything over you but fire," one Chicagoan remembered. "No clouds, no stars, nothing but fire."[3] The fire generated high winds that hurled flaming lumber through the air. "It seemed like a tornado of fire," recalled one survivor.[4] The din of fire, collapsing buildings, church bells, shouting, and terrified animals enveloped the city. Many fleeing citizens tried to carry a few belongings with them. Frightened horses pulling carriages added to chaos in the streets. Families became separated; crying children wandered aimlessly through the crowds. Looters plundered goods from deserted stores. Bridges collapsed under the weight of hundreds of fleeing Chicagoans. "I saw a woman kneeling in the street with a crucifix held up before her and the skirt of her dress burning while she prayed," recalled one Chicagoan. "We had barely passed before a runaway truck dashed her to the ground. Loads of goods passed us repeatedly that were burning on the trucks."[5]

All night long, the fire burned on. The inferno was so large that observers in Indiana could see the glow on the distant skyline. At 7:00 the next morning, fire hydrants went dry as the city waterworks burned to the ground. City residents could do nothing now but hope for rain. Some fled northward, certain the fire would not cross the Chicago River. It did. Others made their way to Lake Michigan and waded out into the water for safety. Flames created temperatures so high that plate-glass windows cracked, iron and steel melted, and limestone construction blocks disintegrated into powder. One eyewitness remembered that "stoves, and sheet and pig iron all melted miserably and ran helplessly down, roaring with rage, to the ground, and there it cooled in all fantastic attitudes and shapes."[6] The blaze raged for more than twenty-fours hours, devouring the wooden city. A cold October rain finally began falling late Monday night. The rain extinguished the flames about 3:00 Tuesday morning.

The most destructive urban fire to date in U.S. history, the Great Chicago Fire was distinguished by the sheer magnitude of the blaze and

The Chicago Fire of 1871 left the downtown in complete ruin, as this view from the corner of Randolph and Market Streets reveals. Buildings could not be repaired; the heart of the city had to be razed to the foundations and constructed anew. This allowed Chicagoans to rationalize the downtown area. Chicago Historical Society, IChi-02808

the extensive loss of property. Although only three hundred people died in the inferno, the fire destroyed the entire downtown section of the city, which included nearly everything between Harrison Street on the south, Chicago Avenue on the north, the two branches of the Chicago River on the west, and Lake Michigan on the east. All told, the burned-out district was about four miles long and one mile wide. The heart of Chicago—including more than seventeen thousand buildings, many of the city's retail stores, hotels, the Board of Trade, the White Stockings' baseball park, the courthouse, the post office, the Tribune Tower, and most of the city's theaters and banks—now consisted of twenty-five hundred acres of smoldering ruins. Financial losses exceeded $250 million, which forced several insurance companies into bankruptcy. The homeless, who had to seek shelter as winter approached, included one hundred thousand of the city's three hundred thousand residents. The devastation seemed so extensive that many thought the city could never recover. John Greenleaf Whittier penned this immediately popular eulogy for the once great city:

Men said at vespers: "All is well!"
In one wild night the city fell;
Fell shrines of prayer and marts of gain
Before the fiery hurricane.

On three score spires had sunset shone,
Where ghastly sunrise looked on none.
Men clasped each other's hands, and said:
"The City of the West is dead!"[7]

But far from being dead, Chicago was about to experience an amazing recovery. Within two years, the city had been completely rebuilt. The scope of the rebuilding project was breathtaking. One historian struggled to communicate what happened in post-fire Chicago: "It is common to see ten or a dozen or fifty houses rising at once; but when one looks upon, not a dozen or fifty, but upon ten thousand houses rising and ten times that number of busy workmen coming and going, and listens to the noise of countless saws and hammers and chisels and axes and planes, he is bewildered."[8] As devastating as the fire had been, it had not touched the sources of Chicago's wealth, namely, its lumber yards, the Union Stock Yards, and most of its grain elevators. Most important, the city's life-lines—the railroads—were unscathed. Business could continue.

Chicago played such an indispensable role in the nation's economy by 1871 that businessmen throughout America had a vested interest in seeing Chicago rebuilt. As one Chicagoan put it, "The capitalists, the mercantile and business interests of this country and of Europe cannot afford to withhold the means to rebuild Chicago."[9] He was right. Businessmen in New York City sent $600,000 to the city to assist in its recovery and sent wagons through the New York City streets to collect spare clothing for needy Chicagoans. Cincinnati raised $160,000 in aid before the fire stopped burning. Milwaukee closed its public schools for one day as the city collected relief supplies. Boston sent $400,000 to the city, Buffalo sent $100,000, and little Lafayette, Indiana, sent $10,000. One Chicago resident called the relief effort "the grandest display of true Christian feeling the world ever saw." He continued, "Here we were, hundreds of thousands of people—houseless, homeless, without food or shelter; and first from all parts of the United States, and then from every country and city in the civilised world money came pouring in till in less that a fortnight we had to telegraph them to stop."[10] Not all Americans wanted to assist Chicago, however. The Sons of Temperance from Urbana, Illinois, believed the inferno was a judgment for the city's refusal to close its saloons on Sunday. One Indiana newspaper thought the fire was divine repayment for William T. Sherman's burning of Atlanta during the Civil War. "God adjusts balances," the newspaper opined. "Maybe with Chicago the books are now squared."[11] Not only was the city almost completely recovered within two years, but the new, post-1871 Chicago enjoyed significant economic advantages over the pre-fire Chicago. By leveling the entire downtown area, the fire allowed Chicagoans to rationalize land use in the city. Before the fire, downtown Chicago was a haphazard and inefficient collection of businesses, homes, warehouses, and barns. The wealthy's impressive mansions stood side-by-side with the poor's clapboard dwellings; downtown office buildings and stores were side-by-side with stables and livestock pens. After the fire, city dwellers moved to outlying areas, and downtown property was devoted almost exclusively to commercial use. With the elimination of thousands of small shanty homes and stables, existing businesses could more easily expand. Property values skyrocketed as investors realized the new Chicago would consist almost entirely of state-of-the-art commercial buildings. With land more expensive, Chicago builders soon invented a new type of building: the skyscraper. Builders built *up,* instead of *out,* to maximize their return on expensive city property.

The fire also enabled Chicagoans to control city fires, of which the 1871 fire had only been the most recent and most cataclysmic. The city council enacted laws in 1872 that prohibited the construction of wooden frame buildings within much of the downtown areas of the city. Chicagoans had noted that, in addition to the many wood structures that were incinerated in the blaze, the cast iron columns and beams in ostensibly fireproof buildings had melted in the intense heat. In the new downtown, terra cotta was applied to buildings' metal frames, thus making them heat resistant. There would be no Second Great Chicago Fire.

An important aspect of rebuilding an incinerated Chicago was providing emergency relief assistance to fire victims. Prominent commercial and civic leaders feared that the relief donations that poured into the city—more than one million dollars worth of clothing, food, and cash—would encourage laziness and dependency if they were distributed carelessly to the city's "undeserving poor." Whether Chicago "should ever recover from the terrible calamity that had swept over it, or whether the ruin should be utter and irrevocable," wrote local journalist Sidney Gay, largely depended upon the "wise and economical distribution of aid."[12]

City leaders therefore carefully controlled the distribution of post-fire relief aid. They prevented the city council from disbursing relief, because councilmen were elected by the people and were, in the eyes of wealthy commercial and civic leaders, too beholden to "interests." Prominent city leaders feared that vote-hungry councilmen would distribute largesse to their constituents, most of whom were immigrants or immigrant-stock Germans and Scandinavians on the devastated North Side, thus winning votes but creating in the process a class of welfare-dependent parasites. Instead, city leaders, most of whom were Anglo-American Protestants, relied upon the independent Relief and Aid Society to distribute the supplies that flooded into the city in the days following the fire. The Relief and Aid Society remained safely out of the reach of elected politicians: it was run by an Executive Committee of fifteen industrialists and businessmen, four lawyers, and one doctor. Powerful Chicagoans such as Mayor Roswell B. Mason believed that this commercial and civic elite was better able to determine what served the public interest than were the base politicians who worked the ethnic wards for votes.

The Relief and Aid Society provided much needed aid to fire victims, but it did so in accordance with the philosophy of "scientific charity." Applicants for aid were examined closely to assess their worthiness. Chicagoans who had demonstrated past entrepreneurial zeal and had owned property were most likely to receive aid; chronically poor Chicagoans who could offer no track record of thrift, investment, steady employment, and financial success often got none. After the initial days of immediate post-fire emergency relief, able-bodied men were granted relief aid only if they were employed. The Relief and Aid Society did not allow a permanently unemployed class of Chicagoans to be dependent upon public charity. When aid recipients made no progress in improving their lot, they were often disqualified from receiving further relief. Eight hundred Chicago families suffered this fate in early 1872.

Many Chicagoans chafed at this heavy-handed distribution of relief funds. German immigrants in the city protested that the Relief and Aid Society harbored Anglo-American prejudices. Native-stock Chicagoans, they charged, had a better chance of receiving aid than did the newcomers of different ethnic backgrounds. This bias posed special hardships on the heavily ethnic North Side that had suffered most in the fire. Several prominent Anglo-American women also rejected the Relief and Aid Society's emphasis on social engineering. Katherine Medill, wife of *Chicago Tribune* publisher and future mayor Joseph Medill, criticized the society for its lack of humanitarian concern. She distributed relief on her own to fire victims, whom she described as "people who are in every way worthy and beyond the Society's rules."[13] Mrs. H. L. Hammond, a Protestant activist and wife of a Chicago Theological Seminary official, likewise operated her own relief agency. Aurelia R. King, wife of prominent Chicagoan and Relief and Aid Society board member Henry King, wrote to out-of-town friends and instructed them to send donations to her and not to the society. It is intriguing that many relief agencies that opposed the policies of the Relief and Aid Society were headed by women. The Chicago Y.M.C.A. and the United Hebrew Relief Association also administered their own post-fire relief agencies.

The battle over post-fire relief—and the underlying battle over who would define Chicago's public interest—suggests that the city was what one historian has called a "smoldering city" in more ways than one. The fire presented the city with a great challenge, but so did latent class divisions and ethnic tensions. It was not a homogeneous and monolithic "people of Chicago" that rose from the ashes to rebuild their city. Rather, it was a people fractured by economic, ethnic, and gender differences that nonetheless managed to rebuild their city.

Civic leaders put a positive face on the post-fire reconstruction, however. The rational distribution of land in the downtown area, the new fire-resistant commercial buildings, and the triumphs of many strong-willed entrepreneurs inspired cheery reports of a post-fire urban renaissance. Thus, only one year after the fire, a local magazine asked rhetorically, "Was not the great fire a blessing in disguise?"[14] The *Chicago Tribune* was even more confident the following year. It agreed with the "common remark" heard about town "that Chicago was set forward ten years by the fire."[15] The city even celebrated the two-year anniversary of the fire—much to the amazement of the *New York Herald,* which was shocked that a city actually celebrated the anniversary of its own destruction. There was reason for celebration. In physical terms, the rebuilt city was far superior to the old one.

Chicagoans began invoking the image of the phoenix to explain their city's miraculous recovery. Like the legendary bird that burned itself on a funeral pyre only to rise again as a youthful creature, Chicago had been reborn by 1874 as the most modern city in the world. London's *Saturday Review* saw in Chicago all the virtues that made the United States the most dynamic nation on the globe. In 1874, it called Chicago the "concentrated essence of Americanism."[16] Seeing Chicago's post-fire grandeur, poet Vachel Lindsay quipped, "The Chicago Fire should occur many times. Each successive time the buildings [emerge] smarter, less expensive, more economic, more beautiful."[17] Although the city's reconstruction resulted in undeniable economic advantages, some Chicagoans realized that such benefits were being purchased at a cost. The *Chicago Tribune* noted in 1873, "The tendency is to be metropolitan in everything—buildings and their uses, stores and their occupants. And village notions are passing away with them." The transformation of Chicago into a modern industrial city—a city devoted to business and commerce—meant the sacrificing of personal relationships. The *Tribune* continued: "We are getting to be a community of strangers. No one expects to know . . . half the audience at the church or theatre, and, as to knowing one's neighbors, that has become a lost art."[18] The remnants of small-town ways had perished in the fire. A massive city rose from the ashes.

THE BOMB

One thing that did perish in later-nineteenth-century Chicago was the city's radical labor movement. In 1886, a bomb exploded at a Haymarket Square labor rally, killing several policemen who had arrived to disperse the protesters. Policemen then fired into the assembly and killed an undetermined number of activists. Perhaps the first famous terrorist bombing in the United States, it confirmed Anglo-Americans' worst suspicions regarding labor unions and marked the zenith of leftist labor activity in America.

To many Anglo-Americans, late-nineteenth-century unionists themselves were probably more alarming than their often modest demands. First, the majority of unionists were immigrants. In Chicago, for example, about two-thirds of the city's 18,400 Knights of Labor members in 1886 were immigrants. Anglo-Americans' disdain for European immigrants easily translated into disdain for organized labor. Many Anglo-Americans were convinced that socialism, communism, and union agitation were motivated, not by legitimate labor grievances here in America, but rather by un-American agitators. In early 1886, the *Chicago Daily News* wrote, "Socialism in America is an anomaly, and Chicago is the last place on the continent where it would exist were it not for the dregs of foreign immigration which find lodgement here."[19] Of course, this was an overgeneralization. One of Chicago's foremost labor radicals, Albert Parsons, claimed ancestors who came to America on the Mayflower's second voyage and fought for Texas during the Civil War.

Parsons notwithstanding, the immigrant stereotype persisted.

Further, union leaders were often labeled as violent anarchists. Believing that every form of government was immoral, anarchists in late-nineteenth-century America were never numerous and always colorful. Some thought the existing world system of oppressive governments would collapse if a significantly earth-shattering "momentous deed" were perpetrated. To this end, anarchists were the modern world's first high-profile terrorists, throwing bombs into crowds in hopes that this would be the "momentous deed." Their most famous acts of violence were assassinations of Czar Alexander II of Russia, Empress Elizabeth of Austria, and U.S. President William McKinley. Some socialist labor leaders grew impatient with their inability to secure power peacefully and reluctantly turned to violence, reinforcing the public notion of unions as hotbeds of anarchist violence.

Anarchism discredited the budding labor union movement. Most unionists were not anarchists, and the Knights of Labor (America's largest labor union with 700,000 members by the 1880s) repudiated anarchism. Native Anglo-American Protestants, however, commonly assumed a link between anarchism, labor unions, and violence. Many Chicagoans cringed when they learned of articles such as this one, which appeared in the city's anarchist newspaper, the *Alarm*, in 1885: "Dynamite! Of all the good stuff, this is the stuff. Stuff several pounds of this sublime stuff into an inch pipe (gas or water pipe), plug up both ends, insert a cap with a fuse attached, place this in the immediate neighborhood of a lot of rich men who live by the sweat of other people's brows and light the fuse. A most cheerful and gratifying result will follow. In giving dynamite to the downtrodden millions of the globe, science has done its best work. The dear stuff can be carried around in the pocket without danger, while it is a formidable weapon against any force of militia, police or detectives that may want to stifle the cry for justice that goes forth from the plundered slaves."[20] Many Chicagoans wrongly assumed all unionists and immigrants embraced these sentiments.

Many Anglo-Americans also stereotyped unionists as atheists. Chicago's Reverend E. A. Adams put it bluntly: "The result of atheism must always be anarchism."[21] By branding the unionists as anti-Christian, it was easier for Anglo-Americans to reject their ideas without evaluation. "Either these people are to be evangelized," warned Chicago evangelist D. L. Moody in 1886, "or the leaven of communism and infidelity will assume such enormous proportions that it will break out in a reign of terror such as the country has never known."[22]

Thus, when Anglo-Americans considered labor unions in the late 1800s, they saw multiple threats to the United States: labor violence, socialist attacks on capitalism, immigrant influence, and godlessness. Because unionists seemed to pose a threat to property, peace, and profits, government nearly always supported management in its conflicts with workers. Policemen and soldiers regularly intervened to help factory owners break strikes. Courts rarely ruled in favor of unionists. At Marshall Field's classy downtown Chicago retail store, customers who were known to be union members were quietly escorted from the emporium by Field's private detectives.

Indeed, unionists found themselves involved in strikes, fights, and shoot-outs. Union newspapers also attracted many writers of socialist or communist persuasion. Much of the labor violence that occurred in America, however, was as much the fault of business owners and policemen as it was of the union members. Antiunion people handled unionists in a way that almost guaranteed violence. Moreover, most union members *were* exploited by their employers. Factory wages were extremely low, working conditions were unsafe, living conditions were atrocious, and employees received no compensation if they were injured or killed on the job. Although urban laborers had reasonable grievances, neither employers nor the government provided relief. The late 1800s was the age of unbridled laissez-faire capitalism.

Labor unrest mounted in post–Civil War Chicago. In 1877, the city saw pitched battles in its streets as local workingmen joined that year's Great Railroad Strike. Tensions remained high in the following years as more immigrants came to Chicago, jobs became scarce, and low wages persisted. Seeking remedies for their plight, the Knights of Labor announced a 1 May 1886 deadline for instituting the eight-hour workday. At one union rally in 1886, twenty-one thousand Chicagoans turned out. A second rally and parade two weeks later drew an entirely different crowd of twenty-five thousand. When the May 1 deadline came, forty thousand Chicagoans went on strike. Several days later, a strike at Cyrus McCormick's International Harvester factory led to the Haymarket bombing.

The bone of contention between McCormick and his workers had always been low wages and the length of the workday. Workers had struck in 1884 when McCormick cut wages 15 percent but then failed to restore wages to their previous levels as promised. The strike led to McCormick's hiring of armed guards, and gunshots were exchanged. McCormick workers struck again in 1886, in part because they sought an eight-hour workday. McCormick refused to negotiate. Instead, he locked the striking men out of his plant and brought in strikebreakers. Those replacement workers filled the factory jobs vacated by the strikers, spelling doom for the union effort.

On 3 May 1886, six thousand striking men were meeting outside the International Harvester plant. The shift changed, and hundreds of strikebreakers poured out of McCormick's plant. The angry strikers, now face-to-face with the men who were taking their jobs, attacked the replacement workers. McCormick had hired private guards for just such an occasion. They and Chicago policemen sprang into action with clubs and pistols. Two men were killed and several more were injured.

Chicago's labor movement mobilized for action. The *Arbeiter-Zeitung,* one of the city's German-language newspapers, immediately printed and distributed more than twelve hundred circulars. Under bold headlines that screamed, "REVENGE! Workingmen, to arms!!" the flyer, printed in both English and German, called for the city's workers to "destroy the hideous monster that seeks to destroy you."[23] A second circular, issued the next morning, exhorted, "Workingmen Arm Yourselves and Appear in Full Force!" Union leaders called a rally to protest the murders. They scheduled it for that night (May 4) in Haymarket Square, which was located on Randolph Street between Desplaines and Halsted. The usually sedate *Chicago Tribune* warned the unionists against responding with violence: "If the Communists of this city are counting on the looseness of our police system and the tendency to proceed against crowds by due process of law, and hope on that account to receive more leniency than in Europe, they have ignored some of the significant episodes in American history. . . . Every lamp post in Chicago will be decorated with a Communistic carcass if necessary to prevent wholesale incendiarism . . . or any attempt at it."[24]

The rally at Haymarket Square saw no "wholesale incendiarism." Perhaps it was because of the *Tribune's* warning or simply because of the steady rain that the 1,500 gathered workers did nothing but listen as speakers extolled the virtues of socialism and anarchism for several hours. Mayor Carter Harrison even visited the meeting, having granted permission earlier for the rally to be held. He strolled about for some time, was convinced that there would be no trouble from this sedate and soggy group, and left. He stopped by the nearby police station and told the chief there that the speakers were finishing up and police intervention would not be necessary. The rain picked up and many left. Only about 300 men remained at Haymarket Square as the last speaker was finishing his harangue. Suddenly, a team of more than 150 Chicago policemen barged into the square. They interrupted the speaker and demanded that all remaining persons go home.

It was then that the bomb exploded. Someone threw it into the midst of the policemen. Police began firing into the crowd, and workers fled for safety. Seven policemen eventually died from the blast, and more than sixty were wounded. The death toll among the workers was unknown; most refused to seek medical treatment for fear of being reported to the police.

Almost overnight, the Haymarket bomb created mass hysteria in Chicago and across the nation. The *New York Times's* headline the next morning read, "Anarchy's Red Hand." The *Albany Law Review* demanded punishment "for the few long-haired, wild-eyed, bad-smelling, atheistic, reckless foreign wretches."[25] The *Philadelphia Inquirer* likewise demanded that Chicago teach the "foreign Anarchists" that the United States did not coddle "cutthroats and thieves."[26] Anglo-Americans took the bombing as proof that law and order was disappearing. They feared America was becoming polluted by the cesspool of European socialism. They increasingly dismissed labor unions as Trojan horses used by immigrant anarchists to destroy America.

Justice was swift and harsh, although many insisted that the word *justice* was inappropriate. Police charged seven local anarchists with murder. All were German immigrants; only one spoke English. Albert Parsons had fled the city after the bombing and escaped arrest, but he returned of his own free will and surrendered himself so he could stand trial with his comrades. There was no evidence that any of the men threw the bomb. Indeed, all eight defendants presented credible alibis that made it clear that they could not have thrown a bomb on the night of 4 May 1886. The identity of both bomb-thrower and bomb-manufacturer was never determined. As the prosecuting attorney said in his closing remarks to the jury, however, it was anarchism that was on trial in Chicago. The prosecution argued that *encouraging* acts of violence was the same as *committing* acts of violence. The city's anarchist newspaper, the *Alarm,* maintained that the accused men's irreligion was also on trial. The *Chicago Daily News* and Anglo-American Protestants throughout the city pointed out that the accused were infidels and enemies of the Christian faith. "The authorities are making a point against them that they do not believe in God," reported one labor sympathizer a week after the riot, speaking of the arrested Haymarket anarchists.[27] For many Anglo-American Chicagoans, the combination of bombs, strikes, socialism, foreigners, and atheism was far too much. The jury deliberated only three hours before finding all eight men guilty of murder. One received a fifteen-year prison sentence; the other seven were sentenced to death.

Petitions for clemency from around America poured into Chicago. The influential journalist Henry Demarest Lloyd headed a national clemency campaign, and Lyman J. Gage, who would later serve as U.S. secretary of the Treasury, lobbied for mercy as well. Requests for clemency even reached the Illinois governor's office from overseas. Despite the conviction on the part of many that the Haymarket defendants were to be punished for their radical political beliefs and not for any crime, pleas for clemency were ignored. Four Haymarket defendants were hanged and one committed suicide while awaiting execution. (George Engel's last words as he stood at the gallows: "Hurrah for anarchy! This is the happiest moment of my life."[28]) Two men had their sentences commuted to life imprisonment because they had officially requested mercy; these men were later pardoned by Illinois Governor John Altgeld in 1893. The funeral for the five executed Haymarket men hailed them as martyrs. Twenty thousand mourners followed the caskets to the train depot, while another two hundred thousand onlookers lined Chicago's streets. A portion of the funeral procession was led by a uniformed war veteran who marched with an American flag draped in black.

Other Chicagoans did not mourn at all. The Commercial Club of Chicago, a club consisting of the city's prominent businessmen, had for several years considered bringing a U.S. military fort to the area, with soldiers who could maintain order in the event of a riot or violent strike. The May 1886 Haymarket bombing drove them to act quickly. Within six weeks of the bombing, with the help of Civil War veteran and Chicago resident General Philip Henry Sheridan, they identified a suitable location for such a fort. The Commercial Club then paid $300,000 for a six-hundred-acre parcel of land in Highwood, a small town twenty-eight miles north of the Loop on the shoreline of Lake Michigan, and donated it to the federal government free of charge for the purpose of constructing a military outpost. Soldiers were rushed from Fort Douglas, Utah, to the uncleared land that would become Fort Sheridan; they arrived three days before the Haymarket executions, pitched their tents, and prepared to fight rioting urban immigrants instead of warring American Indians.

The Haymarket bombing dealt a crippling blow to America's young labor movement, even though the bombing had not been the work of labor union men. The Knights of Labor, for example, immediately denounced the bombers as "cowardly murderers, cutthroats, and robbers" who deserved "no more consideration than wild beasts."[29] But such statements were futile. To most Anglo-Americans, there was little difference between anarchists, immigrants, socialists, communists, and labor unionists. Almost immediately after Haymarket, the Knights of Labor experienced a precipitous decline in membership. At their peak in 1886, they claimed 730,000 members nationally; by 1888, membership had plummeted to 260,000. In Chicago, the death of the Haymarket men decapitated the city's robust labor movement.

Haymarket also intensified anti-immigrant sentiment in Chicago and across the nation. The accused Haymarket bombers confirmed the immigrant stereotype: radical, violent, dangerous, atheistic, and un-American. It became even easier for policemen, soldiers, Pinkerton agents, governors, and presidents to assume an immigrant's guilt (or a unionist's guilt, since the two were often synonymous) when such a stereotype seemed validated by the event at Haymarket Square.

In 1899, a monument was built in the square that honored the fallen Chicago policemen. The bronze image depicted a policeman with upraised hand attempting to establish peace. During the tumultuous 1960s, modern-day anarchists again put Haymarket Square in the news. They blew the statue from its pedestal with bombs in both 1969 and 1970. An outraged Mayor Richard J. Daley relocated the statue to the lobby of the main Chicago police station.

THE FAIR

As if to signal its complete recovery from the Great Chicago Fire of 1871, the city hosted the 1893 World's Columbian Exposition—an event so famous that one recent historian has called it "the most famous fair ever held on American soil."[30] In the middle and late 1800s, expositions were a combination of inventors' showcase, international summit meeting, promotional extravaganza, and entertainment. The host city constructed an impressive (and costly) collection of buildings to house the exposition. Nations from all over the world sent displays designed to impress visitors. Intellectuals from around the world came to these expositions in order to gauge the pulse of human achievement. The common people came to gawk at the amazing sights.

Owing to their enormous expense, world expositions were held only in the world's largest and most affluent cities. London was home to the famous 1851 Crystal Palace Exposition, and New York followed with its own Crystal Palace Exposition in 1853–1854. Philadelphia hosted the 1876 Centennial Exposition, which honored the one-hundredth anniversary of the Declaration of Independence. Paris hosted the 1889 world exposition, unveiling to the world its new Eiffel Tower. Americans sought to host an exposition in 1892 or 1893 that would commemorate the four-hundredth anniversary of Columbus's voyage to the New World. New York was the logical choice, and many laughed when the uncultured frontier city of Chicago requested that *it* host the exposition. "Don't pay any attention to the nonsensical claims of that Windy City," advised Charles A. Dana, who was using the word "windy" to refer to the city's incessant stream of booster rhetoric and self-promoting hot air. "Its people couldn't build a world's fair if they won it!"[31] One New York City cartoon lampooned Chicago's audacious request. The great cities of the United States were pictured as ladies seated around a table. All are vying for a bouquet—marked "World's Fair"—that Uncle Sam will apparently bestow upon one fortunate lass. All the women are beautiful and elegant except for the one labeled Chicago. She is a bony, homely teenager whose evening gown sports a pattern of little pigs (a reference to the city's notorious meatpacking industry). Her bust is gaudily embellished with diamonds. She is demanding the bouquet, her skinny arms grasping for the prize. New York, in contrast, is a cultured woman who looks down at Chicago with an appropriate air of condescension and contempt.

What Chicago lacked in charm and culture, however, it made up for with nerve. The city raised more than ten million dollars to finance the fair, which impressed the U.S. Congress. It granted the Columbian Exposition to Chicago. The city wasted no time in making the fair so impressive that it wowed even the city's harshest critics. Hired to oversee the building project were Frederick Law Olmstead (perhaps the most famous architect in America) and Daniel Burnham. For the exposition's site, they chose Jackson Park—a marshy, undeveloped area of sand dunes and bushes located on Lake Michigan about seven miles south of city hall. In three years, they transformed the area into a state-of-the-art international city. Steel frames gave form to enormous convention halls, and the frames were covered with a white plaster that shone like marble. Domes, vaulted ceilings, arches, columns, and fountains rose out of the Jackson Park marshes. Dubbed the White City for its resplendent plaster buildings, the "city" was built among a beautifully landscaped matrix of lagoons, parks, moving sidewalks, and wide promenades. This marsh-into-oasis metamorphosis was made possible by an army of construction workers that was sometimes twelve thousand strong. These men often labored at night under newly invented electric lights and lived in barracks constructed for them at the Jackson Park site. One of these construction workers was Elias Disney, father of the man who later built amusement parks that would rival the White City's fame.

Not only was it beautiful, it was also big. Chicago's Columbian Exposition, which occupied more than six hundred acres, was three times larger than the largest previous exposition. The 1876 Philadelphia Exposition had attracted 10 million visitors; the Chicago exposition, however, drew 27 million attendees between 1 May 1893 and 30 October 1893. In its final months, the exposition enjoyed an average daily attendance of 150,000. Seventy-two foreign nations sent exhibits to the fair; nineteen of them, along with thirty-eight U.S. states, erected their own buildings to show off their wares. One building at the exposition—the Manufacturers and Liberal Arts Building—was the largest building in the world: it covered forty-four acres of space, contained eleven acres of skylights in its roof, and accommodated 150,000 visitors at one time. Other "theme buildings" housed exhibits in machinery, transportation, agriculture, electricity, mines, anthropology, forestry, aquatic life, and the arts. A Women's Building proclaimed the triumphs of the world's women, while a Children's Building housed both educational exhibits and a functioning nursery (where, in the words of one visitor, "babies are tenderly cared for by sweet-faced nurses in snowy caps and aprons").[32] One building was constructed in downtown Chicago along the lakefront to house the various international parliaments and public speeches that accompanied the fair; this building is the present Chicago Art Institute.

As in all fairs, some exhibits were merely mediocre. Missouri sent a woman who sculpted objects out of butter, visitors to Pennsylvania's exhibit were subjected to a map of the United States made out of pickles, and on the Midway one could see a two-headed pig. These were the exceptions, however. Most visitors were treated to some truly incredible sights. Moveable sidewalks transported visitors over the half-mile pier that reached into Lake Michigan. The Electricity Building glowed at night thanks to nearly 130,000 electric lightbulbs. For visitors who knew only of kerosene lamps and candles, the Electricity Building's lights seemed a miracle. Chicago answered Paris's Eiffel Tower by unveiling the world's first Ferris wheel. Designed by thirty-four-year-old bridge designer George Washington Ferris, it was a monstrous thing that stood 140 feet high, accommodated sixty passengers in each of its thirty-six glass-enclosed cabs, held 2,160 riders at one time, and rotated on a

Millions were dazzled by the 1893 Colombian Exposition, which was often called the White City because of its brilliant plaster neo-classical buildings. In an era when many

feared that the city was a hopeless source of evil ugliness and immortality, the seemingly perfect White City sent a more optimistic message. Chicago Historical Society, IChi-23142

forty-five-ton axle (the largest piece of steel ever forged at that time). Gondoliers in fifteenth-century garb moved serenely across the fair's large lagoons. Exhibits included a reproduction of Christopher Columbus's *Santa Maria,* which was anchored in the South Pond, a demonstration of gold mining in South Africa, electric calculating machines, and Thomas Edison's kinetoscope, a forerunner of the movie projector. Typical of the state-of-the-art displays one could behold at the fair were the awe-inspiring cannons built by Germany's Krupp Iron Works. These were the largest guns ever built: nearly sixty feet long, weighing 127 tons, able to propel shells sixteen miles.

The Midway Plaisance offered visitors a glimpse of life and culture around the globe, as it contained a mock Eskimo village, a traditional Irish cottage, a Java village, a German village (complete with castle, moat, drawbridge, palisades, and peasants' huts), "Old Cairo" (complete with camel drivers), and an African village. For many visitors to the fair, the Midway offered a kind of evolutionary yardstick against which the triumphs of modern man could be measured. Not coincidentally, the most westernized nations' Midway exhibits were located at the Plaisance's east end, nearest the White City; the "least civilized" cultures, such as the African village, were located at the Midway's western end. After strolling amid sod-roofed huts, open cooking fires, and scantily clad natives on the Midway, one stepped into the utopian White City with its electric lights, moveable sidewalks, and glistening faux marble walls. The implicit message regarding the "progress" of the races was unmistakable. "From the Bedouins of the desert and the South Sea Islanders," wrote Marian Shaw, a journalist who toured the Midway, "one can here trace, from living models, the progress of the human race from savagery and barbarism through all the intermediate stages to a condition still many degrees removed from the advanced civilization of the nineteenth century."[33]

Promotional posters billed the exposition as "forming in its entirety the most significant and grandest spectacle of modern times." Most visitors agreed with that assessment. Richard Harding Davis, a leading American journalist, called the fair "the greatest event in the history of the country since the Civil War."[34] One observer from Scotland praised the White City as "perhaps the most flawless and fairy-like creation, on a large scale, of man's invention."[35] A man who traveled all the way from New Zealand to see the exposition left "feeling assured that if I lived to the age of some of the most ancient patriarchs I could never again have a chance of beholding its superior or even its equal."[36] Hamlin Garland described the experience of his elderly parents from the rural Dakotas: "The wonder and the beauty of it all moved these dwellers of the level lands to tears of joy which was almost as poignant as pain."[37] The exposition even overwhelmed American cultural leader Henry Adams, a man not easily overwhelmed. "At Chicago," quipped Adams, "educational game started like rabbits at every building, and ran out of sight among thousands of its kind before one could mark its burrow."[38] Constructed and landscaped in three years, the exposition's utopian city impressed nearly all comers and also turned a profit for its backers.

It is difficult, however, to assess the meaning or the significance of the 1893 World's Columbian Exposition. It was a clear example of the sense of optimism and confidence that pervaded the United States and western Europe around 1900. The world had seen no major world war for almost eighty years. Science and technology were on the march. Medical knowledge was improving. Most Western thinkers thought man could usher in a golden age of peace and prosperity. The White City seemed to capture this confidence that utopia was possible. Significantly, these modern people thought that utopia would be found, not in a garden (as in the biblical Eden), but rather in a city. Consider the *Chicago Tribune*'s farewell as the exposition came to a close. It bid a fond good-bye "to a little ideal world, a realization of utopia, in which every night was beautiful and every day a festival, in which for the time all thoughts of the great world of toil, of injustice, of cruelty, and of oppression outside its gates disappeared, and in which this splendid fantasy of the artist and architect seemed to foreshadow some far-away time when all the earth should be as pure, as beautiful, and as joyous as the white city itself."[39]

There is little doubt that Chicagoans hosted the exposition as a way of promoting the city. They routinely told visitors that the real exhibit was Chicago itself, the urban phoenix that had burned to the ground only twenty years earlier. Influential Chicagoans were so concerned about their city's image that they actually bribed the city's criminals to keep them away from the White City. Any pickpockets caught at the exposition paid an immediate $10 fee to the arresting officer; that gave policemen an incentive to watch the pickpockets. But all pickpockets arrested downtown between the hours of 8 A.M. and 4 P.M. would be immediately released upon arrival at the police station. In other words, pickpockets were given free reign in the city during those hours when visitors would be touring the White City.

In the end, the exposition was a skillful weaving of Chicago boosterism, American flag-waving, and international fair. Visitors came to see what the world (and especially the United States) had to offer. They left convinced that Chicago was one of the world's great cities. In 1964, when Time Incorporated and *Life* magazine published its popular *Life History of the United States,* it entitled its eight-page discussion of the 1893 World's Columbian Exposition "Coming-of-Age Party in Chicago." But what exactly had come of age, and for whom was the party thrown? Was it the United States? Or was it Chicago? The exposition's ambiguity is what made it so important. Perhaps it was only fitting that the White City met its demise in an equally ambiguous fashion. The fair ended just as the United States entered an acute and painful economic depression. Legions of Chicago's poor, unemployed, and homeless squatters took up residence in the abandoned shells of the White City. In July 1894, federal soldiers and striking railroad workers clashed at the abandoned White City, and a raging fire broke out. The inferno engulfed the entire frame-and-plaster White City; city residents traveled to Jackson Park to watch the spectacle. Just as the old frontier Chicago had ended in a great fire, so did the modern city end in fire as well. Only two Columbian Exposition buildings stand today: the former Fine Arts Palace, which functions as the present-day Museum of Science and Industry, and the present-day Art Institute. The exposition's Midway Plaisance remains as well, linking Jackson Park and Washington Park while fronting the University of Chicago. Although little remains from the 1893 fair, its meaning to a growing city and a nation rising to prominence was profound.

* * * *

What do the Great Chicago Fire of 1871, the Haymarket Bombing of 1886, and the World's Columbian Exposition of 1893 tell us? Among other things, they reveal the deep ambivalence and sense of uneasiness that Americans harbored toward cities in the second half of the 1800s.[40] It was during the late nineteenth century that Americans moved in large numbers from the farm to the city, but they made this move with deep reservations. The city was widely perceived as a dangerous, evil, and unnatural place. According to the era's conventional wisdom, gambling halls, labor radicalism, saloons, brothels, and atheism did not flourish in the cornfields of Iowa, the cotton patches of Mississippi, or the family farms of Indiana. Vice and disorder, many Americans assumed, were the special province of the city. "The city has become a serious menace to our civilization," explained Josiah Strong, an influential American minister in the late 1880s, "because in it . . . each of the dangers we have discussed is enhanced, and all are focalized."[41] In his blockbuster 1891 book *Our Country: Its Possible Future and the Present Crisis,* Strong wrote, "Here is heaped the social dynamite; here the roughs, gamblers, thieves, robbers, lawless and desperate men of all sorts, congregate; men who are ready on any pretext to raise riots for the purpose of destruction and plunder."[42] No one could deny the city's commercial successes, but many wondered if they were paying too high a price for economic development.

Perhaps this ambivalence toward the city explains why the fire, the bomb, and the fair captured Americans' imaginations to the extent that they did. The Great Chicago Fire was a disaster so enormous and so sweeping that it seemed the ultimate act of divine judgment, wiping out the very heart of the wicked and unbelieving city. That city leaders could never definitively pin the blame for the fire on Mrs. O'Leary, her cow, or anyone or anything else only seemed to underscore the providential nature of the conflagration. Did not the fire prove that life in the city was unnecessarily dangerous? Did it not prove that the city was excessively and fatally unnatural, an act of human will that would inevitably perish in a judgment of fire? It was in this context that two myths were born. One was the myth of Mrs. O'Leary's cow. It was important that Chicagoans attribute the fire to something other than an act of Providence; it is revealing that they pinned the blame on a poor and careless Irish immigrant and her animal. The second myth proved equally enduring: the myth of the city's Phoenix-like rebirth. The story of the city's rebuilding transformed the fire from disaster into blessing. By dint of their wills, Chicagoans rebuilt their city better than it was before. Humans triumphed over the fire in the long run; the fire did not win. The Great Chicago Fire became an American success story, one that city dwellers could tell themselves in order to put to rest any lingering concerns about the wrongness of the city.

The bomb touched an even deeper nerve. The Haymarket rally itself was not a large one, few people died in the affair, no citywide riot followed the incident, and even prosecutors conceded that blame for the bombing could not be determined. And yet the Haymarket bombing became a national event, because it highlighted deep anxieties regarding labor radicalism, urban unrest, safety, and law and order. The Haymarket bombing pushed to the surface all those things that Americans most feared about their cities. They seemed full of strange immigrants, Europeans who may not fully embrace the "American way" of doing things. They seemed hotbeds of labor unrest, socialism, and communism, and they seemingly posed real threats to the American capitalist system that had allowed many Anglo-Americans to enjoy unprecedented prosperity. Cities seemingly nurtured anarchism and lawlessness, threatening the safety of law-abiding citizens everywhere.

It was essential, then, for the city to respond to the Haymarket bombing swiftly and definitively. Far more than the Haymarket anarchists were on trial in Chicago: the American city was on trial as well. Editorials in the newspapers of other large American cities cried out for death penalties, in part to deter their own labor radicals and in part to vindicate the American city. Order had to be restored. In convicting the accused—although all the defendants presented credible explanations for why they could not have thrown the bomb—the court sought order more than it did justice. Talking about bombs was judged as serious as throwing bombs, because talking about them disrupted urban harmony.

The World's Columbian Exposition was an attempt to show Americans and the world that urban harmony, in the form of a utopian city—the White City—was possible. Good planning and human willpower could in time perfect the city. For example, one of Chicago's most vexing problems—the problem of clean drinking water—was solved ingeniously at the White City. Daniel Burnham constructed a water purification plant at Jackson Park (something the city itself did not have at the time), installed newly invented Pasteur filters on the White City's drinking fountains, and built a 101-mile-long pipe to bring pure mineral water from Waukesha, Wisconsin, directly to the White City. The fair stood as an example of what was possible, as proof that urban disorder was not inevitable. The White City was by design a city of illusions, an answer to those critics who rejected urban life as hopelessly lawless, dirty, and unwholesome. At least in some sense, the Columbian Exposition was born of urban defensiveness. The White City was a vivid display of the indomitable human spirit amid the people's deep reservations about the emerging American city.

The fire, the bomb, and the fair occurred within this context of late-nineteenth-century apprehensions regarding the American city. Urban leaders managed these events to combat the perception that cities were dangerous, immoral, and unnatural. In their capable hands, the events served as redemptive opportunities. Of course, Chicagoans were not alone in this enterprise of legitimizing the urban project; similar urban myths, with similar themes, were crafted in other cities. Perhaps not surprisingly, the anti-urban diatribes of people like Josiah Strong almost disappeared in the early twentieth century. The American city had been validated, in part because of the fire, the bomb, and the fair.

CHAPTER SEVEN

THE NEW

IMMIGRATION,

1880-1920

• Chicago's story is in many ways the story of newcomers to the city: French missionaries and trappers in the 1600s, Anglo-American frontiersmen in the 1700s and early 1800s, Irish laborers and German skilled craftsmen in the first half of the 1800s, German and Bohemian laborers in the immediate post–Civil War years. Even so, nothing compares with the large numbers of immigrants who came to the city in the years between 1880 and 1920. All told, about 2.5 million European immigrants—most from southern and eastern Europe—came to the city during that period.

As late as 1880, the Irish and Germans remained the largest immigrant groups in the city. These pre-1880 immigrants—a product of what historians call "the old immigration"—were quite different from the newcomers who constituted the "new immigration" of the 1880s, 1890s, 1900s, and 1910s. Most of the pre-1880 immigrants hailed from northern and western Europe. Many (for example, the Irish, the British, and Canadians) already spoke English and were familiar with Anglo-American culture. This made it easier for them to assimilate, to transact business with native Anglo-American Chicagoans, or to compete in the local political arena. Other pre-1880 immigrants (for example, Germans) possessed skills that proved invaluable in a growing city that was making the transition from preindustrial frontier town to modern metropolis.

The new immigration, however, brought millions of immigrants to the United States from southern and eastern Europe. The chief peoples in this wave of immigration were Poles, Italians, Bohemians, and Russian Jews. Unlike the Irish, these immigrants spoke no English, and most were penniless and uneducated. They rarely possessed a trade that could translate into a skilled job. The new immigrants were often scorned by both native Anglo-Americans and the older, more established immigrants. Some immigrant groups (such as the Poles) created tightly knit ethnic communities and clung together for support. Other immigrant groups (such as Italians) were often made up of men who arrived without their families, worked for several years, saved their wages, and returned to Europe.

Chicago was not unusual in receiving 2 million European immigrants in the late 1800s and early 1900s. The new immigration was a national phenomenon, and more than 23 million people came to America between 1880 and 1920. By 1910, foreign-born immigrants and their children accounted for more than 70 percent of the populations of New York City, Chicago, Detroit, Cleveland, Boston, Milwaukee, and Buffalo and for between 50 and 70 percent of the populations of San Francisco, Newark, Pittsburgh, St. Louis, Philadelphia, and Cincinnati. A U.S. government survey of twenty-one industries in 1910 discovered that 58 percent of all industrial workers were foreign-born; about two-thirds of these foreign-born workers were "new immigrants" from southern and eastern Europe.

POLES AND GROUP SOLIDARITY

The first Polish immigrants came to Chicago in the 1850s. The number of Poles in the city remained small, perhaps reaching 2,000 by 1870. By 1890, the number of first- and second-generation Poles in Chicago reached 40,000. That number grew to 210,000 by 1910 and to 401,000 by 1930. These Poles came from one of the last feudal societies in Europe and therefore possessed only the rudimentary agricultural skills of peasant serfs. Few were craftsmen, fewer still were professionals, many were illiterate, and all were poor. Polish immigrants moved to American cities that were home to heavy industrial factories, cities such as Chicago and Buffalo. In Chicago, the majority of Poles took jobs in the steel mills, the stockyards, or the city's many factories. They were paid poorly, in part because they took unskilled jobs and in part because employers discriminated against them.

The influx of new immigrants created five distinct Polish neighborhoods in Chicago by 1890. The largest was the Polish Downtown on the Near Northwest Side (close to Division and Ashland Streets). In this small neighborhood three-fourths of a mile long and one-half of a mile wide, 86 percent of the residents were Polish. They were serviced by two of the largest Polish Catholic parishes in the world, St. Stanislaw Kostka and Holy Trinity. The other major Polish neighborhood was located in South Chicago near the city's sprawling steel mills. Seventy-two percent

Table 1. IMMIGRATION TO CHICAGO, 1830–1980

	approx. number of immigrants	largest immigrant groups
1830s	12,000	Germans, Irish, Norwegians
1840s	16,000	Irish, Germans
1850s	55,000	Germans, Irish
1860s	145,000	Germans, Irish, Bohemians, English
1870s	205,000	Germans, Swedes, Bohemians, Canadians
1880s	451,000	Germans, Swedes, Irish, Poles, Norwegians
1890s	587,000	Poles, Russians, Dutch, Italians, Bohemians
1900s	783,000	Russians, Austrians, Poles, Italians, Hungarians
1910s	809,000	Italians, Poles, Czechs
1920s	859,000	Italians, Lithuanians, Poles, Mexicans
1930s	673,000	not available
1940s	526,000	Europeans displaced by World War II
1950s	438,000	English-speaking peoples
1960s	374,000	Hispanics
1970s	230,000	Hispanics, Indians, East Asians

Source: "Introduction: Ethnic Life in Chicago," in Melvin G. Holli and Peter d'A. Jones, eds., *Ethnic Chicago: A Multicultural Portrait,* 4th ed. (Grand Rapids, Mich.: Eerdman's Publishing Company, 1994), 5.

of area residents here were Polish. Other significant Polish communities took root in the Lower West Side (adjacent to major rail lines, several large factories, and the Illinois and Michigan Canal) and two neighborhoods near the Union Stock Yards.

Most noticeable in Chicago's Polish immigrant community was the process of building what scholars have termed "institutional completeness." Polish immigrants created Polish institutions to assist them as they adapted to life in America. The Poles' preference for Polish institutions over preexisting American institutions did not subside as their years in America passed. In many ways, the Poles resisted assimilation.

Polish immigrants to Chicago first created death-benefit societies. These organizations amounted to burial insurance cooperatives: men contributed money to the society each year, and the society pledged to provide the member with a proper Polish burial. By pooling their

Table 2. EUROPEAN-BORN IMMIGRANTS IN CHICAGO, 1890 AND 1920

country	1890	1920
Germany	161,000	112,000
Ireland	70,000	57,000
Sweden	43,000	59,000
Great Britain	38,000	38,000
Czechoslovakia	25,000	50,000
Poland	24,000	138,000
Norway	22,000	20,000
Russia	8,000	102,000
Denmark	7,000	11,000
Italy	6,000	59,000
Austria	6,000	30,000
Lithuania	—	19,000
Netherlands	5,000	9,000
France	2,500	—
Hungary	—	26,000
Greece	—	12,000
Yugoslavia	—	10,000

Source: Melvin G. Holli and Peter d'A. Jones, ed., *Ethnic Chicago: A Multicultural Portrait,* rev. ed. (Grand Rapids, Mich.: Eerdmans Publishing Company, 1984), 548–50.

resources, Poles prevented financial hardships such as paying for expensive burials from being passed on to their surviving families. These death-benefit societies soon expanded and sponsored social activities. Polish immigrants also established building and loan associations. For men and women who had lived as landless serfs in the Old Country, owning a home in Chicago became a priority. Men contributed money to the association until they had accumulated enough funds to make a down payment on a house. The association then extended a low-interest loan to the member. The system worked: the percentage of Polish families who owned their homes was double the citywide average. Poles in Chicago also established an orphanage and industrial school, four Polish cemeteries, two day nurseries, an old-age home, a hospital, and three Polish-language daily newspapers. With the notable exception of their

Table 3. THE CHANGING NATURE OF IMMIGRATION:
OLD AND NEW IMMIGRATION IN CHICAGO, 1860–1920

percentage of total population of Chicago

	Germans	Irish	Scandinavians	East and South Europeans
1860	19%	18%	2%	< 1%
1890	15	6	7	6
1920	4	2	3	14

percentage of foreign-born population of Chicago

	Germans	Irish	Scandinavians	East and South Europeans
1860	39%	36%	4%	< 1%
1890	36	16	16	14
1920	14	6	11	48

Source: Irving Cutler, *Chicago: Metropolis of the Mid-Continent,* 3d ed. (Dubuque, Iowa: Kendall/Hunt Publishing Company, 1982), 55.

workplace, Poles could live in a largely Polish world where they did business with and sought assistance from their countrymen.

Perhaps the most significant and powerful of Polish institutions was the Polish Catholic Church. By 1910, 140,000 out of the 210,000 Poles in Chicago were church members. More so than for any other immigrant group, the church was the focal point of community life in the Polish neighborhoods. At St. Stanislaw Kostka in 1919, for example, seventy-four parish societies—ranging from the Club of St. Rose (which did needlework) to the Court of Frederic Chopin—provided cultural activities for parishioners. Every Polish Catholic church also had its own parochial school. The schools' purpose was to preserve the Polish youths' sense of religious and cultural heritage. While people of other ethnic groups worshiped in Roman Catholic churches and built church-affiliated schools, none were so committed to parochial schools as the Polish. Sixty percent of all Polish children attended parochial schools in

Table 4. IMMIGRATION TO THE TEN LARGEST U.S. CITIES

1860		1890		1920	
city ranked by population	*percent foreign born*	*city ranked by population*	*percent foreign born*	*city ranked by population*	*percent foreign born*
New York	48%	New York	42%	New York	36%
Philadelphia	29	Chicago	41	Chicago	30
Brooklyn	39	Philadelphia	26	Philadelphia	22
Baltimore	25	Brooklyn	33	Detroit	29
Boston	36	St. Louis	25	Cleveland	30
New Orleans	38	Boston	35	St. Louis	13
Cincinnati	46	Baltimore	16	Boston	32
St. Louis	60	San Francisco	42	Baltimore	12
Chicago	50	Cincinnati	24	Pittsburgh	21
Buffalo	46	Cleveland	37	Los Angeles	21

Source: Raymond A. Mohl, *The New City: Urban America in the Industrial Age, 1860–1920,* (Arlington Heights, Ill.: Harlan Davidson, 1985), 20.

1920; by comparison, only one of the ten Italian Roman Catholic parishes even operated its own parochial school.

Because their churches were so important, Chicago's Poles found themselves involved in a bitter fight over their control. At least in theory, the Roman Catholic Church was *catholic*. It claimed to transcend national boundaries and ethnic differences. In practice, however, ethnic divisions within Chicago's Roman Catholic Church were sharp. The Irish controlled the administrative positions within the local Catholic hierarchy, largely because they had come to Chicago first, were numerous, and could speak English. The Polish Catholics chafed at this. They sought to own their churches, to enjoy the leadership of Polish priests, and to determine local church matters for themselves. In short, Poles sought independence and autonomy within the Roman Catholic Church.

The Irish leaders of Chicago's archdiocese refused. They insisted that churches were owned by the archdiocese and that the archdiocese alone appointed priests. What resulted was a protracted struggle between Polish and Irish Catholics in Chicago, a struggle that began almost as soon as the first Polish parish was started in 1869. The battle came to a head in 1916 with the appointment of George William Mundelein, a German American who served as archbishop of Chicago until 1939. A fierce Americanizer, Mundelein was determined to squash all vestiges of ethnic churches in Chicago. He deliberately appointed Polish priests to non-Polish parishes, halted the building of purely national parishes, and standardized parochial school curriculum (which included a policy of instruction in English only). The Poles resisted, and Mundelein backed down. Chicago's Polish Catholics never created the autonomous ethnic parishes they desired, but their unity forced Mundelein to grant them a degree of national separatism. Local Poles won a qualified victory over the indomitable Mundelein, who continued assigning Polish priests to Polish parishes. This decision created de facto Polish national parishes despite Mundelein's desires.

The Poles successfully resisted Mundelein because they displayed a group solidarity that did not weaken. That same unity, however, prevented them from wielding political power and rising to the upper echelons of the local business community, and it has prevented them from producing from among their numbers such professionals as doctors, lawyers, and professors in similar proportion to those produced by other ethnic groups. Refusing to bargain and to ally themselves with other ethnic groups (such as the Irish and Czechs), Poles attempted to vote as a bloc. One historian calls this bloc political behavior a "drive for recognition" on the part of Poles.[1] Although Poles succeeded in electing a few local officials, significant victories eluded them. The bloc strategy failed in a polyglot city like Chicago, where political winners were those who fashioned coalitions of different ethnic groups. Poles lacked the clear majority necessary to carry elections without coalitions, and their ethnic solidarity alarmed other less numerous ethnic groups in the city.

Historian Edward R. Kantowicz makes an intriguing connection between ethnic solidarity and economic success. Perhaps securing the American Dream of upward mobility and personal wealth requires an atomistic, or individualistic, pursuit of success. Poles were community-oriented. Few Polish immigrants invested their meager savings in second-hand goods, loaded those goods into a sack, hopped onto the trolley car early in the morning, rode across town to a different ethnic neighborhood, and spent the day hawking their wares. Chicago's Polish newspapers exhorted its readers to *"Swój do Swego"* ("support your own"). Far from encouraging commercial relationships that transcended ethnic boundaries, such pleas advocated economic nationalism. Poles worked their shifts at the factory and returned home to family and church. Perhaps more than any other ethnic group, Poles defined success in terms of economic stability (but not affluence or prosperity), tightly knit communities (but not individualistic triumphs), and religious (as opposed to secular) security. They were not risk-takers who speculated and invested. Instead, they faithfully labored in their factory and stockyard jobs, content to see their wages rise modestly but steadily. Kantowicz concludes, "If Polish immigrants came to America seeking primarily bread, a home, and a better standard of living for their families, and at the same time they tried to preserve their communal lifestyle as much as possible, the conclusion is inescapable that they got what they wanted and have been successful on their own terms."[2]

ITALIANS AND TEMPORARY IMMIGRATION

Italians first immigrated to Chicago in the 1850s and numbered only 1,400 as late as 1880. When numerous immigrants flooded into the city beginning in the late nineteenth century, Chicago's Italian-born population rose to 5,700 by 1890, 16,000 by 1900, 45,000 by 1910, and 59,000 by 1920. So many Italians relocated to Chicago that the Italian government opened a consular office in the city in 1887. Most of these newcomers were not from the prosperous, industrialized states of northern Italy; rather, they were overwhelmingly poor, illiterate farmers (or *contadini*) from southern and central Italy.

Three immigration patterns distinguished the Italians from most other immigrants. First, Italians, more than any other group of Europeans, planned temporary stays in America. Often a wage-earning male would make the voyage to America alone, work in the United States for five years, save his wages, and return to Italy. Perhaps half of all Italian immigrants returned to Italy as they had planned. This was one reason the city's Italians were long underrepresented in local politics. Although numerous (they supported five Italian-language newspapers), the frequent exodus of immigrants for Italy and their replacement by new, inexperienced men made it difficult for the Italians to organize themselves politically.

Second, many Italian immigrants found work through the *padrone* system. New arrivals would make contact with an Italian labor broker (called a *padrone*) who usually spoke English. The *padrone* would then find work and negotiate wages for his workers. The system worked well for many Italian men: they had no family responsibilities (so they could quickly move from one neighborhood to another to find work), they had no interest in acquiring career skills (because they planned on returning to Italy), and they had little reason to learn English. The system made it easy for the *padrone* to exploit his workers, however. He made his living by skimming a percentage of his workers' wages.

Third, Italian immigrants practiced *campanilismo*. The men from entire villages in southern Italy would often immigrate en masse to America; these men then took up residence with friends, neighbors, and relatives from the Old Country. Chicago reformer Jane Addams observed that often an entire tenement house would be filled with Italian tenants hailing from the same village. In effect, whole villages (minus many wives and children) immigrated intact. For example, men from Naples and Messini lived in Chicago's Near West Side community, immigrants from Palermo and Catania lived on the Near North Side, and men from Genoa lived in the south end of the Loop (near the present-day Merchandise Mart). Settlement patterns such as this enabled first-generation Italian immigrants to preserve much of their ethnic heritage and many of their customs. These immigrants were not isolated, atomized Italians tossed into the American melting pot; they were immigrants who in many ways transplanted their Italian villages to Chicago and preserved traditional folkways.

The largest Italian neighborhood in Chicago—home to one-third of the city's Italians—was located in the Near West Side near Taylor Street and Hull-House. By any measure, this area qualified as a slum. The Italian immigrants' intention to return to Italy accounts for their poor living conditions. Men unburdened by families simply piled into cheap, filthy, overpopulated boarding houses. Few bought their own property. Other Italian neighborhoods, all likewise crowded and dirty, were located at the south end of the Loop and on the Near Northwest Side. Perhaps the most colorful Italian enclave was located on the Near North Side in an area that was known as Little Sicily or Little Hell. It had been an Irish shanty town until the massive immigration of Sicilians to the area at the turn of the century. Centered around West Division Street, the neighborhood was isolated by poor transportation and the river, and it remained virtually untouched by American ways, "a transplantation of Sicilian village life in the heart of a hurrying American city."[3]

Because most Italian immigrants to Chicago were *contadini*, they preferred not to work indoors in the city's steel mills, meatpacking houses, and factories. They instead sought outdoor work, as they had done in Italy. Accordingly, most Italians in Chicago held unskilled jobs as railroad laborers, construction workers, or small-scale fruit and vegetable vendors. Railroad work was especially demanding: twelve-hour workdays, hard labor, bad food, tyrannical foremen, low pay (about $1.50 per day), and housing in railroad boxcars. Carl Sandburg painted this picture of the poor Italian railroad laborer in his poem entitled "Child of the Romans," published in 1916:

> The dago shovelman sits by the railroad track
> Eating a noon meal of bread and bologna.
> > A train whirls by, and men and women at tables
> > Alive with red roses and yellow jonquils,
> > Eat steaks running with brown gravy,
> > Strawberries and cream, eclaires and coffee.
> The dago shovelman finishes the dry bread and bologna,
> Washes it down with a dipper from the water-boy,
> And goes back to the second half of a ten-hour day's work
> Keeping the road-bed so the roses and jonquils
> Shake hardly at all in the cut glass vases
> Standing slender on the tables in the dining cars.

The Italians' apparent lack of preparation for city life led even a sympathetic reformer such as Jane Addams to observe paternalistically, "The South Italians more than any other immigrants represent the pathetic stupidity of agricultural people crowded into city tenements."[4] Italians never wielded much political power in the city, a fact that was attributed by contemporaries to Italians' political backwardness but was more likely a result of their fierce independence. When coupled with the high repatriation rate among Italian immigrants, Italians' reluctance to forge political coalitions with other ethnic groups meant that they were not political leaders in the city.

Perhaps the most surprising aspect about Chicago's Italian immigrants was their relationship with the Roman Catholic Church. With the Church headquartered in the heart of Italy, one would expect Italians to be the most loyal of Catholics. This was not the case for Italians in Chicago. Most southern and central Italians were disaffected with the Roman Catholic Church. In Italy, the church often sided with wealthy landowners who routinely exploited the *contadini*. These impoverished farmers saw the Catholic Church more as an adversary than as an ally.

Local conditions seemed to confirm that perception. It was the city's Irish who controlled the local Roman Catholic diocese, and the Irish church leaders did not accept the Italian newcomers. Having long been alienated from the Catholic Church in Italy, many *contadini* fashioned a folk religion based more on magic, mysticism, and charms than on Christianity. For example, it was common to see Italian immigrants carrying or wearing a *corno*—a goat's horn made of coral—to protect them from the evil eye.

At least initially, Chicago priests in the Italian neighborhoods were horrified by the conspicuous synthesis of pagan and Christian beliefs they saw. Italian priests—who came to Chicago beginning in 1903—were able to reverse this antichurch sentiment. They paid special attention to meeting the immigrants' social and cultural needs and in so doing almost singlehandedly preserved the Italians' sense of community in Chicago. As a result, they won thousands of estranged Catholics back to their church. Whereas the Italian community's commitment to the Catholic Church had been weak in 1900, by 1930 it was strong and vibrant. Together with Italian-language newspapers and Italian benevolent societies, the Church offered guidance to and provided leadership for Italian immigrants in Chicago.

EASTERN EUROPEAN JEWS AND UPWARD MOBILITY

Only about 10,000 Jews lived in Chicago in 1880. Most of these were highly assimilated German Jews, and visitors to Chicago at that time would have been hard-pressed to find a Jewish neighborhood in the city. By 1900, another 70,000 Jews had come to the city, and by 1930 the city's Jewish population had swelled to 275,000. With that number, Chicago boasted the third-largest Jewish population of any city in the world, behind only New York City and Warsaw, Poland. Eighty percent of these recent Jewish immigrants hailed from eastern European areas such as Russia, Poland, and the eastern portions of Austria-Hungary. Most settled southwest of Chicago's downtown and took over an area that had been populated by Germans, Czechs, and the Irish. Bounded by Canal Street, Damen Avenue, Polk Street, and Sixteenth Street, this area became the city's Jewish neighborhood. Housing was cheap, crowded, and dangerous.

The heart of this thriving, squalid, teeming Jewish neighborhood was the corner of Maxwell and Halsted Streets. Hundreds of peddlers

Maxwell Street around 1910, heart of the Jewish commercial district and home to hundreds of street peddlers. Notice the storefront signs in Hebrew. As this photograph shows, some women wore traditional clothing, while others preferred dressing "like the Yankees." Chicago Historical Society, IChi-19155; Barnes-Crosby photograph jammed the street with their pushcarts, wagons, and stands. Potential customers forced their way through the crowds of people and the maze of shouting vendors. Little English was heard on Maxwell Street. All bartered, argued, cursed, and persuaded in Yiddish. One Chicagoan had these recollections of the area:

> The smell of garlic and of cheeses, the aroma of onions, apples, and oranges, and the shouts and curses of sellers and buyers fill the air. Anything can be bought and sold on Maxwell Street. On one stand, piled high, are odd sizes of shoes long out of style; on another are copper kettles for brewing beer; on a third are second-hand pants; and one merchant even sells odd, broken pieces of spectacles, watches, and jewelry, together with pocket knives and household tools salvaged from the collections of junk peddlers. Everything has value on Maxwell Street, but the price is not fixed. It is the fixing of the price around which turns the whole plot of the drama enacted daily at the perpetual bazaar of Maxwell Street. . . . The sellers know how to ask ten times the amount that their wares will eventually sell for, and the buyers know how to offer a twentieth.[5]

The established Jewish immigrant who had accumulated sufficient capital could open a stand on Maxwell Street. One needed an inventory to sell there, but most newly arrived Jews were penniless. Many therefore embraced a job that required little capital and few craft skills: they became door-to-door salesmen. Bernard Horwich, who arrived in Chicago in 1880 at age seventeen, recalled what life was like for these Jewish peddlers:

> They carried packs on their backs consisting of notions and light dry goods, and it was not an unusual sight to see hundreds of them who lived in the Canal Street district, in the early morning, spreading throughout the city. There was hardly a streetcar where there was not to be found some Jewish peddlers with their packs riding to and from their business. Peddling junk and vegetables, and selling various articles on street corners also engaged numbers of our people. Being out on the streets most of the time in these obnoxious occupations, and ignorant of the English language, they were subjected to ridicule, annoyance and attacks of all kinds.[6]

Peddling was difficult, but traveling throughout the various Chicago neighborhoods—and dealing with immigrants from other nationalities—imparted commercial skills to these vendors. Upward mobility would come sooner rather than later for most Jewish immigrants.

For some, economic prosperity came very soon, often within one generation. While most eastern European Jews managed just to scrape by, their children often fared quite well. Joseph Goldberg, for instance, immigrated to Chicago from Russia around 1900. Working in the Maxwell Street area, he bought a blind horse and sold fruits and vegetables. His son, Arthur, served in President John F. Kennedy's cabinet and became a justice of the U.S. Supreme Court. Samuel Paley, who also lived near Maxwell Street, made cigars. His son, William, founded and became president of the Columbia Broadcasting System. David Goodman and Abraham Rickover worked as tailors in Chicago; their sons were musician Benny Goodman and U.S. Naval Commander Hyman C. Rickover. Barnet Balabin, whose father owned a small grocery store near Maxwell Street, became president of Paramount Pictures. It was possible, then, for Jewish immigrants in Chicago to succeed within one generation.

It was Chicago's established German Jewish community that experienced the most conflict with these new Jewish immigrants from eastern Europe. The more recent immigrants were an embarrassment to the established German Jews who had lived in Chicago for several decades. German Jews tended to be cosmopolitan, highly assimilated, and well accepted by Chicago's native Anglo-Americans. Eastern European Jews, in contrast, were provincial and remained wedded to Old World customs. Whereas German Jews dressed much like Anglo-Americans, Jewish men from eastern Europe wore long beards and long black coats, and their wives wore kerchiefs or wigs and billowing black "peasant dresses." German Jews modified their Jewish faith into what would be called Reform Judaism, which meant that they dined with their gentile friends, ate gentile food, and were not averse to shopping or to recreation on Saturday. Eastern European Jews embraced orthodox beliefs, which meant they remained kosher, preserved their Sabbath, and maintained Talmud Torah, or Jewish religious schools. As successful businessmen, the German Jews could match any Anglo-American's scorn for labor radicalism and anarchism. Eastern European Jews, however, were often in the vanguard of Chicago's radical labor protests. As one Chicago rabbi put it, Chicago's Jews were "divided by pecuniary, intellectual, and social distinctions, provincial jealousies, and even religious distinctions and differences."[7]

Motivated by both compassion and self-interest, Chicago's German Jews invested large sums of money in institutions and projects that promised to speed up the eastern European immigrants' assimilation. Sears, Roebuck and Company president Julius Rosenwald, for example, helped fund the Chicago Hebrew Institute in 1908. The institute consisted of classrooms, clubrooms, a library, gymnasiums, assembly halls, and a synagogue. Backers touted the institute as a place where both younger and older Jews could meet and relax. In truth, the German Jewish patrons hoped they could encourage the assimilation of their benighted fellow Jews. The eastern European Jews resented such condescension and established their own support organizations.

By 1910, the flight of eastern European Jews from the Jewish ghetto was on. Many had accumulated substantial savings and could afford better housing. Why did the Jewish immigrants experience such rapid economic success? Perhaps because, more so than any other immigrant group, eastern European Jews came to America without any thought of returning to the Old Country. Anti-Semitism had been rife in eastern Europe, so many European Jews had no desire to return. They therefore threw themselves into their work with a view toward long-term economic success.

Factories and railroad tracks consumed more and more land in the Jewish neighborhoods, which pushed families westward. As the Jews vacated the Maxwell Street area, many African Americans—newly arrived in the "Great Migration" to Chicago from the South that occurred following World War I—took their places. By the 1930s, few Jews remained in what had become, and still is today, a predominantly black community.

GREEKS AND ENTREPRENEURIAL SUCCESS

Chicago was home to a small Greek community in 1880 that numbered only several hundred. Most Greeks lived on the North Side near Clark, Kinzie, and South Water Streets. By 1910, however, fifteen thousand Greeks lived in the city. Although small in comparison to the number of Poles, Italians, or Jews in the city, the Greek community in Chicago was one of the oldest and largest such settlements in the United States. Most of the newer Greek immigrants settled on the Near West Side, displacing Italians and creating a community that came to be known as Greek Town or the Delta. Greek Town was bounded by Halsted, Harrison, Blue Island, and Polk Streets. This description of Greek Town in 1911 suggests a tightly knit community:

Practically all stores bear signs in both Greek and English, coffee houses flourish on every corner, in the dark little grocery stores one sees black olives, dried ink-fish, tomato paste, and all the queer, nameless roots and condiments which are so familiar in Greece. On every hand one hears the Greek language, and the boys in the streets and on the vacant lots play, with equal zest, Greek games and baseball. It is a self-sufficient colony, and provision is made to supply all the wants of the Greek immigrant in as near as possible the Greek way. Restaurants, coffee-houses, barber-shops, grocery stores, and saloons are patterned after the Greek type, and Greek doctors, lawyers, editors, and every variety of agent are to be found in abundance.[8]

Although few in number, the Greeks made an immediate impact on the city. In addition to taking the Italians' housing, they also took their jobs. Contemporaries described the Greek immigrants as so fiercely individualistic that they found it difficult to work harmoniously with others. The "true Greek," observed one Chicago newspaper in the late 1890s, "will not work at hard manual labor like digging sewers, carrying the hod, or building railways. He is either an artisan or a merchant, generally the latter."[9] Many Greeks turned to private business and especially to the fruit-peddling trade. This put them in direct competition with the more numerous Italian peddlers. It was a battle the Greeks won, largely because of their entrepreneurial spirit. One historian observes, "Wherever one [the Greek immigrant] turned in America, the admonition was to work hard, save, invest, succeed, and become independent."[10] By 1895, a local newspaper reported: "The Greeks have almost run the Italians out of the fruit business in Chicago not only in a small retail way, but as wholesalers as well, for the big wholesale fruit houses on South Water Street are nearly all owned by men from the isles of burning Sappho. As a result, there is a bitter feud between these two races, as deeply seated as the enmity that engendered the Graeco-Roman wars."[11] It is estimated that ten thousand of eighteen thousand Greek Chicago men owned their own establishments in 1919.

CZECHS AND PROPERTY OWNERSHIP

The first Czech immigrants, also known as Bohemians, came to Chicago in the 1850s, and by 1870 they had built a significant community of 10,000 members. With the great waves of immigration after 1880, however, their numbers swelled. By 1895, 60,000 Czechs had created a Bohemian enclave known as Pilsen; it was bordered by Sixteenth, Twenty-second, and Halsted Streets and Western Avenue. When that number soared to 110,000 by 1910, Chicago became one of the largest Czech centers in the world, second only to Prague.

The Czechs enjoyed more economic and political success than many other immigrant groups. To begin with, most Czech immigrants were not as poor as other newcomers, nor were they as poorly educated. Only about 2 percent of Czech immigrants were illiterate, compared with an illiteracy rate of 24 percent for all immigrants. Unlike the Italians, Czechs came to Chicago to stay, which translated into an insatiable desire to own property in the city. To this end, they founded numerous Czech building and loan associations that functioned as lending institutions for Czech home buyers; in 1910, 94 of the 197 such institutions in Chicago were owned by Czechs. One 1895 study describes the Czech penchant for penny-pinching and saving:

> Often good artisans were compelled to work for low wages, even $1.25 a day; still, out of this meager remuneration they managed to lay a little aside for that longed-for possession—a house and lot that they could call their own. When that was paid for, then the house received an additional story, and that was rented so that it began earning money. When more was saved, the house was pushed in the rear, the garden sacrificed, and in its place an imposing brick or stone building was erected, containing frequently a store, or more rooms for tenants. The landlord, who had till then lived in some unpleasant rear rooms, moved into the best part of the house.[12]

Such thrift enabled the Czechs to move out of Pilsen into a larger community that became known as Czech California. The enclave took its name from California Avenue, which ran through the community, near present-day South Lawndale. Always determined to own property, Czechs soon owned nearly 80 percent of the buildings in Czech California. They built impressive structures such as Sokol Havlicek-Tyrs (an imposing three-story building that contained a large social hall and a gymnasium), the Pilsen Brewery, Pilsen Park, the Catholic St. Ludmila Church, and the Protestant John Hus Church. Czechs were so dominant in this area that the Czech language was taught in Farragut and Harrison high schools, the two public high schools in the community.

Although Czechs preserved a tightly knit community, they were not separatistic. They freely associated with other ethnic groups. No one personified this Czech attitude toward cooperation better than Anton

Cermak, a Czech who was elected Chicago's mayor in 1931. Unlike the Poles, the Czechs realized that they possessed insufficient numbers to win electoral victories by voting as a monolithic bloc. They fashioned coalitions with other ethnic groups, a strategy that enabled them to elect eighty public officials between 1890 and 1920. Their ultimate political triumph was Cermak's mayoral victory.

SWEDES AND THE DISPERSAL OF AN ETHNIC ENCLAVE

Scandinavian immigrants had long been numerous in Chicago. Many Norwegians and some Danes and Swedes flocked to the city between 1840 and 1870. After 1870, however, the influx of Swedes far outpaced that of other Scandinavians, and Chicago's Swedish population rose to 20,000 in 1880, 43,000 in 1890, and 121,000 in 1920.

What set the Swedes apart from other immigrants is the community that a small group of Swedish pioneers had established in the city before 1880. For example, Swedes in Chicago had founded thirteen ethnic churches in the city by 1880, proof of a vibrant and rooted ethnic life. Their established presence in the city—along with their northern European origins—distinguished them from the other groups migrating into Chicago between 1880 and 1920.

Because a small number of Swedes had planted themselves in Chicago before 1880, however, the settlement patterns of Swedes between 1880 and 1920 differed markedly from that of other new immigrants. When Russian Jews or Poles came to Chicago in the 1880s and 1890s, they were ethnic pioneers. No local Russian or Polish community awaited them. Swedes who came to Chicago in the 1880s, however, found three established Swedish neighborhoods. The largest was Swede Town on the Near North Side, which was bounded by Division, Superior, Franklin, and Larabee Streets and the north branch of the Chicago River; about half of Chicago's original Swedish community resided here. Two smaller communities were located on the Near West Side and the Near South Side. These Swedes had lived in the city for several years and had accumulated cash reserves; they knew the city and spoke at least some English. It was therefore easier for the older Swedes to move out of the downtown area when the waves of new immigrants swept into Chicago after 1880. Most of these established Swedes moved to a ring of better quality homes that were slightly farther away from the Loop.

This small group of pre-1880 Swedish immigrants proved invaluable to later Swedish immigrants. Those immigrants of the 1880s, 1890s, and 1900s benefited from the pathbreaking initiatives of earlier Swedish immigrants and thereby accelerated the community-building process. For example, the older Swedish immigrants fled the inner city and dispersed throughout the outlying regions of the city as the waves of new immigrants came to Chicago; many newer Swedish immigrants—those who came during the "new immigration"—joined them and avoided the downtown slums. The early migration of Swedes to outlying areas inhibited the formation of distinct Swedish enclaves; the only enduring Swedish community was Andersonville, located near Clark Street and Foster Avenue. The dispersal of the majority of Swedish immigrants throughout the Chicago area also quickly assimilated the Swedes, since they distinguished themselves from other immigrants who were forced into older inner-city housing. "The people down there," remarked one second-generation Swedish man, referring to the new inhabitants of his old neighborhood in Armour Square, "began to be nothing but foreigners who cared nothing for making the neighborhood attractive."[13] Thus, between 1880 and 1920, while Poles, Italians, and Greeks were building their distinct ethnic enclaves, Swedes were vacating theirs.

* * * *

Other immigrant groups came to Chicago around 1900 as well. Though this selective survey has omitted discussion of Lithuanians, Austrians, Hungarians, and the Dutch, the theme of this chapter should be clear: a staggering number of immigrants made Chicago their home between 1880 and 1920. Although all major American cities experienced the influx of European immigrants, the number of immigrants coming into Chicago was especially large. By 1900, Chicago had more Poles, Swedes, Czechs, Dutch, Danes, Norwegians, Croatians, Slovaks, Lithuanians, and Greeks than any other city in the United States. It is even more astonishing that the vast number of European newcomers to the city enabled Chicago to proclaim itself at one time or another the largest Lithuanian city in the world, the second largest Czech city in the world, and the third largest Irish, Swedish, Polish, and Jewish city in the world.

Far from existing solely within separate national groups, immigrants from different ethnic backgrounds associated. They worked together in the workplace and also did business with one another, via either the ubiquitous peddler or the multiethnic open-air market. Anglo-American efforts to assist the immigrants—such as Jane Addams's Hull-House or Billy Sunday's missionary outreaches—paid little attention to ethnic boundaries. Moreover, the legal system and local politics threw immigrants together into a world in which ethnicity meant little.

Regardless of nationality, Chicago immigrants shared many common experiences that offer insights into immigration, assimilation, and Chicago itself. Many of these new immigrants succeeded in Chicago only because they worked hard and were painfully thrifty. They worked bad jobs for long hours at low wages, and yet many immigrants still found a way to save part of their income. They invested. They sacrificed immediate gratification for long-term success. They did not spend their children's inheritance. Instead, they bequeathed inheritances to their children, and, accordingly, the children and grandchildren of these new immigrants often did quite well in Chicago.

Another common experience among immigrants to Chicago was that, even if they sought to assimilate (at least to some extent) into American culture, most new immigrants did not want to lose their ethnic distinctiveness. They sustained ethnic churches and synagogues where they found the old language spoken and the old customs practiced. Ethnic newspapers flourished. Nearly every immigrant group established schools (usually religious) that served as transmitters and preservers of their heritage. Although immigrant parents labored long hours for poor wages, they allocated scarce resources to these schools so their children would not forget their roots. Nearly every immigrant group maintained ties with its homeland. Many groups (Italians, for example) sent money back to families in Europe. Others (the Irish) contributed money to European political causes. Still others (Ukrainians) organized paramilitary units that might assist in liberating the motherland in Europe. (The local Ukrainian Sich, for example, outfitted men in military uniforms, drilled in city forest preserves and in wooded areas, and even started an aviation school in the city to train a Ukrainian air corps.) Few Chicago immigrants saw themselves as severing all ties with Europe and refashioning themselves as U.S. citizens. Most foreign-born immigrants instead saw themselves as citizens of two nations.

And yet second- and third-generation immigrants of all ethnic backgrounds assimilated rapidly despite the desires of foreign-born immigrants to preserve their ethnic heritage. To be sure, some (such as Germans) assimilated more rapidly, while others (such as Poles) resisted assimilation. American institutions, however, had a corrosive effect on ethnic particularism. It is perhaps evident how Chicago's public schools—with their standardized, English-based curriculum—helped to assimilate European immigrants. American pastimes, like baseball, also helped. Immigrant children loved the game, and it was an activity in which anyone, regardless of ethnicity, could participate. American economic life also stoked the fires of the melting pot. Immigrants from different countries worked side-by-side and rubbed shoulders in street markets. Addams, speaking of the city's German immigrants, observed that she "found strong family affection between them [foreign-born immigrants] and their English-speaking children, but their pleasures were not in common, and they seldom went out together."[14] In other words, second- and third-generation immigrants loved their foreign-born relatives but found that they had less and less in common with them.

Another common feature of life for turn-of-the-century immigrants to Chicago was that they received virtually no government assistance. In 1900, there was no such thing as food stamps, government-funded low-income housing, unemployment insurance, workmen's compensation, or hospitals that rendered free emergency care to the impoverished. Immigrants came to Chicago penniless. When they needed assistance, they turned to the hundreds of mutual aid societies that the ethnic communities had created themselves. In short, the immigrants helped themselves. It is remarkable that such mutual aid societies were as successful as they were (and they were extremely successful), as they were tantamount to the poor allying themselves and pooling their meager savings to escape poverty. It is to the immigrants' credit that they made such institutions work.

Another vital institution in immigrants' lives was the church or synagogue, which was often the hub of an immigrant community. New Chicagoans often relied upon their houses of worship to preserve old traditions and to maintain a link to the past. Religious schools, whether Catholic parochial schools or Jewish Talmud Torah schools, usually devoted much time to cultural instruction and preservation, often by teaching the mother tongue to immigrants' children. Churches and synagogues were usually established upon an ethnic—and not a multiethnic—basis. The predominantly Irish neighborhood of Bridgeport is a good example of this. Throughout the 1900s, this one-by-one-and-a-half-mile neighborhood was home to ten Catholic parishes of five different nationalities: Irish, German, Bohemian, Polish, and Lithuanian. If you sought a Baptist church in 1920s Chicago, you could choose among churches organized around thirteen different languages.

Also important to immigrants was the saloon. The saloon-to-citizen ratio suggests that one saloon existed for every sixty Chicago families, and about 500,000 Chicagoans used a saloon's services on any given day in the 1890s. The ethnic saloon of 1900 Chicago was far more than a place to buy a beer or a shot of whiskey. Saloons often functioned as community centers for new immigrants. There immigrants could find an established businessman—the barkeeper—who spoke the mother tongue. The barkeeper often served as an informal employment service, connecting available workers with employers. The saloon's owner frequently served as an ethnic bank, lending money to needy immigrants. Newspapers from the mother country could be found at the saloon as well. For the ethnic factory worker seeking a quick lunch during his noon break, the saloons served fast sandwiches and filled lunch pails with beer. When a big room was needed for a wedding, an anniversary celebration, a dance, or a labor union meeting, the saloon often provided it. New immigrants could hardly relax after work in the cramped, dingy, dirty, and smelly tenements that they crowded into; they instead went to the spacious and comparatively clean saloon. On muggy summer nights, immigrants might pay the saloon keeper a nickel to sleep on the cool saloon floors. Chicago's saloon keeper–politicians even received grudging praise from William T. Stead, the English moral reformer who penned *If Christ Came to Chicago* in 1894, a scathing critique of the city's vice and immorality. Stead judged that, unlike the city's wealthy businessmen and church leaders, the saloon keepers practiced the "fundamental principle of human brotherhood which Christ came to teach."[15]

Immigrants in Chicago were not necessarily unhappy. An earlier generation of scholars tended to argue that "the history of immigration is a history of alienation and its consequences . . . [such as] the broken homes, interruptions of familiar life, separation from known surroundings, the becoming a foreigner and ceasing to belong."[16] It is easy to assume that they were miserable when we read descriptions of turn-of-the-century immigrant life in Chicago, like one penned by Jane Addams in 1910: "The streets are inexpressibly dirty, the number of schools inadequate, sanitary legislation unenforced, the street lighting bad, the paving miserable and altogether lacking in alleys and smaller streets, and the stables foul beyond description. Hundreds of houses are unconnected with the street sewer. . . . Many houses have no water supply save for a faucet in the back yard, there are no fire escapes. . . . Meanwhile, the wretched conditions persist until at least two generations of children have been born and reared in them."[17] In considering the hardships faced by most immigrants, we should avoid projecting present-day standards of happiness, which usually include material prosperity, on these people. Moreover, we should avoid seeing the immigrants as passive subjects who did not shape their own experiences. Life in Chicago might have been difficult, but it was often more difficult back in an immigrant's homeland. For example, Russian and Polish Jews in Chicago certainly faced anti-Semitism, but they did not suffer from the state-sponsored pogroms that they experienced in Europe. Perhaps most important, Chicago was a place where hope abounded. Immigrants knew they had a reasonable chance of improving their lot. Carl Sandburg in 1916, in a poem entitled "Happiness," published in 1916, wrote:

> I asked professors who teach the meaning of life
> to tell me what is happiness.
> And I went to famous executives who boss the work
> of thousands of men.
> They all shook their heads and gave me a smile
> as though I was trying to fool with them.
> And then one Sunday afternoon I wandered out
> along the Desplaines River
> And I saw a crowd of Hungarians under the trees with their
> women and children and a keg of beer and an accordion.

In Sandburg's eyes, Chicago's immigrants were not mired in unhappiness. Indeed, the writer claims he found happiness, not in universities or corporate board rooms, but along the banks of a Chicago river among a group of festive immigrants.

CHAPTER EIGHT

PROGRESSIVISM

AND URBAN REFORM,

1890-1915

• Judge Murray F. Turley addressed the Municipal Voters' League, a group of forty thousand concerned Chicagoans that was formed in 1896. "We are trying to rescue the city from a band of conspirators known as the Council 'gang' which is degrading Chicago before all the world," proclaimed Turley. "No city council ever before known in Chicago has attained the degradation of the present one."[1]

Turley and the Municipal Voters' League sought to save the city from the Chicago City Council and their conspirators, the elected city aldermen. They were allegedly degrading the city by means of what Chicagoans called boodle: the selling of municipal favors or privileges (for example, rights to build streetcar tracks along a certain street) by politicians for personal profit. Turley's sense of a noble crusade for righteousness was typical of Progressive Era reformers, who sought to purge their cities of corruption, dishonesty, and bad government.

Between 1890 and 1915, the Progressive movement swept America, manifesting itself in the reform of both national and local politics. Progressive Era reforms aimed at the dislocations that accompanied America's transition from a nation of farmers and artisans to a nation characterized by immigration, industrialization, and urbanization. That transition, which can be dated to around 1900, resulted in problems such as urban slums, poverty, unsafe working conditions, corrupt urban political machines that depended upon ignorant immigrants' votes, and exploitive monopolies. Progressivism was the attempt to address these problems.

Most progressive reformers were well-educated and well-informed middle-class Americans, including many women, journalists, small businessmen, and college professors. Although many flavors of Progressivism existed, several common elements can be identified. Progressives were concerned about the harmful effects of industrialism and big businesses, and therefore they championed social justice concerns. Progressives had great faith that more government intervention in society would benefit all concerned. "The gospel of efficiency" gave Progressive reformers a strategy for addressing problems. Their "scientific" techniques would impose order and organization on chaotic, or inefficient, situations. Good government should be honest, efficient, and managed by professional public servants, they believed, and a scientific approach to governance could cure society's ills.

The dynamics that transformed America and convinced Progressives that reform was needed—immigration, industrialization, and urbanization—were most evident in America's large cities. Accordingly, Progressive reform efforts were numerous in urban America. Some urban Progressives sought moral reform. They were fed up with prostitution, gambling, and the indulgence of politicians who tolerated such sin. Other Progressives fought for urban political reform. These reformers' goals included ending graft, bribes, patronage abuse, and election fraud. They wanted honest businessmen in political office (and not hack politicians) who would manage the city's affairs efficiently. Still other urban progressives desired civic reform. They sought to make the city a safer, cleaner, and more enjoyable place to live. They usually favored extending and improving urban services in order to elevate the quality of urban life.

LOCAL WRITERS, EXPOSÉS, AND THE NEED FOR REFORM

The Progressive movement was fueled by writers and journalists who were dubbed muckrakers. These people exposed the nasty, filthy, unethical underside of life in America. Perhaps most important, the muckrakers ignited the feeling of moral outrage that provided the impetus for many Progressive Era reforms.

One of these muckrakers, Upton Sinclair, immortalized Chicago. A socialist, Sinclair worked as a journalist for a socialist newspaper. Around 1905, the young Sinclair came to Chicago to investigate the Union Stock Yards and the meatpacking industry. Sinclair's purpose, however, was not simply to expose the meatpacking industry but more broadly to expose the exploitive relationship between owners and employees. He intended for his work to be a polemic that supported socialism. What resulted, however, was quite different.

Based upon actual conditions in Chicago, Sinclair's work took the form of a novel. The serialized version of the story began appearing in 1905 and was published as a book in 1906 under the title *The Jungle*. The hero of the book is Jurgis Rudkus, an immigrant from Lithuania who works in Chicago's Union Stock Yards. Sinclair tells a desperate story of how the capitalist system gradually and inevitably crushes poor Jurgis. Sinclair finishes the book by having Jurgis attend a socialist rally. Like Sinclair himself, Jurgis experiences a conversion to the socialist cause, which enables him to see all things clearly.

Americans did not remember Sinclair's not-so-subtle argument for socialism. What they remembered were the disgustingly vivid scenes of unspeakable filth that were a normal part of work in meatpacking plants. Horrified readers realized that they regularly consumed contaminated, spoiled, unclean, and sometimes doctored meat.

> It seemed that they [the meatpacking companies] must have agencies all over the country, to hunt out old and crippled and diseased cattle to be canned. There were cattle which had been fed on "whiskey-malt," the refuse of the breweries, and had become what the men called "steerly"—which means covered with boils. It was a nasty job killing these, for when you plunged your knife into them they would burst and splash foul-smelling stuff in your face; and when a man's sleeves were smeared with blood, and his hands steeped in it, how was he ever to wipe his face, or to clear his eyes so that he could see? . . . [The plant owners] welcomed tuberculosis in the cattle they were feeding, because it would fatten them more quickly. . . . They [the butchers inside the stock yards] would have no nails,—they had worn them off pulling hides; their knuckles were swollen so that their fingers spread out like a fan. There were men who worked in the cooking rooms, in the midst of steam and sickening odors, by artificial light; in these rooms the germs of tuberculosis might live for two years, but the supply was renewed every hour. . . . Worst of any, however, were the fertilizer men, and those who served in the cooking rooms. These people could not be shown to the visitor,—for the odor of a fertilizer man would scare any ordinary visitor at a hundred yards, and as for the other men, who worked in tank rooms full of steam, and in some of which there were open vats near the level of the floor, their peculiar trouble was that they fell into the vats; and when they were fished out, there was never enough of them left to be worth exhibiting,—sometimes they would be overlooked for days, till all but the bones of them had gone out to the world as Durham's Pure Leaf Lard![2]

Soon after publication, Sinclair realized that his story had failed to convey the socialist gospel but had succeeded in exposing the meatpacking industry's atrocious practices. He admitted, "I aimed at the public's heart, and by accident I hit it in the stomach."³ One converted reader of *The Jungle* was President Theodore Roosevelt. The president immediately pushed for federal laws that would impose health standards on the meatpacking industry. Both the Meat Inspection Act and the Pure Food and Drug Act went into effect in 1906.

Sinclair's work proved more important on the national level than it did locally. There was no local equivalent of the federal Pure Food and Drug Act. One writer who did shake up Chicago, however, was the British writer and reformer William T. Stead, who came to the city to attend the World's Columbian Exposition. Appalled by the city's rampant vice, he vented his disgust in his 460-page book, *If Christ Came to Chicago,* published in 1894. Stead was sure that the Savior would have critical words for the city's materialistic young men, who looked to wealthy millionaires as role models. Stead also censured local society women, whom he characterized as lazy and selfish.

Stead was especially shocked by the city's famed Levee, which one historian judged the "most notorious red-light district in the nation."⁴ The Levee contained two hundred brothels as well as numerous saloons, dance halls, pawn shops, and gambling joints. One contemporary who studied the Levee concluded that the district's inhabitants were "morally insane" persons "who fail utterly in conceiving a single thought which is not vile, or an image which is not unspeakable."⁵ Stead's book exposed such local institutions as the famed Everleigh Club. If it was possible to create a classy and respectable brothel, then the Everleigh Club was that place. Located on South Dearborn Street, the fifty-room club sported a music room, a library, a grand ballroom illuminated by cut-glass chandeliers, an art gallery, a dining area suitable for hosting large parties, and exquisite mahogany staircases leading to the more private second floor. A perfume machine added to the club's elegance. Dinners started at $50. The women who labored at the Everleigh Club earned $100 weekly, more than ten times what they would have earned in Chicago's dingy sweatshops.

The *Chicago Tribune* called *If Christ Came to Chicago* "a directory of sin" and urged that it be suppressed. It was not. Stead's book sold ten thousand copies locally almost overnight as Chicagoans devoured the scandalous book. Although *If Christ Came to Chicago* generated a great deal of publicity, it resulted in few moral reform efforts locally. Chicago politicians, taking their cue from the manage-but-not-suppress policies of former mayor Carter Harrison I, rarely engaged in the Progressive Era's moral reform crusades. For the most part, they

regulated vice and were content to confine it within the clearly de-
marcated boundaries of the Levee.

BOODLE, THE MUNICIPAL VOTERS' LEAGUE, AND POLITICAL REFORM

In terms of instigating actual reform, Stead realized more success criticizing local politicians than he did criticizing local prostitutes. *If Christ
Came to Chicago* exposed the corrupt practices of Chicago's aldermen, especially their own form of graft that Chicagoans nicknamed boodle. In
so doing, Stead ignited political reform efforts despite his failure to pro-
voke moral reform.

Boodle was often connected with streetcars. Cable cars first carried
Chicagoans in 1882 along a four-mile stretch of straight track that ran
from near Marshall Field's store to Thirty-ninth Street. By 1893, the
city's streetcar system was the largest in the world, with eighty-six miles
of track that reached from downtown to Jackson Park and the World's
Columbian Exposition. The initial cable car lines carried passengers from
the South Side suburbs into the heart of the city, deposited them near
Field's State Street store, and then looped around on an end-of-the-track
turnaround to return to the South Side. (In this fashion, perhaps
100,000 streetcar riders passed by Field's inviting store windows every
day.) This is how downtown Chicago came to be known as the Loop, a
name derived from the turnaround that appeared fifteen years before elevated streetcar tracks (more commonly referred to then and now as
"the el" or "the L") encircled the downtown area. In addition to this
South Side "L," underworld vice king Mike McDonald owned and operated the Lake Street "L" that ran from today's Laramie Avenue on the
West Side to Market and Madison Streets, and a third company operated
the West Side "L" that ran from Douglas Park, Logan Square, and
Garfield Park into the downtown.[6]

Building streetcars was expensive. Operating them, however, was relatively easy and quite profitable. By 1890, the city desperately needed improved public transportation. The original streetcars had been pulled by
an endless cable that moved between the streetcar tracks; streetcar operators clamped onto the moving cable to propel the car forward and released the cable to stop. New electric trolley cars, however, were more
economical and could reach the hair-raising speed of twenty miles per
hour, doubling the older cars' top speed. Private companies competed

for the right to build new electric streetcar lines in the city. To operate streetcar lines, however, transit, or traction, companies needed to secure the legal right-of-way to city streets in order to build streetcar rails. Competing traction companies would request those rights-of-way from the city council, offering boodle to the aldermen to secure those rights (or franchises). The newspaper estimated that fifty-seven of the city's sixty-eight elected aldermen routinely accepted such boodle.

Spurred on by Stead's book, business and civic leaders declared war on boodle in 1896. They created the 40,000-member Municipal Voters' League and set out to purge the city of those whom Judge Murray F. Turley called "a band of conspirators known as the Council 'gang.'" The Municipal Voters' League and chairman George E. Cole immediately announced a slate of "good government" candidates who would challenge the "boodle aldermen" in the 1896 municipal election. A battle ensued. City newspapers lent the reformers critical support. The incumbent aldermen fought back by filing more than nine hundred libel suits against the Municipal Voters' League for such acts as calling alderman James L. Campbell "a menace to the community," as Cole had done. The reformers won the contest: of thirty-six elected alderman, twenty-six were described by Cole as "aggressively honest men."[7]

The reformers' victory, however, was only partial. Ten of the reelected aldermen were known boodlers. Indeed, Progressive reformers never rid Chicago of all or even most of its corrupt politicians. For example, John Joseph "Bathhouse" Coughlin (elected to the council in 1893) and Michael "Hinky Dink" Kenna (who joined the council in 1897) represented the notorious First Ward, home of the South Side's infamous Levee. Coughlin and Kenna resisted the reformers' best efforts at turning them out of office. Their ability to retain their aldermanic posts symbolizes Chicago's ambivalent record of political reform. "Good government" reformers such as George E. Cole won many battles, but so did the boodle aldermen.

CARTER HARRISON II AND CIVIC REFORM

Chicago's most powerful Progressive Era mayor, Carter Harrison II, personified the city's ambivalence toward political reform. Son of former mayor Carter Harrison I, the younger Harrison reigned as mayor from 1897 to 1905 and again from 1911 to 1915. He had little time for moral reform and proved a lukewarm supporter of political reform, but he steadfastly promoted civic reform. Improving the delivery of urban services to Chicagoans—cleaner water, better sewage disposal, more effective fire protection—was Harrison's passion.

Harrison knew that Chicago's mayors could never dominate local policymaking because political power rested in the hands of aldermen. These men zealously represented their respective wards, dispensing favors to the loyal and withholding them from the errant. Citywide leadership was rare; the good of the city took second place to the good of the ward. Journalist Lincoln Steffens, in his famous 1904 exposé *The Shame of the Cities,* described Chicago politics as "a settlement of individuals and groups and interests with no common city sense and no political conscience."[8] In this balkanized political environment, the successful mayor built coalitions and refrained from alienating powerful interests. He resembled, in some ways, a stagecoach driver attempting to steer a team of wild horses.

Harrison cultivated the image of the efficient, honest businessman-mayor. This was fairly easy to do. The mayor from 1893 to 1895, John Hopkins, had been embroiled in several financial scandals. By eschewing graft, Harrison seemed a veritable puritan when compared to the wanton Hopkins. He also supported the city's Municipal Voters' League and backed the three popular urban reforms of home rule, direct primaries, and the referendum. Harrison also accommodated the political realities of his day by catering to the large immigrant vote. He did this by defending the workingman's right to drink beer on Sunday and refraining from nativist rhetoric.

Harrison's civic reform projects required the city council votes of many aldermen of questionable repute. Chief among these were Coughlin and Kenna. Because they were "Lords of the Levee," they could parade thousands of flophouse residents to the polls on election days to support politicians friendly to the First Ward. One man described the process:

> A few days before the election, the shabby hotels of the First Ward would start swarming with new guests. The arrivals, minus suitcases and often last names, were jammed six to a small room. They slept on a cold floor, with burlap bags as covering. But daytime was a fete. Free liquor, free hops, free prostitutes were theirs for the asking. Come election day, the grateful floaters voted four or five times in different precincts. . . . The morning after election, they came shuffling or reeling into The Workingmen's Exchange to receive a final bonus for their democratic activities. The bonus ran from two to five dollars, depending on the amount of voting done.[9]

The city's moral and political reformers pressured Harrison to wage war on the First Ward. To these Progressives, Coughlin and Kenna typified the immoral aldermen they despised. To reform the First Ward, however, would mean Harrison would lose thousands of votes necessary for his civic reform projects. Harrison made the Faustian bargain: he rejected the moral reformers and to a large extent the political reformers, formed a coalition with the First Ward aldermen and other boodlers, and pursued civic reform.

Harrison killed several corrupt utility company deals, which resulted in lower city utility bills. In the 1880s, an average of two people per day were killed or injured on the city's many street-level railroad tracks; Harrison forced local railroad companies to raise their tracks and run them over the streets on bridges. That move probably saved hundreds of lives and thousands of crippling injuries every year. His parks commission, responding to the lead of Jane Addams's Hull-House, built playgrounds in several inner-city ethnic communities. He also slaked the Progressives' thirst for facts, data, and "scientific information" by establishing Chicago's first Bureau of Statistics and a Municipal Reference Library.

Perhaps Harrison's greatest victory came in his so-called traction wars with Charles Tyson Yerkes, the ruthless multimillionaire who was the subject of Theodore Dreiser's scathing 1914 novel, *The Titan*. Yerkes gained control of several of the city's independently owned streetcar companies and hoped to establish a monopoly over Chicago's electric streetcar business by securing the South Side's Chicago City Railway Company as well. Yerkes improved service in the North and West Sides by leasing two tunnels that ran under the Chicago River and running his streetcars through the tunnels, a change that eliminated delays caused by the swing bridges' yielding to river traffic. It was also Yerkes who built the downtown Union Loop, the elevated streetcar lines that encircled the central business district and created a common downtown streetcar terminal. Many Chicagoans, however, detested Yerkes for his dishonesty and shady dealings. (He had come to Chicago only after serving a prison sentence in Philadelphia for financial improprieties.) Citizens blamed him for poor streetcar service; reformers blamed him for flooding the city council with boodle money. Harrison openly opposed Yerkes, but—as with most municipal matters—decisions regarding the city's streetcars ultimately rested with the city council. Knowing that, Yerkes offered thousands of dollars to aldermen in exchange for monopolistic rights to the city's streetcar business. In order to secure one streetcar franchise, Yerkes gave four aldermen $25,000 each and $8,000 to

Downtown Chicago around 1910. Chicago Historical Society

each of the remaining aldermen who voted for his franchise. The pivotal actors in the Harrison-Yerkes traction wars came down to two figures: "Bathhouse" Coughlin and "Hinky Dink" Kenna. Coughlin and Kenna rejected Yerkes' $150,000 bribe, sided with the mayor, and dealt the multimillionaire a crushing defeat. "Keep clear of th' big stuff," explained Coughlin of the matter. "It's dangerous. Stick to th' small stuff; there's little risk and in th' long run it pays a d——d sight more."[10]

In Progressive Era Chicago, Harrison's civic reform was all that was possible. The failures of his mayoral successors make that clear. Edward Dunne, who followed Harrison into the mayor's office, served from 1905 to 1907 and was a forthright moral and political reformer. Embracing nearly every Progressive reform of the day, Dunne filled the city's appointive positions with political outsiders, university professors, and social workers. He briefly won Chicago the reputation of being the most radical city in America; detractors called Dunne a socialist whose advisors consisted of long-haired men and short-haired women. Dunne turned his attention to the traction fight and advocated the most extreme solution possible: municipal ownership of the city's streetcars. Although such arrangements are commonplace today, they were novel proposals that seemed dangerously socialistic in 1905. Despite cries of protest from private businessmen, Dunne's municipal-ownership solution was wildly popular in Chicago. Hard-core reformers applauded the mayor's vision.

Dunne failed to deliver. Despite the popularity of his proposed solution, he lacked the political savvy to see his proposals through the city council. Moreover, Dunne foundered on the shoals of moral reform. He hoped to steer a middle course between Harrison's policy of open alliance with Coughlin and Kenna, which alienated the dedicated moral reformers, and wholesale war on vice, which would have deprived Dunne of the council votes needed to enact municipal ownership. Harrison had at least won the friendship of the vice lords; Dunne succeeded only in alienating nearly everyone. The fatal blow came when Dunne decided to enforce the Sunday saloon closing laws, to raise the liquor license fees for especially notorious saloons, and to revoke the licenses of about one hundred city saloons. Many Chicagoans turned against Dunne, indicating that beer was more important than city-owned streetcars. Dunne left city hall as a failure.

His successor, Fred Busse, fared little better. Busse served as mayor from 1907 to 1911. His appeal to voters was threefold. First, he was untainted by corruption or dishonesty. (More candid observers said that this was because Busse was a dull bachelor who lived at home with his parents.) Second, Busse presented himself as a businessman's reformer who rejected Dunne's more radical reform proposals. He would solve the municipal ownership debate, not by resorting to socialist solutions, but rather by means of his sharp businessman's acumen. Third, Busse denounced Dunne's moral reform efforts and promised a wide-open city.

Like Dunne, Busse made little headway regarding the streetcar issue. Like Dunne, Busse reluctantly found himself embroiled in political fights that deprived him of his political capital. Most damaging was his succumbing to public pressure and appointing the city's first full-time vice commission. This was tantamount to a declaration of war against Coughlin, Kenna, and the Lords of the Levee. By 1911, Busse had alienated the hard-core Progressives, the immigrants who sought free-flowing beer, and the aldermen from the vice districts. He was dead politically.

The stage was set for Harrison's four-year return to the mayor's office in 1911. He began by displaying the political agility that had marked his earlier terms. He applauded architect Daniel Burnham's urban beautification proposals, thus winning points with the reformers. Aldermen such as Coughlin and Kenna believed that Harrison posed no threat to them, so they supported him as well. Harrison attacked his chief rival, the hard-core reformer and famed University of Chicago professor Charles E. Merriam, as a closet prohibitionist, helping Harrison to win the immigrant vote. Then Harrison crafted a simple campaign promise that appealed to many voters: he would provide cheap utilities to Chicago's hard-working citizens.

Harrison won the election, only to discover that the political environment had changed dramatically since his earlier mayoral tenure. Progressive ideals, especially those regarding political reform, had sunk deeply into Chicagoans. City schoolteachers were dutifully indoctrinating their charges with the Progressive gospel. Arthur Holitischer, a German tourist who visited a city school in 1912, noted: "A little thirteen-year-old Bohemian stands and talks about *recall, referendum, and initiative.* The whipper-snapper ends: 'We must see to it that senators are elected directly. *There is nothing the people need more than direct legislation,'* and sits down at his desk! I'm thunderstruck. What the Devil—are we in the Congress in Washington or an elementary school?"[11] Support for Progressive political reform ran deep in Chicago.

At the same time, the moral reform issue—which Harrison had finessed in the past—now defied compromise. Two things brought the vice issue into the open. One was the vice lords' own lack of discretion. Coughlin and Kenna's annual First Ward Ball, which was a grotesque display of ribaldry, lasciviousness, and decadence, became more and more public each year. The unwritten rule had been that vice had to be kept under wraps. Chicagoans chafed, however, when the First Ward Ball's public parade through the city's streets was led by the ward's two aldermen arm-in-arm with garish prostitutes or when the First Ward's annual party hosted twenty thousand drunken revelers in 1908. Such open vice led to the 1910 creation of the Chicago Law and Order League, which had the avowed purpose of cleaning up the Levee.

Also complicating the vice issue were Mayor Busse's policies. Shortly after Harrison returned to the mayor's office, the vice commission established by Busse released a bombshell report. It disclosed that the vice problem in Chicago was far worse than many had imagined. It announced to a stunned city that one thousand brothels, eighteen hundred pimps and madames, and at least four thousand prostitutes preyed on local residents. It also estimated that annual vice revenues reached $60,000,000.

It is doubtful that Coughlin, Kenna, or even Harrison were surprised. The average Chicago voter, however, was mortified. All knew that prostitution existed in the city; few guessed that the problem was as serious as the vice commission report disclosed. Many Chicagoans demanded a full-scale war on vice, but Harrison equivocated, knowing such a war would spell his political demise. Unable to resist the mounting calls for a massive clean-up operation, Harrison finally succumbed. He closed the famed Everleigh Club in 1912, fired his police chief, reorganized the police department, and sent police into the Levee in 1914. As he expected, Harrison was isolated politically. The hard-core reformers dared not trust the slippery Harrison, and the vice aldermen turned against their former ally. Harrison left office a bitter man in 1915. To the end, Harrison attacked wholesale moral reform as naive and ultimately counterproductive. He later asked rhetorically, "Is Chicago . . . more moral or a better place to live in today than was the Chicago of 1893?" He continued, "Under pressure in 1914 I closed the red light district. . . . My action did not end the evil, it merely scattered it . . . and brought it close to the homes."[12]

JANE ADDAMS AND HULL-HOUSE

Whereas Chicago politicians could claim only qualified successes in their reform efforts, Jane Addams's activities proved enormously successful. Unlike Harrison, Dunne, or Busse, Addams faced no pressure to appease competing interest groups. Few Chicagoans found fault with Addams and her style of reform.

Addams was an Illinois native who graduated from Rockford College in 1882. She was one of a growing number of educated, well-informed, middle-class women who had earned a college degree. Addams, like many other educated women in late-nineteenth-century America, now found herself with a dilemma. Most career paths were closed to women in the 1880s. Women could neither vote nor hold political office. Women ministers, lawyers, factory workers, college professors, and industrialists were unheard of. As a general rule, only young single women worked outside the home in clerical or service jobs; that was not a career, however, as it was expected that these women would return home once they married.

A trip to London in 1887 provided Addams with her life's purpose. There she saw Toynbee Hall, an experimental settlement house founded in 1884 by Oxford University students. The students, all of whom belonged to the upper echelons of society, procured a large home in the heart of London's slums and took up residence there. The project aimed to reduce class antagonisms between the upper and lower classes. To this end, the Oxford students did not dispense charity but rather sponsored social, educational, and cultural activities at Toynbee Hall.

As with many projects, this one was democratized as it crossed the Atlantic Ocean. In 1889, Addams and Rockford College classmate Ellen Gates Starr opened Hull-House in an old mansion on Chicago's South Halsted Street. Their concern was less with class antagonisms than with the hardships confronted by Chicago's numerous immigrants. English-language classes were offered. A dining hall provided inexpensive meals. A gymnasium and Chicago's first public playground afforded recreational opportunities. Guest speakers, many of whom were professors from the University of Chicago, delivered high-brow lectures to assemblies. (The 1903–1904 Sunday evening lecture schedule, for example, included a talk on the English lake country and a recital of "The Alcestes of Euripides.") One immigrant to Chicago later recalled how Hull-House had played a critical role in her childhood: "I remember the red brick Hull House well. My mother used to press three pennies in my hand and send my sister and me two blocks to the House, where we were showered, cleaned, and sent to an 'open air' room to dry off. Later, we spent our three pennies for a bowl of lentil soup, a bologna sandwich, and a glass of milk."[13] Music and dance classes were staples. By 1907, Hull-House occupied thirteen buildings and an entire city block.

Some Hull-House activities were designed simply to make immigrants' lives more bearable. Others helped immigrants adjust to life in Chicago. Still other activities attempted to foster in the immigrants a sense of cultural and ethnic pride. For example, the Hull-House Labor Museum was dedicated to preserving artifacts from immigrants' lives in the Old Country. Addams described the museum as an "educational enterprise which should build a bridge between European and American experiences in such wise as to give them both more meaning and a sense of relation."[14] One exhibit consisted of various European spinning wheels and distaffs. They were displayed next to a demonstration of modern factory spinning. The purpose was to show the immigrants and their children that their work in Europe had constituted a meaningful and necessary stage on the evolutionary path toward modern spinning. Immigrants could be proud that they had served a useful function in Europe and were now playing another vital role in America.

Hull-House demonstrated the compassionate side of the Progressive Era's reform impulse. Despite caring for nearly two thousand people each day, reformers such as Addams were genuinely concerned for the individual immigrant. One Chicago immigrant, this one a budding poet, recalled that the ubiquitous Jane Addams made time for individual conversations with her residents: "We had problems and Jane Addams was always there to straighten them out for us. She was like a mother to us; she was our protector and our advisor. It was a great alliance based on nobility and understanding. . . . One day I showed Jane Addams some of my poetry, some verses I had published here and there. She became interested. She was always ready to give advice."[15] Middle-class women such as Addams, excluded from other vocations by prevailing notions of gender, eschewed comfort to live in the squalid ghettos with thousands of immigrants.

Hull-House also spawned a variety of other urban reform movements. Mary E. McDowell, who founded the University of Chicago Settlement House in 1894, waged a bitter, protracted, and ultimately successful fight against city hall over garbage disposal. The city paid a disposal company $475,000 annually to dump the city's garbage into an enormous pit near McDowell's settlement house. After nineteen years of fighting, she led representatives of the city's major women's organizations into a meeting with Chicago's mayor, who soon halted the trash-dumping practice. The

Hull-House was more than a boarding house. It served as school, infirmary, museum, cultural center, daycare facility, public bath, gathering place, kitchen, and home away from home for hundreds of thousands of Chicagoans. Chicago Historical Society, IChi-19288; Barnes-Crosby photograph

settlement houses also created "milk stations" to guarantee the quality of milk being sold in the city. Lucy Flower and Hull-House's Julia Lathrop helped create a special juvenile court in Chicago. Rather than prosecuting and sentencing young lawbreakers in "adult courts," juvenile courts could draw upon a newly created system of foster homes and detention centers for wayward youths.

Alongside of Addams's secularized social work, both Protestants and Catholics operated institutions that resembled the more famous Hull-House. The Salvation Army operated rescue missions in Chicago by 1892. Edward Fielding left the Salvation Army to form the Volunteers of America in 1896. By 1898, the Volunteers of America mission home in Chicago was lodging about fifteen thousand people per month; Mayor Harrison praised the Volunteers of America for their "good work . . . especially in regard to the waifs and homeless children."[16] Italian Michele Nardi, a former *padrone,* operated Italian relief houses in the city. Nardi's missions included vocational schools for children, morning kindergartens, Sunday schools, sewing schools, and English classes that used the Bible as its textbook. Italian-born Frances Xavier Cabrini came to Chicago in 1899 and opened a school. She returned in 1903 to found Columbus Hospital and later founded Mother Cabrini Hospital, in 1911. For her work among the urban poor, Mother Cabrini later became the Roman Catholic Church's first American saint.

By 1911, 413 settlement houses had been established in the United States, including 32 in Chicago. Although the Henry Street Settlement in New York City had been established first, most turn-of-the-century American settlement houses were patterned after the more famous Hull-House. Until the New Deal in the 1930s, the urban settlement houses in America remained the primary source of assistance for needy city dwellers. Addams's Hull-House continued to function on South Halsted Street until the early 1960s. In 1963, it sold its thirteen buildings to accommodate construction of the University of Illinois's new Chicago campus. The original Hull mansion and a dining hall were preserved as the Hull-House Museum.

ARCHITECTURE, DANIEL H. BURNHAM, AND THE CHICAGO PLAN

One of the Progressive Era's chief themes—a veritable infatuation with efficiency and rational management—extended to the geographical, or spatial, aspects of America's cities. In an attempt to impose order upon ad hoc urban development, many embraced modern city planning for the first time. Their hope was that, instead of cities growing according to the whims of market forces and private investors, professional city planners would ensure orderly, rational urban growth. At the same time, Progressives hoped these planners would be able to preserve some sense of aesthetic balance in the cities. Chicago soon became a leader in what was often referred to as the City Beautiful movement. The driving force behind these efforts was Daniel H. Burnham.

Burnham was by trade an architect, not a city planner. In late-nineteenth-century Chicago, however, local architects were busy redefining and professionalizing their field. Before about 1885, urban architects in the United States were little more than draftsmen. It was not their job to be creative, largely because building technologies did not allow them to be. Many simply designed whatever their clients requested, which resulted in a hodgepodge of urban buildings that were either boringly functional or garishly expressive. What was lacking was a sense of order, rationality, and elegant beauty.

Chicago's architects responded, founding what became known as the Chicago School of Architecture. Led by men such as William LeBaron Jenny, Louis Sullivan, Martin Roche, William Holabird, Dankmar Adler, John Wellborn Root, and Burnham, the turn-of-the-century Chicago School married function and aesthetics. Local architects created useful, practical buildings that were also physically attractive. They also took upon themselves the job of preserving a modicum of beauty in the downtown area. This meant resisting the sometimes less aesthetic impulses of their clients. As the city's self-appointed guardians of order and beauty, the Chicago architects crossed a critical threshold: they regarded themselves as *professionals* who were honor-bound to maintain the standards of their trade. In this regard, they contributed to the phenomenon of professionalization in Progressive Era America.

Unlike New York City architects, who often built plain buildings or imitated European styles, Chicago architects broke all the rules. They used wide glass windows to make their buildings appear lighter. They mastered the science of acoustics and built auditoriums with outstanding acoustical capabilities. Louis Sullivan's Carson Pirie Scott building was designed to entice women customers into the department store: ornamental ironwork decorated both the external facade and the internal radiators, large glass display windows exposed the store's goods to passers-by, and a cavernous entrance was designed to lure pedestrians into the store. Chicago architects also invented the modern skyscraper. They pioneered the technique of sinking sturdy caissons into the soil as foundations for heavy skyscrapers. They invented the steel-skeleton frame building: instead of building walls of brick (which required six-foot-thick walls on big buildings and limited building heights to five stories), a steel frame bore the building's weight, while relatively light walls hung from the frame. Buildings could now soar to unheard-of heights (which required Chicago builders to perfect the elevator). These innovations encouraged further architectural explorations, such as Frank Lloyd Wright's Prairie School.

The Chicago School's overriding architectural themes—rationality, beauty, efficiency, and functionality—were easily translated into urban planning themes. It was this move from architecture to city planning that made Daniel H. Burnham famous. Burnham first displayed his penchant for marrying architecture and planning at the 1893 World's Columbian Exposition, designing and overseeing construction of the magnificent White City. By implication, Burnham's work there had shown that beauty need not be sacrificed for function and that careful planning could yield both beauty *and* functionality.

Burnham's White City launched his career as the foremost apostle of the City Beautiful movement. His municipal redevelopment plans for Washington, D.C., Cleveland, and San Francisco expressed the hallmarks of the City Beautiful movement: wide, uncongested, and beautifully landscaped boulevards to replace the crowded, dingy streets of most major cities; a generous supply of grassy plazas and municipal parks in the downtown area; and grand buildings sporting classical architecture. Burnham returned to Chicago in 1907 and crafted an urban redevelopment plan for his hometown. "Chicago in common with other cities," observed Burnham, "realizes that the time has come to bring order out of chaos incident to rapid growth, and especially to the influx of people of many nationalities without common traditions or habits of life."[17] From the beginning, Burnham's proposals were breathtaking in scope. Planning had to be grandiose, according to Burnham. "Make no little plans; they have no magic to stir men's blood," he counseled urban planners. "Make big plans, aim high in hope and worth, remembering that a noble, logical diagram once recorded will never die, but long after we are gone will be a living thing, asserting itself with ever-growing insistency. Remember that our sons and grandsons are going to do things that would stagger us."[18] He followed his own advice in submitting his 164-page Chicago Plan in 1909. It was nothing if not grandiose. To begin with, the plan did not merely address the needs of the downtown or even the city. Instead, it reached in a sixty-mile radius from Chicago, as Burnham foresaw the extensive suburban growth that would come in the next half century. His Chicago Plan was probably the first truly metropolitan or regional plan in America; heretofore, city planning either confined itself to the city proper or appended parks to the city's fringes.

Burnham advocated replacing the crowded city streets with several wide, landscaped boulevards. He allocated significant parcels of land for city parks, with special attention focused on a proposed twenty-mile-long park that would stretch along the shore of Lake Michigan. To accommodate this new lakeshore park, Burnham called for relocating the city's railroad lines and depots, which at that time ran between Michigan Avenue and the lakefront. Michigan Avenue was to be transformed into "a high-grade shopping street."[19] The Chicago Plan also called for construction of a new civic center and a beautification project for the historically filthy Chicago River. Burnham also anticipated the transportation problems that later confounded metropolitan commuters. Although few Chicagoans owned automobiles in 1909, Burnham recommended both an extensive road system that would connect the suburbs with the central city and a beltway that reached from Kenosha, Wisconsin, to Michigan City, Indiana. Hamlin Garland, who listened to Burnham explain his proposals, said, "I, for one, came to think of him with surprise as a poet, a dreamer, one who was dwelling in the far future."[20]

The audacious scope of the plan almost guaranteed that it would not be implemented in full. Even so, many of Burnham's ideas became reality. Chief of among these was the lakefront park and Burnham's suggestion that a lakefront boulevard follow the shoreline and park. His appeal to Chicagoans for such a showcase avenue proved overpowering: "Imagine this supremely beautiful parkway, with its frequent stretches of fields, playgrounds, avenues, and groves, extending along the shore in closest touch with the life of the city throughout the whole waterfront. What will it not do for us in health and happiness? After it is finished will the people of means be so ready to run away and spend their money in other cities? Where else can they find such delightful conditions as at home?"[21] From Burnham's Chicago Plan was born the city's famous Lake Shore Drive as well as Grant Park, Navy Pier, and Northerly Island. One of Burnham's proposed arterial boulevards was located in almost the same place as today's Eisenhower Expressway. Burnham also proposed double-decked Wacker Drive and Union Station.

Burnham died in 1912 and never saw the Chicago Plan translated into reality. Executing the plan fell to the Chicago Planning Commission, an agency that was born in the wake of the Chicago Plan's publication. The Planning Commission's head, Charles Wacker, devoted much of the remainder of his life to fulfilling Burnham's sweeping plans for Chicago. It was Wacker who oversaw construction of Grant Park during the 1920s, a park built on two hundred acres of lakefront landfill. More than anything else, Burnham's proposals legitimized city planning in Chicago. Residents debated and amended Wacker's activities, but few questioned the salutary nature of urban planning.

* * * *

In 1904, journalist Lincoln Steffens, in *The Shame of the Cities,* described Chicago this way: "First in violence, deepest in dirt; loud, lawless, unlovely, ill-smelling, new; an over-grown gawk of a village, the teeming tough among cities. Criminally it was wide-open; commercially it was brazen; and socially it was thoughtless and raw."[22] Although largely accurate, this assessment fails to express how Chicagoans struggled to reform their city during the Progressive Era. They did not remake their city in twenty years and eradicate all ills. No urban Americans did. But they made some headway in combating some of the most serious problems facing the city. Progressive reform efforts led to many sweeping changes, from fighting corruption to creating a more aesthetically pleasing downtown. The age of Progressive reform reshaped Chicago, and the "teeming tough among cities" smoothed a few of its rough edges.

CHAPTER NINE

WORLD WAR I AND

THE ROARING TWENTIES,

1915 - 1929

• On one level, World War I had little effect on Chicago. America was a combatant in the war for only slightly longer than a year, a period of time insufficient for the nation to mobilize fully for the war. Few local businesses, for example, retooled and converted from peacetime to wartime production. Accordingly, World War I did not have the revolutionary social and economic consequences that World War II did. On another level, however, the war had a significant indirect impact on the city. It unleashed anti-German sentiments that severely affected the city's sizeable German population. The war also drove Chicago employers to hire large numbers of African American laborers, which triggered a historic migration of southern blacks to the city. The war also convinced politicians that ethnic and national allegiances remained strong among the city's numerous immigrants. As they responded to and capitalized upon that reality, enterprising politicians transformed the complexion of local politics. These dynamics, along with the exploits of infamous gangsters such as Al Capone, made the years between 1915 and 1930 momentous ones in Chicago.

THE GREAT WAR AND THE GERMAN COMMUNITY

Contemporaries called the war that erupted in Europe in 1914 the Great War because it was unprecedented in scope. It involved all of Europe's major states (Great Britain, France, Russia, Germany, Austria-Hungary, Italy), many smaller European states (Bosnia, Serbia, Bulgaria, Rumania, Greece, Belgium), the Ottoman Empire, and numerous European ethnic peoples (Czechs, Slovaks, Poles, Croats). After remaining neutral throughout 1914, 1915, and 1916, America declared war on Germany, Austria-Hungary, and the Ottoman Empire in April 1917. By this time, all the major combatants had suffered heavy casualties. When the first American soldiers finally filled European trenches and saw combat in October 1917, their presence tilted the scales in what had been a bloody stalemate. Germany requested an armistice in late 1918 that ended the war.

Hence the American role in the Great War was brief. American soldiers saw battlefield action for only fourteen months. Moreover, America's war mobilization effort proved to be slow and inefficient. Few United States businesses engaged in the thorough, long-term conversion to war production that they would during World War II. To be sure, some Chicago businesses profited handsomely from the war. The magazine *Commerce* reported that, in one thirty-day period during 1917, the army's Depot Quartermaster's Department in Chicago spent more than $100 million on food, clothing, and equipment. Even so, the brevity of the Great War, at least from the American perspective, prevented it from triggering the social revolution within America that World War II later did.

The war's impact on local German Americans, however, was significant. On the eve of World War I, the German community in Chicago was strong and vibrant. German Americans were one of the largest and most highly assimilated ethnic groups in the city, enjoying higher incomes than nearly every other ethnic group and residing in Chicago's nicest neighborhoods. In short, German immigrants had achieved success in Chicago, as they had across the nation. Historian Melvin G. Holli conjectures that in 1914 German Americans were the most favored ethnic group in the United States.[1] German Americans retained aspects of their cultural heritage, such as the city's annual German Day parade, several German-language newspapers, and German names for city streets, schools, hotels, and clubs, but local Germans did not trumpet their ethnicity as did, for example, the Irish.

When American boys went to war to fight Germany and to kill Germans, many Americans became suspicious of German Americans. Hostility against German Americans mounted throughout America, fueled by British propaganda that portrayed Germans as bloodthirsty Huns who bayoneted babies. Anti-German sentiment was so acute nationwide that it resulted in efforts to purge German language from the American vocabulary. Anglo-Americans refused to use the German word *sauerkraut*, instead referring to it as *liberty cabbage*. The *German Shepherd* dog became the *Alsatian* during the war. The *frankfurter* and the *hamburger* sounded like German cities; they became the *hot dog* and the *Salisbury steak*.

Chicago's large German population made the city a hotbed of anti-German sentiment. The annual German Day parade was canceled in 1916. The city's Johann Schiller statue was defaced with yellow paint;

when overly patriotic Chicagoans threatened the Goethe monument, city officials stored the landmark in a warehouse for protection. Some local businesses fired German American employees. The city's Bismarck Hotel renamed itself the Hotel Randolph, while Chicago's Kaiserhof Hotel became the Hotel Atlantic. The Chicago City Council renamed nearly all local streets that sported Germanic names, thus eliminating from the city Berlin, Hamburg, Frankfurt, and Rhine Streets. Goethe Street was one of the few Germanic street names to survive the war.

Chicago's German American community did not respond by fighting back. Local Germans instead distanced themselves from their German heritage. They hoped that the hysteria would pass if they laid low, refrained from drawing attention to their ethnic heritage, and proved themselves model American citizens. Some local German Americans accordingly Americanized their names. Local German social clubs renamed themselves: the Germania Club became the Lincoln Club, and the Kaiser Friedrich Mutual Aid Society became the George Washington Benevolent Aid Society. Indeed, the number of Chicagoans who identified themselves as German dropped dramatically during the war years. In 1910, 191,000 Chicagoans identified themselves as German-born; in 1920 that number fell to 112,000, a decrease far too great to attribute to natural factors or to relocation. Many Chicagoans of German ancestry simply stopped reporting that they were German.

There can be no doubt that the Great War had an immediate impact on the city's German community, and evidence suggests that Chicago's German Americans continued to downplay their ethnicity after the war. Chicago today boasts museums or historical archive depositories for the city's Lithuanian, Ukrainian, Polish, Swedish, Jewish, and black communities. No similar institution documents the city's significant German community, although German Americans made up the largest single ethnic group in Chicago in 1890. Local German Americans apparently felt so vulnerable that they made little attempt to preserve their ethnicity. Chicago's German Americans survived; they did so by sacrificing the preservation of their ethnic heritage.

AFRICAN AMERICANS, THE GREAT MIGRATION, AND THE RIOT OF 1919

World War I had an equally profound effect on Chicago's African American community. Only thirty thousand blacks lived in the city in

1910, making the African American community smaller than the city's Polish, German, Russian, Italian, Swedish, Irish, and Czech communities. About three-fourths of the city's blacks lived in the South Side's "Black Belt." This long, narrow patch of Chicago reached south along State Street for more than thirty blocks and was usually only a few blocks wide.

Travel restrictions related to World War I brought an end to the millions of Europeans immigrating to the United States. That meant that the supply of cheap immigrant labor ended as well. At the same time, many Anglo-American men left their jobs to serve in the military. The labor shortage emboldened some remaining workers to press for higher wages. In order to beat back those wage demands, employers sought a ready supply of eager workers who could function, often unwittingly, as strikebreakers or wage deflators. Faced with that variety of pressures, employers in many northern cities made a historic decision: they hired black laborers.

Throughout the South, blacks responded with zeal. They flooded into northern cities in numbers so great that historians now refer to the exodus as the Great Migration. One scholar goes so far as to describe the movement as "after emancipation . . . the great watershed in American Negro history."[2] All told, 1.5 million blacks left the South for the North between 1910 and 1930. During the years between 1910 and 1920, the black populations doubled in Chicago, Detroit, Buffalo, and Cleveland, while black communities grew by 50 percent in eight other cities. Fifty thousand southern blacks settled in Chicago alone between 1916 and 1919, and an additional 120,000 African Americans settled in the city during the 1920s.

It was not difficult to convince poor southern blacks that Chicago was a veritable Promised Land. In the South, African Americans commonly earned $2 to $3 per week as tenant farmers or as sharecroppers; in Chicago, working men in 1916 earned $2 to $2.50 per day. "The reason why I want to come north," explained one Georgian migrant, "is why that the people don't pay enough for the labor that a man can do down here."[3] Southern blacks also faced oppressive racial discrimination. Chicago promised relief from the injustice that all southern blacks knew firsthand. "When white and black go into the courts of the north," exalted one Georgia man as he spoke wistfully of Chicago, "they all look alike to those judges up there."[4] Thus blacks came north for two reasons: the "push" factor of southern racial discrimination and the "pull" factor of significantly higher wages.

Southern blacks learned that Chicago was a twentieth-century Land of Milk and Honey primarily from the *Chicago Defender*, the city's black newspaper and arguably the most influential black newspaper in pre–World War II America. Founded in 1905 by Robert S. Abbott, a black Georgian who came to Chicago in 1899, the *Defender* was an outspoken critic of southern racial discrimination. Pullman porters, who were usually black and stationed in Chicago, distributed copies of the newspaper as their trains stopped in numerous small southern towns. By 1920, its circulation was 230,000. The *Defender* implored southern blacks to flee their white oppressors and to head north. "I beg you, my brother, to leave the benighted land," read one *Defender* editorial. "Get out of the South. . . . Come north then, all you folks, both good and bad. . . . The *Defender* says come."[5] Blacks did face obstacles in Chicago, the newspaper admitted, "perhaps a few more than their white brother, but none they could not surmount." The real appeal, however, was high-paying employment. "Every kind of labor is being thrown open," the *Defender* reported in 1916.[6]

Southern blacks heeded the calls of prosperity and justice. "My people grab it like a mule grabs a mouthful of fine fodder," reported a black Louisianan.[7] They flooded into Chicago and found jobs in the city's steel mills, food-products industries, Pullman car shops, steam laundries, and tanneries. African Americans entered the meatpacking houses in droves: between 1915 and 1918, the number of blacks employed there skyrocketed from one thousand to twelve thousand. Others took jobs as porters, waiters, servants, janitors, and elevator operators, because even these menial jobs paid better than sharecropping.

Most black Chicagoans lived in one of the most segregated areas in America, the South Side's Black Belt area. Wentworth Avenue was the boundary that separated the Black Belt from the adjoining Irish neighborhood. No one crossed the line. With the notable exception of housing, however, most blacks enjoyed a measure of freedom unparalleled in the South. One African American newcomer recalled getting on a Chicago streetcar for the first time and seeing blacks sitting next to whites. "I just held my breath," she remembered, "for I thought any minute they would start something. Then I saw nobody noticed it, and I just thought this is a real place for Negroes."[8] Writer Langston Hughes, who grew up in the Black Belt, recalled its vibrancy: "South State Street was in its glory then [c. 1918], a teeming Negro street with crowded theaters, restaurants, and cabarets. And excitement from noon to noon. Midnight was like day. The street was full of workers and gamblers, prostitutes and pimps, church folks and sinners."[9]

Of special interest was the black entertainment district, which stretched along State Street from Thirty-first to Thirty-ninth Streets. Referred to as "The Stroll" by locals, this area became one of the jazz capitals of the world. Scattered throughout the Stroll were "black-and-tans," or integrated jazz clubs, which featured black entertainers and were patronized by both black and white customers. In an otherwise strictly segregated city, jazz and dance provided the elixir that made possible interracial talking, flirting, and socializing. The freedom with which the races mixed in these clubs was one reason Chicago (and not New York) became known for its sincere and down-to-earth jazz. "There was a lot more mixing of the races in Chicago at that time than there was in New York," observed "Willie the Lion" Smith, who played for several months in the South Side's Fiume Club. "I sure found the 'toddlin' town' to be real friendly."[10] Louis Armstrong, Joe "King" Oliver, and Jelly Roll Morton performed in such South Side cabarets as the Dreamland Café (with its eight-hundred-person capacity dance floor), the Royal Gardens Café (later renamed Lincoln Gardens), the Sunset (later renamed the New Grand Terrace), the Savoy, and the Plantation Café.

The size of Chicago's rapidly growing African American community eventually provided them with a modicum of political power in the city. Oscar DePriest was elected alderman in 1915, becoming the city's first black city council member. Influential white politicians, such as William "Big Bill" Thompson, who served as Chicago's mayor from 1915 to 1923 and again from 1927 to 1931, began to court the city's African Americans. Thompson's predecessors had no reason for doing so because the city's black community was so small; during the Thompson years, however, the growing black population made courting the Black Belt politically expedient. Thompson curried favor with local blacks through both symbolic acts (such as banning the race-baiting movie *Birth of a Nation* from the city) and substantive acts (such as almost tripling the number of black policemen). By 1919, the South Side's Louis B. Anderson had joined DePriest on the city council and was serving as Mayor Thompson's city council floor leader. Thompson's mayoral reelection in 1919 was due in large measure to his overwhelming support among Chicago's African Americans, which prompted the *Chicago Defender* to crow that it wielded more political power in the city than all the other local newspapers combined.

Despite such victories, the Chicago Riot of 1919 proved that all was not well for blacks in Chicago. At first glance, the uprising of 1919 was a classic race riot that pitted blacks against whites, but the riot was more complicated than that and resists simplistic racial explanations. It was, however, caused by several post–World War I dynamics that existed in multiethnic Chicago.

The 1918 conclusion of World War I brought frustration, not jubilation, to many of Chicago's ethnic groups. Local German Americans, angry, frustrated, and seemingly powerless, watched as the Allies imposed a harsh postwar settlement upon their European countrymen. When President Woodrow Wilson refused to give Italy land that it had been promised in secret wartime deals, local Italians protested the insult to their country. Local Poles and Jews fought openly in city streets over alleged anti-Jewish pogroms in Poland. One June 1919 confrontation saw 8,000 Jews assemble at Twelfth Street and Kedzie Avenue in the Jewish section of Lawndale to fend off an anticipated invasion by 5,000 Poles; police thought the rumor credible enough to dispatch 250 additional officers to the area. One month later, 3,000 Poles filled the streets near Eighty-fourth Street and Buffalo Avenue after hearing a rumor that a local Jewish grocer had killed a Polish boy. The city's Jewish press was so alarmed at what it perceived as anti-Semitism that it spoke of "pogromists" in the city. Local Irish Americans clamored for Irish independence from Great Britain; when Ireland was denied autonomy in the postwar settlement, Chicago's Irish community grew embittered over a war that had seen the Americans assist the despotic British. Former mayor Edward Dunne fanned the aspirations of the city's Irish by joining a delegation that traveled to France after the war to consult with U.S. President Woodrow Wilson about Irish independence. Dunne returned with Eamon De Valera, a noted Irish nationalist, who held three days of rallies and meetings in Chicago only two weeks before the 1919 riot began. De Valera addressed twenty-five thousand Chicagoans in Cubs' Park about Irish nationalism, ethnic pride, and British oppression.

These war-related tensions were exacerbated by economic conditions. In 1919, a brief but sharp economic recession hit the nation at the same time that local workers demanded higher wages and better working conditions. At one time in 1919, 250,000 Chicagoans were on strike, threatening to strike, or locked out by their employers. Even the city's policemen and firemen were considering striking. Returning soldiers found their jobs occupied either by members of European ethnic groups or by blacks. Moreover, white Chicagoans could not help but notice that the city's small Black Belt was no longer small. Virtually no new housing had been constructed during the war years, which meant that the city faced an acute housing shortage. The shortage guaranteed that there would be friction on the borders of ethnic neighborhoods as one enclave attempted to enlarge itself and to secure more housing at the expense of some other group. Nowhere was this more serious than on the South Side, where the black population, which had doubled during the war years, desperately sought more housing. In the two years before the 1919 riot, white Chicagoans had bombed twenty-six homes because African Americans had sought housing in white neighborhoods.

By mid-1919, Chicago was a powder keg of ethnic and racial tensions. Violence might well have broken out between Jews and Poles, and one meatpacking industry official testified before a 1919 fact-finding commission that "he understood there was as much friction between Poles and Lithuanians who worked together in the Yards as between the Negroes and whites."[11] It was racial violence that erupted in July 1919, however. Several black boys were swimming in Lake Michigan at their own "private" spot, a location between the segregated Twenty-fifth Street beach (which was for blacks) and Twenty-ninth Street beach (which was for whites). This time, however, the boys drifted in the direction of the whites-only beach. A white man onshore began throwing rocks at the boys. One of the rocks struck a swimming boy, Eugene Williams, in the forehead, and the unconscious boy slipped under the water and drowned.

Williams's terrified buddies swam to shore and found a black policeman at the Twenty-fifth Street beach. Together, the boys and the policeman marched to the Twenty-ninth Street beach and located the man who had killed Eugene Williams. The white policeman on duty, however, would not arrest the man and refused to permit the black policeman to arrest him. The boys ran back to the African American beach, explained what was happening, and returned with a furious crowd. One black man was arrested, whites and blacks threw bricks and rocks at each other, and gunshots rang out. Six days of citywide rioting began.

White gangs patrolled the city and beat isolated blacks, while African Americans beat whites who dared to venture into the Black Belt. White gunmen drove through the South Side in automobiles, shooting bystanders. John Mills, a black stockyard worker, was riding home when a mob stopped his streetcar and beat him to death. Casmero Lazeroni, an Italian street peddler, was pulled from his horse-drawn wagon and stabbed to death. One white reporter counted six black corpses lying near Fourth Street and Broadway, each with both hands above their heads as though pleading for mercy. The riot only ended when the Illinois National Guard entered Chicago. By that time, fifteen whites and twenty-three blacks had been killed, another five hundred Chicagoans had been injured, and more than three thousand city residents had been left homeless by arsonists. Several other U.S. cities weathered race riots in the summer of 1919, most notably Knoxville, Omaha, and Washington, D.C., but the Chicago riot of 1919 was the largest. In a curious way, however, the Chicago race riot demonstrated the power of the city's growing black community. The riot occurred because African Americans were posing real challenges to members of white ethnic groups, especially in the pursuit of jobs and housing. It was because black Chicagoans were obviously becoming more significant in the local political economy—not because they were weak or marginal—that insecure white Chicagoans lashed out against them. In addition, local African Americans, most of whom were recent migrants from the South, displayed a militancy in defending themselves that they had rarely displayed in Dixie.[12]

The Chicago riot of 1919 was clearly a race riot: all violence was between blacks and whites. The riot must be understood, however, within the context of post–World War I ethnic tensions. It was only in the charged atmosphere of 1919 that violence erupted. For example, when a similar incident occurred in June 1920—two white men were shot and killed in the Black Belt during a black parade—no riot erupted. The summer of 1919, with its seething ethnic tensions, had passed.

Southern blacks had come to Chicago seeking the Promised Land. In some ways, they found it. African Americans certainly enjoyed more civil liberties than they had in the South. They could send their children to schools that, though not as good as schools in the predominantly white neighborhoods, were vastly superior to schools in the South. They were able to vote, which secured for them a small amount of political power. They held jobs that, though inferior to those held by many white Chicagoans, paid much better than jobs in the South. The jobs paid cash wages that provided black Chicagoans with a measure of economic independence that many had never before enjoyed. Unlike many European immigrants who came to Chicago between 1890 and 1915, black migrants quickly embraced the city's mass consumer culture. Black Chicagoans spent their newfound earnings at cabarets, baseball games, department stores, clothiers, and automobile dealers, thereby enjoying a standard of living that was unimaginable among Mississippi sharecroppers or Tennessee tenant farmers. The *Chicago Defender*, however, understated the extent to which black

Chicagoans were marginalized in the local political economy. In the South, African Americans confronted de jure racial discrimination; in Chicago, they confronted an equally formidable system of de facto discrimination, something that became clear when blacks sought adequate housing outside the Black Belt or bore the brunt of angry whites during the 1919 riot. In the 1920s and 1930s, moreover, no one could see the glass ceilings that Chicago's blacks would soon hit. Their occupational advancement, housing possibilities, earnings, enjoyment of social equality, and educational opportunities were sharply limited by Chicago's whites. This would become obvious in the late 1940s, the 1950s, and the 1960s.

THE PROSPEROUS 1920S

During the 1920s, Chicagoans and Americans nationwide enjoyed one of the most prosperous decades in U.S. history. Jobs were plentiful, wages were high, and labor unrest was minimal. Chicago steel mills produced 17 percent of all the steel made in America, and city businesses manufactured one-third of all the radios produced in America. A booming economy meant that more Chicagoans could afford the newfangled automobile. Car registrations in the city jumped from 90,000 in 1920 to more than 400,000 in 1929.

Economic prosperity, the extension of streetcar lines, and the proliferation of the automobile fueled a home construction boom during the 1920s. Local builders' specialty was a single-family dwelling that became known as the Chicago bungalow. Although the 1926 *Home Builders Catalog* described a typical model as having "spacious, well-arranged rooms [that] insure living comfort," 1920s-era Chicago bungalows were small by today's standards: they had two bedrooms, one bathroom, a living room, a dining room, a kitchen, and about one thousand square feet of finished living space.[13] They sported the most modern conveniences, such as ceramic tile bathrooms, built-in kitchen cupboards, bedroom closets, and sometimes an electric chandelier in the living room. The sturdy brick homes were packed into city blocks, often sitting on lots one hundred thirty feet deep but only twenty-five feet wide, with a mere six feet separating adjoining bungalows. In front of the home was a tiny but painstakingly manicured front lawn; behind was an alley designed to facilitate garbage removal that functioned also as urban playground and ball field. Residents often spent warm summer evenings packed onto their small front porches, where they conversed with each other and with neighbors who strolled up and down the sidewalks. One hundred thousand of the popular brick-and-hip-roofed homes were built in the inner-ring suburbs or in the unincorporated areas of Cook County during the decade. The city's Southwest Side, for example, which reached from the Black Belt west to the city limits, became a virtual sea of nearly identical Chicago bungalows. In 1910, Berwyn, Oak Park, and Evanston—all towns adjacent to Chicago but located in Cook County—reported populations of 6,000, 19,000, and 25,000 respectively; by 1930, those three towns had grown to 47,000, 64,000, and 63,000 people, many of whom lived in the modest but functional Chicago bungalow.[14]

Nowhere was 1920s prosperity more evident than in the Loop. The most impressive of the many new downtown buildings was the Merchandise Mart, which was begun in 1928 and completed in 1931. The Mart was the largest commercial building in the world, with ninety-seven acres of floor space. The Stevens Hotel (which sported three thousand rooms and qualified as the world's largest hotel, now known as the Conrad Hilton), the Palmer House, and the Medinah Athletic Club, later renamed the Radisson Chicago Hotel, were some of the most impressive hotels in the world. Other Loop landmarks that were built during the decade include the Wrigley Building, the Tribune Tower, the Palmolive Building (today's Playboy Building), and the Board of Trade Building. In the economic prosperity of the 1920s, money was readily available for the construction of imposing buildings on expensive Loop real estate.

The 1920s were far from idyllic, however. The second Ku Klux Klan made an appearance in Chicago, as it did in many other northern cities. The first Ku Klux Klan, which had flourished in the South in the late 1860s and the 1870s, was a strictly anti-black organization. The second Ku Klux Klan, however, was more of a nativist movement that thrived in the North and the Midwest during the early 1920s. Largely an Anglo-American backlash against the millions of new immigrants who came to America between 1885 and 1915, the second Klan embraced "100 percent Americanism" and attempted to restrict the seemingly growing power of immigrants, Roman Catholics, and Jews. Eighteen Klan organizations flourished in the city, and another twelve functioned in suburban Cook County; area membership was between forty thousand and eighty thousand. This second Klan styled itself as the defender of Christian America and old-fashioned morality. Indeed, the hymn "Onward Christian Soldiers" was sung at a 1922 rally in Oak Park that drew twenty-five thousand Klan members and sympathizers.

PROHIBITION AND THE CHICAGO GANGSTERS

Prohibition took effect in Chicago and across the nation in January 1920. The culmination of nearly a century of temperance advocates' efforts, the Eighteenth Amendment and the subsequent Volstead Act banned the production, sale, and consumption of alcohol. It was the last hurrah of the Progressive movement, the final act of social reform in an era marked by reform. Progressives believed that Prohibition would curtail poverty, strengthen families, reduce crime, and encourage good government. Prohibition was, in the words of President Herbert Hoover, "a great social and economic experiment, noble in motive and far-reaching in purpose."[15]

America's great experiment proved an equally great failure. Middle- and upper-class Americans—those who could afford to pay premium prices—turned alcohol consumption into a status symbol. Far from demonizing alcohol, Prohibition actually glamorized it. Suppliers met the demand. They illegally distilled alcohol, diverted alcohol earmarked for legal uses into beverage production, and smuggled alcohol into the United States. The federal government never invested the kind of resources necessary to enforce Prohibition: at its peak, the Treasury Department employed only three thousand "revenuers" to police a two-billion-dollar industry. In 1925, the Assistant Secretary of the Treasury estimated that his agents seized only 5 percent of all the liquor smuggled into the United States. At the same time, 10 percent of all the government revenue agents were fired for corruption.

As in other large cities, alcohol was easy to find in 1920s Chicago. Prohibition was defied openly and on a large scale, and many Chicagoans were involved in the illegal liquor business either as suppliers or as consumers. Federal law notwithstanding, fifteen city breweries operated at capacity in 1924 and supplied beer to the city's twenty thousand speakeasies, or undercover saloons. Chicagoan Stanley Kell later recalled that bootleggers hid their liquid gold in his church. "I used to go to Sacred Heart Church," remembered Kell. "The man that used to distill the booze and beer used to hide it in the basement of the church. Revenue officers would never believe that the church was the sanctity for the beer. I remember going down in the basement of the church, the beer smell was there. I'd say: what are all those barrels of beer doing here? And good Father Healy, he used to be quite a little devil with all that beer down there."[16] Chicago Police Chief Charles Fitzmorris reported that 60 percent of his police officers were involved in the bootleg business, receiving money from Chicago bootleggers in exchange for their silence. The Genna Gang in the Little Italy neighborhood, for example, paid police officers between $15 and $125 per month, and police captains received $500 monthly.

The story of the city's infamous 1920s gangsters and bootleggers begins with James "Big Jim" Colosimo. The pre-1920 master of Chicago's prostitution and gambling rackets, Colosimo was urged by his associates to expand into the new field of bootlegging with the dawning of the Prohibition era. Colosimo balked, and soon thereafter he was shot to death. His execution was probably ordered by his partner, Johnny Torrio, who resented Colosimo's decision to stay out of the liquor business. Torrio assumed control of Colosimo's empire and immediately expanded into bootlegging. Torrio also hired a young thug from New York City as an assistant. His name was Alphonse Caponi, better known as Al Capone.

Torrio's move into alcohol prompted other Chicago criminals to do likewise, which inaugurated the so-called Beer War. By the mid-1920s, the city was home to at least a dozen major bootlegging gangs. The names of the most powerful gangs indicated the ethnic basis of most operations: O'Banion, Saltis, O'Donnell, Aiello, Genna. The largest was the one established by Torrio, but he was by no means the liquor boss of all of Chicago. The city resembled feudal Europe, with each gang claiming its fief. Gangs might occasionally cooperate to knock off a rival, but they might just as easily turn against former allies. It was survival of the fittest among city gangsters, with two hundred gang killings between 1920 and 1924. When Torrio narrowly escaped an attempt on his life, he retired to the relative safety of southern Italy and turned over his empire to Al Capone. It was Capone who transformed Torrio's operation into a citywide syndicate that controlled almost all alcohol in Chicago. By 1930, Capone and his minions boasted an annual income of seventy million dollars.

In Capone's heyday, gangland murders were routine. The seventy-six slayings in 1926 constituted the highest yearly count. As other organized crime leaders before him had done, Capone paid many city policemen, politicians, and judges for what amounted to permission to sell alcohol. Chicagoans could easily purchase beer or any other form of alcohol; the quickest way to get a drink was simply to ask a policeman for directions to the nearest speakeasy. One undercover Prohibition agent reported that upon arriving in Chicago it took him only twenty-one minutes to purchase alcohol. Crime, corruption, beer, and liquor

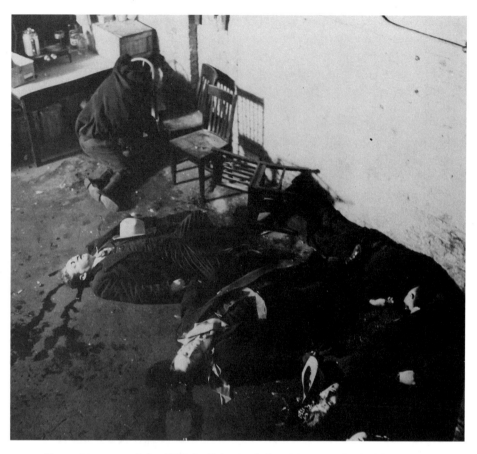

The ruthlessness of the 1929 St. Valentine's Day Massacre shocked both Chicagoans and the nation. For years to follow, "gangland slayings" and "Chicago" were synonymous for many Americans. Chicago Historical Society

were all present in abundance. Not until the infamous St. Valentine's Day massacre of 1929—when Capone's men executed seven members of the O'Banion gang—did Chicago's Beer Wars come to an end. That killing allowed Capone to consolidate his control over the city, making violence less necessary. In some ways, however, the picture of Chicago's lawless Roaring Twenties has been distorted.

Chicago in the 1920s was not a war zone where innocent citizens were gunned down routinely. Law-abiding Chicagoans did not live in fear for their lives. If a Chicagoan stayed away from the gangsters and their illegal business, he or she could walk the city's streets unafraid of crime and violence. Gangland crime was directed almost exclusively against other gang members; gangsters avoided killing innocent civilians and never mugged pedestrians on city streets. This "gangster code of ethics" was displayed in the mid-1920s attempt on Capone's life. Rival gangsters loaded into several cars, drove slowly by Capone's headquarters in Cicero's Hawthorne Hotel, and sprayed thousands of bullets into Capone's room. Rather than shoot over a busy city sidewalk, however, which might kill innocent pedestrians, the gangsters put gunmen with blanks in their guns in the lead vehicle. When that first car slowly cruised past the hotel and fired hundreds of blanks, pedestrians fell to the sidewalk for safety. Gunmen in subsequent cars could now shoot safely over the prostrate pedestrians (in fact, the shooting continued for ten minutes). In the same manner, Chicago's gangsters rarely killed elected officials, policemen, and judges (unless they were taking money from gangsters, in which case they were fair game). To be sure, gangland violence was fierce and widespread. Perhaps the worst aspect of Chicago's gang activity was the atmosphere of lawlessness that it fostered. Even law-abiding citizens could not help but acquire a jaundiced view of the law as they saw gangsters, policemen, politicians, storekeepers, and judges flouting the nation's Prohibition laws.

Initially, in the early and mid-1920s, the public did not demand an end to the city's gangsterism. That changed in 1929 with the St. Valentine's Day Massacre, which presented Chicago in an extremely bad light to the nation. Throughout much of the 1920s, however, most Chicagoans were either unaffected by the gangsters or were their customers. The bootleggers simply provided goods that many otherwise law-abiding Chicagoans demanded. They were not forcing people to drink beer or to come to speakeasies. Al Capone put it this way: "If people didn't want beer and wouldn't drink it, a fellow would be crazy for going around trying to sell it. I've seen gambling houses, too. . . . I've always regarded it as a public benefaction if people were given decent liquor and square games."[17] Capone carefully cultivated a positive public image, living in a modest two-flat at 7244 South Prairie Avenue with his wife, son, mother, sister, and two brothers. He also maintained a palatial Florida vacation estate, but the curious could satisfy themselves that Capone was a decent family man at heart. Capone sometimes paid the medical bills of enemies whom his toughs roughed up, and he occasionally distributed coal, groceries, and clothing to the poor. Many law-abiding Chicagoans saw him as a swashbuckling hero and cheered him when he attended Chicago Cubs baseball games or visited the horseracing tracks. Voters also elected an acknowledged friend of the bootleggers, William "Big Bill" Thompson, to serve as mayor from 1915 to 1923 and again from 1927 to 1931. William Dever, who served as mayor from 1923 to 1927 and declared war on the gangsters, saw his administration crumble in part because of his Prohibition enforcement policies. Breaking Prohibition laws simply was not deemed by the public to be a serious crime.

Chicago in the 1920s provides an excellent stage for viewing the supreme irony of Prohibition. Many Progressive reformers—most of whom were Anglo-American, middle-class, and well educated—pursued Prohibition as a way of limiting the power of European immigrants. Prohibition would ostensibly end the urban machines' beer parties, which would diminish the machines' appeal to immigrant voters and thereby result in lower voter turnout among immigrants. Prohibition also promised to close America's numerous saloons, most of which were owned and operated by immigrants. Instead of further marginalizing immigrants, however, Prohibition simply gave them a new means to gain political and economic power. Immigrants took the lead in supplying thirsty Americans with illegal alcohol.

That was certainly what happened in Chicago. Organized crime had existed in Chicago long before the 1920s and Prohibition. Early "gangsters" such as Mike McDonald had carefully managed the city's vice empire in the post–Civil War years. McDonald, like most of his nineteenth-century cronies, was of Anglo-American heritage. A 1920s study of organized crime leaders in Chicago, however, disclosed that nearly all local gangsters were recent immigrants: 31 percent were Italian, 29 percent were Irish, 20 percent were Jewish, 12 percent were black, and none were native Anglo-Americans. Capone's enormous success rested in his ability and willingness to forge alliances with gangsters from other ethnic groups. Unlike his predecessors and competitors, Capone was willing to work with, for example, black gangsters on the South Side. Capone allowed them to operate their speakeasies and night clubs as long as they purchased their alcohol from Capone's men or gave Capone a percentage of their revenues.

The correlation between newcomers to the city and organized crime is not difficult to understand. These Chicagoans wished to pursue the American Dream of social mobility and affluence as much as anyone. However, they often found their plans blocked by a lack of skills, inadequate education, insufficient financial resources, or Anglo-American discrimination. They therefore turned to a new, wide-open field from which they were not excluded: bootlegging. This industry placed a premium upon toughness and promised big profits. In this light, these newcomers-turned-gangsters appear as stereotypical Americans in terms of their ingenious entrepreneurial spirit and quick mastery of supply-and-demand capitalism.

Also, many newcomers to Chicago shared similar attitudes toward law. In Italy, powerful northern Italians had long used laws as tools of oppression to control southern Italians; most turn-of-the-century Italian immigrants to America were from southern Italy. In a similar manner, Ireland's people regarded law as simply a means employed by the conquering British to subjugate them. Many eastern European Jews, who had endured numerous legally sanctioned pogroms, likewise had an understandably jaundiced view of law. Southern blacks also knew law only as a tool of white oppression. Because of their pre-Chicago experiences, these newcomers to the city tended not to accept laws unquestioningly as embodiments of justice. It is little surprise therefore that these Chicagoans did not attach the same stigma to lawlessness that many Anglo-Americans did. For many newcomers to the city, justice was found only by evading the law. Prohibition seemed to be simply one more unjust law designed only to deprive them of happiness.

The Chicago bootleggers thrived as long as Prohibition lasted. Capone, who was never brought to justice in Chicago, was arrested by federal authorities in 1931 and convicted of income tax evasion. He served almost eight years in federal prison before returning to his home in Miami, where he died of syphilis. Bootlegging continued in Capone's absence, however, until the Twenty-first Amendment repealed Prohibition in 1933. Even then, organized crime did not disappear. Gambling replaced alcohol as the chief source of income for Chicago's underworld. Within one year of the end of Prohibition, the *Chicago Daily News* estimated that the city was home to 7,500 gambling establishments.

BIG BILL THOMPSON AND THE POLITICS OF ETHNICITY

While Chicago's gangsters fought in the streets, its local politicians fought in city hall. Thanks to William "Big Bill" Thompson, the years between 1915 and 1930 were among the most colorful in the city's long history of entertaining politics. Behind Thompson's showboating, however, these proved to be critical years of transition in Chicago politics.

Pre-1915 Chicago politics were very different from post-1931 politics. Before 1915, most local politicians, especially mayors, catered primarily to middle- and upper-class Chicagoans. These wealthy, established, and powerful people—bankers, merchants, lawyers, businessmen, and real estate developers—were the kingmakers in local politics. To be sure, politicians were careful not to antagonize immigrants and working-class voters. They were more careful, however, to avoid alienating the city's commercial-civic elite. Voters displayed little party loyalty, instead rallying around charismatic individuals, such as the two Carter Harrisons. Local politics changed dramatically after 1931, when the Cook County Democratic Party dominated elections by means of its political machine. No longer marginalized, immigrants and working-class Chicagoans became the backbone of the machine. Political victory went, not to charismatic individuals who could elicit personal loyalty, but rather to machine-backed politicians who benefited from voters' loyalty to the machine. These politicians catered to blue-collar voters, often winning their support with urban building programs.

The years between 1915 and 1930 bridged these two strikingly different political eras. The key figure in this transition was Big Bill Thompson, who served as Chicago's mayor from 1915 to 1923 and from 1927 to 1931. To some, Thompson personified the very worst of American politics. He was branded a loud, obnoxious, and uneducated demagogue who appealed to voters' prejudices in his usually successful attempts to win elections. Openly corrupt, he allegedly received significant sums of money from Al Capone. Thompson was the master of the cheap political stunt, a genius at emphasizing style rather than substance. The *Chicago Tribune* stated, "For Chicago, Thompson has meant filth, corruption, obscenity, idiocy and bankruptcy. . . . He has given the city an international reputation for moronic buffoonery, barbaric crime, triumphant hoodlumism, unchecked graft, and a dejected citizenship. He nearly ruined the property and completely destroyed the pride of the city. He made Chicago a byword of the collapse of American civilization. In his attempt to continue this he excelled himself as a liar and defamer of character."[18] A recent scholar of America's cities concludes that Thompson "typified what was wrong with political bosses and machine politics" in urban America.[19]

Thompson was also, however, an extraordinarily successful politician, largely because he did the unprecedented: he unabashedly and vigorously courted the city's many ethnic voters. He had the ability to reduce a complex sociopolitical dilemma into what is today called a sound bite. He was the master of symbolism, which he used to endear himself to the city's polyglot citizenry. He was a political chameleon who unashamedly changed positions to accommodate his constituents; when necessary, he espoused contradictory positions.

During the political climate of World War I, Thompson became convinced that he could win elections by courting the city's immigrant vote. First elected mayor in 1915, Thompson was little different from his predecessors and was even characterized as a reform politician. He fought the local natural gas company and won lower consumer rates. He pledged economy in city hall and reduced the municipal payroll. Like most Republicans, he was not an open supporter of labor unions. He succumbed to pressure from temperance groups and closed the city's saloons on Sunday. By all measures, the early Thompson behaved much as previous mayors had done. By 1917, however, Thompson realized that he was losing his middle-class support. Neither businessmen nor reformers regarded the earthy Thompson as one of their own, especially when he strolled through the city in his Stetson hat and cowboy boots. Their soft support slowly evaporated altogether. When World War I broke out in Europe, however, Thompson realized that ethnic and national loyalties ran deep among the city's many recent immigrants.

Thompson used the war to remake himself politically. He knew that many Chicagoans objected to American entry into the war. The Irish did not wish to aid Britain under any circumstances. The Germans and Austrians opposed going to war against their homelands. Bohemians sought an independent homeland after the war. (When Thomas Masaryk, the famous Czech nationalist, visited the city in 1918, two hundred thousand Chicagoans came out to see him.) Seeing votes he could win, Thompson proclaimed his opposition to American entry into the war. He ingeniously exclaimed that he was an "America First" man: he sought only to advance the interests of the United States and shunned any foreign entanglements. The foreign policy views of an urban mayor mattered little when federal policymakers were deciding American diplomatic policy, but such rhetoric was enormously appealing to Chicago's many ethnic voters.

The only way to appreciate Thompson's skill at what has been called "the politics of image" is to consider several examples of his workmanship. Before swinging a sledgehammer driving the gold spike in 1915 that would signal completion of a new auto speedway in the city, Thompson flashed his union card, to the delight of workingmen throughout the city. In the midst of World War I, French General Joseph Joffre visited the United States, but Thompson refused to extend an invitation to the dignitary. Sensitive to the city's many German American voters, the mayor explained to reporters that Chicago was "the sixth largest German city in the world" and that it would be foolish for any local civic leader to take "the position that all the people are in favor of the invitation."[20] In 1918, Irish Americans nationwide were demanding Irish independence from Great Britain at the conclusion of World War I. Thompson took the occasion to shore up his Irish support by appointing two local Irish Americans to the school board. At the time he explained, "It is difficult to see why we should be indifferent to the situation in Ireland."[21] One week after his victorious 1927 mayoral reelection, Thompson, a Republican, curried favor with the city's large Polish population: he offered the post of assistant city treasurer to Matthew S. Szymczak, a recently defeated Democratic Party candidate for city treasurer. Indeed, Thompson was willing to accommodate all ethnic minorities. In late 1927, he received a group representing the Chippewa, Oneida, Sioux, and Winnebago nations, listened sympathetically to their grievances, and posed for photographs wearing a large Indian headdress. Critics saw these gestures as meaningless political stunts at best and disingenuous demagoguery at worst, but they were actually shrewd responses to the changing nature of Chicago politics. Thompson realized that political victory went to the man who won the city's sizeable immigrant vote.

Thompson never openly criticized U.S. activity in the First World War. He merely refused to support it and instead held to his America First rhetoric. Recent immigrants were grateful to their mayor for establishing a position whereby they could demonstrate a patriotic allegiance to their new homeland (how could someone shouting "America First!" be attacked as unpatriotic?) but nevertheless distance themselves from the war they did not like. Thompson virtually ignored the war and instead initiated one building project after another, much to the delight of the city's ethnic voters. For example, he oversaw construction of a new bridge that linked the Loop with the Near North Side. Upon completion of the bridge, the area experienced a brief renaissance of new construction and business expansion. Between 1915 and 1923, Thompson oversaw the construction of 441 miles of city streets, 230 miles of sidewalks, and 221 miles of sewers. Critics scorned Thompson as unpatriotic, but many ethnic Chicagoans cheered his commitment to building projects that created jobs and patronage.

Thompson's solicitation of the ethnic vote worked. He won reelection in 1919 even though he had alienated most of the city's businessmen. (He had virtually extorted one million dollars from local businesses—

money that went into his campaign fund—by threatening to cancel business licenses. Seething businessmen thus bankrolled Thompson's campaign.) At no time was Thompson's shift to ethnic and class politics more apparent than when he captured the city's growing African American vote. With the help of Oscar DePriest, Thompson established a highly efficient vote-gathering operation in the Black Belt that delivered enormous Thompson majorities. Thompson was careful to reward his faithful black supporters: by the end of his last term, 14 percent of the city's legal department was staffed by African Americans and the number of black Chicago policemen had risen from 50 in 1914 to 137 in 1930.

Thompson's election in 1919 infuriated Chicago's self-proclaimed "better elements." Embarrassed that their mayor was a man whom they regarded as a charlatan and a half-wit, they joined forces to defeat Thompson in 1923. A bipartisan committee selected William E. Dever to run against Thompson. Dever was a model candidate. He was impeccably honest, well bred, and urbane, a prudent reformer who possessed a modicum of political experience. A formidable anti-Thompson coalition took shape that included both Democrats and Republicans. Thompson wisely decided to sit out the 1923 election, and Dever rolled to victory.

The Dever administration was everything that the Thompson administration had not been. Dever proved a sincere good-government reformer and set about cleaning up the mess that he said Thompson had made. He instituted civil service reform, stacked the city school board with reformers, appointed an honest police chief, and built such Chicago landmarks as Midway Airport and Wacker Drive. Gone were Thompson's confrontational politics and gangster payoffs. The national press lauded the artful Dever, who became billed as America's best mayor.

Dever's popularity proved short-lived. He stumbled on the alcohol issue, as other mayors had before him. Dever personally opposed Prohibition, but as a former judge he felt obligated to uphold the law. Somewhat reluctantly, Dever decided to enforce Prohibition to the letter. He proved wildly successful, and within one year national journalists were billing Chicago as the driest city in America. Even the unflappable Al Capone fled Chicago and established his headquarters in suburban Cicero. As the months passed, however, Dever found himself devoting more time to Prohibition enforcement and less time to the reform projects he loved. "I find myself immersed in it [Prohibition enforcement] . . . from morning to night," Dever complained in 1926. "It is almost impossible to give anything approaching good government along general lines [because] this one subject presses so strongly upon our attention."[22] In addition to absorbing all of Dever's time and resources, Prohibition enforcement alienated the city's immigrants, blacks, vice lords, and blue-collar workers. On the eve of the 1927 election, in which he faced a rejuvenated Thompson, Dever staged a massive vice raid. He targeted only Black Belt institutions and arrested more than one thousand African Americans. Thompson did what he did best and "explained" the event in such a manner as to turn ethnic voters against the incumbent Dever: "The Cossacks were trying to bring about a reign of terror. If they do it to Negroes now, how soon before they do it to Jews, to Polacks, to Germans?"[23]

Thompson's decisive 1927 electoral victory over Dever stunned the nation. Members of the national press reported that the nation's best mayor had been defeated by a demagogue. To be sure, Thompson had relied on several outrageous political stunts to win the election. The most infamous was his scandalous remark aimed at Great Britain's King George V. Thompson knew that anti-British sentiment was rife in the city. The local Irish community had always despised all things British, local Germans chafed at the vindictive post–World War I settlement imposed upon Germany by Britain, and many Americans in the 1920s believed that the British had duped them into entering World War I. In 1927, King George set off on a trip to Canada and remarked that he might stop in Chicago to see America's second-largest city. Thompson seized the chance to score points with city voters. He promised to "punch King George in the nose" if he set foot in Chicago. "I want to make the King of England keep his snoot out of America! That's what I want! I don't want the League of Nations! I don't want the World Court! America first and last and always! That's the one issue in this campaign! That's what Big Bill Thompson wants!"[24]

It is difficult to understand how Thompson could turn the king of England into a campaign issue in a Chicago mayoral election. Thompson knew Chicagoans better than most, however, and he knew how deeply ethnic and national loyalties ran. He never intended for his words to be interpreted literally. As historian Douglas Bukowski has argued, Thompson's verbal attack against the king gave ethnic Chicagoans a chance to project their own angers and frustrations on the mayor's feisty defiance of an authority figure. "King" was easily understood as "boss," "millionaire," "policeman," "emperor," "czar," or "kaiser." Thompson's seemingly illogical attack on the king of England was not theater; it was emotional release. Ethnic Chicagoans who were powerless to vent their frustrations enjoyed Thompson's iconoclasm. Thompson also won the 1927 mayoral election by making his usual appeals to the city's immigrants and blacks.

Beer would flow freely in his city, Thompson proclaimed. That pledge helped win him both the immigrant vote and an alleged $260,000 campaign contribution from a relieved Capone. Thompson promised to continue including blacks in his administration, which caused one critic to quip that Thompson was "talking 'America First' and acting 'Africa First.'"[25] Thompson also pledged to remove the highbrow reformers from the school board and to replace them with men preferred by local teachers—a pledge that won him the teachers' votes.

His 1927 defeat of Dever and his return to the mayor's office proved the highwater mark of Big Bill Thompson's illustrious career. He suffered a nervous breakdown in 1928 and accomplished little afterward. Rumors of Thompson's scandalous ties to gangsters circulated; when he died, his safe deposit boxes contained more than $1.5 million in cash. Thompson also had the misfortune of sitting in the mayor's office when the Great Depression began. Like other U.S. cities, Chicago was plunged into a devastating economic tailspin for which Thompson had no answers.

Despite the lackluster record of Thompson's final mayoral term, he had a permanent effect on city politics. The city's commercial-civic elite reluctantly admitted that Chicago's voters no longer looked to them for political leadership. Never again would they play the kingmaker role as they had before the Thompson era. Thompson's unabashed distribution of patronage jobs to supporters (in his early years as mayor, Thompson made thirty-one thousand temporary job appointments to backers) convinced other city politicians that patronage wins elections. Thompson's astounding electoral victories proved that the central reality of Chicago politics was its factious and decentralized character and that such a political environment rewarded conciliators who could keep many parties happy. All this confirmed to politicians that a successful political machine could thrive in the city. Anton Cermak succeeded Thompson as mayor in 1931, relying upon his newly created political machine. That machine was built upon Thompson's twofold recipe for political success: loyal ethnic support and urban building projects. It was Thompson, then, who sowed the seeds of the vaunted Cook County Democratic Party machine. Cermak, Edward Kelly, and Richard J. Daley would reap the harvest.

CHAPTER TEN

THE GREAT DEPRESSION,

WORLD WAR II,

AND SUBURBAN GROWTH,

1929 - 1955

• In late 1934, Chicago's Century of Progress Exposition drew to a triumphant close. Held on 427 acres of artificially created lakeshore land, the world's fair used the occasion of the city's one hundredth birthday to celebrate scientific progress. A total of thirty-nine million visitors marveled at eighty-two miles of exhibits that included a two-hundred-foot-tall thermometer, an African diamond mine, dinosaur skeletons, trendy Art Deco buildings, and Sally Rand's risque fan-dancing. One mile away, in the Loop, fourteen thousand public school teachers rioted. Facing another depression-era school year that would include suspended paychecks, they stormed downtown banks, demanded paychecks, and picketed the city's financial district. Police used tear gas to disperse the teachers. Perhaps the message was that a century of progress does not eliminate turmoil.

That message aptly describes the years between 1929 and 1955. The city was first rocked by the Great Depression; during World War II and the postwar years, it enjoyed economic prosperity. The famous Chicago political machine, which was born in the early 1930s, both flowered and faltered during the next twenty years. An issue that plagued the city for years to come—de facto racial segregation and the controversy over housing for the growing African American population—came to the fore in the 1940s. By the 1950s, many whites were fleeing the city for the new middle-class suburbs. Chicagoans were not so confident in 1955 that they had embarked upon a second century of progress.

ANTON CERMAK AND THE BIRTH OF THE MACHINE

Anton Cermak, who served as Chicago's mayor from 1931 to 1933, stands in stark contrast to nearly all his mayoral predecessors. Born near

Prague to Czech parents in 1873, Cermak came to Chicago as an infant and lived in both the city's ethnic neighborhoods and a small coal-mining town fifty miles southwest of the city. As a young man, he sold wares from a horse-and-wagon along city streets; he developed into a rough and intimidating man with few social graces. At one local Democratic Party convention in 1915, for example, Cermak had a disagreement with West Side leader Timothy J. Crowe. After exchanging personal insults, Cermak asked Crowe to step out in the hall so they could settle their differences. Associates of both political leaders were able to prevent them from coming to blows. One contemporary commented, "Cermak was not a very nice man."[1] Nor was he a gifted public speaker. Cermak seemed the opposite of Chicago's pre-1931 mayors, who tended to be charismatic and affable.

Cermak realized, however, that a winning personality was unnecessary if one managed an efficient political machine. The urban political machine—something found in American cities from New York to San Francisco to Nashville—approached city politics in the same way that a business approaches selling its products. Just as a business has one chief executive officer at the top of its decision-making pyramid, so the machine has one man, the boss, who operates the machine. Bosses were the chief brokers in the sale and purchase of urban political power. They employed middle- and lower-level managers, such as ward captains and precinct workers, to conduct the day-to-day affairs of the machine. Like the businessman, the boss sold products to his "consumers," only his customers happened to be voters. These products included efficient government, public works projects, urban jobs, municipal services, and humanitarian aid. In return, the voters "paid" for these services with votes. In the final analysis, the boss brought order and rationality to the often chaotic world of urban politics.

The machine was so named because of its mechanical efficiency. Every election day, the machine's numerous workers hit the streets to ensure that promachine voters came to the polls. Well-run machines such as Chicago's proved extraordinarily effective in securing lopsided votes. With the machine firmly entrenched in city hall, private businesses were forced to cooperate with the machine on its own terms, as machine opponents were rarely victorious. Private businesses therefore made generous campaign contributions to the machine in order to win a municipal building contract or to prevent unfavorable city council action. That money made it unnecessary for machine politicians to rob the taxpayers or to steal from the city treasury. Any machine expenses were funded by the campaign contributions of private businesses.

Political machines were often viewed as undemocratic. Many believed that they violated the spirit of free, uncoerced elections and camouflaged bribery and extortion as campaign contributions. At the same time, however, the machines delivered on their promises to the voters. Machines provided jobs, built buildings, and offered assistance to the poor. Machines were responsive to voters' needs, which is why many voters willingly trudged to the polls to reelect machine candidates. Diligent machine workers earned the sincere loyalty of voters. As Cermak put it, "Only lazy precinct captains steal votes."[2] With thousands of dollars pouring into the machine's coffers from private businesses, politicians had little need to engage in the petty corruption that had long roused the ire of urban reformers.

In order for a political machine to operate, one did not need a charismatic speech maker like Big Bill Thompson or an artful balancer like Carter Harrison II. What was needed instead was an efficient, organized disciplinarian like Anton Cermak. A veteran of city politics, Cermak took his cue from Thompson. He saw how Thompson won elections by appealing to the city's numerous and various ethnic groups. Cermak's insight was simple. He convinced the city's many ethnic communities that by cooperating with one another they could together build a political machine that would deliver enormous tangible benefits. Cermak warred against the factionalism and strife that would render his machine ineffective; he nurtured unity and collaboration.

Cermak turned to the Cook County Democratic Party (CCDP) to build his machine. Immigrants, Catholics, and Jews had long leaned toward the Democratic Party, and Cermak wisely made his political machine synonymous with the CCDP. Poor eastern and southern European immigrants tended to vote for Democrats already; they became the heart of Cermak's political organization. The CCDP also made running the machine easier. With no party in place, businessmen would need to give their "campaign contributions" to individual politicians. In Cermak's Chicago, however, they could make a campaign donation to a private organization, namely, the CCDP. Had there been no CCDP, it would have been up to individual politicians to disburse funds equitably throughout the machine. With the CCDP in place, however, funds could be disbursed efficiently. The CCDP also provided a necessary buffer for machine politicians. City hall itself was kept clean as a whistle; any questionable financial dealings could take place in the privacy of the CCDP. Cermak seized control of the Cook County Democratic Party in 1928, began building his machine, and prepared for his 1931 run for the mayor's office.

Cermak won the 1931 mayoral election by two hundred thousand votes and became the only foreign-born mayor in the city's history. Some of his positions were predictable. As a Czech American in an immigrant city, Cermak despised Prohibition. (The *Chicago Tribune* called him "the wettest man in Chicago," which was a forceful statement, considering that he shared the city with Big Bill Thompson and Al Capone.) Cermak also championed such perennial reform concerns as administrative efficiency and fiscal restraint. What was new, however, was the way his machine recast the Democratic Party along ethnic lines. Campaigning against the ultimate campaigner in Thompson, Cermak depersonalized politics and stressed the advantages of organizational unity.

Perhaps most surprising was the young machine's effectiveness. Cermak used it to provide a higher level of urban services and to improve life for city residents. Waste, extravagance, and political corruption were minimized. Cermak prided himself on his masterful command of nearly any policy issue. When political opponents tried to smear Cermak with the old politics of personality and rhetoric, Cermak silenced them with a blizzard of facts, research reports, and the conclusions of his many blue-ribbon commissions. "Tony really saw himself as a corporate executive," recalled one insider, "and he thought it was stupid for the top guy not to know everything that was happening."[3] Cermak's opponents also learned that, in order for a machine to work, its opponents must be squashed.

EDWARD J. KELLY, THE DEPRESSION, AND THE MACHINE

Cermak served as mayor for less than two years. In 1933, he accompanied President Franklin D. Roosevelt on the president's visit to Miami. An assassin fired several shots at Roosevelt; they missed the president but killed the mayor. Despite Cermak's death, the machine continued to function. CCDP regulars continued to do their jobs as they had while Cermak was alive. Efficient machines could survive changes in top-level personnel, and Cermak's confidant and assistant, Pat Nash, guided the city through a smooth and uneventful transition. Nash and the CCDP chose Edward J. Kelly as Cermak's replacement, and Kelly presided over the city from 1933 until 1947 without losing an election.

Kelly had made a name for himself in the 1920s as president of the city's South Park Board and chief engineer of the Sanitary District. He and his board had overseen the refurbishing of Grant Park from eyesore to oasis and had brought such attractions as the Shedd Aquarium, the Adler Planetarium, Buckingham Memorial Fountain, and Soldier Field to the lakeshore area. Because he had headed that board, Kelly had been the chief benefactor of illicit "appreciation money" from grateful private businesses. In a curious way, the ill-gained fortune Kelly acquired while president of the South Park Board made him a good choice for mayor. In Chicago parlance, he already had his. Kelly had banked enough money from South Park Board bribes and kickbacks that it was believed he would not succumb to financial temptations as mayor.[4]

The first half of Kelly's administration was dominated by attempts to cope with the Great Depression. The economic tailspin began with the stock market crash of late 1929, and at least some Chicagoans suffered immediately. Howard Worthington, who was working at the time in a LaSalle Street financial institution, recalled, "A friend of mine was making $25,000 a year. They cut him to $5,000. He walked right over the Board of Trade Building, the top, and jumped."[5] The depression had crippled the city by 1931; the city, concluded one scholar, "during the worst moments, virtually ceased to function."[6]

Homelessness reached epidemic proportions. Many Chicagoans lost their homes to banks, as foreclosures in the city jumped from 3,100 in 1929 to 15,200 in 1933. Evictions provoked riots. Chicagoan Lew Gibson recalled an event in the early 1930s: "You couldn't walk three doors without walking into people's furniture [because it had been placed on the sidewalk]. . . . They evicted a lady, she was sick and she had ten or twelve children. They sit her out in the middle of the street. White, colored, they came from everywhere, they had a meeting in front of the house. What I saw was thousands of people gather there and put these people back in their home. They turned the gas and light on and took up a collection. The police wagon drove into a crowd and turned into a riot. I heard the shots. Four people were killed."[7] Shanty towns with homes constructed of cardboard and scrap lumber appeared around the city. One was located at the edge of the Loop on Randolph Street; another three hundred Chicagoans lived in a so-called Hooverville located at the garbage dump at Thirty-first and Cicero Avenues. By late 1931, fifteen hundred Chicagoans slept on the lower level of the Michigan Avenue bridge. "Several hundred homeless unemployed women sleep nightly in Chicago's parks," began one 1931 story in the *New York Times*.[8] Some social workers resorted to herding the homeless into abandoned buildings that lacked water, electricity, heating, and plumbing.

At the root of the homelessness problem was unemployment. By

1932, the unemployment rate in the city had soared to the unprecedented level of 40 percent. The fortunate few who were able to retain their jobs labored for only half of their former incomes. Unemployment was especially acute among the city's African American citizens. Sixty-two percent of all jobs held by blacks qualified as unskilled and service work in 1935 (as compared to 17 percent of all jobs held by whites), and those working unskilled and service jobs were more susceptible to layoffs during tough economic times. One million Cook County residents (or almost one-third of all Chicagoans) received relief money between 1934 and 1937. As late as 1939, industrial production across the nation had returned to 84 percent of its 1929 level; industrial production in Chicago, however, had rebounded to only 77 percent of its 1929 level. Even nonindustrial jobs, such as construction jobs, were scarce. In 1926, 43,000 residential units were built in the city; in 1933, only 137 units were constructed, and only 8,000 new housing units were built in the entire period between 1931 and 1938. Building construction was so slow that many of the city's architectural draftsmen turned to building doll houses.

Like Americans nationwide, Chicagoans experienced deprivation during the 1930s. Ben Isaacs later recalled the humiliation of seeking public welfare: "I didn't want to go on relief. Believe me, when I was forced to go to the office of the relief, the tears were running out of my eyes. I couldn't bear myself to take money from anybody for nothing. If it wasn't for those kids—I tell you the truth—many a time it came to my mind to go commit suicide. . . . I would go stand on that relief line, I would look this way and that way and see if there's nobody around that knows me. I would bend my head low so nobody would recognize me."[9] "There is not a garbage-dump in Chicago which is not diligently haunted by the hungry," wrote journalist Edmund Wilson of the *New Republic*. "Last summer, when the smell was sickening and the flies were thick, there were a hundred people a day coming to one of the dumps, falling on the heap of refuse as soon as the truck pulled out . . . [devouring] all the pulp that was left on the slices of watermelon and cantaloupe till the rinds were thin as paper." Wilson recalled one widow who frequented the dump and hunted for old, discarded meat as well as fruits and vegetables: "She would always take off her glasses so that she couldn't see the maggots."[10]

This was the situation Kelly encountered when he assumed Cermak's job in city hall. Kelly did not end the depression in Chicago, but in his first few years as mayor he did an outstanding job of stabilizing the situation. Political columnist Arthur Krock wrote in 1936, "Chicago still has relief problems, slums, poverty, and great groups of the unemployed. But the difference between present conditions and those in 1932 is the difference between black and white."[11] Kelly's success also ensured the continued vitality of the Democratic machine, in part by winning for the machine the grudging acceptance of the city's business community. Business leaders would never heartily endorse the machine, but at least it had restored some financial stability. Kelly's success also drove a stake in the heart of local Republicans. When Kelly trounced his Republican challenger in the 1935 mayoral election by a lopsided 799,000 to 167,000 count, the Republican loser was amazingly frank: "There isn't much to say except that the results confirm what had been repeatedly published—that the Republican party is completely disintegrated. In fact, there is no local Republican party."[12] Only eight years earlier, Republican Big Bill Thompson had defeated local Democrats at the polls. That was how dominant the machine had become only two years after Cermak's death.

Far from collapsing during the difficult depression decade, the Cook County Democratic Party machine grew stronger. This can be explained in part by the fact that Kelly and the machine gradually won about half of Chicago's black vote. The black community nationwide made a historic shift during the 1930s, deserting the Republican Party, the Party of Lincoln, for the first time and voting for Democrats. Black Chicagoans were less enamored with the local Democratic Party than they were with the national Democratic Party, as local Democrats hid their racism and bigotry behind a thin veneer of New Deal rhetoric. Black support for the CCDP came grudgingly and much later than the support of other voters in Chicago. Immigrant-stock Chicagoans gave overwhelming majorities to the machine, but blacks gave only narrow electoral majorities to Democratic machine candidates. Even so, this stands in stark contrast to the 1920s and the Thompson years, when black Chicagoans voted overwhelmingly Republican.

In the 1940s, Kelly was able to command between 50 and 60 percent of the black vote with the help of William Dawson. Born in Albany, Georgia, in 1886, Dawson graduated from Fisk University in Nashville, Tennessee, and then moved to Chicago to attend law school. After serving in World War I, Dawson earned his law degree and entered the rough-and-tumble world of Chicago politics. He began as a Republican, but by 1939 he had switched to the Democratic Party. By 1942, the Kelly/Nash machine tabbed Dawson as their man in the growing black South Side. The machine replaced its white Second Ward committeeman with Dawson. Dawson preferred national office to a local one: he won election to the U.S. House of Representatives in 1942 and remained in that position for twenty-seven years until his death in 1970. Although New York City's Adam Clayton Powell was the nation's most visible and outspoken black politician during the 1940s and early 1950s, perhaps the most powerful black politician in America during that time was Chicago's Dawson. Much like Chicago's Jesse Jackson in the 1980s and 1990s, Dawson became a national political figure: he traveled the nation campaigning for Harry S Truman in the 1948 presidential campaign, proved especially valuable to Truman in the South by persuading black voters to stick with the Democratic Party, and even served on the Democratic National Committee. Dawson's political clout in Chicago, however, was never as great as his national profile would suggest.[13]

Dawson had hitched his political fortunes to the Kelly/Nash machine. As long as Kelly was mayor, Dawson enjoyed significant political power. In return for delivering the black vote to machine candidates, the CCDP placed a few blacks on the Chicago Housing Authority board, gave several blacks seats on school boards, appointed a small number of black judges, and promoted some blacks to supervisory positions in the police department. The machine never really empowered the African American community, however, and it would be inaccurate to conclude that the CCDP dealt justly with black Chicagoans. The recently coined word "tokenism" best described the morsels thrown to the city's African Americans during the 1940s and early 1950s. Kelly's policies, although minimal by today's standards, were unprecedented in his day.

Kelly's small acts of kindness comported nicely with Dawson's low expectations. A status quo politician who rarely made race an issue, Dawson never demanded progress in race relations and in the 1950s disagreed with the National Association for the Advancement of Colored People's agenda for racial change. "Noncommittal, evasive and seldom takes an outspoken stand on anything. Bill Dawson is, by all odds, ultraconservative," said the *Chicago Defender.*[14] Dawson realized that he delivered few goods to black Chicagoans and did not challenge the city's formidable system of de facto racial segregation. He defended his willingness to go along with the machine despite its shoddy treatment of African Americans by explaining that blacks had no alternative but to work with the CCDP. "We must play the game according to the rules," said Dawson. "I always play it that way and I play with my team. If you are on a baseball team you stick with your team or you may not be able to play much longer."[15] The local NAACP sharply criticized Dawson in the mid-1950s for his unwillingness to press for racial justice. Dawson responded the next year—a year in which the local NAACP elected a new president—by ordering his six hundred precinct captains to join the NAACP and to vote as a bloc to oust the incumbent president who had scolded him. Dawson won this battle and silenced the NAACP.

Dawson's power on the South Side strengthened Edward Kelly's machine, as did Kelly's efforts to solidify the machine's financial base by establishing a cozy relationship with organized crime. When Prohibition ended in 1933, most gangsters returned to the old standbys of gambling and prostitution. The New Deal's protection of labor unions in the 1930s also made labor racketeering increasingly profitable for organized crime. In exchange for political protection, gambling houses and bookies usually split their profits with the machine. That meant that anywhere from $12 to $20 million annually poured into the machine from gambling alone. Chicagoans who wished to gamble could, and, because it was managed effectively, there was little violence associated with gambling. The machine returned a significant portion of this money to the community in the form of constituent assistance, such as the famed chicken-and-shoes welfare baskets. "One thing we ever got from the bad times is the shoes from the Democratic Party," recalled Noni Saarinen, a Finnish immigrant who endured the depression in Chicago. "During election, somebody had brought the basket with the chicken and shoes for my son. One friend of ours used to tease when the boy had those shoes on. He says they are Democratic Party shoe. That's the only thing we ever got."[16] Such small acts of assistance endeared the machine to many city voters.

Kelly also secured millions of dollars for the city in the form of federal New Deal programs. Nearly all of this money was controlled by the machine, which in turn dispensed it to friends and withheld it from enemies. President Franklin D. Roosevelt gave Kelly and the machine such power because, after Kelly's 1935 landslide victory, the machine's political clout was unquestionable. Roosevelt realized that Kelly was the most powerful Democrat in the state of Illinois and could deliver more than a half-million votes on election day. (In Chicago's Twenty-fourth Ward, for example, the vote in the 1936 presidential election favored Roosevelt by an astonishing twenty-nine thousand to seven hundred margin, prompting Roosevelt to call it "the number one ward in the Democratic Party.") These political realities compelled Roosevelt to court Kelly; millions of federal dollars helped secure a fruitful marriage. Roosevelt grew to value Kelly's political advice and often consulted the Chicago mayor.

Kelly warmed to the charismatic Roosevelt and enjoyed his companionship. By the mid-1930s, the Chicago mayor's most popular campaign speech was entitled "Roosevelt Is My Religion."

The New Deal was extraordinarily valuable to Chicago. One of the government's antidepression programs, the Works Progress Administration, brought forty thousand jobs to the city. The machine controlled all those jobs. The WPA and a second New Deal program, the Public Works Administration, embarked on myriad construction projects around the city. For example, during the 1930s the WPA and PWA constructed the seventeen-mile-long Outer Drive (later renamed Lake Shore Drive) along Lake Michigan, landscaped Lincoln Park, built the State Street subway, erected thirty new public schools, introduced the first three public housing projects to the city, enlarged Midway Airport, and built several new parks. For Chicago's unemployed legions, such projects provided much-needed jobs and paychecks. Grateful Chicagoans thanked Mayor Kelly and the machine.

New Deal largesse was not the only reason Chicagoans supported the machine. Kelly proved a capable politician as he teamed up with Pat Nash, Anton Cermak's old adviser, to provide outstanding leadership for the CCDP. Nash wielded behind-the-scenes power and kept the machine functioning on a day-to-day basis. Kelly was the visible face of the machine, devoting his time to campaigning, backslapping, ribbon-cutting ceremonies, and fruitful chats with Washington New Dealers. Perhaps Kelly's greatest political asset was his ability to admit errors, repent publicly, and seek forgiveness, a graciousness that enabled him to turn enemies into friends. No incident illustrates this better than Chicago's 1937 Memorial Day Massacre. At one 1937 strike in Chicago, edgy policemen fired into a crowd of strikers, killing ten men and wounding thirty others. Kelly immediately defended his policemen and blamed the unrest on leftist labor agitators. The federal government investigated the affair and concluded that both Kelly and his policemen, however, had been at fault. In a supreme act of contrition, Kelly met with local labor union officials. He apologized, offered them protection from future police interference (in other words, permission to strike, which was a major concession), and sought only official forgiveness for city hall's role in the shooting. The unionists obliged and later worked for the machine in local elections. Even more remarkable, one steelworker who had his eye shot out in the 1937 Memorial Day Massacre gave Kelly a public radio endorsement in the mayor's 1939 reelection campaign. Such mayoral acts of mea culpa helped the machine pass through what could have been rough waters.

WORLD WAR II

America's World War II home front experience was quite different from that of World War I. The United States was slow to enter World War I and fought for less than two years. As a result, the American home front never fully mobilized for that war effort. Americans did not enter the Second World War until late 1941, but many American businesses had been supplying war supplies to Great Britain since early 1940. Partial mobilization in mid-1941 turned into full mobilization by the end of the year; the United States remained in the war until its end in mid-1945.

Full mobilization began with preparation for enemy air attacks. When air raid sirens sounded, Chicagoans extinguished all lights and sought cover under beds or in air raid shelters. Sixteen thousand volunteer air raid wardens policed the city, searching for the careless who endangered the city's safety by leaving a lamp burning. Chicago journalist Mike Royko was nine years old when the war started. He recalled the air raids from a child's perspective: "The siren would go off and everybody would turn off the lights. He [the air-raid warden] would go around the neighborhood banging on doors and yelling, 'Your lights are on.' He'd write down people's names if they had a little light on in their apartments. I didn't like this. My parents were downstairs running the tavern, so I'd have to turn out those d——d lights. My younger brother and I would sit there in this absolutely pitch-black apartment. We were afraid that if we didn't the air-raid warden would come by and the FBI would come and terrible things would happen."[17] If Royko was more afraid of the air raid warden than he was of the Japanese or the Germans, older Chicagoans remembered that the drills brought the war close to home. The air raid drill and blackout "does something to you. It is a personal experience," remembered one Chicagoan. "There is no personal fear. But the war is no longer far off in London or Chungking."[18]

Perhaps most important, World War II ended the Great Depression, something the New Deal had been unable to do. WPA and PWA work programs prevented Chicagoans from becoming as impoverished as they could have been, but those programs never created prosperity. What did create prosperity were the many war supply contracts that the government placed with private businesses. In order to outfit its armed forces, the government needed an enormous supply of shoes, socks, shirts, pants, jackets, belts, blankets, medicine, and food. It also needed specialized war materials such as tanks, machine guns, artillery shells, fighter aircraft, aircraft carriers, and submarines. Thousands of businesses produced these materials and sold them to Washington at a handsome profit.

In Chicago, for example, the Stewart-Warner Corporation converted from producing automobile parts to making fuses, ammunition boxes, practice bombs, and instrument panels. The Pressed Steel Car Company and the Pullman-Standard Car Manufacturing Company built tanks. International Harvester converted from manufacturing farm machinery to building military tractors, aircraft torpedoes, artillery shells, and huge refrigeration units. Elgin National Watch, possessing expertise in intricate timepieces, made detonation fuses for antiaircraft shells. Abbott Laboratories turned out a new miracle drug for use on the battlefield: penicillin. The new one-square-mile Dodge-Chicago plant on South Cicero Avenue (where the Ford City Shopping Center would later be built) cost $100 million to construct and employed thirty-one thousand people; it manufactured aircraft engines for B-29 Superfortress bombers. The twenty-nine thousand workers at Cicero's Western Electric plant developed radar systems, and the city's forty electronics factories produced half of all the nation's military communications equipment.

War supply contracts pumped nine billion dollars into Chicago's economy, a sum that in the 1940s was almost unthinkably large. Fulfilling the contracts not only put nearly all Chicago men to work but also gave jobs to three hundred thousand local women who filled jobs vacated by men in the military. War-related business also had unanticipated economic benefits. One local corporation, Douglas Aircraft, built 655 C-54 transport planes during the war years. It constructed runways to test its aircraft in Orchard Park, a rural community two miles beyond the city's northwest corner. Later, during the 1950s, the city purchased the old World War II–era runways and transformed the area into O'Hare Airport.

The war brought other kinds of economic activity to Chicago as well. The military required many specialized products that no private business could readily produce; accordingly, Washington funded new industrial and manufacturing facilities devoted to war production. After the war ended, the federal government sold these facilities to the private businessmen who operated them for a nominal fee. These publicly funded industrial and manufacturing facilities were virtual gifts to local communities that had seen little new construction during the long depression decade. By the end of 1943, 267 new facilities had been built in Chicago, and more than 1,000 factories had expanded their production capacity.

Table 5. TOP TEN U.S. CITIES IN VALUE OF WAR SUPPLY CONTRACTS, JUNE 1940 TO SEPTEMBER 1945

city	dollar value of war-related contracts
New York City	$18.8 billion
Detroit	13.9 billion
Los Angeles	9.6 billion
Chicago	9.2 billion
Philadelphia	6.6 billion
Boston	4.7 billion
Buffalo	4.6 billion
Cleveland	4.4 billion
Baltimore	4.1 billion
San Francisco/Oakland	4.0 billion

Source: Robert G. Spinney, *World War II in Nashville: Transformation of the Homefront* (Knoxville: University of Tennessee Press, 1998), 23.

The federal government also built, refurbished, and maintained military facilities across the nation—some as training bases, some as recruitment centers, some as military hospitals. More than $100 million of federal money went toward constructing such facilities in Chicago. One-third of all the men who served in the U.S. Navy during the war visited the Great Lakes Naval Training Center in North Chicago. Army inductees were trained at Fort Sheridan, and ten thousand pilots received training at the Glenview Naval Air Station. The military actually bought the city's Stevens Hotel, at that time the world's largest with three thousand rooms, and used it briefly as a barracks. It and the nearby Congress Hotel together housed fifteen thousand soldiers at one time.

One indicator of the city's wartime prosperity was the renewed migration of southern blacks to the city. Much as World War I had initiated the Great Migration of southern blacks to northern cities, World War II encouraged similar relocations. More than two hundred thousand African Americans came to Chicago between 1940 and 1950, swelling the city's black population to twice its 1930 level. During peak times, more than two thousand southern blacks arrived in the city weekly.

Table 6. TOP TEN U.S. CITIES IN VALUE OF PUBLICLY FINANCED INDUSTRIAL AND MANUFACTURING FACILITIES, JUNE 1940 TO JUNE 1945

city	dollar value of new facilities
Chicago	$926 million
New York City	786 million
Detroit	708 million
St. Louis	478 million
Philadelphia	427 million
Los Angeles	404 million
San Francisco/Oakland	374 million
Louisville	357 million
Houston	350 million
Buffalo	325 million

Source: Spinney, *World War II in Nashville,* 25.

African Americans would later recall that their wartime employment affected them both financially and psychologically. Chicagoan Lois Arthur reminisced about her wartime job:

> I used to be afraid, too, when my children were smaller. I used to say, "Oh, I would like to do something. I would like to vote differently, but maybe I better not. Maybe this will be changed and it'll be good."
>
> I stopped being afraid when I got my first good job. When I got my first big, good—I don't say a big one—the best I ever had, when I got in the defense plant in World War II. I got a good salary. And I didn't even realize then how wonderful it was not to be afraid. I didn't even realize it until . . . later days. But all of a sudden I was just automatically doing what I wanted to do, for the first time since I had the children. But it was money. It was a good, fat paycheck, taking it home every week . . . every week. And it made me feel, well, I was free.[19]

The 1940s also proved to be a seedtime for future reform. George Houser and James Forman founded the Chicago Committee on Racial Equality (CCRE), a group that served as a prototype for the more famous

Congress On Racial Equality (CORE). The CCRE gingerly tested racial discrimination in downtown restaurants and even engaged in what might be called sit-ins. Meaningful progress in civil rights, however, would not come until much later.

In the early years of World War II, one might have predicted that southern blacks would relocate to Chicago. Few could have guessed that Japanese Americans would make their first significant appearance in the city during the war years. In early 1942, the federal government rounded up 110,000 Japanese Americans from the western states and interned them in guarded detention camps, fearing they were still loyal to Japan and therefore posed a threat to the security of the United States. Later, many of these imprisoned Japanese Americans were allowed to relocate to cities far from the West Coast. Nearly thirty thousand moved to Chicago and became the city's Japanese American pioneers. Most were settled in "buffer zones" between white and black neighborhoods in the South Side's Kenwood community or along North Clark Street, which divided the North Side's affluent Gold Coast from slums to its west. Local newspapers supported the Japanese resettlement, local employers eagerly hired the new arrivals, and overt discrimination against the hardworking Japanese was rare. "Simply by looking at the sidewalk you can tell where the Japanese live," marveled one Chicagoan, "because they keep not only the front yard, but also the sidewalk, clean."[20]

Italian Americans were less fortunate. Whereas the city's German Americans had been targets of suspicion during World War I, Italian Americans came under fire in World War II. America was at war with Italy, and some doubted the loyalty of Italian Americans. Chicago's Italians responded much as the city's Germans had responded to World War I pressures: they quickly assimilated. Second-generation Italian Americans in particular were Americanized by the war.[21] Ethnic hostilities had escalated in the city during the First World War, but Chicagoans successfully defused similar tensions during World War II. The *Civilian Defense Alert,* a publication of the city's civilian defense organization, explicitly praised both Italian Americans and German Americans for their loyal support of the war effort.

The Second World War also brought a new entertainment to the city. Many major league baseball players enlisted in the armed forces or were drafted, which meant that professional baseball teams were forced to field a motley assortment of athletes who were unfit for military service. Chicago Cubs owner Philip K. Wrigley feared that major league baseball would not survive the war. As a hedge against the possible bankruptcy of his Cubs team and in an attempt to keep interest in baseball alive, Wrigley in 1943 created the All-American Girls Baseball League (AAGBL). The new league opened in small Chicago-area towns like Kenosha, Racine, South Bend, and Rockford and later fielded teams in Chicago, Milwaukee, Minneapolis, Muskegon, Kalamazoo, Grand Rapids, Fort Wayne, Peoria, Battle Creek, and Springfield. Former major league stars such as Jimmie Foxx were hired as managers. The league survived from 1943 to 1954, at its peak playing in ten cities and drawing one million fans in a season. For Wrigley, however, the AAGBL was strictly a business venture. When it became obvious that major league baseball and the Cubs would survive the war and remain profitable, Wrigley withdrew from the AAGBL.

KELLY'S GRACEFUL EXIT AND THE KENNELLY YEARS

All was not well on Chicago's World War II home front. Edward Kelly was losing his sure grip on city politics, in part because Pat Nash had died in 1943. Nash's gift had rested in smoothing friction among ambitious Chicago Democrats. When Nash died, however, no one stepped up to perform the role of mediator, and discord mounted within the Cook County Democratic Party. Other Chicagoans grew increasingly uncomfortable with Kelly as the machine's connections to organized crime were publicized. The city's public schools were a disaster, so much so that the regional review board threatened to revoke the accreditation of area high schools. Standards in the schools had slipped because the machine gave jobs within the school system to unqualified precinct workers. Improved economic conditions also meant that fewer Chicagoans were dependent upon machine assistance, which freed them to criticize the machine.

It was the race issue, however, that ultimately spelled political doom for Kelly. Chicago's brand of segregation was seen most strongly in the area of housing. All knew the location of (and few crossed) boundaries that separated black neighborhoods from white ones. Racially restrictive residential covenants were also used to prevent blacks from living in white neighborhoods. These legal arrangements, which affected perhaps 80 percent of the city, prevented homeowners from selling, leasing, or renting their property to certain groups (usually to blacks). Even the University of Chicago, a bastion of liberalism, supported such tools of segregation; university board members helped write such covenants for the Woodlawn area in the 1920s. Confined to the Black Belt, African Americans had to deal with a limited supply of housing. When the city's black population doubled during the 1930s and 1940s, the housing supply became grossly inadequate. Desperate African Americans sought housing outside the Black Belt. Kelly defended his loyal Black Belt voters, demanding that Chicago be a city with "open housing" standards, that is, housing based on nondiscrimination.[22]

Chicago's blacks, argued Kelly, should be free to rent and to purchase any housing they desired. He therefore ordered city policemen to protect blacks as they integrated previously all-white neighborhoods. Many of the city's whites, especially ethnic Germans, Irish, and Poles who lived on the South Side, were furious. They resisted the unwelcome invasion of their neighborhoods by blacks, which they called "blockbusting." With Kelly's stance on open housing alienating much of the machine's core constituency, the machine did what it had to do to survive: it dumped Kelly in the 1947 election and instead backed Martin Kennelly.

Loyal to the bitter end, Kelly did not protest. He never considered running for reelection without the machine's backing. Instead, the mayor of fourteen years reportedly said, "The Organization made me. It built me up. It put me where I am. If it's better for the Organization for this thing to be, then so be it."[23] Kelly began campaigning for Kennelly, who swept to victory backed by the machine.

THE CREATION OF THE AMERICAN BLACK GHETTO

Martin Kennelly was an anomaly among modern Chicago mayors. He was incorruptible and soft-spoken. He rarely drank, and he lived in an apartment with his widowed sister. Although he was the machine candidate, he fought the CCDP from the mayor's office. Only one year into Kennelly's administration, the *Saturday Evening Post* marveled at the city's "new moral climate." It was a climate created largely by the squeaky-clean Kennelly. One contemporary remarked that the saintly Kennelly "never should have been mayor of Chicago." Instead, he said, "He should have been a cardinal or monseigneur."[24]

The CCDP chose Kennelly for the mayor's office for just this reason. The machine sought respectability. It had to extinguish the controversies involving corruption, cronyism, and money from organized crime. Kennelly agreed to run as the machine's candidate on one condition: his hands would not be tied by commitments to the organization. The machine agreed to give Kennelly free rein, and a curious eight years followed. Kennelly championed various reforms (his favorites were civil service reform, vice crackdowns, school reform, and better accounting procedures) but accomplished little because he lacked machine backing. The machine continued to function, but Kennelly prevented the organization from accomplishing what it had in the Kelly years. At the end of eight years, Kennelly had provided the machine with much-needed breathing space. The organization was able to shake off its negative image, regroup, and return one of its own to the mayor's office in 1955.

In the meantime, neither city hall nor the machine provided vigorous leadership for the city. This proved especially tragic with regard to race relations in the city. Kennelly inherited the open housing dilemma that had spelled Kelly's political doom, and, at least from the perspective of white politicians such as Kennelly, the situation only worsened in the 1950s. After the city's black population doubled between 1940 and 1950, it increased another 65 percent from 492,000 in 1950 to 813,000 in 1960. Housing conditions in the South Side became unbearable, and blacks sought housing in previously all-white neighborhoods. African Americans managed to break into the West Side—the city's so-called second ghetto—as many Jews and other eastern European ethnic groups moved to the suburbs, pushing the area's black population from 380 in 1940 to 114,000 in 1960; during the same period, the area's white population declined from 102,000 to 11,000. During the 1950s, an average of three-and-a-half city blocks per week shifted from white-majority to black-majority ownership. In the South, the flashpoints of racial conflict were public schools, public accommodations (such as buses), and voting; in Chicago, the flashpoint was segregated housing.

A few months after Kennelly took office in 1947, rioting broke out near the Chicago Housing Authority's Fernwood Park Homes over such blockbusting. More race riots occurred in Park Manor and Englewood in 1949 when small contingents of African Americans attempted to move into these all-white neighborhoods. The 1951 riot in Cicero, just outside the city's western border, made national and international headlines. When a single black family moved into a large all-white apartment complex, angry whites engaged in several days of burning and looting in the apartment building. Order was only restored when 450 National Guardsmen and 200 local policemen subdued the crowd. The riot was front-page news in newspapers as far away as Southeast Asia. A resident of Ghana apparently read of the violence as well. He wrote a letter from Africa to the mayor of Cicero denouncing the city's "savagery" and seeking an "apology to the civilized world."[25]

Kennelly was indecisive. He did not embrace Kelly's courageous but politically suicidal policy of protecting blacks seeking housing in white neighborhoods, but neither did he side with segregationist whites. His middle-of-the-road course, dubbed a policy of "appeasement and persuasion," angered both blacks and whites. It also enabled white Chicagoans, who were far less indecisive, to control the situation. What followed the 1951 riot was the quiet but calculated creation of a carefully circumscribed black ghetto on the city's Near West and South Sides. The black community that had developed in the South Side between 1910 and 1930 had formed and grown in an ad hoc fashion, the response to a swelling in the city's black population. This was not the case with the South Side and West Side ghettos that took shape after 1940. The Chicago Housing Authority (CHA), the city council, and even the University of Chicago made sure that black Chicagoans would stay in the South Side.

The federal government's new post–World War II urban redevelopment programs provided the means for keeping blacks in the ghettos. Federal money assisted major cities in demolishing blighted neighborhoods and in replacing substandard housing with low-income public housing. In Chicago, that meant leveling dilapidated homes on the South and West Sides and replacing them with towering high-rise housing complexes. The city council, the Metropolitan Sanitary District, and the Illinois Commerce Commission all possessed veto power over proposed public housing sites; the CHA extended virtual veto power to aldermen in whose wards a housing complex was being considered before suggesting sites to the city council. This system resulted in forty-nine of fifty-one approved public housing sites between 1955 and 1966 being located in all-black areas. The CHA, the one institution that might have challenged the city's formidable de facto housing segregation, catered to white desires. The city council followed suit. Government decisions effectively reinforced and solidified the city's black ghettos. One example of such decision making demonstrates the city's complicity in housing segregation. Donald Howard, a black World War II veteran, moved his family into the all-white Trumbull Park Homes in 1953. Escalating and sustained white violence against his family created a crisis that demanded resolution. An investigative committee appointed by the city council concluded, "The Howard family has come to stand as a symbol of all the tensions . . . in the Trumbull Homes area; and its removal therefore should be expedited in the interests of tranquility."[26] With no assistance forthcoming from the CHA or city hall, the Howards left the complex four months later. National outcry over the housing conflicts in Chicago never materialized, however, as the birth of the civil rights movement in the South shifted the nation's attention.

Kennelly's abandonment of the black community caused African American voters to question their allegiance to the CCDP. Kennelly then added insult to injury by attacking two important black institutions. One was the "policy wheel" business, or the operation of private lottery games in the South Side. Hundreds of such petty gambling syndicates provided black Chicagoans with inexpensive entertainment, just as white Chicagoans enjoyed numbers games and betting on horses on the North and West Sides. Kennelly attempted to close down these black gambling businesses. The other Kennelly target was the so-called jitney cab. White taxi cabs drivers rarely ventured into the South Side, so black-owned and unlicensed jitney cabs provided much-needed trans-portation in the black community. Kennelly attempted to shut down these unlicensed cabs that were ostensibly depriving the city of money. A furious William Dawson had seen his political power shrink with the replacement of Kelly with Kennelly; now he saw Kennelly deprive his political organization of money from the policy wheel operators, a chief source of its income. Dawson's organization took in perhaps $10,000 every month from policy operators, which Dawson then returned to the community as informal welfare and assistance money. Dawson con-fronted the CCDP and threatened to withhold his support from Ken-nelly in the 1951 election unless the machine pledged that the 1951–1954 mayoral term would be Kennelly's last. A young Richard J. Daley watched as Dawson successfully challenged the machine; when Daley became mayor in 1955, he methodically stripped the African American politician of his clout so he would not face similar challenges.

The 1950s were bleak years for Chicago's African Americans. Kennelly treated them shoddily, unlike Kelly. The housing problem grew worse, and black attempts to seek housing outside the Black Belt exposed the depth of de facto segregation in Chicago. Black laborers earned less than whites for similar work. The one South Side black man with power, William Dawson, chose to embrace rather than to challenge the status quo. At the same time, however, few doubt that black Chicagoans en-joyed a rich and vibrant community in the part of Chicago that came to be called Bronzeville. As Vernon Jarrett, an esteemed African American journalist who once resided in Bronzeville, commented, "The ghetto used to have something going for it."[27] White hostility created among blacks a sense of racial unity. Thousands of black businessmen prospered in the 1950s, in part because white discrimination guaranteed them a loyal customer base. Middle- and upper-middle-class blacks could not flee Bronzeville for the suburbs, so they continued to live in close proximity to the black working class. This prevented neighborhood deterioration in many South Side neighborhoods. Black nightclubs, restaurants, stores, theaters, churches, and other recreational and social opportunities thrived. Perhaps above all else, hope and optimism flourished in 1950s Bronzeville. "It was economically poor," recalled John Stroger, the first black president of the Cook County Board of Commissioners, speaking of the South Side in the 1950s, "but spiritually and socially rich. People had hope that things would be better."

Journalist and political observer Alan Ehrenhalt concludes that black Chicagoans today—when compared with their 1950s predecessors—are freer, confront less oppression and discrimination, and enjoy more individual liberties. But they have lost the virtues of community that they enjoyed in the 1950s.[28] Timuel Black, a lifelong Chicago civil rights activist who settled in the South Side in 1919, agrees. "I would say at this point in my life and experience," reflected Black, then in his seventies, "that we made a mistake leaving the ghetto. Speaking of 1950s Bronzeville, Black recalled: "Within this area we created parallel institutions. We had our own churches, clubs, businesses and our own political base. We built all this because we didn't think we would be welcome outside the community because of our experiences in the South. There was no real strong urge to leave the community because we had everything we needed in our own back yard. . . . We were a village. We were, as the saying goes, 'Our brothers' keepers.'"[29]

THE CREATION OF THE AMERICAN WHITE SUBURB

The relocation of whites to the new suburbs prevented the open housing controversy from completely fracturing the city. Whites abandoned older and less desirable inner-city housing, which made these dwellings available to the growing black population. Exodus from the inner city and growth of outlying areas was not new, both having occurred since 1850, especially between 1890 and 1915. The cycle had been repeated many times in the city's history: newcomers would seek the cheapest housing available (usually older inner-city housing), and the people residing in that inexpensive housing, usually for a generation, would have accumulated sufficient resources to relocate to newer and better housing farther away from the Loop. In 1945, African Americans were the city's most recent newcomers, many having arrived between 1915 and 1945. Blacks did what Poles, Russians, and Italians had done before them—they occupied the cheapest housing in the city.

In the decade immediately following World War II, this movement of people from the inner city to the suburbs accelerated for a number of reasons. By 1945, new home construction had been negligible for fifteen years, leaving the city with a severe housing shortage. Developers knew they could sell hundreds of newly built homes quickly, so they sought large tracts of land where they could construct multihome subdivisions. The search for vast expanses of undeveloped land necessarily drove these builders into the suburbs. Post–World War II prosperity also made the automobile affordable. Most Chicagoans owned at least one automobile, which made commuting from the suburbs manageable. Federal programs for veterans also made buying a new home in the outlying areas easier. Before World War II, most home buyers were required to make a down payment of 50 percent and amortize their mortgages over less than ten years; with a Veterans' Housing Administration loan, war veterans could purchase a home with a down payment of 5 percent or sometimes even with no down payment and amortize their mortgage over fifteen or twenty years. The Federal Housing Administration also liberalized its home mortgage policies in 1955.

Park Forest was a typical postwar Chicago suburb. Built in 1947 on unoccupied farmland, Park Forest occupied four square miles of land, was located thirty miles south of the Loop, and became home to twenty-six thousand suburbanites. Nine out of ten couples there were parents, and nine out of ten children were under age thirteen. In 1952, the community included 682 small two-bedroom duplexes designed for renters and 1,300 larger single-family ranch-style homes that sold for $12,000. Unlike the row houses in Chicago that included almost no yards and fronted busy streets, Park Forest's homes included yards, trees, sidewalks, and quiet roads. Developers also included shopping centers, schools, and churches in the neighborhood. Park Forest's developers actually made little profit on the homes they sold and the duplexes they rented. They made most of their money by providing water to the community (because the developing company also owned the community water works) and by collecting 10 percent of total sales at the Park Forest shopping center. In other words, as William H. Whyte put it in his famous 1956 book *The Organization Man,* "the developers were building a city to provide a sort of captive market—a constantly replenished, unsatiable reservoir of 30,000 people, most of whom would ever be poised at that stage when families just begin to lay up possessions."[30]

Building a suburban community such as Park Forest, however, posed unusual difficulties. All of the residents would be new to the community (because the community itself had been only recently created), so no one would know each other. New renters and home buyers might be reluctant to move into a barren community of strangers. After consulting with psychologists, developers marketed Park Forest as an extraordinarily *friendly* place where personal relationships grew like weeds. As William Whyte put it, they advertised happiness, not homes. Consider one 1952 promotion:

> a cup of coffee—symbol of
> PARK FOREST!
> Coffeepots bubble all day long
> in Park Forest. This sign of
> friendliness tells you how much
> neighbors enjoy each other's company—
> feel glad that they can share their daily
> joys—yes, and troubles, too.
> Come out to Park Forest where small-
> town friendships grow—and you still live
> so close to a big city.[31]

Other Chicago suburbs followed the Elmhurst model. Residents of this sleepy town, founded in the 1840s and located fifteen miles west of the city limits, had ignored Chicago (and Chicagoans had ignored Elmhurst) for years. Blacksmiths could be found plying their trade in the rural town as late as 1950. In 1952, however, developers bought Emery Munson's cornfield and did something no one had ever done in Elmhurst before. They divided the farm into 365 small lots, built mostly two-bedroom ranch houses on each lot, and sold them for $14,000, or a little less than $20,000 for homes with a garage, to Chicagoans fleeing the city. All the homes sold in less than one month. Like the developers of Park Forest, the developers of Elmhurst equated suburban living with happy family living: "Here in Elmhurst," read the promotional literature, "has been developed an entire community where the whole family can share a spirit of togetherness, based upon the soundest family values."[34] Elmhurst's old-timers thought the new subdivision conflicted with *their* family values, however. They did not like the new Emery Manor subdivision, the suburbanites it attracted, or the flooding problems created by all the new concrete and asphalt. They resisted when the same developers proposed a second and larger Elmhurst subdivision, Brynhaven, in 1954. The developers won their campaign to build, and 132 acres of southern Elmhurst was transformed into 500 more suburban homes. Elmhurst's population swelled, leading long-time residents to grumble that Elmhurst was "no longer a small town where you can be sure that there is no one on the streets who does not belong there."[35] Park Forest and Elmhurst were not unique: similar growth was seen in the town of Skokie, which grew from 7,200 people in 1940 to more than 59,000 by 1960, and throughout DuPage County, whose population skyrocketed from 41,000 in 1950 to 155,000 in 1960.

Suburban commuters depended upon their automobiles and therefore demanded more and larger roads. As late as 1925, only thirteen paved roads led out of the city and only two miles of road could carry four lanes of traffic satisfactorily. The Congress Street Superhighway (later renamed the Eisenhower Expressway, a thoroughfare originally proposed by Daniel Burnham in his 1909 Plan of Chicago), the Edens Expressway, and the Calumet Skyway, later renamed the Chicago

Table 7. POPULATION OF CHICAGO AND ITS SUBURBS, 1920–1970

	Chicago	percent change	metropolitan Chicago outside of city limits*	percent change
1920	2,702,000	—	693,000	—
1930	3,376,000	+25%	1,073,000	+55%
1940	3,397,000	+1	1,173,000	+9
1950	3,621,000	+7	1,557,000	+3
1960	3,550,000	-2	2,671,000	+72
1970	3,369,000	-5	3,612,000	+35

* This area consists of the non-Chicago portions of Cook, McHenry, Lake, DuPage, Kane, and Will Counties.

Source: Irving Cutler, *Chicago: Metropolis of the Mid-Continent,* 3d. ed. (Dubuque, Iowa: Kendall/Hunt Publishing Company, 1982), 277.

Skyway, were all constructed between 1945 and 1958. So was the Grant Park underground garage, now made necessary by the armies of commuting Loop employees.

Suburbs and cars encouraged another phenomenon: the fast-food hamburger restaurant. Ray Kroc, a milkshake-mixer salesman and a suburban Chicago native, watched Mac and Dick McDonald do a booming business in their small San Bernardino, California, hamburger-and-shake joint. Kroc brought the concept home and opened the first McDonald's franchise in 1955 in suburban Des Plaines, about ten miles away from what had been Emery Munson's Elmhurst cornfield. Kroc soon bought the franchise rights from the McDonald brothers and perfected the art of squeezing ten burgers out of a pound of meat and selling them for fifteen cents each.

* * * *

By the mid-1950s, Chicago was a city in flux. The economy was good. Many whites were fleeing to the suburbs. Racial tensions were mounting as the growing black population expanded into white neighborhoods. The Loop had seen little new construction since the 1920s; most of the money seemed to be going to the suburbs. Some thought the city might be stagnating. Times were ripe for a strong, dynamic politician who would provide leadership for Chicago. Times were ripe for Richard J. Daley.

CHAPTER ELEVEN

RICHARD J. DALEY

AND THE CITY THAT WORKS,

1955-1976

•   For many Americans in the late 1950s, the 1960s, and the early 1970s, the name Richard J. Daley was synonymous with Chicago. Daley was elected mayor in 1955 and then went on to win reelection in the city's next five mayoral contests. No mortal could remove him from the mayor's office; only a fatal heart attack in 1976 did that. Daley was the undisputed boss of Chicago, the man who perfected the Cook County Democratic Party machine. He controlled everything and overlooked nothing. As the last of the big city bosses in America, Daley might well have been the best in American history at doing what he did: using a political machine to govern a large city.

THE PROBLEM: INNER-CITY STAGNATION

Many Chicagoans were pessimistic in 1955. Enthusiasm, growth, and new construction were found in the suburbs and noticeably absent in the inner city. Not one major new building had gone up in the Loop between 1945 and 1955. Wealthier residents were fleeing the city for the suburbs and being replaced by poorer residents who required more in the way of welfare services. One of the many causes for despair was the city's surfeit of substandard housing. A 1950 survey revealed that the city's 1.1 million housing units included 64,000 units that should be demolished, 180,000 that lacked essential sanitary facilities, and more than 300,000 that had been built before 1900. Louis Kurtz described the Black Belt in 1945: "I have seen pitiful, pathetic, deplorable, rotten and damnable shacks, hovels, lean-tos and hell-holes in my travels, but when you see these Negro families huddled together like cattle in dilapidated wood sheds, garages, ankle-shift huts made of old lumber, old tin signs, cardboard and whatever could be picked up and fastened together as a shelter, one cannot help but realize that, rotten and deplorable as all slum areas are, the 'Black Belt' of Chicago beats them all when it comes to misery at its worst!"[1] The *New Republic* reported in 1951 that, under Mayor Martin Kennelly, "adequate housing, real civil-service reform and trimming of unnecessary city expenditures are no closer today than they were at the end of the Kelly administration." In 1953, the national magazine described Kennelly as "affable and ineffectual . . . numbed by an inability to take firm action for fear of hurting someone's feelings."[2]

Chicago struggled, as did most large American cities. During the 1950s, cities throughout the nation were burdened by an outdated industrial infrastructure, substandard housing, and suburban flight. Most urban political machines, incapable of dealing with these vexing mid-twentieth-century problems, breathed their last. Academics and pundits wondered aloud whether the American city had become ungovernable. They placed much of the blame on the city's decentralized and inefficient political system, a system that privileged parochial neighborhood concerns over citywide interests. A. J. Liebling, for example, concluded in 1952 that Chicago "is less one town than a loose confederacy of fifty wards. Communication between residents of the different wards is limited by the pronounced tendency of immigrant groups . . . to coagulate geographically."[3] Chicago journalist Mike Royko, also speaking of the pre-Daley years, referred to these tightly knit ethnic communities as "ethnic states," and, he observed, "The ethnic states got along just about as pleasantly as did the nations of Europe."[4] During the city's 1955 mayoral campaign, the executive director of the Independent Voters of Illinois issued a clarion call for bold municipal leadership. He concluded with a favorable assessment of one mayoral candidate: Richard J. Daley.

DALEY'S SOLUTION: THE MACHINE

Richard J. Daley was Chicago personified. He was born in 1902 in Bridgeport, an Irish kid in one of the world's largest Irish communities. He also died in Bridgeport; his funeral was held in the same Roman Catholic church where he had been baptized and married. The son of working-class parents, Daley grew up in tough neighborhoods. Those who remember the young Daley recall that he was diligent, hardworking, thorough, and unextraordinary. He was reliable but not charismatic. As an adult, he attended mass daily before showing up for work at city hall. He never swore publicly and was never seen drunk.

Like many ethnic Chicagoans, Daley realized as a young man that politics offered a promising future. In the arena of politics, family, ethnicity, modest means, and a lack of gentility did not close doors. Daley began at the bottom of the political ladder and worked his way up slowly: aldermanic scribe, chief assistant to Cook County treasurer, Hamburg Athletic Association president, Chicago representative to the state legislature in 1936, state senator, budget director for Governor Adlai Stevenson, Cook County clerk, and ward committeeman of Bridgeport's Eleventh Ward. In 1953, Daley was elected chairman of the Cook County Democratic Party.

As head of the CCDP, it was Daley who controlled the party's 1955 mayoral nomination. He pushed out Kennelly, promoted himself as the machine's candidate, and won the election. The new mayor let it be known that the inefficient Kennelly days were over. He threw down the gauntlet to the city council, pledging to use his veto power if the city's aldermen refused to support the CCDP's initiatives. Neither Kelly nor Kennelly had ever vetoed any council action. Daley also demanded that the city council transfer much of its executive power to the mayor's office. To top things off, Daley insisted on remaining head of the CCDP while serving as mayor. As both party chief and mayor, he could impose organization and efficiency on the city's political system and make it yield results.

Daley's consolidation of power in the mayor's office was aided by two demographic phenomena. Throughout the 1930s and 1940s, the CCDP machine's fiercest opposition had always come from the middle-class white Protestants who lived on the city's outlying edges. During the 1950s, however, many of these Chicagoans left the city for new homes in the suburbs. A similar relocation of machine opponents was precipitated by the 1948 *Shelley v. Kraemer* decision, which outlawed racially restrictive housing covenants. This allowed the black middle and upper classes to flee the South Side in search of better housing elsewhere. The black middle class had provided South Siders with viable alternatives to machine candidates; when they fled the Black Belt, poor African Americans had little choice but to submit to machine rule. With his political hand strengthened by the flight of the white anti-machine Protestants and the black anti-machine middle class, Daley was able to turn his attention to something that neither Kelly nor Kennelly could do: waging war against opponents within the machine.

This was not a naked grab for power by a megalomaniac, nor did Daley seek power in order to pad his bank account. Over the next twenty years, millions of dollars were spent investigating Daley. Many assumed that such a powerful man had to be making money illicitly, but no evidence ever pointed to financial impropriety on Daley's part. Daley sincerely sought to make Chicago a great city and to assist hard-working, blue-collar Chicagoans like his neighbors in Bridgeport. He knew he needed political power to accomplish those ends. The lessons of the Kennelly years had been clear to all: the machine was impotent and the city unmanageable unless a strong mayor imposed discipline and provided leadership. All agreed that, without firm leadership at the top, political power would be diffused among the city's fifty aldermen. Each would be most concerned with the interests of his own ward, not with the overall welfare of the city, making the pursuit of citywide goals impossible. Most observers in the 1950s assumed that no one man could crack the whip and make the city's many elements operate in harmony. Daley centralized political power in his own hands so he could crack the whip loudly and thereby accomplish things for the city he loved so much. "The old bosses were not interested in what was good for the public welfare," said Daley in 1963. "They were interested only in what was good for themselves. . . . We're the first of the new bosses."[5]

Daley had run for mayor in 1955 as a reform candidate, earning endorsements from both Martin Kennelly and Illinois governor Adlai Stevenson. As mayor, Daley proved to be a liberal pragmatist and a social conservative. He was a political liberal in that he believed government should take an active role in improving the lives of the people. His bevy of young, energetic assistants briefed him on issues and kept him well supplied with creative proposals. There would be no stagnation in the Daley administration. The mayor was a political pragmatist in that he compromised, cut deals, and tried to give something to everybody. He won back political opponents when possible. He freely granted favors and influence in exchange for the power needed to get things done. In social matters such as racial integration, Daley proved conservative and almost reactionary. Moreover, all agreed that he was a hard worker. As journalist David Halberstam quipped, "He is at early Mass when his enemies are still sleeping, and he is still working on city problems at night when they've all gone to bed or are out drinking."[6]

Daley also knew how to cut his losses when necessary, to sacrifice portions of the machine to keep the remainder alive, and to turn setbacks into victories. One example of this political agility was his handling of the 1960 Summerdale scandal. City policemen were caught operating a burglary ring, and rumors abounded that the scandal would spread to hundreds of city policemen. Daley had long defended his police force from charges of corruption; the Summerdale scandal exposed Daley as ignorant, naive, or a liar. Daley responded by firing the city police chief and replacing him with University of California criminology professor Orlando W. Wilson, an expert in progressive law enforcement. Wilson radically restructured the police department by ending all city hall control of the department and eliminating all department patronage positions, and he halted even small-scale graft. Wilson's reforms deprived the machine of many valuable patronage jobs in the police department—as Daley had anticipated—but it also put an end to local criticism and salvaged the remainder of the machine. The national press hailed Daley as a wise statesman and reformer, and machine regulars saw Daley as a shrewd operator who had amputated an appendage to keep the body alive.

THE ACCOMPLISHMENTS:
MAYOR DALEY BECOMES "DICK THE BUILDER"

Almost overnight, Daley turned Chicago around. He began by eliminating the petty graft that had become commonplace in city hall. Before 1955, for example, anyone who wished to install or to pave a driveway needed a driveway permit. These permits were obtained from city aldermen, who routinely charged between $500 and $20,000 for each permit. Daley immediately took that prerogative out of the aldermen's hands, because he did not want his administration tainted with graft and scandal. City hall began issuing the permits for a uniform fee of $2.75.

Daley also embarked immediately on a massive building campaign that rejuvenated the Loop, provided jobs for many Chicagoans, and pumped new money into the city's economy. Even Daley's harshest critic, Mike Royko, admitted that Daley's first four years as mayor were "four of the busiest, most frantic years City Hall had ever seen without people being indicted."[7] Street lighting was improved. Roads were repaved. Double construction shifts worked to finish the new Congress Street Superhighway (later named the Eisenhower Expressway). More policemen and firemen were hired. Set in motion were myriad additional projects: new high-rise apartments, public housing for the poor, improved medical services, new Loop parking garages, mechanical street

Here is Mayor Richard J. Daley doing what he did best: building. During his tenure, Daley oversaw numerous public works projects that both improved the city's infrastructure and provided jobs for local constituents. Chicago Historical Society

sweepers, a new downtown convention center, modernized lake docking facilities. Historian Paul M. Green judges that "no other major American city at the time created as much public policy enthusiasm as Chicago."[8] By 1959, the city's newspapers were praising Daley as "Dick the Builder." "He had a kind of worship for the pouring of concrete," recalled a local politician. "He liked physical things. He was not interested in ideas, but in getting skyscrapers into the Loop he was effective."[9] Even the city's business community lauded Daley. Businessmen, who had originally harbored deep reservations about the Irish politician from Bridgeport, fearing that he would be another machine stooge, were pleasantly surprised by his determination to revitalize the Loop and his businesslike attitude toward governing the city. Proof of Daley's acceptance among the business community was his 1959 reelection committee: its three cochairmen were the president of United Air Lines, the president of the Association of Western Railroads, and the chancellor of the University of Chicago.

Building continued after 1959. Perhaps no project demonstrates Daley's builder mentality more than O'Hare Airport. Midway Airport, the busiest in the world in 1950 but still adequate for the city's needs, was conveniently located close to the downtown Loop. In 1946 the city had purchased Douglas Aircraft's old airfield, which was located several miles beyond the city's northwest corner, but had done little with the property. Daley set about to turn the ten-square-mile park into the largest airport in America. At the time, no other U.S. city possessed a large airfield located far outside the central business district; all had arrangements similar to Midway Airport. Daley anticipated extraordinary municipal growth, however, and he therefore developed his airport in the wilderness. Daley's project was a smashing success. The airport's parking garage alone represented a formidable undertaking: the largest in the world, it could accommodate 12,500 cars on seventy-nine acres of parking space. O'Hare was a state-of-the-art airport that brought national attention to the city and, not coincidentally, created thousands of new patronage jobs for the machine.

Daley's building projects entirely reshaped Chicago. Rivaling O'Hare Airport in scope were the city's many expressways. "Dick the Builder" presided over the opening of the Eisenhower, Kennedy, Dan Ryan, and Stevenson Expressways. Urban renewal projects and low-income housing enabled Daley to make some improvement in the quality of the city's housing. A 1950 survey had determined that 28 percent of the city's housing units were dilapidated; by 1967, that figure had dropped to 10 percent. Under Daley's watch, the revitalized Loop became home to impressive downtown buildings such as the Marina City Towers, the John Hancock Building, the First National Bank Building, the Sears Tower, the Standard Oil Building, and Water Tower Place. The University of Illinois Circle Campus was also built in the city during the Daley years. Daley even inaugurated an impressive downtown public art project that brought outdoor sculptures by Pablo Picasso, Marc Chagall, and Alexander Calder to the Loop. Chicago enjoyed these improvements with no budget deficits, the highest possible ratings for its municipal bonds, and relatively stable real estate taxes.

Daley's motto as mayor was "good government is good politics." He meant that the surest way to political success was to deliver the goods. Clean, effective government won votes. Even Daley's severest critics admitted that his machine made Chicago a cleaner, wealthier, better-paved, and better-lit city. Unlike America's other large cities, which seemed to be falling apart in the 1950s, Daley's Chicago thrived and became known as *the city that works*.

Daley also knew how to make the city proud of itself. A case in point was the mayor's 1959 reception of England's Queen Elizabeth. With the national and European press watching, Daley orchestrated a masterful show. The city built a special landing dock on Lake Michigan to receive the royal entourage and even dredged portions of the lake so the royal ship would dock smoothly. Daley marked off the streets on which the queen would travel and had them scrubbed. He also had all concrete gutters replaced along the parade route and all relevant traffic lights repainted. At the formal reception, Daley donned a spanking white tuxedo and looked smashing next to the glamorous queen. Daley knew the show was not really for the queen; it was for his constituents. They proudly watched their mayor—a tough Irish kid from Bridgeport—dine with the queen of England. The scene exemplified what Chicago novelist Saul Bellow once said of Daley: "He was like Chicago itself in many ways . . . tough, even crude at times. Yet he had a hidden sophistication and genuine talent and intelligence. I think a lot of Chicagoans are like that, living up to the lowbrow image when they're really not lowbrows at all."[10] Chicagoans saw themselves in their mayor.

THE DAY-TO-DAY WORKINGS OF THE DALEY MACHINE

Daley brought a staggering number of projects to fruition by managing an effective machine. The machine gave Daley what amounted to dictatorial powers in the city. Milton Rakove, a professor of political science who also worked at the lower levels of the machine, bluntly states, "What is probably true of Daley's five terms as mayor is that Chicago has lived for two decades under a constitutional monarchy."[11] Daley was able to acquire such absolute power in part because the voters of Chicago freely gave it to him. Daley never lost a mayoral election, and he won most of them by landslides. Chicagoans proved the validity of Daley's "good government is good politics" maxim. He got things done, so they wanted him as mayor. Furthermore, Daley's machine met the everyday needs of Chicago's voters. After all, voters ultimately controlled the machine's political destiny; the machine was careful to take care of them.

How Daley's machine catered to the needs of the voters is a subject that deserves some attention. Consider this extended observation by Rakove of what happened one evening in the office of one of the machine's ward committeemen. Vito Marzullo was a seventy-seven-year-old grandfather when Rakove observed him in 1975. Marzullo, who had been involved in city politics since 1920, now reigned as ward committeeman of the city's West Side Twenty-fifth Ward. He had run for office eighteen times and only faced an opponent once, defeating him by a fifteen thousand to one thousand margin. Rakove recalled:

> A precinct captain ushered in a black husband and wife. "We got a letter here from the city," the man said. "They want to charge us twenty dollars for rodent control in our building." "Give me the letter. I'll look into it," Marzullo replied. The captain spoke up. "Your daughter didn't vote on November fifth. Look into it. The alderman is running again in February. Any help we can get, we can use."
>
> The telephone rang. Marzullo listened and said, "Come to my office tomorrow morning." He hung up. "She's a widow for thirteen years. She wants to put her property in joint tenancy with her daughter. The lawyer wants a hundred dollars. I'll have to find someone to do it for nothing. . . ."
>
> Another captain ushered in a constituent. "Frank has a problem. Ticket for violation of street sweeping." "Tell John to make a notation," Marzullo said. "You'll have to go to court. We'll send Freddy with you." The constituent thanked Marzullo and left.
>
> The captain from the 16th precinct brought in a young black man who had just graduated from college and was looking for a job. "I just lost fifteen jobs in the city," Marzullo said. "How about private industry?" said the captain. "His family has been with us a long time." "Bring him downtown

tomorrow," Marzullo instructed the captain. "I'll give him a letter to the —––––– Electric Company. They may have something." The young man left.

"Last time I ran, the Polish priest from St. Anne's took my petitions and got all the nuns to sign them," Marzullo said. "He had a paralyzed woman in a wheelchair who couldn't go to Mass because she couldn't get her chair over the curb in front of the church. I had the city build a ramp over the curb for her."

A Polish truck driver came in. "I was laid off three weeks ago," he told Marzullo. "I've got six children." Marzullo countered, "I lost two truck drivers and three laborers this week. The city budget is being held down. We have to keep taxes down. But come down to my office in City Hall tomorrow morning. I'll see if there is an opening in street sweeping or snow plowing." "We got ten votes in my building," said the man. "If we get you a job, let your conscience be your guide," the alderman advised.

The last captain came in with a sickly looking black woman. "Mamie," he said, "I want you to meet my great alderman and your great alderman. If he can help you, he'll do it."

"Alderman," Mamie said, "I need food stamps. I've been in the hospital three times this year. They're giving me pills, but I can't afford to eat."

"You have to get food stamps from your case worker," Marzullo explained. "I can't help that." Turning to County Commissioner Charley Bonk, "Charley, give her a check for fifty dollars for food." And to Mamie, "If you need more come back again." "God bless you!" Mamie responded as she went out the door.[12]

Explaining his business, Marzullo stated: "Anybody in the 25th needs something, needs help with his garbage, needs his street fixed, needs a lawyer for his kid who's in trouble, he goes first to the precinct captain. If the captain can't deliver, that man can come to me. My house is open every day to him. . . . I'm not an intellectual, but I love people. I'm not elected by the media, the intellectuals or do-gooders. I'm elected by my people. Service and communication. That's how my ward is run. . . . I never ask for anything in return. On election day, I tell my people, 'Let your conscience be your guide.'"[13]

The machine was diligent to secure its most precious commodity: votes. Years of favors were repaid with five minutes in the voting booth, and the machine made sure the votes came in. Jay McMullen, a reporter for the *Chicago Daily News* (and later husband of Mayor Jane Byrne), recorded the 1964 election day activities of Arthur W. Varchmin, a fifty-four-year-old Democratic precinct captain in the Thirty-fifth Ward.

Varchmin explained:

> "People in my precinct don't have to worry about a thing. All they have to do is call me. That's how I do business. I get the streets patched, for example. This morning, I turned in a bunch of curbs that need repairs.
>
> "I was out one Saturday morning after the election checking up to see if the complaints I reported were taken care of.
>
> "I do maybe 150 favors a year. I have 15 notebooks at home with the list of favors I've done for my voters. Each time a voter calls me for a favor I get his phone number. I helped one woman get her citizenship after she had been trying for five years. I made seven trips downtown with her. . . ."

Election day is the time for voters to return Varchmin's favors and he does a neat job of collecting. Before the election he has visited every household, followed up with a letter. Then a second letter of reminder hits each home the day before the election.

This isn't enough. On election day, Varchmin has seven people working for him. Several are "runners" who go to remind people who have not voted to come to the polls. Names of these are compiled by Varchmin's checkers at the polling place.

> "I sent a letter out the day after the election thanking them for coming out and assuring them that I'll continue to serve them. This is what gets people to come and vote. They find out you're strictly business. . . ."

What does Varchmin get out of it? Not exactly a cushy patronage job, but a comfortable one as assistant clerk of the Chicago City Council, working in the "bullpen" outside the council chambers. Easy work, good hours, enough pay to live on.[14]

Was there anything unethical or improper about this way of doing politics? The machine in effect bought votes with its acts of assistance. But in one sense, all politicians offer their constituents something in exchange for votes. The Chicago machine was simply more blatant in its quid pro quo arrangements. More problematic were the patronage jobs that most machine regulars held. These lower-level workers were not elected public officials and therefore needed full-time jobs. Moreover, those "full-time" jobs could not require too much time because ward and precinct work was quite time-consuming. One plum patronage job was that of bridge tender. These men were paid for raising and lowering the bridges that spanned the Chicago River and were paid even during the long winter when no ships could ply the frozen Chicago River. Another nice patronage job was that of elevator operator, a job made easier by the fact that many "operated" automatic elevators. During the 1960s, the CCDP controlled between twenty thousand and forty thousand patronage jobs. This was not an efficient use of city revenues, because few patronage workers were qualified for their jobs and little was expected of them. Taxpayer money was used to pay the salaries of part-time political workers.

Financial corruption in the machine was rife. Machine workers took bribes, kickbacks, and campaign contributions from appreciative businessmen. It was understood that directing one's business toward machine regulars usually resulted in machine blessings. Daley himself instructed his men, "Don't take a nickel—just show them your business card."[15] Insurance proved an especially lucrative business venture. Chicago businesses needed insurance, and state-regulated rates eliminated competition. A ward committeeman or precinct worker often opened up an insurance office in the heart of his territory. The individual might know nothing about insurance, but that mattered little. He simply needed an office with his name on the door and one employee who knew how to draft insurance policies. Buying one's insurance from the machine regular was certainly legal, although businessmen probably felt pressured to buy their insurance from the ward committeeman. Machine regulars also raised money through what can only be called petty extortion. Alderman Marzullo raised $35,000 every year by selling advertisements in his annual "ad book." Businesses in his ward purchased advertisements at $100 per page, filling up the 350-page book. This was not illegal, but businessmen knew they would incur the machine's wrath if they did not participate.

The machine could indeed display wrath. Voters were supposed to support machine candidates; voter mutiny was not tolerated. Because the machine was vitally connected with the city's many municipal departments, it could apply pressure on Chicagoans who fought the machine. Neighborhoods that voted against the machine might find the city slow to repair streets or to install needed traffic lights. Individuals felt the machine's pressure as well. In the 1963 mayoral election, for example, Daley faced a stiff challenge from Polish alderman Benjamin Adamowski. Shortly before the election, a restaurant owner in one of Chicago's Polish neighborhoods posted a large "Adamowski for Mayor" sign in his front window. A machine precinct captain stopped by the restaurant the same day the sign appeared and asked the restaurant owner to remove the sign. The owner refused. The precinct worker returned the next day and again asked the owner to remove his sign; the owner again refused. The precinct captain did not return the third day. Instead, city building inspectors showed up and checked the restaurant for violations of the city's building code. Chicago possessed one of the nation's toughest building codes for just such an occasion. The building inspectors demanded that $2,100 in plumbing improvements alone be made to the building. No one would have known if the restaurant owner had secretly voted for Adamowski. A big sign in the front window, however, was unacceptable.

Daley's Chicago was home to other injustices. Vote fraud, for example, was common. The machine rarely resorted to tampering with ballot boxes or submitting fraudulent absentee ballots in local elections. It did not need to. Most Chicagoans readily gave their votes to the machine. In critical national elections, however, vote fraud was more common. The most famous example of this was the 1960 presidential election. Democrat John F. Kennedy carried Illinois by a slim ten-thousand-vote margin, thus winning the state's electoral votes and narrowly defeating Republican Richard M. Nixon. The Democrat carried the state only because he enjoyed an enormous four-hundred-thousand-vote margin over the Republican in Chicago. Few doubted that vote fraud created such a huge margin of victory; for example, some city precincts reported more votes for Kennedy than it had registered voters. Kennedy later said that Daley had won him the election.

Other injustices existed. Local court judges were part of the machine, and they rarely disappointed their benefactors in city hall. The machine also had connections with organized crime. Daley forced vice to go underground and stay out of public sight, but he made no attempt to chase it out of Chicago. He judged that unrealistic. The machine, however, also tolerated open alliances between its regulars and organized crime. First Ward Democratic committeeman John D'Arco, for example, was a longtime associate of Mafia gangsters. Daley maintained an "intelligence division" that gathered information on political enemies. It was an open secret that Chicago police took bribes from bars, prostitutes, and bookies. Chicago motorists routinely handed policemen their driver's license with a ten-dollar bill wrapped around it, which resulted in their receiving a warning rather than a citation. During Daley's last full term in office, seven machine aldermen, including Daley's floor leader, were convicted of job-related crimes. Daley's press secretary of nineteen years, who operated a monopoly on advertising billboards at O'Hare Airport, was also convicted of job-related crimes, although the conviction was later overturned. Daley's chairman of the Chicago Housing Authority board, Charlie Swibel, borrowed fifty million dollars from Chicago's Continental Bank. He used the loan to develop chic and trendy Marina City, but Continental Bank never asked Swibel to repay the entire loan. Instead, $3.4 million was simply forgotten. Perhaps it was no coincidence that the CHA kept its sizeable deposits in Continental Bank and that Swibel blocked other board members' attempts to deposit CHA funds with other banks. Although Daley himself was investigated, no evidence of financial improprieties was ever uncovered.

All major cities were home to similar injustices. These sins cannot be attributed wholly to the machine or to Daley. What seems most disturbing to modern-day observers, however, is that Daley and his machine managed such vice rather than warred against it. Daley was a pragmatist who expected people to do bad things. He harbored no illusions that he could eliminate prostitution, shut down organized crime, or root out graft. Instead, he forced such sin to go underground and to stay out of the public eye. Daley refused to fight such wars for two reasons: they were unwinnable, and they would prevent him from accomplishing what was possible.[16]

Many also bristle at Daley's old-fashioned privileging of authority, discipline, and obedience. For a generation of post–World War II Americans, however, such characteristics were considered virtues. Some judged Daley's moral code—which Royko described as "Thou shalt not steal, but thou shalt not blow the whistle on anybody who does"—as hypocritical; others saw it as expressing loyalty.[17] Chicagoans accepted the proposition that someone had to wield authority if things were to get done. Daley's constituents liked the fact that their mayor was a faithful family man who might tolerate some indiscretions but never tolerated adultery. Royko wrote of Daley, "If one of his aides or handpicked officeholders is shacking up with a woman, he will know it. And if that man is married and a Catholic, his political career will wither and die. That is the greatest sin of all. You can make money under the table and move ahead, but you are forbidden to make secretaries under the sheets. He has dumped several party members for violating his personal moral standards."[18] On one occasion, a machine regular had spent much of the evening in a bar. He received a telephone call while he was at the bar and was shocked to hear a familiar voice. "This is Mayor Daley," the voice boomed. "Your wife is rather upset. I think you'd better get home."[19] The moral code that Daley upheld in his administration was one of the things Chicagoans in the 1950s, 1960s, and 1970s respected about their mayor. But Daley's support was far from universal.

WHEN THE CITY DIDN'T WORK:
THE MACHINE'S BIGGEST FAILURES

Daley did not adapt well to the new political mood of the late 1960s and early 1970s. These were the tempestuous years of Martin Luther King Jr., Abbie Hoffman, the Black Panthers, the civil rights movement, hippies, and the anti–Vietnam War protest movement. Young liberals, intellectuals, and minority group activists often took positions motivated by moral or ideological concerns. They sought deep-seated social change and demanded that old wrongs be righted immediately. Daley, in contrast, was a political pragmatist. He worked by compromising, dealing, and exchanging favors for other favors. According to Daley, interest group demands must always be subordinated to the good of the overall community. Inflammatory rhetoric (which usually ended up in the evening newspaper) was foreign to the world that Daley knew, in which negotiations took place in closed-door, smoke-filled rooms.

Daley and his machine failed when they confronted groups that would not compromise or issues that could not be compromised. This put him on a collision course with the ideologically motivated activists of the late 1960s and early 1970s. Because civil rights workers and Vietnam protestors believed they were fighting for lofty principles, they refused to compromise. Instead of requesting, they demanded. This both mystified and infuriated Daley. He sought quiet meetings with leaders to negotiate agreements in which no one lost political face. Activists in the late 1960s organized loud protest marches through city streets, sought national publicity, and created embarrassing confrontations. The machine (and, more specifically, Daley himself) proved too inflexible to work constructively with these activists.

Consider, for example, Daley's response to the 1966 Chicago campaign of Martin Luther King Jr. As far back as the 1940s, the open housing issue had victimized the city's African Americans and bedeviled Chicago politicians. South Side blacks were confined to a rigidly segregated Black Belt, and yet the city's black population increased dramatically while its white population declined. During the 1960s alone, the white population decreased by 505,000 while the black population increased by 300,000. The concentration of African Americans in South Side housing also created a highly segregated public school system. Unlike southern cities, Chicago did not formally segregate students into "white schools" and "black schools." Its policy of assigning children to "neighborhood schools" nevertheless resulted in de facto school segregation due to the city's sharply segregated neighborhoods. A 1958 article in the NAACP's journal *Crisis* reported that 70 percent of the city's elementary schools were "predominantly white," 21 percent were "predominantly black," and only 9 percent were "mixed." Black Chicagoans also clearly needed more housing and pressed into historically all-white areas, but whites refused to surrender their neighborhoods.

Daley saw a solution: high-rise housing projects. He would demolish dilapidated houses in the Black Belt and replace them with clean, modern, tall apartments. In the late 1950s and early 1960s, this seemed to solve the problem. It kept African Americans within their designated areas and yet created desirable and affordable housing. Housing projects sprang up in the Black Belt, none more incredible than Robert Taylor Homes. Begun in 1960 and located about four miles south of the Loop, Robert Taylor Homes became the largest public housing complex in the world. It consisted of twenty-eight identical buildings, each sixteen floors high, that housed a total of twenty-seven thousand black Chicagoans. Critics later condemned the buildings as little more than vertical ghettos. In the early 1960s, however, they were clean, safe, and spacious by the standards of the day. Both black and white Chicagoans regarded the high-rise apartments as a housing savior.

Robert Taylor Homes typified Daley's approach to a vexing question. Confronted with the open housing dilemma, his predecessors had either supported open housing (and alienated whites) or opposed open housing (and angered blacks). Daley did neither; he opted for a building project. Daley refused, however, to address the fundamental issue of racial discrimination. He therefore allowed the issue to fester and to gain momentum. The "ghettos in the sky" approach bought peace for a short period of time, but it did not deal with the underlying problem.

Daley still felt little compulsion to address racial discrimination when Martin Luther King Jr. came to Chicago in 1966. King's Chicago campaign that year marked a turning point in the modern civil rights movement. King and his organization, the Southern Christian Leadership Conference (SCLC), had spent the previous decade working exclusively in the South. By 1965, King's victories had helped to largely end de jure segregation in Dixie. King then turned to the North, with Chicago—and especially its impoverished Near West Side—as his first target. In the North, however, King faced a different situation. Federal courts could compel Georgians to change their unconstitutional laws, but they could not compel Chicagoans to change their discriminatory attitudes. Instead of attacking discriminatory laws, King found himself attacking poverty, trash in alleys, and poor housing. To be sure, white racism played a large part in the desperate plight of black Chicagoans, but so did cultural, educational, structural, and economic issues. King had a clear goal in Birmingham; his goal in Chicago was more elusive. Some of King's advisors, like Bayard Rustin, feared that the job in Chicago was too vexing for the SCLC. In the aftermath of the Watts race riot in Los Angeles, however, King felt obligated to introduce nonviolent protest to a northern black ghetto.

King was also hamstrung by a fractured black community in Chicago. Many black leaders—ministers, businessmen, politicians, and labor leaders—displayed ambivalence toward King's crusade or simply opposed him. Factions within the city's heterogenous African American community often balked at cooperating with one another. Poor blacks in the "second generation" ghetto on the Near West Side had little in common with the better-established and largely middle-class black community on the South Side. Compounding this lack of solidarity within the black community was an unwillingness on the part of many black Chicagoans to participate in a nonviolent protest movement. In the South, King's call for peaceful marchers had secured widespread grassroots participation. This was not the case in Chicago.

Moreover, King had never before encountered an opponent like Daley. King's protest strategies succeeded because white southerners overreacted, responded with violence, and won King nationwide support. Daley was too cool. When King initially appeared in Chicago, the mayor welcomed him with the key to the city. "Your goals are our goals," Daley publicly announced to the stunned King.[20] Daley convened meetings with King and sought suggestions for solving the city's racial problems. Daley publicly invited King to show him where poor housing existed, and he dutifully sent his men hustling to the buildings that King indicated. The evening news once showed King shoveling piles of garbage that had accumulated in one of the city's South Side alleys; the next day, Daley dispatched sanitation workers to the area to remove all debris. Television viewers saw the mayor accommodating King's every request. King became increasingly flustered, as he was unable to generate the obstructionism that might have won federal intervention. One contemporary said that King's battle with Daley was like a fighter punching a cloud: no blows hit home, all were simply absorbed.

Daley had seemingly defeated the invincible King when the "Hydrant Riots" broke out. The 1966 summer was hot, sultry, and uncomfortable. To escape from the oppressive heat, Chicagoans had always opened fire hydrants and allowed children to frolic in the streets. This was part of city life, as normal as approaching the ward committeeman for a job. In the summer of 1966, however, city workers went into several black neighborhoods and closed the open hydrants. Fights broke out between African Americans and city workers. Policemen intervened, and the fights escalated. Snipers appeared on building rooftops. Two blacks were killed, dozens more were injured, and five policemen were hurt. Looting began to spread through the city. On the riot's second day, the police chief said he could not control the chaos, and the National Guard was called in.

This was not the kind of situation that King had sought, but it dramatized racial friction in the city. The pressure on Daley mounted. As the rioting and looting raged, King was for the first time in the driver's seat. King was in a position to capitalize on black discontent and national sympathy and to extract real concessions from city hall. Then he made a tactical mistake—a mistake the shrewd Daley used to defeat King. Edwin Berry, a black Chicagoan who assisted King during the Chicago Campaign, recalls the fateful meeting: "He [Daley] asked us what we thought could be done. We were worried about now, right now, so we didn't go back to the big problems. We told him to turn on the hydrants, put spray nozzles on them, and start giving black people safe passage to pools in white neighborhoods."[21] Daley's response, explained Mike Royko, gave the civil rights leaders exactly what they had requested:

> Now there was a program, and Daley liked it. Give them water. He had a whole lake right outside the door. Even before the riots ended a few days later, City Hall had embarked on a crusade to make Chicago's blacks the wettest in the country. Portable swimming pools were being trucked in. Sprinklers were attached to hundreds of hydrants, and water was gushing everywhere. The city's department of planning mobilized to launch a long-range program of black wetness. The Chicago Park District joined in. So did the Fire Department. Suddenly the entire city administration was thinking wet. One cynical civil rights worker said, "I think they're hoping we'll all grow gills and swim away."[22]

Daley presented himself as the cooperative mayor giving in to black demands. The black leaders had requested water, and he had obliged. Of course, he had ignored the broader questions of open housing and racial discrimination.

Daley had bested King, and King knew it. The civil rights leader began looking for a graceful way of extracting himself from the city without making it look as if his first campaign in a northern city had failed. King threatened to do what everyone knew would elicit a violent response from local whites: he proposed leading protest marches through all-white neighborhoods such as Cicero. The threat resulted in a conference between Daley and King and a subsequent document that the two men signed. The so-called Summit Agreement was a face-saving device for King, and Daley understood that. King held up the piece of paper and said that city hall had pledged itself to the goal of open housing. King left the city in late 1966; three months after he had gone, one of Daley's men publicly announced, "There is no Summit Agreement."[23]

Daley had defeated King and his seventeen-month-long Chicago campaign. White Chicagoans cheered their mayor. Indeed, Daley swept the 1967 mayoral election with his usual landslide margin. King had warned Daley before the Chicago campaign, "Our vote can and will be the balance of power." Daley, however, carried all fifty city wards, including each predominantly black ward.[24] In the following years, Daley and the machine made some minor concessions to the city's growing black population. More patronage went to loyal African Americans, and by 1971 the city treasurer and sixteen of the city's fifty aldermen were black. Unlike his predecessors, however, Daley and the machine no longer relied upon William Dawson to deliver the black vote. Daley himself dispensed patronage directly to black committeemen in the primarily black wards, thereby bypassing Dawson and cutting off his source of political power. The black wards were represented in the city council by aldermen so pliable, conservative, and pro-Daley that they were originally dubbed "The Silent Seven" and "Daley's Dummies." The machine also gave cash to loyal African American pastors and their struggling churches, provided they remained supportive of the machine. Patronage, political office, and cash did not add up to substantive gains for the city's African Americans, however. A system of de facto segregation thrived in the city that was every bit as discriminatory as the de jure segregation that had prevailed in the South. For example, in the late 1950s blacks were only accepted in six of the metropolitan area's seventy-seven hospitals, and five of those six hospitals treated African Americans only on a quota basis. Likewise, a 1973 study revealed that the Chicago public school system was the most segregated of eighty-one northern school systems.

Daley's refusal to address racial discrimination in the city was one of the machine's glaring failures. The other was Daley's handling of protesters at the 1968 Democratic Convention. To appreciate the drama of what the national press called "The Battle of Chicago," one must recall the charged atmosphere of 1968. Nationwide protests against the Vietnam War were mounting. Both Martin Luther King Jr. and Senator Robert Kennedy had been assassinated a few months earlier; King's assassination had prompted race riots in numerous American cities. With King dead, the control of the black civil rights movement shifted to militant blacks such as Stokely Carmichael, H. Rap Brown, and Eldridge Cleaver. Policemen were often referred to as pigs, and young protesters spoke of armed revolution. Many Americans not given to apocalyptic fears thought that the United States was coming unraveled.

In August of this tumultuous year, the Democratic Party held its national convention to nominate its 1968 presidential candidate. Everyone knew there would be anti–Vietnam War protestors at the meeting, so Daley's Chicago was selected as the host city. Only Chicago offered a "safe" venue for such an explosive convention. The mayor had already demonstrated that he would not tolerate civil unrest in his city. In the April 1968 aftermath of King's assassination, rioters burned and looted Chicago's West Side black communities. City police resorted to force as they attempted to control the bedlam, and they ultimately wounded forty-eight black Chicagoans and killed four more. It was at this time that Daley uttered perhaps his most memorable and infamous words: he instructed his police to "shoot to kill" all arsonists and "shoot to maim" looters. Critics howled at the mayor's calloused "shoot to kill" order, but all press secretary Earl Bush could do was scold the media by telling them that they "should have printed what he meant, not what he said."[25] As Daley seemingly prepared for similar riot control techniques with the approach of the Democratic Convention, few could have misunderstood what the mayor meant. He put his twelve-thousand-man police force on twelve-hour shifts, kept six thousand Illinois National Guardsmen in reserve outside the city, and outfitted his law enforcement people with rifles, bayonets, tear gas, flamethrowers, bazookas, and machine guns. It was the largest military presence in a U.S. city since the Civil War.

As convention delegates poured into Chicago, so did what might have been the most impressive collection of young activists, radicals, protestors, hippies, and Yippies in American history. Some ten thousand antiwar protesters came to the city and "brought the city to the edge of anarchy."[26] They were led by such luminaries as Tom Hayden, David Dellinger, Jerry Rubin, Rennie Davis, Abbie Hoffman, Bobby Seale, Lee Weiner, and John Froines. Some of the youths were hardened revolutionaries, and some were so eccentric that they were difficult to take seriously. The majority were college students who planned to march, chant, and sing but intended no real trouble. The youthful protesters, armed only with guitars, North Vietnamese flags, and marijuana, were baffled by the heavily armed policemen and National Guardsmen. "Chicago was an armed camp," recalled one protester. "We just couldn't quite get it through our heads that all that force was being lined up against us. It was too abstract; it was too absurd."[27]

The convention lasted several days. Youths had several run-ins with city police as they congregated at Grant Park. On one occasion, police removed their badges so they could not be identified, routed protesters at Lincoln Park, and slashed the tires of thirty nearby automobiles that bore "McCarthy for President" stickers. (Eugene McCarthy was the outspoken antiwar candidate for the Democratic presidential nomination.) None of this grabbed national headlines, however. The antiwar protesters planned their big charge to coincide with the convention's final night, the night when Vice President Hubert H. Humphrey would receive the Democratic Party's nomination for president, because all the major television network and newspaper reporters would be present. Protesters would chant, "The whole world is watching!" with the full confidence that it was, thanks to television. The Battle of Chicago would be seen around the globe.

Many of the young protestors assembled at Grant Park. Daley had denied them a parade permit, but they still marched toward the convention site, the old Chicago Amphitheater. As twilight fell on the city, several thousand young people turned onto Michigan Avenue and surged toward the convention. Chants of "Peace Now! Peace Now!" echoed through the Loop. As they pushed down Michigan Avenue, they were met near Balbo Street by a police line. Thousands of Daley's blue-helmeted policemen stood shoulder-to-shoulder, nightsticks drawn, blocking the young peoples' path. The students stopped short of the police line and began taunting the police. After several tense minutes—with television news cameras rolling—the policemen exploded into the group of protesters.

Protesters tried to turn and run, but the streets were so packed that no one could move. Policemen grabbed people and beat them with nightsticks. Tear gas was fired. Some protesters threw bottles and stones at the policemen. Protesters who tried to surrender were beaten anyway, as were elderly bystanders and journalists who happened to be on Michigan Avenue at the time. "For no reason that could be immediately determined,"

The 1968 Democratic National Convention brought convention delegates, presidential hopefuls, youthful protestors, and these barbed-wire-equipped National Guard jeeps to Chicago. Before the convention was over, Chicago Police and the National Guard waged pitched battles with protestors in the city streets. Chicago Historical Society

the *New York Times* reported, "the blue-helmeted policemen charged the barriers, crushing the spectators against the windows of the Haymarket Inn, a restaurant in the hotel. Finally the window gave way, sending screaming middle-aged women and children backward through the broken shards of glass."[28] Police paddy wagons began forcing their way into the pandemonium, and policemen beat protesters again as they threw them into the wagons. Chaos reigned on Michigan Avenue as thousands of policemen chased protesters through the streets. The sidewalks were littered with crumpled bodies, and tear gas hung heavy in the air. The major television networks cut away from their coverage of the convention to show ninety million horrified Americans what was happening in Daley's Chicago.

The fallout from the Battle of Chicago was enormous. The *Chicago Daily News* criticized Daley's "security overkill" and the "police state" atmosphere in the city. The *Chicago Sun-Times* condemned the policemen's "unlawful acts."[29] "Miraculously, no one was killed by Chicago Mayor

Richard Daley's beefy cops," said *Newsweek* magazine, "who went on a sustained rampage unprecedented outside the unreconstructed boondocks of Dixie."[30] *Nation* magazine called Daley a "Fascist proprietor of a police state" who had "lost touch with the times."[31] The staid *New York Times* opined that Daley's use of force "brought shame to the city, embarrassment to the country."[32] Even Daley supporters were embarrassed. Congressman Roman Pucinski, who hailed from a conservative northwest Chicago area, said, "We survived the Chicago fire; we will survive this."[33] The President's Commission on Violence later investigated the riot and concluded that much of the violence had been the result of what it termed "police riot." Daley did not help his cause when, in defending his police department in the riot's aftermath, he uncorked one of his most famous malapropisms. "Gentlemen, get this thing straight for once and for all," he explained to reporters. "The policeman isn't there to create disorder. The policeman is there to preserve disorder."[34]

Fallout from the riot was not only enormous; it was also permanent. Historian Godfrey Hodgson contends that the riot was instrumental in making American journalists more liberal and supportive of dissent. Influential journalist Tom Wicker concluded that the 1968 Democratic Convention was "the place where all America was radicalized."[35] Such events understandably received extraordinary attention in the news media. What is remarkable is how the 1968 Democratic Convention became an identifying event for Daley's Chicago. In other words, many use the Battle of Chicago as a window through which to see the *real* Daley and the *real* nature of the machine. The behavior of Daley's policemen in the summer of 1968 is offered as evidence that machine politics, especially when the machine was headed by an all-powerful boss such as Daley, was wicked.

It is unfair to regard this one event as emblematic of Daley's Chicago. Nor does this one event, reprehensible as it might be, discredit the entire twenty-one-year administration of Daley. It does illustrate quite vividly, however, some of Daley's chief shortcomings. For all of his political shrewdness, he could not adjust to new situations. The young protesters could not be bargained with, nor could Daley simply ignore them. He viewed authority the way parents of young children sometimes do: authority successfully defied once breeds future defiance.

Perhaps *Nation* magazine was right when it said that Daley had lost touch with the times. Daley was a man reared in the tough, authoritarian, no-nonsense world of World War I–era Chicago. He could not be flexible with young, disrespectful, pot-smoking, long-haired individuals waving North Vietnamese flags. He could not simply ignore the antics of Jerry Rubin, who brought a pig to the city and told the news media that he would nominate the pig for president. ("If our president gets out of line, we'll eat him," said the Yippies of their pig-candidate.)[36] Many laughed at Rubin, but Daley fumed. Had Chicago's mayor responded with heavy-handed and authoritarian measures in the 1930s, 1940s, or 1950s, national criticism probably would not have been shrill and unrelenting. But times had changed, and Daley had not. It is only fair to add, however, that Daley himself realized that he could have handled the situation better. "I was wrong," Daley secretly admitted to powerful Illinois politician Adlai Stevenson III. "We over-reacted."[37] Moreover, most Chicagoans supported Daley's actions in the summer of 1968, and a majority of the city's major newspapers actually praised the mayor. For example, the *Chicago Tribune* wrote, "For enforcing law and order, Mayor Daley and the police deserve congratulations rather than criticism. . . . Chicago did not invite these street fighters to come here in the hope of disgracing the city."[38] Nor was Daley's support limited to the city. A nationwide public opinion poll conducted immediately after the convention revealed that only 21 percent of those interviewed deemed the Chicago police department's handling of the young protesters inappropriate. But Daley's performance at the Democratic National Convention altered the course of the nation in the late 1960s and has forever affected the way Americans will remember Richard J. Daley.

THE MACHINE TRANSFORMED: DALEY'S TWILIGHT YEARS

Despite crises such as King's Chicago campaign and the 1968 Democratic Convention, Daley's machine continued to win elections by comfortable margins. It could still do what it did best: provide basic urban services to most Chicago residents. In 1971 *Newsweek* described Chicago, stating, "Chicago is that most wondrous of exceptions—a major American city that actually works. While breakdowns in essential services have become almost a daily event elsewhere, Chicagoans enjoy virtually an uninterrupted supply of urban amenities. They commute to work on the nation's most ingeniously integrated transportation system. . . . Chicago's streets are probably the cleanest and best-illuminated on the metropolitan scene; its police and fire departments are ranked by professionals as among the most effective in the world."[39] Many Chicagoans still had good reasons for supporting Daley. He remained an able city administrator and a crafty politician, providing the city with urban services and political stability. He was not flashy, polished, charismatic, and silver-tongued like his peer, Mayor John V. Lindsay of New York City. Yet, in an era when large U.S. cities were confronting intractable administrative and financial problems that rendered them virtually ungovernable, Daley's Chicago was one of the few major cities that thrived. New York City, for example, stumbled into colossal financial woes shortly after Lindsay left office, largely due to Lindsay's unwise fiscal policies; Detroit, Cleveland, Cincinnati, and Philadelphia all faced financial crises as well during the 1970s. Daley's Chicago, by contrast, was efficient, well managed, and fiscally prudent. Whereas Lindsay watched helplessly as his New York City was paralyzed by a teachers' strike, Daley intervened and resolved a 1971 Chicago teachers' strike after only four days. (Daley brought the opposing sides to city hall, put them in separate rooms, and shuttled back and forth between rooms facilitating a resolution.) "He is a man who knows how to keep the machinery running," judged the *Chicago Daily News* in a 1971 endorsement of Daley's reelection bid, "how to maintain and extend and improve the city's superb physical plant, how to keep it prosperous and on the move. In these achievements, he stands unique among the mayors of the nation's great cities."[40]

Daley also remained in power because he found new political formulas for winning elections. Between 1955 and 1967, the machine's strategy for winning was twofold: run competitive races in the mostly white West and North Sides and pile up huge electoral majorities in the black South Side. Beginning in the mid-1960s, however, the machine's African American vote declined precipitously. Blacks resented Daley's dismissal of Martin Luther King Jr. in 1966, his "shoot to kill" and "shoot to maim" orders in the 1968 riots, and the 1969 police raid that led to a one-sided gunfight and the suspicious deaths of two popular Black Panther leaders, Fred Hampton and Mark Clark. Blacks also resented the not-so-subtle racial segregation practiced by the Chicago Housing Authority. In 1969, the fifty CHA housing projects located in black neighborhoods reported 91 percent black occupancy, while the four CHA projects in white neighborhoods reported between 93 and 99 percent white occupancy. No one doubted that Daley actively maintained the city's formidable system of de facto racial segregation. In 1971, the CHA released a list of 275 sites in white neighborhoods that were suitable for low-cost public housing. Whites were horrified that an all-black housing project might come to their neighborhood; Daley quickly rejected all 275 sites as unacceptable. Finally, Ralph Metcalfe, a black Daley man active in the South Side machine, turned against the machine in the early 1970s when a friend (a South Side dentist) was beaten by white policemen during a routine traffic stop. Metcalfe rallied black opposition to the machine.

By the early 1970s, the machine had lost much of the black vote. Daley compensated by winning more of the white vote, since the same positions that alienated the mayor from black Chicagoans endeared him to many of his white constituents. The machine's strategy for success now called for the nonparticipation of many black voters and the securing of most white votes in the city. These political dynamics encouraged Daley and the machine to be even more supportive of the conservative white position. By 1974, for example, Daley—the archetypical law-and-order politician—defied court orders to implement affirmative action programs in the police department. To many national observers, Daley was a stubborn man desperately out of touch with the times; to local observers, however, Daley was a shrewd politician who was very much in touch with political winds in his city. A journalist once asked Michael Madigan, a thoughtful machine committeeman from the South Side, to name the smartest political move he had ever witnessed. "Probably Mayor Daley's move from the left to the right as the country moved from the left to the right," responded Madigan. He continued: "When Daley was first elected he was a liberal. He enjoyed strong support from the black wards. As late as 1963, were it not for the black wards, he would have lost to Benjamin Adamowski for mayor. But in the mid-sixties there was a shift in public sentiment from the left to the right. He moved very adroitly to reflect that. The convention disorders, and the position he took relative to the hippies and Yippies, clearly positioned himself on the right. His statement on arsonists was reflective of his view that society was becoming less tolerant of criminality and lawlessness."[41] Relying upon an overwhelming majority of the white vote weakened the machine. Numerous white reformers, liberals, and machine enemies would not vote for the machine under any circumstance. The number of such die-hard Daley critics mounted after 1970 as one after another of Daley's closest associates were implicated in financial scandals. In 1974, Daley's press secretary of eighteen years, Earl Bush, was indicted on charges of extortion for his secret ownership of a company that had enjoyed a monopoly on advertising at O'Hare Airport since 1962. Although Bush's conviction was later overturned, many nonetheless suspected financial improprieties. County Clerk Edward J. Barrett and three aldermen—all Daley men—were indicted on either fraud or extortion charges. In 1973, Daley transferred city insurance policies to the firm where his son worked; commissions from those policies earned the firm $500,000. Daley fumed when some suggested the transfer was unethical. The indignant mayor countered that he was only trying to help his son.

Although these financial dealings were not new, times had changed. Americans grew increasingly critical of politicians in the Vietnam and Watergate era. Terms such as "conflict of interest" entered the public discourse. Suddenly, activities that had long been an accepted part of politics (such as the mayor helping his son by giving him lucrative city business) were now regarded as unethical. The rules of political propriety and legitimacy were changing, and these rules did not bode well for the machine. It began to look more and more corrupt.

Daley remained in power, however. In his last mayoral campaign, the 1975 election, he clobbered his three primary opponents by winning 58 percent of the vote; he won 78 percent of the vote in the general election. Despite his eroding support in the city's black community, he still won all the black wards in the general election (indeed, he won all fifty wards) as well as endorsements from the *Chicago Defender* and the Chicago-based *Ebony* and *Jet* magazines. National political leaders still courted the powerful Daley. After his 1975 reelection, for example, Democratic presidential hopeful Morris K. Udall reaffirmed the mayor's role as a national political leader. "I wouldn't say Daley's the whole ball game any more," quipped Udall, "but he's still a good piece of it."

No politician ever ousted Daley from the mayor's office. In 1976, Daley suffered a heart attack and died. He had spent the last twenty-one years of his life doing what he loved most: being boss of Chicago. The funeral was a national event, attended by the vice president of the United States, president-elect Jimmy Carter, cabinet members, congressmen, governors, and mayors. Thousands of Chicagoans lined up in bitterly cold weather to view Daley's body, which lay in state. *Washington Post* reporter Haynes Johnson remarked, "To be in Chicago for Richard Daley's funeral is to understand, in a way, what it was like in China when Chairman Mao died."[42]

Was Richard J. Daley a good or bad mayor? To many, Daley was the worst of all possible mayors: a corrupt, power-hungry, mean-spirited, reactionary, boorish political hack. Others agreed with Chicago writer and elder statesman Studs Terkel: "He's marvelous when it comes to building things like highways, parking lots, and industrial complexes. But when it comes to healing the aches and hurts of human beings, Daley comes up short."[43] A 1985 poll of informed academics and journalists, however, ranked Daley as the best mayor in the city's history, far outdistancing the second-place finisher and leaving Daley in a class by himself. Such debates ultimately come down to how one defines "good mayor" and "bad mayor." Most agree, however, with the assessment of Daley's biographer, historian Roger Biles. On the one hand, Daley was a master at delivering urban services. He was an administrator and negotiator without peer, and he created a stable business environment that resulted in impressive economic prosperity. Only Daley earned for his home the epitaph "the city that works." Despite the misdeeds of associates and an occasional favor that he bestowed upon his sons, Daley was a scrupulously honest politician who steered clear of financial and moral improprieties. On the other hand, Daley failed to adjust to the changing realities of Chicago, especially those relating to its growing black population. Rather than addressing such problems as de facto segregation and race-related poverty, he ignored them and at times made them worse. Daley pushed African Americans to the margin of the city's political economy, which meant that the city worked for fewer and fewer of its citizens.

The machine would never be the same after Daley's death, nor would Chicago. Daley's assistants attempted to keep the machine alive, but they failed. Daley's death marked the passing of an era in Chicago history.

CHAPTER TWELVE

THE TRANSITIONS OF
THE POST-DALEY YEARS,
1976-1997

•   The Democratic National Convention returned to Chicago in 1996. This was the first presidential nominating convention to be held in the Windy City since the infamous 1968 Democratic National Convention—the nationally televised convention that had been marred by student protestors and what government investigators later described as a "police riot." More than anything else, the 1996 convention demonstrated how much Chicago had changed in twenty-eight years.

In 1968, Mayor Richard J. Daley had refused to allow youthful antiwar protesters in his city; in 1996, Mayor Richard M. Daley, the original Daley's son, established a small, fenced-in "protest pen" close to the convention site where all demonstrations were held. Activists signed up for one-hour time slots and protested to their hearts' content. In 1968, the older Daley had denounced the protesters as hippies, drug addicts, traitors, and bums; in 1996; the younger Daley attended a "Day of Healing" gathering, sharing the stage with such leaders of the 1968 demonstrations as Tom Hayden, Bobby Seale, John Froines, and Rennie Davis. If anything, the 1996 convention remembered the protesters at the 1968 convention almost as heroes. "However unwelcome you may have felt 28 years ago in the middle of a very troubled time," intoned the conciliatory Daley in 1996, alluding to the behavior of his father, "you are welcome today."[1] In 1968, the Chicago Police force—99 percent male and 83 percent white—had often instigated violent clashes with protestors. In 1996, the Chicago Police force—20 percent female, 25 percent black, 10 percent Hispanic—was a model of restraint, thwarting the protesters' persistent attempts at getting arrested. As the nation observed the 1996 convention on television, they were treated to numerous reminders of the 1968 convention. The comparison only underscored how different the two Chicagos were.

POLITICAL INSTABILITY AND THE POLITICS OF TRANSITION

During the Daley years of the late 1950s, the 1960s, and the early 1970s, many Chicagoans had grown accustomed to stability as well as to building projects and landslide Democratic victories. Local politician William Singer observed in 1975 that people voted for Richard J. Daley and the Cook County Democratic Party machine, "not because the precinct captain forced or cajoled them, but because they made a decision that they were for Daley. They felt a great sense of stability in knowledge of what they had. . . . It was an incredible thing. There was an enormous stability factor."[2] That stability came to an end with Daley's death in 1976. As the supremely powerful figure in the CCDP, Daley had been able to control the ambitions of his assistants. They were more or less content with their secondary status, because unseating Daley was unthinkable. With the boss gone, however, local politicians began to war with one another. Daley had controlled the mayor's office for more than twenty years, between 1955 and 1976; over the next fifteen years, five different mayors ascended to city hall. Transition replaced continuity; uncertainty replaced stability.

Michael Bilandic, a shy, careful, competent lawyer who worked hard, succeeded Daley as mayor in 1976. His chief qualification for office was his devotion to Daley and the machine. Bilandic was not a bad mayor. He kept the city on a straight course, even if he did not provide dynamic leadership. His undoing was the fabled blizzard of 1979. A series of record-breaking snowstorms hit the city, and the following cold spell only worsened conditions. For all Daley's faults, even his critics admitted that he had made Chicago the city that works. Buses ran on time. Sewers were adequate. Streets were kept clean. Snow had always been removed. The January 1979 snowstorms, however, paralyzed Chicago. City workers were unable to remove the snow before the ice set in. For almost two months, city life slowed to a crawl as snow and ice enveloped the city. Garbage piled up on city streets, streets were impassable, and delivery trucks could not resupply stores. In his first opportunity to prove that he could handle crises as Daley had, Bilandic failed. He was the mayor who made the city stop working. Chicagoans might tolerate corruption or an occasional police riot, but they would not tolerate a failure in basic urban services such as snow removal.

The Bilandic years gave the wobbling CCDP machine time to fall apart. Jane Byrne took advantage of this in 1979 when she defeated Bilandic and the machine to win the mayor's office. Byrne's victory marked the first time that the machine had lost a mayoral election since its birth in 1931. Byrne had little political experience, having risen quickly through the ranks to become a leader in the CCDP. Mayor Richard J. Daley had taken a liking to Byrne (he probably hoped she would shore up his support among both women and the city's "lace curtain" Irish) and had ushered her into the CCDP's inner circles. In 1979, however, she ran for mayor against the incumbent Bilandic as an anti-machine candidate. Two things led to her historic victory. First, she capitalized on mounting anti-machine sentiment in the city's black and liberal districts. Second, her feisty, wisecracking, mud-in-your-eye style made her an attractive candidate. Working-class Chicagoans liked the 5'3" blond woman's spunk, combativeness, and sharp tongue. For example, while many politicians routinely lamented the city's dilapidated public housing projects, Byrne actually moved into the city's notorious Cabrini-Green projects for a brief but highly publicized stay.

Byrne's splashy tactics did not translate into effective municipal leadership. She proved an ineffective leader who was further hobbled by a faltering national economy. Labor unrest buffeted the city, as transit workers, teachers, and firefighters all went on strike during her reign. The business community grew especially frustrated with Byrne, blaming her for creating an uncertain business environment. To her credit, Byrne bit the bullet and made several difficult decisions. She eliminated more than one thousand municipal jobs in a cost-cutting maneuver and raised city taxes. Byrne also increased the number of minorities serving in city hall. In the end, however, Byrne abandoned her anti-machine and reformist agenda. She made an alliance with Alderman Edward Vrdolyak, the new head of the CCDP, because she needed city council votes in order to accomplish anything at all. One minute she was the fiery, confident, anti-machine fighter who was nicknamed "Attila the Hen"; the next she was courting the remnants of the old machine and seemingly consigning the city to politics as usual. The zigzag course wearied Chicagoans by 1983. The *Chicago Tribune* characterized her mayoral reign as "creative, chaotic, dramatic, devastating, exciting, excruciating . . . historic."[3] She had three chiefs of staff, three press secretaries, and three police superintendents during her four-year term. Local journalist Gary Rivlin recalled that she acted decisively but then reversed herself six months later.[4] Historian Melvin G. Holli agrees: "Few politicians in Chicago's history could match Byrne for her zaniness, madcap, and daring acts that were to mar the solid and substantive acts of her administration. Unfortunately for her, too many Chicagoans mistook her style for her substance."[5] Like Bilandic, Byrne failed to win reelection to the mayor's office.

Just as Byrne's 1979 mayoral victory seemingly signaled the end of machine rule in Chicago, Harold Washington's 1983 victory seemingly signaled the end of white rule. Washington's stunning triumph also marked something of a zenith of black political power in the city.

Before Washington and the 1983 mayoral election, African Americans had never been free agents in the market of Chicago politics. First William Dawson had controlled the black vote from the early 1940s until the early 1960s. Dawson had secured a handful of patronage jobs for his constituents but not justice, equality, and first-class citizenship. Then Daley began dispensing patronage personally, stripping Dawson of his power and making black political leaders dependent upon the Irish mayor from Bridgeport. Black activists denounced Daley's control of the Black Belt as "plantation politics." One black politician who left the machine characterized Daley as a "plantation master . . . who keeps his darkies loyal to him by doling out small political favors . . . [and] playing the same old 'divide and conquer' game his forefathers experienced when they made some slaves 'house servants' and kept others out in the field."[6] Beginning with the racial tumults of the late 1960s, the machine began relying more upon the white vote, and crumbs fell from city hall's table with less frequency because the machine no longer needed the black vote. The result was widespread black political disaffection and apathy. The seemingly hopeless situation caused many black Chicagoans to become nonparticipants in the political system.

Local black activists came alive politically at precisely this time. The 1972 National Black Political Convention in nearby Gary, Indiana, sounded a call-to-arms to African Americans nationwide. The convention signaled the involvement of African Americans in electoral politics—and not simply in schools, bus terminals, and housing—and called for the civil rights movement and the struggle for "Black Power" to proceed. Ralph Metcalfe, an Olympic medal winner turned politician who inherited William Dawson's mantle as chief broker of black votes in Chicago, broke with the machine in 1972 when a friend was brutalized by white policemen. Metcalfe announced himself as a political independent, explaining his dramatic political rebirth by quipping, "It's never too late to be black."[7] Perhaps the most important factor in the political reawakening of black Chicagoans was Cook County State's Attorney Edward Hanrahan's defeat in his 1972 reelection bid, the first citywide defeat of a CCDP machine candidate during Daley's mayoral reign. Black

Chicagoans blamed Hanrahan for what they regarded as the police murder of popular Black Panther Party leaders Fred Hampton and Mark Clark. For the first time, a majority of local African Americans abandoned the Democratic Party and voted for a Republican.

This new enthusiasm translated into few tangible political victories. Two distinct groups of black political activists in Chicago—the coalitionists and the nationalists—remained at odds with one another and could not agree on a common political strategy. Coalitionists avoided antagonizing white lakefront liberals, refrained from militant rhetoric, and launched biracial initiatives with white political leaders. Nationalists were tired of cooperating with whites and moderating their rhetoric. They tended to be ideologically motivated, disdained compromise, and frequently used bombastic language that alarmed whites. With prominent blacks sharply divided over these two approaches, a lack of local political leadership caused most black voters to grow disaffected. They stayed away from the polls in droves despite the fact that they composed one-third of the city electorate by the 1970s. This explains why the unextraordinary Michael Bilandic easily defeated Harold Washington in the 1977 mayoral primary: only 27 percent of registered black voters bothered to participate in the election. Things would be different in 1983.

Washington had been an African American lieutenant in the CCDP's Black Belt machine since 1954. He also served in the Illinois legislature for the fourteen years prior to his 1983 campaign. A graduate of the Northwestern University Law School, Washington both backed machine candidates and cultivated his own power base within Chicago's black community. Washington's break with the machine came in 1977 when he openly criticized the CCDP for failing to reward blacks sufficiently. Knowing his days of machine support were over, Washington divorced himself from the CCDP and transformed himself into the candidate of the city's black community. His drubbing in the 1977 election, however, revealed to all—and especially to Washington—that black Chicagoans were not sufficiently united to elect a black mayor.

Mayor Jane Byrne's treatment of African Americans contributed to Washington's stunning 1983 mayoral victory. During the first half of her administration, Byrne had won the cautious praise of many blacks. For example, she had named Renault Robinson, an African American, to the board that oversaw the Chicago Housing Authority and created a black majority on the board. It had been Robinson's racial discrimination suit that had forced the city to establish hiring and promotion quotas in the city police department, so his appointment was especially galling to whites and especially gratifying to blacks. With her 1983 reelection only seven months away, however, Byrne faced a difficult battle against Richard M. Daley, the former mayor's son. Perhaps in an attempt to shore up her waning support in white ethnic communities, Byrne reversed course and reinstalled a white majority on the CHA board. Black community leaders portrayed this as a betrayal of African Americans, a clear and easily understood event that they could use to mobilize black Chicagoans. They were right: Byrne's snubbing of blacks angered and galvanized local African Americans into a political force. Coalitionists and nationalists momentarily put aside their differences.

Almost all black political leaders in Chicago knew that Washington was their only viable mayoral candidate. Two problems emerged. First, Washington did not want to run. He remembered his crushing 1977 mayoral defeat and the low voter turnout among blacks. It was only after much cajoling and pleading that Washington agreed to consider running, but in return for his concession he requested that one condition be met: he wanted to see fifty thousand new black registered voters. This was a problem that could be resolved with relative ease. An enormous and enormously successful voter registration campaign ultimately registered 140,000 new black voters before the 1983 Democratic mayoral primary.

The second problem was more vexing. Jesse Jackson, who had made his home in Chicago since the mid-1960s, was perhaps the most widely known national black political figure in 1980, and many outsiders assumed that Jackson was the logical choice to be the first black mayor of Chicago. Jackson assumed that as well. He continually reminded local black political leaders that he was available and deserving of the nomination. Whatever divisions plagued local black leaders, however, they agreed on one thing: Jackson was unacceptable as a mayoral candidate. Most black Chicago leaders despised Jackson's egotistical, demagogic, attention-grabbing style. They thought that he abandoned projects before they were completed, lured by the prospects of some new situation. Jackson also had a habit of getting carried away by his own rhetoric, promising much more than he could ever deliver. "For months it has become clear that Jackson simply cannot tolerate another black man being more prominent in Chicago," observed Vernon Jarrett, a leading black journalist in the city.[8] In the end, Jackson reluctantly accepted Washington's candidacy and refrained from killing the campaign with intemperate remarks.

Finally, after much prodding, Washington threw his hat into the 1983 Democratic mayoral primary. For much of the campaign, the two front-running candidates—Jane Byrne and Richard M. Daley—gave Washington little chance of winning. Byrne and Daley focused on winning the white vote while ignoring the South Side, a decision that divided the city along racial lines. Black voters were infuriated at being disregarded by the two white front-runners; Byrne's and Daley's decision effectively turned Washington's candidacy into something resembling a religious crusade in the black community. Instead of resolving the deep coalitionist-nationalist tension among black civic leaders, Washington harnessed it. Coalitionists ran a campaign headquarters in the Loop, while nationalists headed up campaigning in the Black Belt. The white media rarely ventured into the black communities and rarely listened to the pulse of Chicago's black community, the black-operated radio stations. White Chicagoans therefore did not hear the nationalists' sometimes inflammatory campaign rhetoric, which was aired on those radio stations. Whites heard the coalitionists' words instead. This proved to be one of the keys to Washington's victory: the strong rhetoric needed to mobilize disaffected black voters rarely reached (and therefore rarely alarmed) white voters.

One month before the Democratic mayoral primary, whites suddenly realized that Washington had a real chance of winning the primary. With the possibility of a black mayor looming, race became the paramount issue in the primary. Ed Vrdolyak, chairman of the CCDP, foresaw that whites would split their votes between the incumbent Byrne and Daley and thereby give the election to Washington. Vrdolyak bluntly appealed to white voters: "A vote for Daley is a vote for Washington. It's a two-person race. It would be the worst day in the history of Chicago if your candidate . . . was not elected. It's a racial thing. Don't kid yourself. I'm calling on you to save your city, to save your precinct. We're fighting to keep the city the way it is."[9] Washington appealed to blacks and white liberals. Just before the primary election, Washington said, "There are some who believe that I should avoid the race issue. But I will not avoid it because it permeates our entire city and has devastating implications. . . . I'm running to end Jane Byrne's four-year effort to further institutionalize racial discrimination in this great city."[10]

Washington mobilized the city's black churches, hoping they could encourage disaffected black voters to return to the polls. The churches responded, turning out the black vote in record numbers. Byrne (with 388,000 votes, or 34 percent) and Daley (345,000 votes, or 30 percent) split the white vote as Vrdolyak had predicted; Washington captured 85 percent of the black vote to win the Democratic primary (424,000 votes, or 36 percent). A jubilant Jesse Jackson, speaking to blacks at a victory celebration, told them, "It's our turn!"

In heavily Democratic Chicago, where 78 percent of the voters identified themselves as Democrats, winning the Democratic Party's nomination almost always meant that one had captured the office. The general election was a mere formality, and Republicans were so outnumbered that they often did not run candidates against Democrats. Not true in 1983. The specter of Chicago's first black mayor pushed many white Chicagoans—many of whom had never voted for a Republican in their lifetime—to support the Republican mayoral candidate, Bernard Epton. Even the CCDP and the vestiges of its machine refused to back the winner of their own party's primary and instead backed the white Republican. Epton, who had won the Republican mayoral primary with a total of eleven thousand votes, had originally planned to open three campaign offices in the city; the legions of white voters now frantic to see the white Epton elected compelled the Republican to open thirty campaign offices. "The people in my area," explained Anthony Laurino, a Democratic committeeman in a predominantly white ward, "just don't want a black mayor—it's as simple as that." Another white Chicagoan from the mostly white Southwest Side explained that whites he knew had been "pushed out of their neighborhoods two or three times by blacks." He concluded, "This is a chance to get even."[11]

The Washington-Epton mayoral contest quickly became one with a single issue: skin color. Epton, however, was no white supremacist. A wealthy Jewish lawyer from the liberal lakefront area, Epton was a fiscal conservative but a social liberal who often sided with Democrats. The *Chicago Defender,* the city's black newspaper, had already praised Epton's civil rights record, and Epton himself declared, "I do resent anyone who would vote for me because I'm white. This is one city that should not be divided." Epton repudiated the efforts of those whom he called "white racist Democrats," who supported him merely "to save Chicago from the blacks." He declared, "I have no desire to win a vote, because an opponent is black and I am white. A bigot is a bigot, and I want no part of it."[12]

Despite Epton's protestations, the 1983 mayoral election divided the city along racial lines and engendered intemperate, racially insensitive language on both sides. Epton himself did not make race an issue in the election, but he did focus his attacks upon Washington's character. (The Illinois Supreme Court had suspended Washington's law license for one year in 1970, and Washington had served a brief jail sentence for failing to file income tax returns for several years in the 1970s.) Regardless of

Epton's personal desires to keep race out of the election, many Epton supporters made open or thinly veiled appeals to race. Some wore t-shirts that read, "Vote right—Vote white." On Palm Sunday, former vice president Walter Mondale arrived in the city and attempted to attend a worship service with Washington at the Northwest Side's St. Pascal's Roman Catholic Church. They confronted an angry white mob and the words "NIGGER DIE" spray-painted on the church door. Epton condemned the overt display of racism, disavowed connection with the incident, and apologized if any of his people were involved. It was difficult, however, to ignore what everyone knew was the real issue in the campaign. Epton's own campaign slogan, which appeared in television ads, was "Epton for mayor. Before it's too late." Epton denied that the slogan carried racial connotations, claiming he had crafted it before he knew Washington would be his opponent. "Before it's too late," according to Epton, referred to the city's impending financial crises. Many were unconvinced. In the campaign's closing days, Washington contributed his own controversial advertisements. One television spot included photos of a Ku Klux Klan rally and the Kennedy and King assassinations. Interspersed between these scenes was footage of Epton supporters deriding Washington and Mondale at St. Pascal's Church. "There are moments in our history when we are thoroughly and profoundly ashamed," intoned the ads. "One of those moments may be happening in Chicago right now."[13] This "ashamed commercial," as Washington's staff dubbed it, appealed to the consciences of white voters. A vote for Epton, they were made to feel, was a vote for the KKK, racists, and assassins. The message it conveyed to voters was, reject bigotry by voting for Washington.

Washington won the mayoral election by a slim margin: of 1.3 million votes cast, Washington's margin of victory was a mere 46,000 votes. Seventy-three percent of all blacks in the city voted; at least 95 percent gave their votes to Washington. Voting was so heavy in one South Side black precinct that an election judge telephoned the Board of Elections in mid-afternoon and asked if they should close their doors, since every registered voter in the precinct had already cast a ballot. Sixty-seven percent of all whites voted, with Epton receiving 88 percent of those votes. With most whites voting for Epton and most blacks voting for Washington, the city's growing Hispanic population played a critical role in the election.[14] Hispanic Chicagoans cast 82 percent of their votes for Washington in the general election; only 15 percent had given their vote to Washington in the Democratic primary. Washington also won the white

Mayor Harold Washington campaigning. The first African American mayor of Chicago, it took four years for Washington to consolidate his control over a hostile city council. He eventually prevailed and saw significant accomplishments before suddenly dying in office. *Chicago Tribune*

vote in Epton's home district, the liberal lakefront areas, where the white backlash vote was small and the "ashamed commercials" probably had their greatest impact.

Washington's election meant that Chicago had its first black mayor. It also meant the end of all semblance of cooperation between the mayor's office and the city council. During the Daley years, the city council—packed full of aldermen beholden to the CCDP—had been little more than a rubber stamp organization that followed the mayor's lead. Neither Bilandic nor Byrne possessed Daley's power, but because they both did business with the CCDP machine they never found themselves at loggerheads with the city council. Washington encountered a different situation. Of the city council's fifty members, Washington could count on twenty-one aldermen to vote with him. The remaining twenty-nine aldermen opposed the newly elected mayor and were loyal to alderman and CCDP chief Ed Vrdolyak. What resulted were four and a half fractious and discordant years in the city, years that led the *Wall Street Journal* to dub the city "Beirut on the Lake." Basing his spoof of the city council on the popular *Star Wars* movies that were showing at the time, a local comedian christened Chicago's municipal politics "Council Wars." The eloquent Washington was dubbed Harold Skytalker ("may the clout be with you") while Vrdolyak became "evil Lord Darth Vrdolyak." City council proceedings became predictable. Washington or one of his aldermen would introduce a proposal that would be defeated by a 29–21 margin. Then Vrdolyak or one of his aldermen would introduce a counterproposal that would pass by a 29–21 margin. Next Washington would veto the Vrdolyak measure. Thirty-four votes were required to override a mayoral veto, and Vrdolyak could only garner twenty-nine. Washington and Vrdolyak took turns storming into the council chambers, dropping verbal bombshells, and criticizing each other. The city council even sought (unsuccessfully) Washington's impeachment. For all the sound and fury, neither the mayor nor the city council provided leadership or accomplished much.

Few Chicagoans were happy with the mayor's first term and the protracted deadlock. About half of Washington's loyal aldermen considered defecting, charging that Washington failed to dispense patronage to them. Washington also labored under the burden of unrealistically high black expectations. Many black Chicagoans expected Washington to be a Moses who would lead his people through a social and economic revolution. In the world of urban politics, however, dramatic change is rare. "Being the first black mayor," quipped Maynard Jackson, Atlanta's first black mayor and a veteran politician who had himself faced exceedingly high expectations, "is what you wish on your worst enemy."[15] At one time during Washington's mayoral term, a poll indicated that one-third of all Chicago's black voters wished that Richard J. Daley were still mayor.

After four years of battling with Vrdolyak and the remnants of the CCDP, Washington easily won reelection as mayor. He soundly defeated Vrdolyak in the 1987 Democratic mayoral primary, so much so that some of Vrdolyak's aldermen defected to the Washington camp and Vrdolyak—the head of the CCDP—quit the Democratic Party to become a Republican. In addition to winning the black vote, Washington proved popular with Hispanic voters and captured 20 percent of the white vote.

Enjoying a 67 percent public approval rating, Washington consolidated his power in the city, secured an effective majority in the city council, and began to register accomplishments. He pushed through a tough city ethics ordinance and demanded an unpopular tax increase to put the city on a sound fiscal course. He also appointed African Americans to many high-level positions, including police superintendent, city corporation counsel, Chicago Housing Authority chairman, Chicago Transit Authority chairman, city budget director, and park district director.

In the final analysis, however, Washington's accomplishments did not match his rhetoric. Defenders point out that it took Washington four and a half years to consolidate his mayoral power. To be sure, even the most cynical of Chicagoans admired the nerve of a black man who marched—smiling and waving—in St. Patrick's Day parades wearing a "Sons of St. Patrick" sash. The city saw few improvements in public housing during the Washington years, however, and the public schools probably deteriorated during Washington's reign. Washington proved to be a first-class politician but only a second-class administrator and city manager.

It is hard to imagine a bumpier course of events during Chicago's transition from the old Daley machine to post-Daley politics. Daley had died suddenly, Bilandic had fumbled during the blizzards, Byrne had handed the machine its first mayoral defeat ever in 1979, Washington had given political power to black Chicagoans in 1983, and the city council had ground to a halt for months. Things did get bumpier, however. Washington died unexpectedly in November 1987 at the age of sixty-five. State law required the city council to select his successor from among sitting aldermen. The predominantly white council realized that Washington's successor ought to be black, and two men emerged as front-runners: Timothy Evans and Eugene Sawyer. Evans was an outspoken, flashy leader considered by many to be Washington's right-hand man. Washington's true confidant, however, was the quiet, capable Eugene Sawyer, who was also an old Daley man. Chicagoan Monroe Anderson described him this way: "Eugene Sawyer was a nice man. A little quiet, but very nice. And somewhat boring."[16] Twenty-three white aldermen and six black aldermen joined to name Sawyer as Washington's successor.

Evans's supporters—among them Jesse Jackson, who had rushed home from the Persian Gulf to enter the debate over Washington's successor—were furious. They painted Sawyer as the white man's candidate and the Uncle Tom mayor who would betray his people. The true heir to the mayor's chair, they maintained, was Evans. The Evans faction's criticism of Sawyer was so damning that Sawyer was never able to govern effectively. He was permanently crippled by local African Americans' charge that he was selling out his own people. African American political leaders in the city were never able to mend their fences, and the alliance of coalitionists and nationalists died with Washington. Chicago muddled through two years of a hamstrung Sawyer administration before Evans gained a court order that forced an early mayoral election. Richard M. Daley, Richard J. Daley's son, defeated Sawyer in the Democratic Party's 1989 mayoral primary and went on to win the general election—the first white candidate in a major U.S. city to defeat a black incumbent.

Daley was a welcome relief to many Chicagoans of all colors. He was a calm moderate who refused to engage in the rhetoric and race-baiting that had marked city politics for the past decade. For example, he offered no harsh criticism of Sawyer as he challenged him for the Democratic Party's nomination. Daley correctly sensed that Chicagoans were weary of name-calling and mudslinging. He instead offered a businesslike demeanor, leadership, and, perhaps most important, stability. He promised to make the city work again, pledging "a strong dose of common sense."[17] After defeating Sawyer in the primary, he defeated Timothy Evans in the 1989 special election that Evans's people had secured. African American political leaders had predicted turmoil if Richard M. Daley—the man they dubbed "the Pharaoh's son"—ascended to the mayor's office. By 1991, however, Daley's moderation and even-handedness had won him a two-to-one approval rating among local blacks. He even garnered endorsements from the city's African American newspaper, the *Chicago Defender*.

Following his special election victory in 1989, Daley went on to win reelection in 1991 and 1995. Daley the Younger turned out to be a different kind of mayor than his father. Richard M. Daley saw himself as a chief executive officer or a manager, not a political boss. To that end, he made efficient management of the city his goal. By 1996, he had balanced seven city budgets in a row. He eliminated patronage jobs, the primary source of his father's political power. (Daley controlled only about one thousand of the city's forty-one thousand jobs in 1996.) Daley also cut payrolls in several city departments, implemented innovations in city management, and even privatized some public works jobs, such as janitorial services, drug abuse counseling, operation of O'Hare's parking garages, and the junking of abandoned cars. His father would never have done these things, as they would have crippled the CCDP by eliminating patronage. Richard M. Daley had no machine to protect, however; he knew he had to win the public's confidence. In addition to streamlining city hall, Daley also pursued economic growth and job expansion. His probusiness platform won him generous (and legal) campaign contributions from businessmen. His careful attention to urban details such as sanitation, public schools, and city streets (two-thirds of which were repaved between 1989 and 1998) won him a reputation as a capable administrator.

How different is Richard M. Daley from his father? Consider some of his actions. For city employees, the younger Daley approved the extension of city benefits to homosexual couples who lived together, treating homosexual "spouses" and heterosexual spouses on equal terms. It is difficult to imagine Richard J. Daley even considering such a measure. The younger Daley also aggressively endorsed affirmative action programs in the city, a position that endeared him to many local blacks. "I think you have to give this mayor high marks; he's trying to reach out to all communities," commented Jesse Jackson Jr., son of the Reverend Jesse Jackson. "Mayor Daley has supported affirmative action while others have opposed it for years. For this mayor to be so progressive is to his infinite credit."[18] In addition, Daley granted neighborhoods a great deal of autonomy in his ongoing neighborhood restoration program, which has spent two billion dollars in twenty different Chicago neighborhoods. Perhaps, like his son, Richard J. Daley would have built Grecian pillars in Greek Town as part of a neighborhood restoration project, but it is doubtful the senior Daley would have flown Puerto Rican flags in Humboldt Park, as his son did. Richard M. Daley broke all precedents with his neighborhood development plan on North Halsted Street, the city's gay district. Here Daley budgeted $3.2 million to renovate eight blocks, commissioned public artwork that explicitly celebrated gay pride, and installed decorative electric lights in the color of the gay-pride flag. No one can say that the Irish Catholic kid from Bridgeport had not adapted to the times.

The Richard M. Daley era seems to have marked an end to the rancorous, turmoil-filled politics that occurred between 1976 and 1989. The secret to Daley's success is combining careful attention to the details of urban governance with liberal support of the city's many communities. His no-frills management of the city earned him American City and County's 1997 Municipal Leader of the Year award. Perhaps Daley is the first of a new breed of politicians in Chicago. Unlike his father, he has no machine to guarantee reelection. He relies only on his record to win votes. Unlike Byrne and Washington, he is not a charismatic speaker who rouses audiences with fiery orations. He is instead a pragmatist who earns grudging respect for his quiet management of the city. Few characterize Daley as creative or imaginative, but even his critics agree that he has proved a sensible and competent urban manager.

WARD POLITICS IN THE POST-MACHINE ERA

If Richard M. Daley is indeed a new breed of politician, there remain plenty of the old breed in Chicago. The machine of the 1960s is dead, but some old machine regulars have adapted quite well to new political realities. Dick Mell is one such survivor.[19] Mell is Chicago's Thirty-third Ward alderman, a position he has held since 1975. With an army of campaign workers that numbers one thousand and a perennial campaign fund, Mell is the undisputed king of the 2.5-square-mile ward near Kedzie Avenue and Irving Park. His fifty-six thousand constituents know that if they need a stop sign installed, a tree trimmed by the city's forestry bureau, a curb fixed, a fee waived, a road resurfaced, a zoning ordinance changed, or an unsightly garage demolished, they can count on Mell. More than half of all the legislation introduced by Mell in the city council deals with either streets or sidewalks, and Mell and his fellow aldermen waive, reduce, or refund about one million dollars in city fees annually through special city council legislation. Perhaps four hundred of Mell's campaign workers hold city or state jobs.

In many ways life has changed little for Mell since the demise of the machine. "To me, politics is a game of pluses," says Mell. "You identify your plus voters and get them to the polls." Mell wins votes by doing favors for his constituents; they pay him back with votes. This was how Daley's machine operated in the 1950s. Mell also has ties to criminal elements. People in his ward are fearful of gangs, and Mell calls himself "probably the biggest gangbuster in the world." Nevertheless, Mell employed a top gang leader, Ray Rolon of the Maniac Latin Disciples, as a precinct worker. One could even reach Rolon by leaving messages with Mell's secretary. Mell also earns money off the liquor business, much as the machine did during the Daley years. His constituents think their ward has too many noisy bars and taverns, and Mell quickly agrees with them. Although Mell controls the all-important liquor licenses in his ward, as do many aldermen, he nevertheless quietly works behind the scenes to keep those businesses open and even to bring new ones into the ward, because grateful liquor store and bar owners give campaign contributions to aldermen who help them secure liquor licenses. Perhaps the presence of this kind of "appreciation money" explains why 324 candidates filed to run for the city's fifty aldermanic seats in 1990, even though the job pays only $40,000 per year.

What has changed for Mell is that he no longer acts as a cog in the CCDP machine. He is now an independent operator, an alderman who looks out only for himself and his ward. He makes deals with other aldermen and votes against them when necessary. There is no longer an organization to keep aldermen such as Mell in line. Like Europe's feudal lords of old, aldermen exercise absolute sovereignty over their small fiefdoms, sometimes collaborate with neighboring power brokers, and sometimes go to war with those same neighboring political leaders. That means that Mell can pursue the interests of his constituents with reckless abandon and thereby win their undying loyalty, which is one reason Mell has had only one serious election challenge since 1979. At least in some ways, the balkanized structure of Chicago politics—forty-nine other aldermen are in much the same position as Mell—is similar to the political environment of 1900. Like Carter Harrison II, who also followed his father into the mayor's office, Richard M. Daley must create working coalitions among fiercely independent aldermen such as Mell.

URBAN PROBLEMS: CRIME, EDUCATION, AND THE ECONOMY

As is true for many large U.S. cities, Chicago has faced troubled times during the 1970s, 1980s, and 1990s. One especially troubling problem in post-1976 Chicago has been crime. The 936 murders registered in the city in 1992 marked the highest total since 1974. Perhaps even more disturbing was a recent demographic profile of city murder victims: 80 percent were African Americans and 25 percent were under the age of twenty-one. Young Chicagoans are being reared in a culture in which violent crime, prison sentences, and early death are normative. Author Alex Kotlowitz recently asked a classroom of Chicago youngsters how many had ever witnessed a shooting or stabbing; all but three raised their hands. The high crime rate has had economic consequences as well, scaring potential investors away from the inner-city areas that need investment most. One fast-food restaurant in the city closed after being robbed nine days in a row by nine different assailants. Entrepreneurs, retailers, and banks have abandoned whole portions of the inner city, preferring to do business in the suburbs.

Along with crime, the pitiful state of public schools has also encouraged flight to the suburbs. U.S. Secretary of Education William Bennett proclaimed Chicago's public schools the worst in the nation in 1987, and, despite reform efforts, they have improved little since then. By the early 1990s, the public schools (which educated more than 400,000 pupils) had a dropout rate of 44 percent. In an attempt to raise educational standards, the city Board of Education purposed in 1996 to end the practice of "social promotion." New policies required students to demonstrate seventh-grade-level proficiency in reading and in math in order to move on to high school. In a typical eighth-grade class at the city's Donoghue Elementary School that year, only eleven of forty students had scores high enough to matriculate to high school. Margaret A. Tolson, principal of a city elementary school, explains how the crime and education problems are related: "We've also had a couple of stabbings. And the difficult thing about it has been when you return the child who was stabbed to the same classroom with the child who did the stabbing, it's difficult to ask them to concentrate on what they need to concentrate on."[20] One city high school went so far as to order plastic utensils for its lunchroom after a small lunchroom riot. Given the tragic state of public education, it is little surprise that an estimated one Chicago adult in three was functionally illiterate in the mid-1990s.

A third major problem confronted by post-1976 Chicagoans has been the city's economic woes. Like many midwestern cities in the Rustbelt, Chicago has been experiencing the transition from an economy based on industry and manufacturing, which proved so vibrant in the years before 1970, to an economy based on service and technology. Such transitions are difficult, especially when they are hindered by high levels of functional illiteracy among the labor force. The city has lost 60 percent of its manufacturing jobs since 1960: it lost a total of 123,000 jobs between 1973 and 1977, 150,000 more between 1979 and 1983, and another 83,000 between 1990 and 1993. On Chicago's West Side at midcentury, for example, a Western Electric plant employed 43,000 Chicagoans, while an International Harvester factory employed 14,000. By the mid-1990s, both plants were closed, a circumstance that has had many repercussions in the community: the unemployment rate rose to nearly 50 percent, almost half of the available housing in the area has been abandoned, and the high school dropout rate soared to 59 percent. This economic malaise has affected the Loop as well: as late as 1993, the central business district suffered from a 21 percent vacancy rate, the highest figure since the Great Depression.

At the same time, Chicago's recent economic malaise has led to the growth and prosperity of its suburbs. High technology businesses such as American Telephone and Telegraph, Bell Laboratory, Amoco Research Center, Argonne National Laboratory, and Fermi National Accelerator Laboratory have located along the East-West Tollway in DuPage County. Honeywell, Motorola, Northrup Defense Systems, Pfizer, and Western Electric have relocated to metropolitan Chicago's so-called Golden Corridor, a strip that reaches into Northwestern Cook County along the Northwest Tollway between O'Hare Airport and Elgin and has brought prosperity to the communities of Elk Grove Village, Schaumburg, Rolling Meadows, Arlington Heights, Palatine, and Hoffman Estates. The number of jobs in Lake County, located one hour north of the Loop, has increased 53 percent between 1983 and 1992; Abbott Laboratory, Baxter Travenol Laboratory, Sara Lee, and the corporate offices for Walgreen drug stores, for example, are all located in Lake County.

In 1991, DuPage County was judged the number-one real estate growth county in the Midwest, and Lake County ranked second. If the suburbs are included in analyses of Chicago's economy, then the picture does not look so bleak. By the 1990s, the Chicago area boasted the fourth highest number of information technology jobs, trailing California, New York, and Texas. Indeed, one team of scholars concluded in the mid-1980s that, if the entire Chicago metropolitan region was treated as though it were a country, Chicagoland's "gross national product" would rank as the eleventh largest in the world.[21]

The suburbs, however, are a long distance from perhaps the bleakest side of Chicago, namely, its public housing projects. By 1976, the Chicago Housing Authority was the city's largest landlord and the second largest landlord in the nation: it supervised 140,000 tenants (or 4.5 percent of the city's population) in more than 42,000 housing units. Richard J. Daley might well have been an administrative genius who made Chicago the city that works, but his cynical mismanagement of the city's public housing was scandalous. A 1982 federal study reported that CHA properties were in a state of woeful disrepair and were plagued by excessive operating costs and staggering deficits. What caused the problem? By the mid-1960s, Daley and the CHA had ceased attempting to provide quality housing for the city's poor. The CHA's sole purpose for existing, according to the federal report, was the "acquisition of as many Federal . . . dollars as possible for the creation of patronage jobs and financial opportunities."[22] The report could have added that by the late 1960s Da-

Table 8. POPULATION OF THE SIX-COUNTY CHICAGO METROPOLITAN AREA, 1970–1990

	1970	1980	1990	1970–1990 percent change
Chicago	3,400,000	3,000,000	2,800,000	- 18%
non-Chicago part of Cook County	2,094,000	2,254,000	2,305,000	+ 10
DuPage County	488,000	659,000	782,000	+ 60
Lake County	383,000	440,000	516,000	+ 35
Will County	248,000	324,000	357,000	+ 44
Kane County	251,000	278,000	317,000	+ 26
McHenry County	112,000	148,000	183,000	+ 63

ley and the CHA were using federally subsidized low-income housing to maintain the city's rigidly segregated neighborhoods. Largely because of the high-rise projects, a mid-1990s University of Chicago study indicated that Chicago was the most racially segregated city in the nation (in 1995, 70 percent of all African Americans in the city lived in census blocks whose populations were greater than 90 percent black). By the 1990s, all agreed that the projects were catastrophic failures. The housing units themselves were dismal, filthy, and poorly maintained; many contained walls that were no more than cinder blocks. When a group of Communist officials from the Soviet Union visited the Henry Horner Homes during construction in 1955, they were horrified that the walls consisted of exposed block and not plaster. "We would be thrown off our jobs in Moscow if we left unfinished walls like this," said I. K. Kozvilia, the Soviet minister of city and urban construction.[23]

The high-rise projects had offered Spartan, safe, and desirable housing when they were first constructed. By the 1970s, however, they had fallen into a state of wretched disrepair. Doors were missing, windows were broken, appliances did not work, and water ran from sink and tub spigots twenty-four hours a day. Chain-link fencing was installed on exposed outside walkways and balconies as a safety measure, but it made the projects look and feel like prisons. In Henry Horner Homes, a putrid smell wafted up into the apartments from the basement. Gwen Anderson, the housing manager of the complex, inspected the dank, dark basements of the six buildings of the Henry Horner Homes complex in 1989. A portion of her report to CHA superiors on the basements' contents reads:

> An estimated two thousand (2000) appliances:
>
> Refrigerators—some new, with the insulation pulled out, missing motors, aluminum freezer compartments missing, electrical cords ripped out, some standing in pool of water and rusting away.
>
> Ranges—some stacked wall to wall—floor to ceiling and barring entry into the storage room, parts missing (doors, burners, grates, boiler trays, knobs, panels, etc.), standing in the pools of water and rusting away.
>
> It should be noted also that these appliances were heavily infested with roaches, fleas. Cats were bedding and walking the rafters (pipes) and dead rodents and animals were lying in the storage areas, stench and putrid odor abounded. (The manager became nauseated to the point of intensely vomiting for relief, and could not continue the inspection until after being revived.) Soiled female undergarments and paraphernalia with foul odors were lying around. No equipment presently in use by staff could be used to withstand this odor beyond a minute![24]

The projects depressed entire areas of Chicago. "There were no banks, only currency exchanges, which charged customers up to $8.00 for every welfare check cashed," reported Alex Kotlowitz as he surveyed the area around Chicago's projects in 1987. He added, "There were no public libraries, movie theaters, skating rinks, or bowling alleys to entertain the neighborhood's children. For the infirm, there were two neighborhood clinics . . . [that] teetered on the edge of bankruptcy and would close by the end of 1989. Yet the death rate of newborn babies exceeded infant mortality rates in a number of Third World countries, including Chile, Costa Rica, Cuba, and Turkey."[25] One recent study concluded that nine CHA projects were among the ten poorest neighborhoods in the United States. The area was so poor that, when Mother Teresa visited it in 1982, she assigned nuns from her Missionaries of Charity to work at the city's Henry Horner Homes. Gangs ruled the projects, sometimes charging residents a fee to bring groceries into their own high-rise buildings or to use their own elevators. Fortified by the highly lucrative drug trade, these gangs were so well armed and ruthlessly violent that police often stayed away from the projects. When several children fell out of high-rise windows in 1993, the CHA sent crews to install window guards. Gangs drove them away with gunfire.

In the late 1990s, the CHA admitted that rehabilitating the projects was hopeless. Studies indicated that it was cheaper to provide subsidized private housing than to operate the city's notorious Robert Taylor Homes complex. A 1997 report confirmed that abysmal poverty was commonplace in the housing complexes: only 4 percent of the residents in Robert Taylor Homes were employed, and the average income for residents was a paltry $5,905. The CHA began demolishing several high-rises and slated the entire twenty-eight-building Robert Taylor Homes complex for demolition over the next fifteen years.

URBAN PROMISE:
GENTRIFICATION, REFORM, AND ECONOMIC DEVELOPMENT

The years between 1976 and 1997 have not been ones of unmitigated woe in Chicago. Many positive signs suggest that the city is alive and well, as ready as any large urban area to enter the twenty-first century. For one thing, many of the city's old ethnic neighborhoods have experienced a new vitality in the 1990s. During the 1970s and 1980s, gentrification—the process of renovating older and less desirable neighborhoods—was confined primarily to the lakefront areas. By the mid-1990s, a second layer of gentrification was emerging near the University of Illinois's Chicago campus in the West Side and extending north through Wicker Park and Bucktown. The old Little Italy neighborhood, which had seemed hopelessly blighted in the 1970s, made a revival in the 1990s. For the first time in thirty years, local banks began moving back into the West Side. Sparkling new multiscreen movie theaters opened in the West Side's Lawndale and the South Side's Chatham and Chicago Lawn communities in late 1997; the Lawndale theater, for example, boasted ten screens and cost $10 million. City officials believe these are the first upscale theaters to be constructed in these areas in thirty years, and city hall claims that its innovative tax incentive programs are what made these projects possible. The Near North Side has seen a rash of new high-rise condominium construction in the 1990s in response to the Loop's recent prosperity. About two hundred of the area's eighteen hundred new dwellings will be in the Bristol, a forty-one-story building whose condominiums will cost between $230,000 and $1.3 million each. The many young adults moving into these newly refurbished areas may well be forming the nucleus of a new urban middle class, one that resides in stable, integrated neighborhoods such as Edgewater. "The old strict ethnic lines on which neighborhoods were once formed are breaking up," observes Joseph Epstein, a resident of the city for more than half a century. He adds, "Once upon a time, if you told me where you lived in Chicago I could tell you, with a fair degree of accuracy, your family income, religion, ethnicity and whether you ate in the dining room or the kitchen. No more. The biggest ethnic group in Chicago just now seems to be the young, that transient class."[26] Among those breathing new life into the city are Hispanic immigrants.[27] As late as 1960, Chicago's Hispanic population numbered only 56,000 (less than 2 percent of the city's total population). By 1990, that number had soared to 535,000 (19 percent of city's population); with continuing immigration, it was projected that one-fourth of all Chicagoans would be Hispanic by 2000. Only New York City and Los Angeles claim larger Hispanic populations than Chicago.

Chicago's Hispanics—as many new immigrants before them throughout the city's history—seemed ill equipped to trigger an economic renaissance. In 1990, 71 percent of the city's non-Hispanics were high school graduates and 22 percent possessed college degrees; the comparable numbers for the city's Hispanics were 41 percent and 7 percent, respectively. Hispanics, however, have proved both hardworking and willing to take low-paying entry-level jobs—the formula for success embraced by European immigrants in 1900—and they have injected new economic vitality into many downtown neighborhoods. Chicago's Hispanics possessed a gross purchasing power of between eight and nine billion dollars in the 1990s. The average household income stood at $33,000, which was 8 percent higher than the national Hispanic average. The community supported two Spanish-language newspapers in the 1990s, *La Raza* (published by Uruguayan Luis Rossi, with a mid-1990s circulation of 150,000) and *¡Exito!* (published by the *Chicago Tribune*, with a circulation of 80,000), and one Spanish-language television station. The formerly Czech and Polish neighborhood of South Lawndale had fallen on hard times by the 1970s; Hispanic

Table 9. HISPANIC POPULATION OF METROPOLITAN CHICAGO,
1980 AND 1990

	1980	*1990*	*percent change*
Mexican	256,000	353,000	+ 38%
Puerto Rican	112,000	120,000	+ 7
Cuban	12,000	10,000	- 17
other	43,000	63,000	+ 47
total	422,000	546,000	+ 29

Source: Jorge Casuso and Eduardo Camacho, "Latino Chicago," in Melvin G. Holli and Peter d'A. Jones, *Ethnic Chicago: A Multicultural Portrait* (Grand Rapids, Mich.: Eerdmans Publishing Company, 1994), 369.

(largely Mexican) immigrants transformed the community into the prosperous enclave of Little Village. Home to nearly seventy thousand Hispanics in 1990, housing values there doubled between 1990 and 1995. By the 1990s, the commercial heart of the neighborhood, Twenty-sixth Street, generated more tax revenue than any other retail area in the city except for Michigan Avenue. The formerly Bohemian neighborhood of Pilsen is now a vibrant Hispanic community featuring taquerias, pushcarts carrying paletas, and colorful wall murals in the tradition of Diego Rivera.

Many Hispanic immigrants have also left the city for the more economically prosperous suburbs; for example, 63 percent of local Mexican immigrants live outside the city limits in such suburbs as Aurora, Waukegan, Joliet, and Elk Grove Village. Those Hispanics who have remained in the city earnestly protect their communities from developers and gentrification plans that they deem are not in their own best interests. For example, the University of Illinois's Chicago campus had been built in the late 1960s by displacing the city's Italian American Taylor Street neighborhood and small Hispanic community. When the school announced plans for more expansion in the mid-1990s, some local Hispanics feared more housing displacement and escalating property taxes, and they opted to press for a quid pro quo: acquiescence to university expansion in exchange for guarantees of more jobs earmarked for community residents and financial commitments to neighborhood development. The small and marginalized Hispanic community possessed no

Table 10. HISPANIC COMMUNITIES IN CHICAGO, 1990

	Hispanic population	Percentage of community that is Hispanic
South Lawndale/Little Village	69,000	85%
Logan Square	54,000	65
West Town	53,000	61
Lower West Side/Pilsen	40,000	88
Humboldt Park	29,000	43
New City/Back of the Yards	20,000	38
Belmont Cragin	7,000	30
Hermosa	16,000	68
Albany Park	15,000	31
Chicago Lawn	14,000	28

Source: Casuso and Camacho, "Latino Chicago," in Holli and Jones, *Ethnic Chicago,* 347.

such negotiating power in the late 1960s; by the mid-1990s, they clearly enjoyed a great deal of clout in Chicago politics.

Chicago is also home to one of the strongest black middle-class communities in America. Although the largely African American housing projects receive most of the media's attention, only about one-third of the city's blacks could be classified as poor. Twenty percent of local blacks are members of the upper class, and 45 percent are middle class. The city boasts one of the largest populations of black homeowners in the nation, as tours through the South Side's Pill Hill, Roseland, Washington Heights, Gresham, and Chatham neighborhoods suggest. The affluence of these virtually all-black communities often stun visitors, says Lee Nunery, an assistant vice president of a Chicago bank and a resident of Chatham. "When friends from work come out here, they're absolutely shocked. They say, 'Geez, you have grass and trees and squirrels. This is kind of like Wilmette, isn't it? It's kind of like Evanston, isn't it?' They say, 'Geez, the house is nice.' I say, 'What did you expect, jungle vines?'"[28] When the Dominick's grocery store chain, one of the largest in Chicago, proposed building a store in Chatham, it had to submit first to demands set forth by Chatham's well-organized civic leaders: the manager of the store must be black, at least 80 percent of the management team must be African American, most employees must be hired from the neighborhood, and company officials must meet with community leaders every three months. Dominick's consented.

Despite this apparent success in creating a stable middle-class black community, some fear that Chatham is dying—or at least graying—because young families are moving to integrated neighborhoods such as Lake Point Tower, Outer Drive East, and Lincoln Park. Others applaud the migration as the ultimate fruit of the 1960s civil rights movement. "When I was active in civil rights, we were talking about an integrated America," said seventy-three-year-old Judge Leighton. "I thought we were struggling for the very thing that to some extent is happening now [the exodus of African Americans from all-black communities to integrated ones]. And I have a great deal of difficulty mustering any feeling of regret about this."[29]

Many in the mid-1990s also believed that the city's economy had finally turned the corner. They saw the city as having endured a twenty-year-long restructuring period that was slow, painful, and necessary. Although many jobs had been lost, the productivity of the city's manufacturing sector doubled from 1969 to 1993. The overseas export business had expanded noticeably, probably doubling in volume between 1987 and 1991. All this suggests that local businesses had become leaner and more competitive. By the mid-1990s, the city had apparently even regained some of the lucrative convention and tourist business that it had lost to Sunbelt cities in the 1970s and 1980s. Between 1987 and 1997, Chicago's convention attendance rose 65 percent from 2.8 million to 4.6 million, an increase that allowed city hotels to record 1997 occupancy levels that were the highest since 1966. Politicians were quick to claim credit for this economic renaissance, and few denied that they had made economic development a priority. One local government official was amazed by the "machinations of state and regional agencies" that "subordinated everything else to economic development."[30] Although few Chicagoans in the mid-1990s were willing to declare local economic woes cured, many thought they could finally see the light at the end of the tunnel.

In 1990s Chicago, any optimism must be tempered with strong doses of caution. Wealth and poverty remain unevenly spread throughout the city. In particular, the task of inner-city redevelopment—certainly one of the city's most pressing needs—is far more difficult than most imagine. Three things must usually happen before blighted areas undergo significant redevelopment. First, wealthy outsiders, who are usually white suburbanites, must be persuaded to invest in run-down inner-city communities. Second, residents of the target area, most of whom are black, must accept the intervention of the outside investors. Locals usually have little control over investors' redevelopment plans and often chafe at what they regard as a new form of colonialism. Third, local politicians must be willing to see the redevelopment plans proceed. Even if they do not help the process along, they must at least refrain from blocking the project. Investors, residents, and politicians must all cooperate if redevelopment projects are to succeed, and it is easy and common for one of the three parties to block the endeavor.

Inner-city residents have grown increasingly reluctant to accept the redevelopment plans of outsiders. They charge that such plans often replace existing housing with office buildings, parking lots, parks, and expensive apartments. Poorer residents are simply displaced. Accordingly, they often drive hard bargains and wring significant concessions from developers before consenting to urban redevelopment projects in their neighborhoods. The recent redevelopment battle in the Near West Side is an example of this process. In this dingy area near the old Chicago Stadium, half the adults had no high school diploma, half the men were unemployed, and more than half of the families lived on earnings below the poverty level. When the Chicago Bears considered building a new football stadium there, however, area residents displayed their impressive political savvy and killed the proposal. Then the Chicago Bulls and Blackhawks proposed a new basketball and hockey area. Before residents consented to construction of the United Center, they secured sixteen replacement houses at $235,000 each, a no-interest loan of $600,000 to develop seventy-five new townhouses, a new park, a new library, and a grant of $200,000 to develop retail businesses on Madison Street. Such investments seem to have paid off. The Near West Side economy began to boom in the late 1990s, and the high-end residential real estate market looked rosy. Fancy restaurants began to lure customers to West Randolph Street, and the number of jobs in the area rose 20 percent from 1990 to 1995. Area residents have also benefited from the sports arena in ways they never expected. When the Bulls basketball team fined Dennis Rodman $104,000 (or two-games' pay) for using profanity and allowing his swearing to be aired on television, team officials gave the money to a Near West Side community group to renovate the homes of long-time community residents. Eighty-year-old Margaret Glenn, a resident of West Jackson Boulevard for fifty years, acquired a new wrought-iron fence and a refurbished facade for her aging home. "I love Rodman because he gave me all this," quipped Glenn. "He can say anything he wants to say."[31]

Some believe that Chicago is a dying city with a bleak future. Such pessimistic prognoses often stem from comparing today's city with an idealized version of the city, perhaps the Chicago of the 1950s. The city will never return to its glory days, these critics claim. This claim overlooks how the Chicago of 1890 bore little resemblance to the Chicago of 1840, and how the Chicago of 1960 differed significantly from the Chicago of 1925. If history teaches us anything, it is that the Chicago of 2030 will look little like the Chicago of 1990. The only constant throughout the city's history has been change. Chicago has successfully adapted to new situations and responded to new challenges.

Yet some things seem to have changed little. Carl Sandburg accurately captured the city's brawling, earthy, unpretentious character when he christened Chicago "The City of the Big Shoulders" in 1914. That same spirit seemingly persists today. Author Scott Turow, for example, called the city "The Capital of Real Life" in 1996. "People tell me that they like Chicago, extolling it as 'a real place, a real city,'" writes native Chicagoan Turow. "That it is. . . . No glamour, no jive. It's not like either of the coastal megalopoli, the one in southern California, or the universe and city of New York; it can't compete. It is a particularly Chicago thing that the baseball team for which I root with near-religious fervor has not won the World Series in the entire 76 years that the Cubs have played at Wrigley Field. New York City is the city of winners; Chicago's where there are losers too. L.A. is the home of stars. Just Plain Folks live in Chicago."[32] Although Chicago is no longer the Hog Butcher for the World, the Stacker of Wheat, or the Nation's Freight Handler as it was in 1914, some of Sandburg's words seem as appropriate today as they did almost a century ago:

> And having answered so I turn once more to those who sneer
> at this my city, and I give them back the sneer and say to them:
> Come and show me another city with lifted head singing so proud
> to be alive and coarse and strong and cunning.

NOTES

●

1: THE EARLY WORLD OF CHIGAGOU

1. The word *Chigagou* first appears in the diaries of the French Jesuit missionary Jacques Marquette. The word was Marquette's attempt to spell phonetically the American Indians' name for this place. My spelling is in no way an official spelling; others spell it *Chicagou* and *Chicagoua*. For a spirited discussion of how the city of Chicago got its name, see John F. Swenson, "Chicagoua/Chicago: The Origin, Meaning, and Etymology of a Place Name," *Illinois Historical Journal* 84 (Winter 1991): 235–48.

2. Bessie Louise Pierce, in *A History of Chicago: The Beginning of a City, 1673–1848*, vol. 1 (Chicago: University of Chicago Press, 1937), 3–5, estimates that Mud Lake extended from present-day Harlem Avenue and West Forty-seventh Street to Kedzie Avenue and West Thirty-first Street.

3. For more on the Native American inhabitants of the Chicago area, see Charles W. Markman, *Chicago before History: The Prehistoric Archaeology of a Modern Metropolitan Area* (Springfield, Ill.: Illinois Historic Preservation Agency, 1991); William C. Sturtevant, ed., *Handbook of North American Indians,* vol. 15 (Washington, D.C.: Smithsonian Institution, 1978). A good discussion of intertribal warfare—even in the face of a growing number of hostile white settlers—is found in Roger L. Nichols, *Black Hawk and the Warrior's Path* (Arlington Heights, Ill.: Harlan Davidson, 1992), 1–20.

4. Chicago Department of Development and Planning, *Historic City: The Settlement of Chicago* (Chicago: n.p., 1976), 3.

5. Thomas A. Meehan, "Jean Baptiste Point du Sable, The First Chicagoan," *Journal of the Illinois State Historical Society* 56 (1963): 441.

6. These details are sketchy and therefore disputed. For an alternative version, see Meehan, "Jean Baptiste Point du Sable," 442.

7. Quoted in Donald L. Miller, *City of the Century: The Epic of Chicago and the Making of America* (New York: Simon and Schuster, 1996), 45.

8. Quoted in Miller, *City of the Century,* 46.

9. Pierce, *History of Chicago,* I, 11.

2: CHIGAGOU BECOMES CHICAGO

1. I use the term *Anglo-American* to designate those people who populated the British colonies in North America. Most of these colonists, at least in the 1700s, were British, Scottish, or Scotsmen who settled in Ireland (that is, the Scots-Irish).

2. Between 1750 and 1850, Americans referred to Ohio, Indiana, Illinois, Michigan, Wisconsin, and Minnesota as "the Northwest." To present-day readers, such terminology (while historically accurate) can be confusing. Historians therefore refer to the northwest of the 1780s as "the Old Northwest."

3. Kentucky had no colonial legislature or assembly at this time because the territory was too sparsely populated to be organized formally. This band of Kentuckians therefore sought a commission from the Virginia government, who held a vague claim to all lands to the west.

4. Meehan, "Jean Baptiste Point du Sable," 447.

5. Cultural exchanges between Indians and settlers in Chigagou were common. Anthropologist James A. Clifton, in "Chicago Was Theirs," *Chicago History* 1 (Spring 1970): 8, noted that a group of Potawatomi in Kansas in 1962 greeted one another with *bon jour.*

6. Chicago Department of Development and Planning, *Historic City,* 5; Meehan, "Jean Baptiste Point du Sable," 451.

7. The ceded tract was bounded by present-day Fullerton Avenue on the north, South Thirty-first Street on the south, Forty-eighth Avenue on the west, and Lake Michigan on the east.

8. Whistler's grandson was James Abbott McNeill Whistler, the famous American artist who painted *Arrangement in Gray and Black: Portrait of the Artist's Mother,* commonly called *Whistler's Mother.*

9. Robert Cromie, *A Short History of Chicago* (San Francisco: Lexicos, 1984), 17.

10. David Lindsey, "The Founding of Chicago" *American History Illustrated* 8 (December 1973): 28.

11. In 1815, the U.S. government estimated that Illinois was home to 4,800 Potawatomi, 3,200 Sac, 2,400 Winnebago, 1,600 Kickapoo, and 1,200 Fox.

12. Simon Pokogon, son of the Potawatomi chief whose men attacked Fort Dearborn, observed, "When whites are killed, it is a massacre. When Indians are killed, it is a fight." Quoted in Richard C. Lindberg, *Quotable Chicago* (Chicago: Onion Press, 1996), 33.

13. The British had been involved in almost constant war with France since the late 1790s. Napoleon's conquest of Europe only intensified the European war. By 1814, Britain was exhausted from its lengthy and costly war with France.

14. Cromie, *Short History of Chicago,* 32.

15. Many Enlightenment thinkers (for example, John Locke, Jean Jacques Rousseau, and Voltaire) rejected the traditional belief that humans were born with sinful natures. Instead, they believed that all humans were born as "blank slates," or tabulae rasae. They believed humans are born neither good nor bad, but rather neutral. Humans who grow up in good environments tend to be good; those who live in bad environments tend to be less good. Many Enlightenment thinkers theorized that men who live in pristine, noble environments are usually the most noble of men. The North American wilderness was allegedly a prime example of such a blissful, pure environment. The Enlightenment thinkers' view of *noble savages,* the term they used for the Native Americans, then, was quite complimentary. Although lacking in education and culture, they believed, such men were unstained by the sins of modern society.

16. Louise Christopher, "Henry Whitehead, Circuit Rider," *Chicago History* 5 (Spring 1976): 5.

17. William Cronon, *Nature's Metropolis: Chicago and the Great West* (New York: W. W. Norton, 1991): 26.

18. Bessie Louise Pierce, ed., *As Others See Chicago: Impressions of Visitors, 1673–1933* (Chicago: University of Chicago Press, 1933), 28.

19. Quoted in Miller, *City of the Century,* 53.

20. Cromie, *Short History of Chicago,* 30; and Lindsey, "The Founding of Chicago," 30. Lindsey attributes the statement to Major Stephen Long.

21. Kenan Heise and Ed Baumann, *Chicago Originals: A Cast of the City's Colorful Characters* (Chicago: Bonus Books, 1995), 10.

22. Quoted in Miller, *City of the Century,* 53.

23. Cromie, *Short History of Chicago,* 42.

24. Ibid.

25. Pierce, *As Others See Chicago,* 74.

26. Anselm J. Gerwing, "The Chicago Indian Treaty of 1833," *Journal of the Illinois State Historical Society* 57 (1964): 122.

27. Heise and Baumann, *Chicago Originals,* 9. One scholar judges that the Potawatomi were fiercely independent and resisted assimilation. He writes that "they went voluntarily and with some sense of anticipation," eager to capitalize on the new opportunity offered them west of the Mississippi River (Clifton, "Chicago Was Theirs," 12).

28. Gerwing, "Chicago Indian Treaty of 1833," 127.

29. See Jacqueline Peterson, "The Founding Fathers: The Absorption of French-Indian Chicago, 1816–1837," in Melvin G. Holli and Peter d'A Jones, eds., *Ethnic Chicago: A Multicultural Portrait,* 4th ed. (Grand Rapids, Mich.: Eerdmans Publishing Company, 1994), 48–56.

30. Patrick E. McLear, "'. . . And Still They Come': Chicago from 1832–36," *Journal of the West* 7 (1968): 399.

31. Lindsey, "Founding of Chicago," 33.

3: BOOM, BUST, AND RECOVERY IN EARLY CHICAGO

1. Cromie, *Short History of Chicago*, 48–49.

2. The portage dilemma was the problem of transporting goods across the portage. If the bog was not flooded, transported goods had to be unloaded, moved by land to the opposite side of the portage, and reloaded onto boats. It often took several days to cross the ten-mile-long portage.

3. Pierce, *As Others See Chicago*, 83.

4. Cromie, *Short History of Chicago*, 48. Wright's phrase, "burst in a natural way," referred to land prices climbing so high that they eventually collapsed on their own accord. He implies that Jackson's specie circular forced land prices to collapse before they rose as high as they could have risen.

5. Craig Buettinger, "The Rise and Fall of Hiram Pearson: Mobility on the Urban Frontier," *Chicago History* 9 (Summer 1980): 112.

6. Cronon, *Nature's Metropolis*, 14.

7. Quoted in Daniel J. Boorstin, "The Businessman as an American Institution," in Alexander B. Callow, ed., *American Urban History: An Interpretive Reader with Commentaries* (New York: Oxford University Press, 1969), 138.

8. Quoted in William L. Downard, "William Butler Ogden and the Growth of Chicago," *Journal of the Illinois State Historical Society* 75 (Spring 1982): 47.

9. Quoted phrases from Pierce, *History of Chicago*, I, 204.

10. Ibid., 205.

11. Cromie, *Short History of Chicago*, 53.

12. Quoted in Miller, *City of the Century*, 67.

13. Cronon, *Nature's Metropolis*, 57.

14. Ernst Ekman, "Fredrika Bremer in Chicago in 1850," *Swedish Pioneer Historical Quarterly* 14 (October 1968): 238.

15. Irving Cutler, "The Jews of Chicago: From Shetl to Suburb," in Holli and Jones, *Ethnic Chicago*, 124. The number of German Jews in the city numbered around 1,500 in 1860.

16. Ekman, "Fredrika Bremer in Chicago in 1850," 242.

17. Pierce, *History of Chicago*, I, 258.

18. For example, Illinois law prohibited blacks from testifying in trials where whites were either defendants or plaintiffs. State laws also mandated that free blacks in Illinois carry proof of their status. If a questioned black failed to prove he was not a fugitive slave, he was incarcerated while newspaper advertisements proclaimed the capture of a possible runaway. If no slave owner stepped forward to claim his property, the jailed black was sold at auction to recoup the costs for jailing him.

19. In this regard, the Chicago churches typified American churches across the nation. Both the Presbyterian and Baptist denominations split nationwide, each forming an abolitionist northern church and a proslavery southern church.

20. Quoted in Lindberg, *Quotable Chicago*, 3.

21. Cronon, *Nature's Metropolis,* 57.

22. Pierce, *History of Chicago,* I, 204.

23. Cronon, *Nature's Metropolis,* 58.

24. The Whig Party flourished in the late 1830s, the 1840s, and the early 1850s. Initially an anti-Andrew Jackson party, it became a party that favored a more proactive state and national government.

25. Cronon, *Nature's Metropolis,* 63.

4: CHICAGO CONQUERS THE MIDWEST

1. Quoted in Lindberg, *Quotable Chicago,* 4.

2. Ibid., 3.

3. Cronon, *Nature's Metropolis,* 53.

4. Ekman, "Fredrika Bremer in Chicago in 1850," 238.

5. Pierce, *As Others See Chicago,* 150.

6. Noah Brooks and P. J. Staudenraus, "'The Empire City of the West': A View of Chicago in 1864," *Journal of the Illinois State Historical Society* 56 (1963): 342–43.

7. Pierce, *As Others See Chicago,* 230.

8. The Galena and Chicago Union never reached Galena as planned. Another railroad company, the Illinois Central, ran track to the town in 1854. Rather than compete with one another over the relatively small Galena market, the two rails worked out a cooperative arrangement.

The world's first commercial steam railway had begun operating in England in 1825, but by 1840 only 3,300 miles of track existed in all of the United States. During the 1840s, 6,000 more miles of track were built; by 1860, total rail mileage in the United States had jumped to 30,600.

9. Quoted in Downard, "William Butler Ogden and the Growth of Chicago," 54.

10. Cronon, *Nature's Metropolis,* 308.

11. Ibid., 71.

12. Ibid., 70.

13. Pierce, *As Others See Chicago,* 123.

14. Cronon, *Nature's Metropolis,* 91.

15. Ibid., 207–8.

16. Frederic Trautmann, "Arthur Holitischer's Chicago: A German Traveler's View of an American City," *Chicago History* 12 (Summer 1983): 44.

17. William S. Peterson, "Kipling's First Visit to Chicago," *Journal of the Illinois State Historical Society* 63 (1970): 296.

18. Quoted in Miller, *City of the Century,* 209.

19. Brian McGinty, "Mr. Sears and Mr. Roebuck," *American History Illustrated* (June 1986): 36.

20. Cronon, *Nature's Metropolis*, 338.

21. For a full discussion of this subject, see Arnold Lewis, *An Early Encounter with Tomorrow: Europeans, Chicago's Loop, and the World's Columbian Exposition* (Chicago: University of Illinois Press, 1997). These stories are recounted by Lewis.

22. Quoted in Douglas Bukowski, *Big Bill Thompson, Chicago, and the Politics of Image* (Urbana: University of Illinois Press, 1998), 107–8.

23. Garry Wills, "Chicago Underground," *The New York Review* (21 October 1993): 16.

5: LIFE IN A CITY ON THE MAKE

1. Ethnocultural issues dominated city as well as national politics. This explains why voter turnout during the 1880s and 1890s was the highest ever in U.S. history, routinely topping 80 percent of all eligible voters. When politics moved from ethnocultural questions to the policy debates of the Progressive Era (1900–1920), voter turnout dropped significantly.

2. Richard Wilson Renner, "In a Perfect Ferment: Chicago, the Know-Nothings, and the Riot for Lager Beer," *Chicago History* 5 (Fall 1976): 161.

3. In the mid-1850s, the Know-Nothings enjoyed many victories nationally. For example, they captured the Massachusetts legislature and elected more than forty U.S. congressmen.

4. Quoted in Theodore J. Karamanski, *Rally 'round the Flag: Chicago and the Civil War* (Chicago: Nelson-Hall Publishers, 1993), 173.

5. Cutler, "The Jews of Chicago," in Holli and Jones, *Ethnic Chicago*, 129–30.

6. Michael Funchion, "Irish Chicago: Church, Homeland, Politics, and Class—The Shaping of an Ethnic Group, 1870–1900," in Holli and Jones, *Ethnic Chicago*, 57.

7. David L. Protess, "Joseph Medill: Chicago's First Modern Mayor," in Paul M. Green and Melvin G. Holli, eds., *The Mayors: The Chicago Political Tradition*, rev. ed. (Carbondale: Southern Illinois University Press, 1995), 267 n. 12.

8. Quoted in Miller, *City of the Century*, 449.

9. Dick Griffin, "Opium Addiction in Chicago: 'The Noblest and the Best Brought Low,'" *Chicago History* 6 (Summer 1977): 108.

10. Quoted in Miller, *City of the Century*, 436.

11. Katherine R. Morgan, "'We Do Have to Work Hard,'" *Chicago History* 26 (Spring 1997): 28.

12. Quoted in Miller, *City of the Century*, 122.

13. Frank J. Piehl, "Chicago's Early Fight to 'Save Our Lake,'" *Chicago History* 5 (Winter 1976–1977): 225.

14. Bessie Louise Pierce, *A History of Chicago: From Town to City, 1848–1871*, vol. 2 (Chicago: University of Chicago Press, 1940), 333.

15. Both quotations are from Carl Abbott, "'Necessary Adjuncts to its Growth': The Railroad Suburbs of Chicago, 1854–1875," *Journal of the Illinois State Historical Society* 73 (Summer 1980): 121-22.

16. Quoted in Cronon, *Nature's Metropolis,* 354–55.

17. Peter Levine, *A. G. Spalding and the Rise of Baseball* (New York: Oxford University Press, 1985), 37.

18. Ibid., 46.

19. Comiskey catered to the city's Irish. When he built the original Comiskey Park in 1910, he laid a green brick as the new parks' cornerstone. At the cornerstone ceremony, the park's architect kneeled on a piece of sod that had been transported to Chicago from Ireland.

20. Stan Barker, "Paradises Lost," *Chicago History* 22 (March 1993): 29.

21. Bessie Louise Pierce, *A History of Chicago: The Rise of a Modern City, 1871–1893,* vol. 3 (Chicago: University of Chicago Press, 1957), 509–10.

22. Quoted in James Gilbert, *Perfect Cities: Chicago's Utopias of 1898* (Chicago: University of Chicago Press, 1991), 186.

23. Perry Duis, *Chicago: Creating New Traditions* (Chicago: Chicago Historical Society, 1976), 58.

24. Paula Lupkin, "A Temple of Practical Christianity," *Chicago History* 24 (Fall 1995): 22–41.

25. Levine, *A. G. Spalding and the Rise of Baseball,* 32.

26. Heise and Baumann, *Chicago Originals,* 82.

27. Pierce, *As Others See Chicago,* 120. In Chicago's German neighborhoods, many stores and beer gardens remained open.

28. Bruce C. Nelson, "Revival and Upheaval: Religion, Irreligion, and Chicago's Working Class in 1886," *Journal of Social History* 25 (1991): 236.

29. Heise and Baumann, *Chicago Originals,* 35–36.

30. Ibid.

31. Thomas Godspeed, quoted in Miller, *City of the Century,* 256.

32. Ibid., 225.

33. Quoted in Gilbert, *Perfect Cities,* 192.

34. Quoted in ibid., 193–95. The depression of 1893 destroyed Turling-ton Harvey in late 1893, a turn of events that ended his control of Harvey, Illinois. The citizens of Harvey soon established self-government in their town and promptly voted to allow the sale of alcohol. Although its status as a Christian utopia was extremely short-lived, Harvey continues to function as a Chicago suburb.

35. Quoted in Miller, *City of the Century,* 238.

36. Quoted in ibid., 544.

37. Theodore Dreiser, *The "Genius"* (New York: John Lane, 1915), 37.

38. Stevenson Swanson, ed., *Chicago Days: 150 Defining Moments in the Life of a Great City* (Wheaton, Ill.: Catigny First Division Foundation, 1997), 79.

6: THE FIRE, THE BOMB, AND THE FAIR

1. Cromie, *Short History of Chicago*, 81.

2. Quoted in Karen Sawislak, *Smoldering City: Chicagoans and the Great Fire, 1871–1874* (Chicago: University of Chicago Press, 1995), 1.

3. Cromie, *Short History of Chicago*, 85.

4. David Lowe, ed., *The Great Chicago Fire in Eyewitness Accounts and 70 Contemporary Photographs and Illustrations* (New York: Dover Publications, 1979), 22.

5. Ibid., 22.

6. Ibid., 86.

7. Pierce, *History of Chicago*, III, 3.

8. Lowe, *Great Chicago Fire*, 5.

9. Cronon, *Short History of Chicago*, 346.

10. Pierce, *As Others See Chicago*, 220.

11. Cromie, *Short History of Chicago*, 92.

12. Quoted in Sawislak, *Smoldering City*, 85.

13. Ibid., 110.

14. Cronon, *Short History of Chicago*, 346.

15. Pierce, *History of Chicago*, III, 63.

16. Ibid., 19.

17. Quoted in Lindberg, *Quotable Chicago*, 38.

18. Pierce, *History of Chicago*, III, 63.

19. Bruce C. Nelson, "Anarchism: The Movement behind the Martyrs," *Chicago History* 15 (Summer 1986): 4.

20. Finis Farr, *Chicago: A Personal History of America's Most American City* (New Rochelle, N.Y.: Arlington House, 1973), 143–44.

21. Nelson, "Revival and Upheaval," 241.

22. Ibid., 242.

23. Pierce, *History of Chicago*, III, 277.

24. Farr, *Chicago: A Personal History*, 144.

25. Both quotations in Burton Schindler, "The Haymarket Bomb," *American History Illustrated* (June 1986): 24.

26. Pierce, *History of Chicago*, III, 280.

27. Bruce Nelson agrees with the *Alarm* that the atheism of the accused played a vital role in their trial and execution. See Nelson, "Revival and Upheaval," 247.

28. Quoted in Lindberg, *Quotable Chicago*, 178.

29. Pierce, *History of Chicago*, III, 280.

30. Cronon, *Nature's Metropolis*, 341.

31. Quoted in Lindberg, *Quotable Chicago*, 40.

32. Marian Shaw, *World's Fair Notes: A Woman Journalist Views Chicago's 1893 Columbian Exposition* ([St. Paul, Minn.]: Pogo Press, 1992), 64.

33. Quoted in Shaw, *World's Fair Notes*, 56.

34. Donald L. Miller, "The White City," *American Heritage* (July/August 1993): 71.

35. Cronon, *Nature's Metropolis*, 342.

36. Ibid.

37. Pierce, *History of Chicago*, III, 511.

38. Farr, *Chicago: A Personal History*, 194.

39. Pierce, *History of Chicago*, III, 510–11.

40. A full discussion of this subject is found in Carl Smith, *Urban Disorder and the Shape of Belief: The Great Chicago Fire, the Haymarket Bomb, and the Model Town of Pullman* (Chicago: University of Chicago Press, 1995).

41. Quoted in J. John Palen and Karl H. Flaming, ed., *Urban America: Conflict and Change* (New York: Holt, Rinehart and Winston, 1972), 54.

42. Quoted in Miller, *City of the Century*, 493.

7: THE NEW IMMIGRATION

1. Edward R. Kantowicz, *Polish-American Politics in Chicago, 1888–1940* (Chicago: University of Chicago Press, 1975).

2. Edward R. Kantowicz, "Polish Chicago: Survival through Solidarity," in Holli and Jones, *Ethnic Chicago*, 197.

3. Irving Cutler, *Chicago: Metropolis of the Mid-Continent*, 3d ed. (Dubuque, Iowa: Kendall/Hunt Publishing Company, 1982), 101.

4. Jane Addams, *Twenty Years at Hull-House* (1910; rpt., New York: Penguin Books, 1981), 170.

5. Cutler, "The Jews of Chicago," in Holli and Jones, *Ethnic Chicago*, 135.

6. Ibid., 134.

7. Thomas Sowell, *Ethnic America: A History* (New York: HarperCollins, 1981), 81.

8. Andrew T. Kopan, "Greek Survival in Chicago," in Holli and Jones, *Ethnic Chicago*, 266–67.

9. Ibid., 277.

10. Ibid., 276.

11. Ibid., 277.

12. Cutler, *Chicago: Metropolis of the Mid-Continent*, 80.

13. Quoted in Anita R. Olson, "A Community Created: Chicago Swedes, 1880–1950," in Holli and Jones, *Ethnic Chicago*, 116.

14. Addams, *Twenty Years at Hull-House*, 171.

15. Quoted in Miller, *City of the Century*, 535.

16. See, for example, Oscar Handlin's famous book, *The Uprooted: The Epic Story of the Great Migration That Made the American People* (New York: Gosset and Dunlap, 1951), from which this quotation comes.

17. Addams, *Twenty Years at Hull-House*, 82–83.

8: PROGRESSIVISM AND URBAN REFORM

1. George D. Bushnell, "The Buzz Saw Reformer," *Chicago History* 18 (Fall 1989): 93.
2. Upton Sinclair, *The Jungle* (1906; rpt., New York: Doubleday, 1981), 96–99.
3. Sinclair, *The Jungle*, vi.
4. Jon C. Teaford, *The Twentieth-Century American City*, 2d ed. (Baltimore: Johns Hopkins University Press, 1993), 28.
5. Teaford, *Twentieth-Century American City*, 29.
6. The first city streetcars were powered by machine-drawn cables or by horses. They were replaced with electric cable cars in the 1890s.
7. Quoted in Bushnell, "The Buzz Saw Reformer," 94, 95.
8. Raymond A. Mohl, *The New City: Urban America in the Industrial Age, 1860–1920* (Arlington Heights, Ill.: Harlan Davidson, 1985), 106.
9. Bill Granger and Lori Granger, *Lords of the Last Machine: The Story of Politics in Chicago* (New York: Random House, 1987), 32.
10. Investor Samuel Insull finally consolidated the city's many streetcar lines into one Chicago Rapid Transit Company in the 1920s. The streetcars passed from private to public ownership in the 1940s with the creation of the Chicago Transit Authority.
11. Trautmann, "Arthur Holitischer's Chicago," 50.
12. Edward R. Kantowicz, "Carter H. Harrison II: The Politics of Balance," in Green and Holli, *The Mayors*, 30.
13. Kopan, "Greek Survival in Chicago," in Holli and Jones, *Ethnic Chicago*, 285.
14. Addams, *Twenty Years at Hull-House*, 172.
15. Kopan, "Greek Survival in Chicago," in Holli and Jones, *Ethnic Chicago*, 285.
16. Norris Magnuson, *Salvation in the Slums: Evangelical Social Work, 1865–1920* (Grand Rapids, Mich.: Baker Book House, 1990), 62.
17. Teaford, *Twentieth-Century American City*, 42.
18. Cutler, *Chicago: Metropolis of the Mid-Continent*, 274–75.
19. Swanson, *Chicago Days*, 95.
20. Ibid., 94–95.
21. Farr, *Chicago: A Personal History*, 294.
22. Addams, *Twenty Years at Hull-House*, x.

9: WORLD WAR I AND THE ROARING TWENTIES

1. Melvin G. Holli, "German American Ethnic and Cultural Identity from 1890 Onward," in Holli and Jones, *Ethnic Chicago*, 102–3.
2. Allan H. Spear, *Black Chicago: The Making of a Negro Ghetto, 1890–1920* (Chicago: University of Chicago Press, 1967), ix.
3. James R. Grossman, "African-American Migration to Chicago," in Holli

and Jones, *Ethnic Chicago,* 304–5.

4. Ibid., 307.

5. David M. Kennedy, *Over Here: The First World War and American Society* (New York: Oxford University Press, 1980), 283.

6. Quotations are from Grossman, "African-American Migration to Chicago," in Holli and Jones, *Ethnic Chicago,* 310.

7. Swanson, *Chicago Days,* 84.

8. Quoted in James R. Grossman, *Land of Hope: Chicago, Black Southerners, and the Great Migration* (Chicago: University of Chicago Press, 1989), 119.

9. Quoted in Grossman, *Land of Hope,* 117.

10. Quoted in William Howland Kenney, "Chicago's 'Black-and-Tans,'" *Chicago History* 26 (Fall 1997): 6.

11. Quoted in Bukowski, *Big Bill Thompson,* 100.

12. Grossman, *Land of Hope.*

13. Daniel J. Prosser, "Chicago and the Bungalow Boom of the 1920s," *Chicago History* 10 (Summer 1981): 91.

14. In 1910, the non-Chicago parts of Cook County were home to 220,000 people. Suburban Cook County's population grew to 351,000 by 1920 and 606,000 by 1930.

15. Michael E. Parrish, *Anxious Decades: America in Prosperity and Depression, 1920–1941* (New York: W. W. Norton, 1992), 98.

16. Studs Terkel, *Hard Times: An Oral History of the Great Depression* (New York: Random House, 1970), 492.

17. Parrish, *Anxious Decades,* 107.

18. Jay Robert Nash, *Makers and Breakers of Chicago from Long John Wentworth to Richard J. Daley* (Chicago: Academy Chicago Publishers, 1985), 244.

19. Carl Abbott, *Urban America in the Modern Age: 1920 to the Present* (Arlington Heights, Ill.: Harlan Davidson, 1987), 22.

20. Quoted in Bukowski, *Big Bill Thompson,* 62.

21. Quoted in ibid., 74.

22. John R. Schmidt, "William E. Dever: A Chicago Political Fable," in Green and Holli, *The Mayors,* 92.

23. Bukowski, *Big Bill Thompson,* 186.

24. Nash, *Makers and Breakers of Chicago,* 242.

25. Douglas Bukowski, "Big Bill Thompson: The 'Model' Politician," in Green and Holli, *The Mayors,* 75.

10: THE GREAT DEPRESSION, WORLD WAR II, AND SUBURBAN GROWTH

1. Paul M. Green, "Anton J. Cermak: The Man and His Machine," in Green and Holli, *The Mayors,* 99.

2. Ibid., 110.

3. Ibid., 107.

4. For example, Soldier Field cost $8 million to build on park district land; a similar stadium built in Los Angeles at about the same time cost $1.7 million. Such projects resulted in Kelly earning a whopping income of $450,000 in 1927 and 1928.

5. Terkel, *Hard Times,* 487.

6. Roger Biles, "Edward J. Kelly: New Deal Machine Builder," in Green and Holli, *The Mayors,* 112.

7. Studs Terkel, *Division Street: America* (New York: Random House, 1967), 130.

8. David A. Shannon, ed., *The Great Depression* (Englewood Cliffs, N.J.: Prentice-Hall, 1960), 14–15.

9. Terkel, *Hard Times,* 485–86.

10. Teaford, *Twentieth-Century American City,* 78.

11. Biles, "Edward J. Kelly," in Green and Holli, *The Mayors,* 114.

12. Ibid.

13. The extent of William Dawson's political power is a subject of much controversy. The traditional view maintained that Dawson headed a black submachine and delivered votes to the CCDP in exchange for patronage. The more recent view, which I embrace, has been championed by William J. Grimshaw in *Bitter Fruit: Black Politics and the Chicago Machine, 1931–1991* (Chicago: University of Chicago Press, 1992), 69–87.

14. Quoted in James L. Cooper, "South Side Boss," *Chicago History* 19 (Fall and Winter 1991): 73.

15. Quoted in Grimshaw, *Bitter Fruit,* 5.

16. Terkel, *Hard Times,* 181.

17. Studs Terkel, *"The Good War": An Oral History of World War II* (New York: Random House, 1984), 133.

18. Richard R. Lingeman, *Don't You Know There's a War On?* (New York: G. P. Putnam's Sons, 1970), 48.

19. Terkel, *Division Street,* 188.

20. Masako Osako, "Japanese Americans: Melting into the All-American Melting Pot," in Holli and Jones, *Ethnic Chicago,* 426.

21. Dominic Candeloro, "Chicago's Italians: A Survey of the Ethnic Factor, 1850–1990," in Holli and Jones, *Ethnic Chicago,* 244.

22. Kelly also supported racial integration in the city's public schools.

23. Emmett Dedmon, *Fabulous Chicago: A Great City's History and People* (New York: Random House, 1953), 349.

24. Arnold R. Hirsch, "Martin H. Kennelly: The Mugwump and the Machine," in Green and Holli, *The Mayors,* 135.

25. Quoted in Arnold Hirsch, "The Black Struggle for Integrated Housing in Chicago," in Holli and Jones, *Ethnic Chicago,* 383.

26. Quoted in Arnold R. Hirsch, "Massive Resistance in the Urban North: Trumbull Park, Chicago, 1953–1966," *Journal of American History* 82 (September 1995): 530.

27. Quoted in Alan Ehrenhalt, *The Lost City: Discovering the Forgotten Virtues of Community in the Chicago of the 1950s* (New York: HarperCollins, 1995), 140.

28. Quoted in ibid., 140.

29. Quoted in the *Chicago Tribune,* 9 October 1997.

30. William H. Whyte, *The Organization Man* (New York: Simon and Schuster, 1956), 282–83.

31. Ibid., 284–86.

32. Quoted in Ehrenhalt, *Lost City,* 194.

33. Quoted in ibid., 195.

11: RICHARD J. DALEY AND THE CITY THAT WORKS

1. Harold M. Mayer and Richard C. Wade, *Chicago: Growth of a Metropolis* (Chicago: University of Chicago Press, 1969), 378.

2. Paul M. Green, "Mayor Richard J. Daley and the Politics of Good Government," in Green and Holli, *The Mayors,* 151.

3. Quoted in ibid., 146.

4. Mike Royko, *Boss: Richard J. Daley of Chicago* (New York: Dutton, 1971), 30–31.

5. Ehrenhalt, *Lost City,* 41.

6. Quoted in Milton Rakove, *Don't Make No Waves—Don't Back No Losers: An Insider's Analysis of the Daley Machine* (Bloomington: Indiana University Press, 1975), 50.

7. Royko, *Boss: Richard J. Daley of Chicago,* 97.

8. Green, "Mayor Richard J. Daley and the Politics of Good Government," in Green and Holli, *The Mayors,* 155.

9. Roger Biles, *Richard J. Daley: Politics, Race, and the Governing of Chicago* (DeKalb: Northern Illinois University Press, 1995), 227.

10. Dedmon, *Fabulous Chicago,* 410.

11. Rakove, *Don't Make No Waves,* 88.

12. Ibid., 120–22.

13. Ibid., 118–20.

14. Ibid., 127.

15. Ehrenhalt, *Lost City,* 47.

16. This point is ably made in Ehrenhalt, *Lost City,* 8–58.

17. Royko, *Boss: Richard J. Daley of Chicago,* 53.

18. Ibid., 24–25.

19. Rakove, *Don't Make No Waves,* 48.

20. William J. Grimshaw, "Harold Washington: The Enigma of the Black

Political Tradition," in Green and Holli, *The Mayors*, 190.

21. Royko, *Boss: Richard J. Daley of Chicago*, 154.

22. Ibid., 154–55.

23. Ibid., 158.

24. Rakove, *Don't Make No Waves*, 263.

25. Quoted in Biles, *Richard J. Daley*, 147.

26. "'Battle of Chicago'—and the Consequences," *U. S. News and World Report* (9 September 1968): 42.

27. Terry H. Anderson, *The Movement and the Sixties: Protest America from Greensboro to Wounded Knee* (New York: Oxford University Press, 1995), 217.

28. Ibid., 224.

29. "'Battle of Chicago'—and the Consequences," 43.

30. Godfrey Hodgson, *America in Our Time: From World War II to Nixon, What Happened and Why* (New York: Random House, 1978), 371.

31. Raymond R. Coffey, "Dossier on Daley," *Nation* (7 October 1968): 328–29.

32. Anderson, *The Movement and the Sixties*, 225.

33. Royko, *Boss: Richard J. Daley and Chicago*, 193.

34. Quoted in Biles, *Richard J. Daley*, 161.

35. Quoted in Anderson, *The Movement and the Sixties*, 224.

36. Quoted in Biles, *Richard J. Daley*, 152.

37. Quoted in ibid., 164.

38. "'Battle of Chicago'—and the Consequences," 43.

39. Melvin G. Holli, "The Daley Era: Richard J. to Richard M.," in Green and Holli, *The Mayors*, 218.

40. Quoted in Biles, *Richard J. Daley*, 184.

41. Quoted in Grimshaw, *Bitter Fruit*, 21.

42. Paul Kleppner, *Chicago Divided: The Making of a Black Mayor* (DeKalb: Northern Illinois University Press, 1985), 91.

43. Biles, *Richard J. Daley*, 227.

12: THE TRANSITIONS OF THE POST-DALEY YEARS

1. *Chicago Tribune*, 26 August 1996.

2. Holli, "The Daley Era: Richard J. to Richard M.," in Green and Holli, *The Mayors*, 219.

3. Melvin G. Holli, "Jane M. Byrne: To Think the Unthinkable and Do the Undoable," in Green and Holli, *The Mayors*, 175.

4. Gary Rivlin, *Fire on the Prairie: Chicago's Harold Washington and the Politics of Race* (New York: Henry Holt and Company, 1992), 69.

5. Holli, "Jane M. Byrne," in Green and Holli, *The Mayors*, 178.

6. Quoted in Steven F. Lawson, *Running for Freedom: Civil Rights and Black*

Politics since 1941, 2d ed. (New York: McGraw-Hill, 1997), 209–10.

7. Quoted in Rivlin, *Fire on the Prairie*, 15.

8. Quoted in ibid., 163.

9. Kleppner, *Chicago Divided*, 177.

10. Ibid., 173.

11. Both quotations in Rivlin, *Fire on the Prairie*, 186.

12. Kleppner, *Chicago Divided*, 201.

13. Quoted in ibid., 230–31.

14. In 1987, 44 percent of the city's registered voters were black, 48 percent were white, and 8 percent were Hispanic.

15. Quoted in Rivlin, *Fire on the Prairie*, 308.

16. Monroe Anderson, "The Sawyer Saga: A Journalist, Who Just Happened to Be the Mayor's Press Secretary, Speaks," in Green and Holli, *The Mayors*, 199.

17. John R. Coyne Jr., "Vouchers and the Pharaoh's Son," *National Review* (29 April 1991): 25.

18. Despite public officials' commitment to affirmative action programs, racial tensions remain difficult to resolve. A good example of this is the Chicago Police Department. In 1976, a federal judge mandated an affirmative action program designed to increase minority employment within the department. At first glance, the program seems to have been a smashing success. Whereas in 1973 only 17 percent of all police officers were black and 1 percent were women, by 1988 those numbers had risen to 37 percent and 17 percent, respectively. In the 1990s, however, the city's police department is rife with dissension. White officers have sued the city for reverse discrimination, charging that they have been passed over for promotions solely because of their skin color. Minorities have also complained, charging that they are excluded from leadership positions by discriminatory evaluation procedures. Jackson quoted from http://chicago.digital city.com/tales/people/daley/daley7.htm.

19. The following discussion, including quotations, is taken from *Chicago Tribune*, 26 August 1996.

20. LeAlan Jones and Lloyd Newman with David Isay, *Our America: Life and Death on the South Side of Chicago* (New York: Scribner, 1997), 167.

21. Gregory D. Squires, Larry Bennett, Kathleen McCourt, and Philip Nyden, *Chicago: Race, Class, and the Response to Urban Decline* (Philadelphia: Temple University Press, 1987), 38.

22. Quoted in Biles, *Richard J. Daley*, 231.

23. Alex Kotlowitz, *There Are No Children Here: The Story of Two Boys Growing Up in the Other America* (New York: Doubleday Anchor Books, 1991), 22.

24. Ibid., 240.

25. Ibid., 12.

26. Joseph Epstein, "A Secret Good Place," *Newsweek* (2 September 1996): 14.

27. The term *Hispanic* is used to refer to Mexican, Puerto Rican, Cuban, and other Spanish-speaking peoples from Central and South American. It implies a

unity that does not exist; Mexicans, Puerto Ricans, and Cubans, for example, display significant cultural, political, and economic differences.

28. William Braden, "Chatham: An African-American Success Story," in Holli and Jones, *Ethnic Chicago,* 342–43.

29. Braden, "Chatham: An African-American Success Story," in Holli and Jones, *Ethnic Chicago,* 345.

30. Squires, Bennett, McCourt, and Nyden, *Chicago: Race, Class, and the Response to Urban Decline,* 37.

31. Quoted in *Chicago Tribune,* 7 June 1998.

32. Scott Turow, "The Capital of Real Life," *Newsweek* (9 September 1991): 47.

BIBLIOGRAPHY

•

BOOKS

Abbott, Carl. *Urban America in the Modern Age: 1920 to the Present.* Arlington Heights, Ill.: Harlan Davidson, 1987.

Addams, Jane. *Twenty Years at Hull-House.* New York: Penguin Books, 1981.

Allswang, John M. *A House for All Peoples: Ethnic Politics in Chicago, 1890–1936.* Lexington: University Press of Kentucky, 1971.

Anderson, Terry H. *The Movement and the Sixties: Protest America from Greensboro to Wounded Knee.* New York: Oxford University Press, 1995.

Avrich, Paul. *The Haymarket Tragedy.* Princeton: Princeton University Press, 1984.

Barrett, James R. *Work and Community in the Jungle: Chicago's Packinghouse Workers, 1894–1922.* Urbana: University of Illinois Press, 1987.

Bensman, David, and Roberta Lynch. *Rusted Dreams: Hard Times in a Steel Community.* New York: McGraw-Hill, 1987.

Biles, Roger. *Big City Boss in Depression and War: Mayor Edward J. Kelly of Chicago.* DeKalb: Northern Illinois University Press, 1984.

———. *Richard J. Daley: Politics, Race, and the Governing of Chicago.* DeKalb: Northern Illinois University Press, 1995.

Bluestone, Daniel. *Constructing Chicago.* New Haven: Yale University Press, 1991.

Bowly, Devereux. *The Poorhouse: Subsidized Housing in Chicago, 1895–1976.* Carbondale: Southern Illinois University Press, 1978.

Buder, Stanley. *Pullman: An Experiment in Industrial Order and Community Planning, 1880–1930.* New York: Oxford University Press, 1967.

Bukowski, Douglas. *Big Bill Thompson, Chicago, and the Politics of Image.* Urbana: University of Illinois Press, 1998.

Burg, David F. *Chicago's White City of 1893.* Lexington: University Press of Kentucky, 1976.

Chicago Department of Development and Planning. *Historic City: The Settlement of Chicago.* Chicago: n.p., 1976.

Cromie, Robert. *A Short History of Chicago.* San Francisco: Lexikos, 1984.

Cronon, William. *Nature's Metropolis: Chicago and the Great West.* New York: W. W. Norton, 1991.

Cutler, Irving. *Chicago: Metropolis of the Mid-Continent.* 3d ed. Dubuque, Iowa: Kendall/Hunt Publishing Company, 1982.

Dedmon, Emmett. *Fabulous Chicago: A Great City's History and People.* New York: Random House, 1953.

Diner, Steven J. *A City and Its Universities: Public Policy in Chicago, 1892–1919.* Chapel Hill: University of North Carolina Press, 1980.

Drake, St. Clair, and Horace R. Clayton. *Black Metropolis: A Study of Negro Life in a Northern City.* Revised and enlarged edition. Chicago: University of Chicago Press, 1993.

Dreiser, Theodore. *The "Genius."* New York: John Lane, 1915.

Duis, Perry. *Chicago: Creating New Traditions.* Chicago: Chicago Historical Society, 1976.

———. *The Saloon: Public Drinking in Chicago and Boston.* Urbana: University of Illinois Press, 1983.

Ebner, Michael H. *Creating Chicago's North Shore: A Suburban History.* Chicago: University of Chicago Press, 1988.

Ehrenhalt, Alan. *The Lost City: Discovering the Forgotten Virtues of Community in the Chicago of the 1950s.* New York: HarperCollins, 1995.

Einhorn, Robin L. *Property Rules: Political Economy in Chicago, 1833–1872.* Chicago: University of Chicago Press, 1991.

Farr, Finis. *Chicago: A Personal History of America's Most American City.* New Rochelle, N.Y.: Arlington House, 1973.

Gilbert, James. *Perfect Cities: Chicago's Utopias of 1893.* Chicago: University of Chicago Press, 1991.

Granger, Bill, and Lori Granger. *Lords of the Last Machine: The Story of Politics in Chicago.* New York: Random House, 1987.

Green, Paul M., and Melvin G. Holli. *The Mayors: The Chicago Political Tradition.* Rev. ed. Carbondale: Southern Illinois University Press, 1995.

Grimshaw, William J. *Bitter Fruit: Black Politics and the Chicago Machine, 1931–1991.* Chicago: University of Chicago Press, 1992.

Grossman, James R. *Land of Hope: Chicago, Black Southerners, and the Great Migration.* Chicago: University of Chicago Press, 1989.

Heise, Kenan, and Ed Baumann. *Chicago Originals: A Cast of the City's Colorful Characters.* Chicago: Bonus Books, 1995.

Hines, Thomas S. *Burnham of Chicago.* Chicago: University of Chicago Press, 1979.

Hirsch, Arnold R. *Making the Second Ghetto: Race and Housing in Chicago, 1940–1960.* Cambridge: Cambridge University Press, 1983.

Hodgson, Godfrey. *America in Our Time: From World War II to Nixon, What Happened and Why.* New York: Random House, 1978.

Holli, Melvin G., and Paul M. Green, eds. *The Making of the Mayor: Chicago, 1983.*

Grand Rapids, Mich.: Eerdmans Publishing Company, 1984.

Holli, Melvin G., and Peter d'A. Jones, eds. *Ethnic Chicago: A Multicultural Portrait.* 4th ed. Grand Rapids, Mich.: Eerdmans Publishing Company, 1994.

Homel, Michael W. *Down from Equality: Black Chicagoans and the Public Schools, 1920–1941.* Urbana: University of Illinois Press, 1984.

Jones, LeAlan, and Lloyd Newman, with David Isay. *Our America: Life and Death on the South Side of Chicago.* New York: Scribner, 1997.

Kantowicz, Edward R. *Corporation Sole: Cardinal Mundelein and Chicago Catholicism.* Notre Dame: University of Notre Dame Press, 1983.

———. *Polish-American Politics in Chicago, 1888–1940.* Chicago: University of Chicago Press, 1975.

Karamanski, Theodore J. *Rally 'round the Flag: Chicago and the Civil War.* Chicago: Nelson-Hall Publishers, 1993.

Keating, Ann Durkin. *Building Chicago: Suburban Developers and the Creation of a Divided Metropolis.* Columbus: Ohio State University Press, 1988.

Keil, Hartmut, and John B. Jentz, eds. *German Workers in Chicago: A Documentary History of Working-Class Culture from 1850 to World War I.* Urbana: University of Illinois Press, 1988.

Kennedy, David M. *Over Here: The First World War and American Society.* New York: Oxford University Press, 1980.

Kenney, William Howland. *Chicago Jazz: A Cultural History, 1904–1930.* New York: Oxford University Press, 1993.

Kleppner, Paul. *Chicago Divided: The Making of a Black Mayor.* DeKalb: Northern Illinois University Press, 1985.

Kotlowitz, Alex. *There Are No Children Here: The Story of Two Boys Growing Up in the Other America.* New York: Doubleday, 1991.

Lemann, Nicholas. *The Promised Land: The Great Black Migration and How It Changed America.* New York: Random House, 1991.

Levine, Peter. *A. G. Spalding and the Rise of Baseball.* New York: Oxford University Press, 1985.

Lewis, Arnold. *An Early Encounter with Tomorrow: Europeans, Chicago's Loop, and the World's Columbian Exposition.* Urbana: University of Illinois Press, 1997.

Lindberg, Richard. *Chicago by Gaslight: A History of Chicago's Netherworld, 1880–1920.* Chicago: Academy Chicago Publishers, 1996.

———. *Quotable Chicago.* Chicago: Onion Press, 1996.

Lingeman, Richard R. *Don't You Know There's a War On?* New York: G. P. Putnam's Sons, 1970.

Lissak, Rivka Shpak. *Pluralism and Progressives: Hull-House and the New Immigrants, 1890–1919.* Chicago: University of Chicago Press, 1989.

Lowe, David, ed. *The Great Chicago Fire in Eyewitness Accounts and 70 Contemporary Photographs and Illustrations.* New York: Dover Publications, 1979.

McCaffrey, Lawrence J., et al. *The Irish in Chicago.* Urbana: University of Illinois Press, 1987.

McCarthy, Kathleen D. *Noblesse Oblige: Cultural Philanthropy in Chicago, 1849–1929*. Chicago: University of Chicago Press, 1982.

Magnuson, Norris. *Salvation in the Slums: Evangelical Social Work, 1865–1920*. Grand Rapids, Mich.: Baker Book House, 1990.

Markman, Charles W. *Chicago before History: The Prehistoric Archaeology of a Modern Metropolitan Area*. Springfield: Illinois Historic Preservation Agency, 1991.

Meyer, Harold M., and Richard C. Wade. *Chicago: Growth of a Metropolis*. Chicago: University of Chicago Press, 1969.

Meyerowitz, Joanne J. *Women Adrift: Independent Wage Earners in Chicago, 1880–1930*. Chicago: University of Chicago Press, 1988.

Miller, Donald L. *City of the Century: The Epic of Chicago and the Making of America*. New York: Simon and Schuster, 1996.

Miller, Ross. *American Apocalypse: The Great Fire and the Myth of Chicago*. Chicago: University of Chicago Press, 1990.

Mohl, Raymond A. *The New City: Urban America in the Industrial Age, 1860–1920*. Arlington Heights, Ill.: Harlan Davidson, 1985.

Nash, Jay Robert. *Makers and Breakers of Chicago from Long John Wentworth to Richard J. Daley*. Chicago: Academy Chicago Publishers, 1985.

Nelli, Humbert S. *Italians in Chicago, 1880–1930: A Study in Ethnic Mobility*. New York: Oxford University Press, 1970.

Nelson, Bruce C. *Beyond the Martyrs: A Social History of Chicago's Anarchists, 1870–1900*. New Brunswick, N.J.: Rutgers University Press, 1988.

Newell, Barbara Warne. *Chicago and the Labor Movement*. Urbana: University of Illinois Press, 1961.

Nichols, Roger L. *Black Hawk and the Warrior's Path*. Arlington Heights, Ill.: Harlan Davidson, 1992.

Pacyga, Dominic A. *Polish Immigrants and Industrial Chicago: Workers on the South Side, 1880–1922*. Columbus: Ohio State University Press, 1991.

Parot, Joseph John. *Polish Catholics in Chicago, 1850–1920: A Religious History*. DeKalb: Northern Illinois University Press, 1981.

Parrish, Michael E. *Anxious Decades: America in Prosperity and Depression, 1920–1941*. New York: W. W. Norton, 1992.

Philpott, Thomas Lee. *The Slum and the Ghetto: Neighborhood Deterioration and Middle-Class Reform, Chicago, 1880–1930*. New York: Oxford University Press, 1978.

Pierce, Bessie Louise. *A History of Chicago: The Beginning of a City, 1673–1848*. Vol. 1. Chicago: University of Chicago Press, 1937.

——. *A History of Chicago: From Town to City, 1848–1871*. Vol. 2. Chicago: University of Chicago Press, 1940.

——. *A History of Chicago: The Rise of a Modern City, 1871–1893*. Vol. 3. Chicago: University of Chicago Press, 1957.

——, ed. *As Others See Chicago: Impressions of Visitors, 1673–1933*. Chicago: University of Chicago Press, 1933.

Platt, Harold L. *The Electric City: Energy and the Growth of the Chicago Area, 1880–1930.* Chicago: University of Chicago Press, 1991.

Rakove, Milton L. *Don't Make No Waves—Don't Back No Losers: An Insider's Analysis of the Daley Machine.* Bloomington: Indiana University Press, 1975.

———. *We Don't Want Nobody Nobody Sent: An Oral History of the Daley Years.* Bloomington: Indiana University Press, 1979.

Ralph, James. *Northern Protest: Martin Luther King, Jr., Chicago, and the Civil Rights Movement.* Cambridge: Harvard University Press, 1993.

Rivlin, Gary. *Fire on the Prairie: Chicago's Harold Washington and the Politics of Race.* New York: Henry Holt and Company, 1992.

Royko, Mike. *Boss: Richard J. Daley of Chicago.* New York: New American Library, 1971.

Ruth, David E. *Inventing the Public Enemy: The Gangster in American Culture, 1918–1934.* Chicago: University of Chicago Press, 1996.

Rydell, Robert W. *All the World's a Fair: Visions of Empire at American International Expositions, 1876–1916.* Chicago: University of Chicago Press, 1984.

Sawislak, Karen. *Smoldering City: Chicagoans and the Great Fire, 1871–1874.* Chicago: University of Chicago Press, 1995.

Schmidt, John. *"The Mayor Who Cleaned Up Chicago": A Political Biography of William E. Dever.* DeKalb: Northern Illinois University Press, 1989.

Shannon, David. *The Great Depression.* Englewood Cliffs, N.J.: Prentice-Hall, 1960.

Shaw, Marian. *World's Fair Notes: A Woman Journalist Views Chicago's 1893 Columbian Exposition.* St. Louis: Pogo Press, 1992.

Sinclair, Upton. *The Jungle.* New York: Doubleday, 1981.

Siry, Joseph. *Carson Pirie Scott: Louis Sullivan and the Chicago Department Store.* Chicago: University of Chicago Press, 1988.

Smith, Carl S. *Urban Disorder and the Shape of Belief: The Great Chicago Fire, the Haymarket Bomb, and the Model Town of Pullman.* Chicago: University of Chicago Press, 1995.

Sowell, Thomas. *Ethnic America: A History.* New York: HarperCollins, 1981.

Spear, Allan H. *Black Chicago: The Making of a Negro Ghetto, 1890–1920.* Chicago: University of Chicago Press, 1967.

Squires, Gregory D., Larry Bennett, Kathleen McCourt, and Philip Nyden. *Chicago: Race, Class, and the Response to Urban Decline.* Philadelphia: Temple University Press, 1987.

Strickland, Arvarh E. *History of the Chicago Urban League.* Urbana: University of Illinois Press, 1966.

Sturtevant, William C. *Handbook of North American Indians.* Vol. 15. Washington, D.C.: Smithsonian Institution, 1978.

Swanson, Stevenson, ed. *Chicago Days: 150 Defining Moments in the Life of a Great City.* Wheaton, Ill.: Catigny First Division Foundation Books, 1997.

Tanner, Helen Hornbeck, ed. *Atlas of Great Lakes Indian History.* Norman: University of Oklahoma Press, 1987.

Tarr, Joel A. *A Study in Boss Politics: William Lorimer of Chicago.* Urbana: University of Illinois Press, 1971.

Teaford, Jon C. *The Twentieth-Century American City.* 2d ed. Baltimore: Johns Hopkins University Press, 1993.

Terkel, Studs. *Chicago.* New York: Pantheon Books, 1985.

———. *Division Street: America.* New York: Random House, 1967.

———. *"The Good War": An Oral History of World War II.* New York: Random House, 1984.

———. *Hard Times: An Oral History of the Great Depression.* New York: Random House, 1970.

Tuttle, William M., Jr. *Race Riot: Chicago in the Red Summer of 1919.* New York: Atheneum, 1970.

Wade, Louise Carroll. *Chicago's Pride: The Stockyards, Packingtown, and Environs in the Nineteenth Century.* Urbana: University of Illinois Press, 1987.

———. *Graham Taylor: A Pioneer for Social Justice, 1851–1938.* Chicago: University of Chicago Press, 1964.

Whyte, William H. *The Organization Man.* New York: Simon and Schuster, 1956.

ARTICLES

Abbott, Carl. "'Necessary Adjuncts to Its Growth': The Railroad Suburbs of Chicago, 1854–1875." *Journal of the Illinois State Historical Society* 73 (Summer 1980): 117–31.

Ahrens, Arthur R. "How the Cubs Got Their Name." *Chicago History* 5 (Spring 1976): 39–44.

Bach, Ira J. "Pullman: A Town Reborn." *Chicago History* 4 (Spring 1975): 44–53.

Barker, Stan. "Paradises Lost." *Chicago History* 22 (Spring 1993): 26–49.

Bates, Beth Tompkins. "The Brotherhood." *Chicago History* 25 (Fall 1996): 4–23.

"'Battle of Chicago'—and the Consequences." *U.S. News and World Report* (9 September 1968): 42–43.

"Battleground Chicago." *Newsweek* (3 April 1995): 26–33.

Best, Wallace. "The *Chicago Defender* and the Realignment of Black Chicago." *Chicago History* 24 (Fall 1995): 4–21.

Boorstin, Daniel J. "A. Montgomery Ward's Mail-Order Business." *Chicago History* 2 (Spring–Summer 1973): 142–52.

Bourassa, J. N. "The Life of Wah-bahn-se: The Warrior Chief of the Pottawatamies." *Kansas Historical Quarterly* 38 (1972): 132–43.

Branch, Taylor. "The Uncivil War." *Esquire* (May 1989): 89.

Brown, Lizzie M. "The Pacification of the Indians of Illinois after the War of 1812." *Journal of the Illinois State Historical Society* 8 (1916): 550–58.

Buettinger, Craig. "The Rise and Fall of Hiram Pearson: Mobility on the Urban Frontier." *Chicago History* 19 (Summer 1980): 112–17.

Bushnell, George D. "When Chicago Was Wheel Crazy." *Chicago History* 4 (Fall 1975): 167–75.

———. "Buzz Saw Reformer." *Chicago History* 18 (Fall 1989): 86–96.

Cain, Louis P. "The Creation of Chicago's Sanitary District and Construction of the Sanitary and Ship Canal." *Chicago History* 8 (Summer 1979): 98–110.

Christopher, Louise. "Henry Whitehead, Circuit Rider." *Chicago History* 5 (Spring 1976): 2–11.

Clayton, John. "How They Tinkered with a River." *Chicago History* 1 (Spring 1970): 32–46.

Clifton, James A. "Chicago, September 14, 1833: The Last Great Indian Treaty in the Old Northwest." *Chicago History* 9 (Summer 1980): 86–97.

———. "Chicago Was Theirs." *Chicago History* 1 (Spring 1970): 4–17.

Coffey, Raymond R. "Dossier on Daley." *Nation* (7 October 1968): 328–31.

Conniff, Richard. "Chicago: Welcome to the Neighborhood." *National Geographic* (May 1991): 50–77.

Cooper, James L. "South Side Boss." *Chicago History* 19 (Fall–Winter 1990–1991): 66–81.

Coyne, John R., Jr. "Vouchers and the Pharaoh's Son." *National Review* (29 April 1991): 25–26.

Cudahy, Brian J. "Chicago's Early Elevated Lines and the Construction of the Union Loop." *Chicago History* 8 (Winter 1979–1980): 194–205.

Downard, William L. "William Butler Ogden and the Growth of Chicago." *Journal of the Illinois State Historical Society* 75 (1982): 47–60.

Duis, Perry R. "Chicago Chronicles." *Chicago History* 14 (Winter 1985–1986): 57–67.

———. "Symbolic Unity and the Neighborhood: Chicago during World War II." *Journal of Urban History* 21 (January 1995): 184–217.

———. "Yesterday's City: Prey for Work." *Chicago History* 18 (Spring 1989): 60–72.

Edmunds, R. David. "The Prairie Potawatomi Removal of 1833." *Indiana Magazine of History* 68 (1972): 240–53.

Ekman, Ernst. "Fredrika Bremer in Chicago in 1850." *Swedish Pioneer Historical Quarterly* 14 (October 1968): 234–44.

Erenberg, Lewis A. "'Ain't We Got Fun?'" *Chicago History* 14 (Winter 1985–1986): 4–21.

Farmelo, Graham. "The Day Chicago Went Critical." *New Scientist* 136 (28 November 1992): 26–29.

Frazier, Arthur H. "The Military Frontier: Fort Dearborn." *Chicago History* 9 (Summer 1980): 80–85.

Garrow, David J. "'I March Because I Must.'" *Chicago History* 17 (Spring–Summer 1988): 24–45.

Gems, Gerald R. "Not Only a Game." *Chicago History* 18 (Summer 1989): 4–21.

Gergen, David. "A Bridge to Nowhere." *U.S. News and World Report* (9 September 1996): 64.

Gerwing, Anselm J. "The Chicago Indian Treaty of 1833." *Journal of the Illinois State Historical Society* 57 (1964): 117–42.

Green, Paul M. "Making the City Work: Machine Politics and Mayoral Reform." *Chicago History* 14 (Fall 1985): 58–72.

Griffin, Dick. "Opium Addiction in Chicago: 'The Noblest and the Best Brought Low.'" *Chicago History* 6 (Summer 1977): 107–16.

Harris, Neil. "Dream Making." *Chicago History* 23 (Summer 1994): 44–57.

Hirsch, Arnold R. "Massive Resistance in the Urban North: Trumbull Park, Chicago, 1953–1966." *Journal of American History* 82 (September 1995): 522–50.

Hoffman, Dennis E. "Watchdog on Crime." *Chicago History* 23 (Spring 1994): 4–15.

Kelly, Jack. "Gangster City." *American Heritage* (April 1995): 65–88.

Kenney, William. "Chicago's 'Black-and-Tans.'" *Chicago History* 26 (Fall 1997): 4–31.

Kohl, Johann Georg. "Yesterday's City: Chicago's Geography." *Chicago History* 22 (Spring 1993): 62–72.

Lamb, John M. "Early Days on the Illinois and Michigan Canal." *Chicago History* 3 (Winter 1974–1975): 168–76.

Lewis, Russell. "Chicago Goes to War." *USA Today Magazine* (July 1993): 51–55.

Lindberg, Richard. "The Evolution of an Evil Business." *Chicago History* 22 (July 1993): 38–53.

———. "Yesterday's City: The South Side's Baseball Factory." *Chicago History* 18 (Summer 1989): 60–72.

Lindsey, David. "The Founding of Chicago." *American History Illustrated* 8 (1973): 24–33.

Long, E. B. "Camp Douglas: 'A Hellish Den'?" *Chicago History* 1 (Fall 1970): 82–95.

Lupkin, Paula. "A Temple of Practical Christianity." *Chicago History* 24 (Fall 1995): 22–41.

Mahoney, Olivia. "Black Abolitionists." *Chicago History* 20 (Spring–Summer 1991): 22–37.

McGinty, Brian. "Mr. Sears and Mr. Roebuck." *American History Illustrated* (June 1986): 34–37, 48–49.

McLear, Patrick E. "'. . . And Still They Come': Chicago from 1832–36." *Journal of the West* 7 (1968): 397–404.

Meehan, Thomas A. "Jean Baptiste Point du Sable, The First Chicagoan." *Journal of the Illinois State Historical Society* 56 (1963): 439–53.

Meyer, Alfred H. "Circulation and Settlement Patterns of the Calumet Region of Northwest Indians and Northeast Illinois." *Annals of the Association of American Geographers* 44 (September 1954): 245–74.

Miller, Donald L. "The White City." *American Heritage* (July/August 1993): 70–87.

Miranda, Rowan A. "Post-Machine Regimes and the Growth of Government: A Fiscal History of the City of Chicago, 1970–1990." *Urban Affairs Quarterly* 28 (March 1993): 397–422.

Moore, Mike. "The Incident at Stagg Field." *Bulletin of the Atomic Scientists* 48 (December 1992): 11–15.

Morgan, Katherine R. "'We Do Have to Work Hard.'" *Chicago History* 26 (Spring 1997): 22–39.

Nelli, Humbert S. "John Powers and the Italians: Politics in a Chicago Ward, 1896–1921." *Journal of American History* 57 (June 1970): 67–84.

Nelson, Bruce C. "Anarchism: The Movement behind the Martyrs." *Chicago History* 15 (Summer 1986): 4–19.

———. "Revival and Upheaval: Religion, Irreligion, and Chicago's Working Class in 1886." *Journal of Social History* 25 (1991): 233–53.

Nichols, Roger L. "The Black Hawk War in Retrospect." *Wisconsin Magazine of History* 65 (1982): 238–46.

Peterson, William S. "Kipling's First Visit to Chicago." *Journal of the Illinois State Historical Society* 63 (1970): 290–301.

Piehl, Frank J. "Chicago's Early Fight to 'Save Our Lake.'" *Chicago History* 5 (Winter 1976–1977): 223–32.

Prosser, Daniel J. "Chicago and the Bungalow Boom of the 1920s." *Chicago History* 10 (Summer 1981): 86–95.

Reardon, Patrick T. "Solid Citizens." *Chicago Tribune Magazine* (7 June 1998): 12–19.

Renner, Richard Wilson. "In a Perfect Ferment: Chicago, the Know-Nothings, and the Riot for Lager Beer." *Chicago History* 5 (Fall 1976): 161–70.

Santoli, Al. "The Nguyen Family." *Chicago History* 23 (Winter 1994–1995): 22–35.

Schindler, Burton. "The Haymarket Bomb." *American History Illustrated* (June 1986): 20–27.

Schneirov, Richard. "Chicago's Great Upheaval of 1877." *Chicago History* 9 (Spring 1980): 2–17.

Schnell, J. Christopher. "Chicago versus St. Louis: A Reassessment of the Great Rivalry." *Missouri Historical Review* 71 (1977): 245–65.

"Segregation and Cities." *Society* 33 (September/October 1996): 2–3.

Smith, Carl S. "Cataclysm and Cultural Consciousness: Chicago and the Haymarket Trial." *Chicago History* 15 (Summer 1986): 36–53.

Smith, Nina B. "'This Bleak Situation': The Founding of Fort Sheridan, Illinois." *Illinois Historical Journal* 80 (Spring 1987): 13–21.

Staudenraus, P. J. "'The Empire City of the West': A View of Chicago in 1864." *Journal of the Illinois State Historical Society* 56 (1963): 340–49.

Stodghill, Ron, III. "Bringing Hope Back to the 'Hood." *Business Week* (19 August 1996): 70–73.

Street, Paul. "Packinghouse Blues." *Chicago History* 18 (Fall 1989): 68–85.

Swenson, John F. "Chicagoua/Chicago: The Origin, Meaning, and Etymology of a Place Name." *Illinois Historical Journal* 84 (Winter 1991): 235–48.

Trautmann, Frederic. "Arthur Holitischer's Chicago: A German Traveler's View of an American City." *Chicago History* 12 (Summer 1983): 36–50.

Vecoli, Rudolph J. "*Contadini* in Chicago: A Critique of *The Uprooted.*" *Journal of American History* 51 (December 1964): 404–17.

Wade, Richard C. "The Enduring Chicago Machine." *Chicago History* 15 (Spring 1986): 4–19.

Watterson, John S. "Chicago's City Championship: Northwestern University vs. The University of Chicago, 1892–1905." *Chicago History* 11 (Fall–Winter 1982): 161–74.

Weisberger, Bernard. "The Forgotten Four Hundred: Chicago's First Millionaires." *American Heritage* 38 (November 1987): 34–44.

Williams, Mentor L. "The Chicago River and Harbor Convention, 1847." *Mississippi Valley Historical Review* 35 (1949): 607–26.

Wills, Garry. "Chicago Underground." *New York Review of Books* (21 October 1993): 15–22.

Winger, Stewart. "Unwelcome Neighbors." *Chicago History* 21 (Spring–Summer 1992): 56–72.

Ziemer, Linda. "Chicago's Negro Leagues." *Chicago History* 23 (Winter 1994–1995): 36–51.

Zochert, Donald. "Heinrich Schliemann's Chicago Journal." *Chicago History* 2 (Spring–Summer 1973): 173–81.

INDEX

Abbott, Robert, 169
abolitionism, 40–42
Adams, Henry, 119
Addams, Jane, 132, 143–44, 157–60
Adler, Dankmar, 161
Adler Planetarium, 191–92
affirmative action, 238, 254, 283
African Americans, 94, 167–72,185–87,
    193–94, 200–2, 204–8, 213–15,
    227–28, 231, 237–38, 244–45,
    264–65, 272. *See also* abolitionism;
    affirmative action; Black Panthers;
    Bronzeville; *Chicago Defender;*
    William Dawson; Great Migration;
    Race Riot of 1919
Alarm, 108, 111
Algren, Nelson, 97
Alliance Movement, 63–64
Altgeld, John, 112
American Fur Company, 21, 24, 29–30
American Temperance Society, 40
amusement parks, 87
Anderson, Louis B., 170
Armour, Philip, 58, 61
Arnold, Schwinn & Company, 86
Astor, John Jacob, 21, 24

Baker, Ray Stannard, 96
balloon-frame construction, 67
baseball, 142–43
    All-American Girls Baseball
        League, 202–3
    Chicago Cubs, 85
    Chicago White Stockings, 84–86, 90
Beaubien, Mark, 23–24, 26, 36
Bellow, Saul, 97, 220
Berwyn, Ill., 175
Bilandic, Michael, 242, 245
Bismarck, Otto von, 46
Black Hawk. *See* Black Hawk War
Black Hawk War (1832–1833), 26–29,
    33
Black, Timuel, 208
Boone, Levi D., 72–73
Boynton, Paul, 87
Bradwell, Myra, 91–92
Bridgeport, 31, 38, 71, 214
Bronzeville, 207–8
Buckingham Memorial Fountain,
    191–92
Buffalo, N.Y., 32
bungalow, 174
Burnham, Daniel, 114, 155, 161–64, 211

Bush, Earl, 232, 238
Busse, Fred, 155–56
Byrne, Jane, 242–47

Cabrini, Frances Xavier, 160
Camp Douglas, 74
canal. *See* Chicago Sanitary and Ship
   Canal; Illinois and Michigan Canal
Capone, Al, 177–82, 185, 187
Century of Progress Exposition
   (1933–1934), 188
Cermak, Anton, 139–40, 187–91
"Chicago" (Sandburg), 3, 97–98, 267
Chicago Anti-Slavery Society, 41
Chicago Art Institute, 115
Chicago Board of Trade, 54
Chicago Committee on Racial Equality,
   201–2
Chicago Daily American, 39–40
Chicago Daily News, 78, 107, 111, 181,
   234, 237
Chicago Defender, 94, 168–70, 173–74,
   195, 239, 248, 253
Chicago Democrat, 43, 81
Chicago Fire, 63, 76, 80, 99–107, 113, 121
Chicago Journal, 43
Chicago Legal News, 91–92
Chicago Magazine, 50
Chicago Renaissance, 97
Chicago Sanitary and Ship Canal, 83
Chicago School of Architecture, 160–64
Chicago School of Literature. *See*
   Chicago Renaissance
Chicago Sun-Times, 234
Chicago Times, 84
Chicago Tribune, 43, 63, 71–72, 76, 85,
   100, 107, 110, 119, 149, 182, 191,
   236, 243, 262
Cicero, Ill., 205–6, 231
Cincinnati, Ohio, 73
Civil War, 57, 73–76, 104, 272
Clark, George Rogers, 14–15
Clark, Mark, 237, 245

Cleveland, Grover, 96
Cole, George E., 151
Colosimo, James "Big Jim," 177
Colvin, Harvey D., 76
Comiskey, Charles A., 85, 275
Congress on Racial Equality, 201–2
Cook County Democratic Party (CCDP)
   182, 187, 189–90, 280
      pre-1952, 190–91, 194–97,
         203–4, 207
      1952–1976, 215, 220–26
      post-1976, 242–45, 247–48,
         250–51, 255–56
Coughlin, John Joseph "Bathhouse,"
   77, 151–56

Daley, Richard J., 113, 207, 213–44,
   251
Daley, Richard M., 241, 246–47,
   253–55, 258
D'Arco, John, 225
David, Jefferson, 27, 74
Dawson, William, 194–96, 207, 231,
   244, 280
De Valera, Eamon, 171
Democratic National Convention
      1968, 231–36
      1996, 241
DePriest, Oscar, 170, 185
Dever, William, 180, 185–87
Dreiser, Theodore, 96–97, 153
Du Sable, Jean Baptiste Pointe, 15–16
Dunne, Edward, 154–55, 171
Dyer, Thomas, 73

Elmhurst, Ill., 210–11
Emerson, Ralph Waldo, 37
Englewood, 205
Epton, Bernard, 248–49
Erie Canal, 32, 47, 51
ethnocultural politics (late nineteenth
   century), 70–79, 274
Evans, Timothy, 252–53

Evanston, 81, 175
Everleigh Club, 149

Ferris wheel, 115–16
Field, Marshall, 63, 81, 92–93, 109, 175
Forman, James, 201
Fort Dearborn, 16–23, 27
Fort Dearborn Massacre (1812), 20–21, 270
Fort Sheridan, 112, 200
French and Indian War. *See* Great War for Empire
Fugitive Slave Law, 42

gangsters (1920s), 177–81
Garfield Park, 86
Glenview Naval Air Station, 200
grain industry, 48, 52–54
Grange Movement. *See* Alliance Movement
Grant Park, 163–64, 191–92, 233
Great Depression (1930s), 192–93, 196–98
Great Lakes Naval Training Center, 200
Great Migration (1910–1930), 137, 167–69
Great Railroad Strike (1877), 94, 109
Great War for Empire, 14

Hampton, Fred, 237, 245
Hanrahan, Edward, 244–45
Harper, William Rainey, 81
Harrison, Carter, I, 76–79, 110, 149
Harrison, Carter, II, 151–57, 160
Harvey, Ill., 95, 275
Haymarket bombing, 107–13, 121–22
Heald, Nathan, 19–20
Hispanic community, 249, 251, 262–64
Holabird, William, 161
Hopkins, John, 152
horse racing, 86
Hubbard, Gordon Saltonstall, 24–25, 33

Hughes, Langston, 169
Hull-House, 153, 157–60

If Christ Came to Chicago (Stead), 144, 149–50
Illinois and Michigan Canal, 24–25, 31–33, 35–36, 38, 42, 44, 48, 50, 55
immigrants
    Czechs (Bohemians), 71, 138–40
    Eastern European Jews, 133–37
    German Jews, 38–39, 75, 87
    Germans, 38–39, 62, 71–76, 123, 165–67
    Greeks, 137–38
    Irish, 38–39, 62, 71–76, 123
    Italians, 130–33
    Norwegians, 39
    Poles, 71, 124–30
    Scandinavians, 71
    Swedes, 39, 140–41

Jackson, Andrew, 22, 32–34, 272
Jackson, Jesse, 246, 248, 252
Jackson, Maynard, 251
Jackson Park, 114, 120
Japanese American community, 202
Jenny, William LeBaron, 161
Joliet, Louis, 8–10
Jungle, The (Sinclair), 147–49

Kelly, Edward J., 191–97, 203–4, 215, 280
Kenna, Michael "Hinky Dink," 151–56
Kennedy, John F., 225
Kennelly, Martin, 204–8, 214–16
King, Martin Luther, Jr., 227–31, 237
Kinzie, John, 18–19
Kipling, Rudyard, 60
Knights of Labor, 107–9, 112–13
Know-Nothing (American) Party, 39, 42, 72–73, 274
Kroc, Ray, 212
Ku Klux Klan, 175

La Salle, Robert Cavelier Sieur de, 10–11
Lager Beer Riot (1855), 72–73
Lake Shore Drive, 163, 197
Lincoln, Abraham, 27, 51, 75, 94
Lindsay, Vachel, 106–7
Literary Budget, 71
Lloyd, Henry Demarest, 112
Loop, 150, 175, 212, 213, 217–20, 257–58
Lovejoy, Elijah, 41
Loyola University (St. Ignatius College), 81
lumber industry, 48, 54–56
lumberyards, 103
Lutherans, 87

McCormick, Cyrus, 52–53, 109–10
McCormick reaper, 52–53, 74
McDonald, Mike, 74, 76, 150, 180
McDowell, Mary E., 159–60
mail-order catalog industry, 62–66
Marquette, Jacques, 8–10, 269
Mason, Roswell B., 105
Mazullo, Vito, 221–22, 224
meatpacking industry, 56–62
Medill, Joseph, 76–77, 105
Medill, Katherine, 105–6
Mell, Dick, 255–56
Mencken, H. L., 97
Merchandise Mart, 175
Merriam, Charles E., 156
Metcalfe, Ralph, 237–38, 244
Midway Airport, 7, 185, 219
Mondale, Walter, 249
Moody, D. L., 88–90, 95, 108
Moody Bible Institute, 89
Mundelein, George William, 129
Municipal Voters' League, 146, 151–52
Museum of Science and Industry, 120

narcotics, 78
Nardi, Michele, 160

Nash, Pat, 191, 197, 203
National Black Political Convention (1972), 244
Native American Indians, 5–6, 8–9, 11, 16, 18, 19–23, 26–29
    Fox, 11
    Illinois, 5–6, 8–9
    Iroquois, 6
    Miami, 6, 16, 19–21
    Potawatomi, 6, 15, 18–21, 26, 28–29
    Winnebago, 19, 21
Navy Pier, 163
Nixon, Richard, 225
Northerly Island, 163
Northwestern University, 81, 86, 245

Oak Park, Ill., 175
Ogden, William B., 34–35, 48–49
O'Hare Airport, 199, 219
Olmstead, Frederick Law, 83, 114
open housing crisis (1950s), 203–7
Ouilmette, Antoine, 18

panic of 1837, 34, 36, 49
Park Forest, Ill., 209–10
Park Manor, 205
Parsons, Albert, 107, 111
Plan of Chicago (1909), 162–64, 211
Populist Movement. See Alliance Movement
portage, 7, 9–11, 24–25, 31–32, 68, 272
Potter, Palmer, 63, 93
presidential election
    1936, 196
    1960, 225
prohibition movement
    1800s, 40, 70–73, 81
    1920s, 176–81, 185–87, 191, 196
public housing, 228, 237, 258–61
public schools, 80–81, 257
Pullman, George, 93–96
Pullman, Ill., 95–96

Pullman Strike (1894), 96

Race Riot of 1919, 170–73
railroads, 48–51, 53–55, 57, 60–61, 273
Relief and Aid Society, 105–6
religion, 40, 87–91, 143
Revolutionary War. See War for Independence
Reynolds, John, 27
Riverside, Ill., 83
Riverview Park, 87
Robert Taylor Homes, 228
Roche, Martin, 161
Rockefeller, John D., 81
Roebuck, Alvah, 64–65
Roman Catholics, 39, 71–72, 75–76, 87, 90
Roosevelt, Franklin D., 191, 196
Roosevelt, Theodore, 149
Root, John Wellborn, 161
Rosenwald, Julius, 137
Rush Medical College, 36

St. Ignatius College (Loyola University), 81
St. Louis, 6, 31–32, 48, 50–51, 53, 73
St. Valentine's Day Massacre, 178
saloons, 72–73, 76–78, 143–44, 155
Salvation Army, 160
Sandburg, Carl, 3, 97–98, 132, 145, 267
Sankey, Ira, 89
Sawyer, Eugene, 252–53
Sears, Richard, 64–65
Second Great Awakening, 40
Shedd Aquarium, 191–92
Sheridan, Philip Henry, 112
Sherman, Francis C., 73
Sinclair, Upton, 147–49
Sister Carrie (Dreiser), 97
skyscrapers, 104, 162
Soldier Field, 191–92, 280
Spalding, Albert G., 84–85
Stagg, Amos Alonzo, 86

Stanton, Edwin, 74
Starr, Ellen Gates, 158
Stead, William T., 91, 144, 149–51
Steffens, Lincoln, 152, 164
Strong, Josiah, 120–21
suburban growth, 83, 208–12
Sullivan, Louis, 161
Summerdale Scandal (1960), 216–17
Sunday, Billy, 90
Swibel, Charlie, 225–26
Swift, Gustavus F., 58, 60–61
Swing, David, 87–88

Temperance Movement (1800s). See Prohibition Movement
Teresa, Mother, 260–61
Thomas, Hiram W., 87–88
Thompson, William "Big Bill," 170, 180–87, 190–91
Tonty, Henri de, 10–11
Torrio, Johnny, 177
Treaty of Chicago (1833), 27–28
Treaty of St. Louis (1816), 21
Turow, Scott, 267

Underground Railroad, 41
Union Stock Yards, 56–60, 103
University of Chicago, 81, 86, 158, 203–4
University of Illinois Circle Campus, 220, 261, 263
urban renewal, 261–62

Varchmin, Arthur, 222–23
Volunteers of America, 160
Vrdolyak, Edward, 243, 247, 251

Wacker, Charles, 164
War for Independence, 14–15, 17
War of 1812, 19–21
Ward, Aaron Montgomery, 63–65
Washington, Harold, 244–52
Wayne, Anthony "Mad Anthony," 16

Wentworth, John "Long John," 30, 35, 73, 75, 78–79

Western Citizen, 41

Weyerhauser, Frederick, 56

Whistler, John, 16–17, 19, 270

Whittier, John Greenleaf, 102–3

Whyte, William H., 209

Wilson, Orlando W., 217

Women's Christian Temperance Movement, 81

Woodlawn, 204

World War I, 62, 165–67, 198, 200

World War II, 198–203, 209

World's Columbian Exposition, 76, 88, 90, 113–20, 122, 150, 162

Wrigley, Philip K., 202–3

Yerkes, Charles Tyson, 153–54

Y.M.C.A., 89, 106